13|95

8080
MICROCOMPUTER
EXPERIMENTS

8080
MICROCOMPUTER
EXPERIMENTS

Howard Boyet

Professor, Electrical Engineering
Pratt Institute
Brooklyn, New York

dilithium Press   Portland, Oregon

Dedicated to Nina
— *Je vous en dirai des nouvelles*

© COPYRIGHT, dilithium Press   1978

10 9 8 7 6 5 4 3 2 1

Library of Congress catalog card number: 78-60613

dilithium Press
P.O. Box 92
Forest Grove, Oregon 97116

ISBN: 0-918398-08-8

Printed in the United States of America

Contents

Chapter 4
Single Stepping and Its Importance—Experiments ●   141

Chapter 5
Interfacing Experiments: Controlling Input/Output Devices With a Microprocessor—Microcomputer: The Need for Device Select Pulses, Latching, and Tri Stating; Data Acquisition, Storage, Read-out; Status Bits; Interrupt Jamming; Control Signal Generation • 171

Preface

The age of the microprocessor-microcomputer may well be known as the Second Industrial Revolution. The First Industrial Revolution introduced the machine. The microprocesor-microcomputer now gives the machine a brain capable of making decisions under a very large variety of variable and varying conditions. This development has probably its greatest significance in control applications of every conceivable kind limited only by man's imagination. Industry has been quick to pick this up, particularly as the cost and size of the microprocessor and memories decrease rapidly and to the point where their incorporation into tools, machines, devices, medical instruments, displays, autos, instruments, traffic lights, test sets, manufacturing processes, appliances, measurement-data acquisition-processing systems, computer terminals, telephone systems, electronic games, etc. becomes economically totally feasible. The substitution of software (programs to implement decision and control) for hardware (relays, electronmechanical systems, etc.) makes the microcomputer extremely attractive in the areas of cost, reliability, and process control efficiency optimization. Economics now makes it imperative for a company to incorporate the microprocessor wherever possible in its product line and/or manufacturing processes to insure its very survival. Competition will undoubtedly exert pressure on other countries to follow suit—a glance at balance of trade figures in any newspaper's financial section makes that clear. The conclusion seems inescapable: the microprocessor tidal wave, world wide, is only beginning. *Business Week* (March 14, 1977) sees microprocessors growing at a rate of more than 110% annually through 1980 with unit sales going from 638,000 in 1975 to between 26 and 35 million microprocessors annually by 1980. They further see the installed number of microcomputers rising from zero in 1973 to 60 millions systems by 1980. And the real acceleration, they predict, will come after 1980 when the large volume markets go into full production.

The microprocessor-microcomputer revolution may well be the single most important and far-reaching technological development for civilization to the present time. Everybody's, but everybody's, life will sooner than later be affected by it in labor saving devices and in controls of processes and information flow of every kind. And who knows the ways it will affect our whole life-style and social structure. The changes may well be profound.

Industry is now in the process of a crash retraining program of its engineers. Seminars in and out of house are being given on a vast scale. They serve a vital and important purpose. After the two-, three-, or five-day seminar the participant is usually in a good position to follow up by himself and continue his learning in the areas of digital electronics and microprocessors that are of relevance to his interests and areas of applications. Engineers and scientists of every kind, (let alone possibly the general public ultimately—at a different level) must get into this new field,—and now. The microprocessor is of vital importance to the electrical engineer, the mechanical engineer, the chemist and chemical engineer, the physicist, the biologist, the medical researcher, the social scientist, the industrial engineer, the instrumentation and controls engineer, the computer scientist, the field representative, the marketing man, the technician—it cuts across all lines and for varying reasons[27]. Programmable instant control of, and decision-making for, a process, device, system or measurement under a wide variety of variable and varying conditions is basically the common factor. The engineer, for the first time, has to be both software *and* hardware oriented. The microprocessor-microcomputer allows no other possibility.

The effect on colleges and their curricula will have to be just as great if they are to prepare their engineering and science students for a whole new emphasis that industry is initiating and demanding[27]. Microprocessor courses, theory *and* laboratory, will very soon start working their way into the curricula of various departments. This is one field where, for the newcomer, *reading* about the subject is almost of no use; *hands* on the microcomputer-microprocessor itself with a good, motivating group of software and interfacing experments is the *only* way. Otherwise the field will remain a mystery and leave the student with a certain fear of a subject that appears, at first sight, very complex. And indeed the learning gap to be filled in going from the random logic computer to the microprocessor-microcomputer-microcontroller technology is probably far bigger than was the case, for example, in the transition from the vacuum tube to the transistor, as far as engineering use and applications are concerned[27]. My own recent experience has indicated that industry is gobbling up those graduating students who have hands-on experience with the microprocessor. Colleges, of course, cannot and will not ignore the realities of the job market[27]. The microprocessor will be found wherever electronics is needed and used.

It is the purpose of this book to present a concise, hard-hitting, significant, and motivating group of experiments covering the basic and fundamental essentials of the microprocessor-microcomputer. It should ideally serve the student, professor, industry engineer, sales person, scientist, technician, or administrator new to the field. The experiments focus on the 8080 microprocessor. Learning with the 8080 should smooth the task of mastering other microprocessors—the 8085, the 6800, the Z-80, the 6502, etc. The basic microcomputer architecture and the programming *concepts* are the same. (Appendices F and H have pertinent remarks and discussion on the Intel 8085 and its relation to the 8080. Remarks are also made in Appendix H indicating the interfacing adaptations required to perform the experiments in this book with the 8085, and how it can be made to interface with standard memories—peripherals. Naturally, the programming presents no difficulties, as the 8085 and 8080 use the same instruction sets, with the exception of two added instructions with the 8085).

While the experiments have been performed specifically on the E & L Instruments Inc. MMD-1 8080 microcomputer trainer, the software and single stepping experiments (Chap. 3 and 4) can be done on any 8080 based system, and the interfacing experiments (Chap. 5) can be done on another 8080 system as is, or at most with simple adaptations, as long as the data bus and address bus are accessible. The requirements and adaptations are given in Appendix H (See also Chap. 5, sections 5-2(C) and 5-2(G) and Figs. 11, 12, and 34). No such modifications are necessary if the microcomputer provides: 1) control signals [see section 5-2(G), Chap. 5], 2) device codes from a decoder [section 5-2(C), Chap. 5], 3) accessibility to the data and address busses, 4) a keyboard and encoder with bootstrap PROM to write programs into RAM. If such is the case, all the experiments in this book can be implemented directly. While the Intel 8080 instruction set (Appendix B) is used exclusively, the reader should be able to adapt the experiments to the instruction sets of other microprocessors, with corresponding interfacing changes, should he choose to do so. Octal address and instruction coding in the programming is used throughout. It has certain important advantages for the beginner from a pedagogical standpoint. The 8080 instruction list in Appendix B is presented with both octal and hexadecimal encoding of the instructions. The student can program any experiment in this book in Hexa if he so desires. Octal to Hexa keyboard adapters are available.

The book should allow the student to work and progress by himself at home if he has an assembled trainer; or to cover perhaps 25–50% of the material in the 2 to 5 full day type of industry seminar and then continue with the rest of the material on his microcomputer at home or at work; or to cover all the experiments in a one semester lab course (3 hours per week) at the university or college level. It is also well suited to the needs of technicians. The book can serve as a starting point, as well as a point of departure, for the professor who needs to get into this field and organize a laboratory quickly. The experiments presented will undoubtedly suggest others to him depending on his own tastes and needs. References and a partial list of vendors are presented in the Appendices, as are integrated circuit chip and display pin configurations (Appendix A).

It is organized in such a way that enough theory is presented in Chaps. 1 and 2 to simplify the understanding of the microprocessor-microcomputer, its architecture, and bootstrapping, and again in the right places, as needed, before new groups of experiments are presented in Chaps. 3, 4, and 5. The theoretical approach is not intended to be exhaustive—references (Appendix E) are provided for further reading where the student feels the need for it. The book can stand on its own in that the theory presented is sufficient to allow the student to perform the experiments with complete understanding, and give him a good grasp of the workings of the microprocessor-microcomputer and how it is used in software—interfacing to affect control functions.

Chapter 3 is devoted mostly to software experiments illustrating the power of the micrcomputer in control and decision-making. The student is exposed there exclusively to machine and assembly/symbolic language programming in which the control results and effects are displayed at ports 0, 1, and 2 of the MMD-1 trainer. Chapter 4 is devoted to single-stepping of programs in which the experiments reveal many of the architectural aspects of microcomputers (data and address bus flow, machine cycle execution, fetch, execution, and "extra" bytes), as well as the peculiarities of individual instructions and of interfacing details. Single stepping provides the basis for a real understanding of the microprocessor and its instruction set. Chap. 5 integrates the material of Chaps. 3 and 4 into interfacing experiments in which the microcomputer interacts with I/O devices: device selecting; I/O instructions; jam interrupts; data acquisition; status bits and control signals; control of counters, machines and process rates; function generators; demultiplexing; calculators; etc., are covered. *Chapter 5 puts it all together.*

The book is an outgrowth of lectures and hands-on experiments given by the author at industry seminars as well as in the laboratory with his students at Pratt Institute, Brooklyn, N.Y. Fundamentals are stressed. The power of the microcomputer in control and decision-making through software and interfacing with the I/O device is constantly brought out in the experiments. No previous experience with microprocessors or even computers is necessary. The experiments should bring the student along, from scratch, to a solid level of accomplishment and understanding as well as pre-pare him for going on to the areas of microprocessor applications and specialized problems.

I wish to thank Mr. Ron Katz, E. E. senior at Pratt Institute, (present affiliation: Bell Telephone Laboratories) for many pene-trating discussions and invaluable suggestions. Any errors or misconceptions are my own. The support and confidence of Dr. Eleanor Baum, chairman of the electrical engineering depart-ment at Pratt Institute and Richardson Pratt Jr., president of Pratt Institute, are gratefully acknowledged. This book would not be possible without their support of a microprocessor laboratory. I wish, also, to thank the many Pratt students and participants in my seminars through-out industry, colleges, and government agencies for their suggestions, support, and encouragement. Interacting with them was most stimulating.

Finally, my deepest appreciation to my friend and colleague, Prof. Nina Kurtis of Pratt Institute, for her constant encouragement, moral support, suggestions, and help.

The author wishes to acknowledge the following sources for their help; Intel Corporation, E & L Instruments Inc., Texas Instru-ments Inc., National Semiconductor Corp., Hewlett Packard Co., and Gernsback Publications.

A WORD OF CAUTION

When the "bug" "bytes" it itches. Let's hope that in passing through these "gates", and in fanning out to the inputs to euphoria and power, your domestic and social life and habits will not suffer too much . . . never mind—let the chips fall where they may (as long as +5V. and ground are connected).

Howard Boyet
May, 1978
New York City, N. Y.

The 8080 Microprocessor Chip (courtesy of Intel Corp.)

Parts List for Experiments

Chapters 1 and 2: Theory only.

Chapter 3: All software experiments use the output ports on the MMD-1 or equivalent 8080/8085 system, except the following experiments which require the components noted:

Expt 3-4(a),(b),(c),(d): A7525(Tip 29) transistor (1), 1KΩ resistor, 8Ω speaker (these items are optional if one wants audio output).

Expt 3-5(d): 74150 (1), 74154 (1), 7404 (1), 1KΩ resistors (8), LEDs (8).

Chapter 4: 7476 or 7474 (1), clock source or pulse, matrix or 7-segment displays (6) for address and data bus to monitor octal bytes (can be E&L 7-segment LR-4 outboards or HP 5082-7300 matrix displays). Alternative to the 7476 (7474), clock or pulser, is the E&L LR-50 single stepper outboard.

Chapter 5: **Expt 5-2(a):** 7490 (1), pulser or clock source (1), 7404 (1), matrix or 7-segment display (1).

Expt 5-2(b): 7490 (2), 74154 (1), 7404 (1), pulser or clock source, 7-segment or matrix display (2).

Expt 5-2(c): 74154 (1), 7474 (1), Resistor 1KΩ (1), LED (1).

Expt 5-2(d): 7475 (2), 7404 (1), 8 LEDs or three 7-segment displays.

Expt 5-2(e): 74154 (1), 7475 (2), 7404 (1), 16 LEDs or six 7-segment displays.

Expt 5-2(f): 7474 (1), 7432 (1), 1KΩ resistors (2), LEDs (2).

Expt 5-2(g): slide switches (4), 8095 (1).

Expt 5-2(h): 8095 (2), slide switches (8).

Expt 5-2(i): 8095 (4), slide switches (8), 8212 (1), 7404 (1), 7474 (1).

Expt 5-2(j): 8095 (2) and items in Expt 5-2(e).

Expt 5-2(k): 8095 (1), slide switches (4), 7475 (1), 7402 (1), LR4 outboard (1) <u>or</u> 7448 (1) plus HP 5082-7740 7-segment display plus 7 1KΩ resistors.

Expt 5-2(l): 8202 (1), LEDs and 1KΩ resistors (8 each), single stepping circuit (1). (See items listed under Chapter 4 heading.)

Expt 5-3(a): D to A converter (1), voltage source (15V), .5KΩ POT, scope, 8Ω speaker.

Expt 5-3(b): Software.

Expt 5-3(c): 8095 (1), slide switches (4).

Expt 5-3(d): Same as 5-3(c).

Chapter 1

Review of Binary and Octal Number Systems, and the Pertinent Digital Logic and Digital Components*

A hands-on mastery of the microprocessor-microcomputer requires an understanding of some elements of programming, computer architecture, and digital logic design (interfacing with Input/Output devices). The aim of this book is to present the essential theory behind these various aspects so as to make possible a rapid practical understanding of the microprocessor and its uses, and to successfully perform the wide range of experiments involving software, hardware, and interfacing presented. Hands-on involvement with the experiments in the various chapters is *the* goal of this book. Machine, assembly, and symbolic language are essential for microprocessor mastery at the present time and this subject will be introduced in this and other chapters. No higher languages are discussed or needed. Elements of digital logic and digital components are presented in this chapter—enough to get going. The essentials of microcomputer architecture as they pertain to the writing and execution of programs and the control of data to and from input-output devices are presented in the next chapter. It is beyond the scope of this book to present a complete theory of programming, languages, computer architecture, or logic

*For theory and experiments see Ref. 17, Appendix E.

design. References are given in Appendix E for further reading in these various fields where the student deems it necessary. Chapters 3, 4, and 5 are then devoted to numerical software and interfacing experiments with further theory introduced where needed.

1.1 BINARY, OCTAL, AND DECIMAL REPRESENTATIONS OF NUMBERS (DATA OR INSTRUCTION BYTES)— OCTAL CODING

In a decimal system there are ten distinct numbers 0, 1, 2, 3, 4, 5, 6, 7, 8, 9; in the binary system just two 0, 1; in the octal system there are eight 0, 1, 2, . . . 7. The *bases* are 10, 2, and 8, respectively. The computer's digital components and elements work on just two states 1 or 0 (on or off, true or false, *5 volts* or *ground*). The advantage in using binary elements should be clear: Two different states are less complicated than 8 or 10 different states as far as electronic implementation. Thus the "machine language" is in binary. However, the world understands decimal, and the keyboard, is often in octal for reasons that will soon be apparent. To appreciate this recall that

$$(586)_{10} = 5 \times 10^2 + 8 \times 10^1 + 6 \times 10^0 \text{ (decimal)}$$

while

$$(101)_2 = 1 \times 2^2 + 0 \times 2^1 + 1 \times 2^0 \text{ (binary)} = 5_{10}$$

and

$$(271)_8 = 2 \times 8^2 + 7 \times 8^1 + 1 \times 8^0 = (185)_{10}$$

Consider further the *byte* (a string of 8 "bits" in binary, each bit being a 1 or a 0), also called a *word*. For example,

$$\text{Byte} = 10111001$$

The decimal weights of each position starting from right to left are clearly 2^0, 2^1, 2^2, 2^3, 2^4, 2^5, 2^6, 2^7, or from left to right 128, 64, 32, 16, 8, 4, 2, 1. Adding these numbers taking due account of the 1's and 0's in the byte would give the decimal number 185.

Hence the binary byte $(10111001)_2 = (185)_{10}$. But note that we could group the byte into sections of 3 bits as $\widehat{10}\,\widehat{111}\,\widehat{001}$ (zero being understood to the left of the MSB—"most significant bit"—here a 1). Using the fact that

$$(\widehat{001})_2 = 0 \times 2^2 + 0 \times 2^1 + 1 \times 2^0 = 1$$

$$(\widehat{111})_2 = 1 \times 2^2 + 1 \times 2^1 + 1 \times 2^0 = 7$$

$$(\widehat{010})_2 = 1 \times 2^1 + 0 \times 2^0 = 2$$

and taking these groups independently of each other would give the octal representation of $10111001 = (185)_{10}$, namely $\widehat{10}\,\widehat{111}\,\widehat{001}$ $= (271)_8$. We note the subscript 8, indicating octal, because the complete possible range of each group can go from 0 (000) to 7 (111) and everything in between; i.e., 8 different values.

Note further that $(271)_8 = 2 \times 8^2 + 7 \times 8^1 + 1 \times 8^0 = (185)_{10}$. Thus Byte $= (10111001)_2 = (271)_8 = (185)_{10}$ are equivalent. We thus have three different ways to represent a byte or a number (and there are others as well—hexadecimal for example—which we won't discuss here), namely binary, octal, or decimal and they are all equivalent. Computers, to the present time, work with 1's and 0's, i.e., in binary (machine) language. But this language would be tedious for *us* to work with, given the long string of 1's and 0's to be punched in to the computer to represent a data, or an instruction, or an address byte (see Chap. 2). Errors could easily be made. It would also be somewhat difficult to work with decimal, as we would have to convert the binary to decimal and vice versa and that takes time (we would not wish to convert every 8 bit instruction or address byte into decimal or vice versa). But punching in a program in octal is particularly simple because the conversion from machine (binary) to octal and vice versa is easy. Thus, at a glance, $(365)_8 = (\widehat{11}\,\widehat{110}\,\widehat{101})_2$ and $(\widehat{01}\,\widehat{101}\,\widehat{111})_2 = (157)_8$. To sum up, taking the previous example, the computer works on $(10\,111\,001)_2$, our keyboard (through which we enter the program or instructions or addresses) works on $(271)_8$, and the world *understands* results in decimal, i.e. $(185)_{10}$. (The 10 111 001 might represent an *address* in memory, i.e. the 185th location, or the *code* for an *instruction* (to add, subtract, or clear a register, etc.), or be an actual *data* number—here $(185)_{10}$—to be entered into memory and then worked on as in multiplication.) It should be clear that when an instruction, or address, or data byte is entered via the keyboard in octal form, e.g. $(234)_8$, keys 2, 3, and 4 are pressed in succession and a keyboard *encoder* in the microcomputer converts $(234)_8$ to binary, i.e. $\widehat{01}\ \widehat{011}\ \widehat{100}$ for machine use internally. These 8 bits then *flow* on the 8 bit *data bus* to registers where they may be stored, or to memory where they may be stored as *data* or *instruction* bytes (see next chapter)—or if the 8 bits represent an *address* in memory then the byte $(234)_8 = 01\ 011\ 100$ would flow on the *address bus* to "point" to a particular memory location ("address") at which we may want to store the *next* byte keyed in (an instruction or data byte). But we are getting ahead of ourselves. These aspects are covered in the next chapter.

Some facts should be noted as we work with 8 bits:

$$00\ 000\ 000 = \quad (0)_{10} = (000)_8$$

$$00\ 000\ 001 = \quad (1)_{10} = (001)_8$$

$$00\ 000\ 010 = \quad (2)_{10} = (002)_8$$

$$00\ 000\ 011 = \quad (3)_{10} = (003)_8$$

$$\ldots\ \ldots\ \ldots = \quad \ldots$$

$$\ldots\ \ldots\ \ldots = \quad \ldots$$

$$11\ 111\ 111 = (255)_{10} = (377)_8$$

Thus there are $(256)_{10}$ *different* possible numbers in an 8 bit byte $(2^8 = 256)$. Further, the octal number after $(017)_8 = \widehat{00}\ \widehat{001}\ \widehat{111}$ *has* to be $00\ 010\ 000 = (020)_8$ where $(017)_8 = (15)_{10}$ and $(020)_8 = (16)_{10}$. Likewise after $(077)_8$ follows $(100)_8$, the first representing $(63)_{10}$ and the second $(64)_{10}$. The numbers 8 and 9 do not exist in octal. $(137)_8$ is followed by $(140)_8$.

Note the binary addition rules $0 + 0 = 0, 0 + 1 = 1, 1 + 0 = 1, 1 + 1 = (2)_{10} = (10)_2$. Thus we speak of $1 + 1$ having a sum of 0 with a carry of 1. On this basis we see that by using

$$\begin{array}{ccc} 1 & & 0 \\ \underline{+\ 1} & \text{and} & \underline{-\ 1} \\ 10 & & 11 \\ \uparrow & & \uparrow \\ \text{carry} & & \text{borrow} \end{array}$$

$$017 = 00\ 001\ 111$$
$$\underline{+\quad 1} \qquad \underline{\qquad +\ 1}$$
$$00\ 010\ 000 = (020)_8$$

$$(200)_8 = 10\ 000\ 000$$
$$\underline{-\quad 1} \qquad \underline{\qquad -\ 1}$$
$$01\ 111\ 111 = (177)_8$$

$$(277)_8 = 10\ 111\ 111$$
$$\underline{+\quad 1} \qquad \underline{\qquad +\ 1}$$
$$11\ 000\ 000 = (300)_8$$

and finally

$$(377)_8 = 11\ 111\ 111$$
$$\underline{+\quad 1} \qquad \underline{\qquad +\ 1}$$
$$1\ 00\ 000\ 000 = (000)_8$$

In the latter case the final carry, 1, is in the 9th bit which does not exist in an 8-bit data bus, so we ignore it (it does exist in a *carry flip flop*—a "flag"—see Chap. 3). Likewise,

$$(000)_8 = 00\ 000\ 000$$
$$\underline{-\quad 1} \quad \underline{1 \qquad\quad -\ 1}$$
$$11\ 111\ 111 = (377)_8$$

The final borrow, 1, is ignored in the 9th bit.

It should be mentioned that while octal coding has important pedagogical advantages for the beginning student, hexadecimal coding is also in use. We will not concern ourselves with hexadecimal in this book, although the 8080 instruction list given in Appendix B is in both octal and hexa. It should also be noted that E & L Instruments has an add-on keyboard adapter ("HEX Key Pad") for their MMD-1 which allows programming directly in hexa. *All experiments in this book can be done in hexadecimal if so desired. Just use the list in Appendix B.*

1.2   REVIEW OF GATES, FLIP-FLOPS, LATCHES, DECODERS, REGISTERS, TRISTATES, REGISTER TRANSFERS, ENCODERS

It is not the purpose here to delve into the digital electronics behind diode gates, diode-transistor logic gates (DTL), Resistor-

Transistor logic gates (RTL), Transistor-Transistor logic gates (TTL), Emitter Coupled Logic gates (ECL), MOSFET gates, CMOS gates, or integrated circuits. Nor are we here concerned how flip-flops, latches, tristates, decoders, registers, etc. are realized from such gates. The reader is referred to references 1, 2, 3, 4, 14, 16, 17, 23, 24, 28, 31, and 32 in Appendix E. Our aim is to describe briefly what gates, latches, flip-flops, registers, etc. do and what their properties are to the extent that they will concern us in microprocessor-microcomputer work, especially as they pertain to the theory of Chap. 2 and the interfacing experiments of Chaps. 4 and 5. We thus treat them, for our purposes here, as black boxes obeying certain "truth tables."

Gates

In most microprocessor-microcomputer work (TTL) the bit 1 represents +5 volts and the bit 0 represents ground (0 volts). It is, therefore, well to keep this in mind as we briefly review the truth table properties of the following gates (A and B are inputs to the gate, F its output):

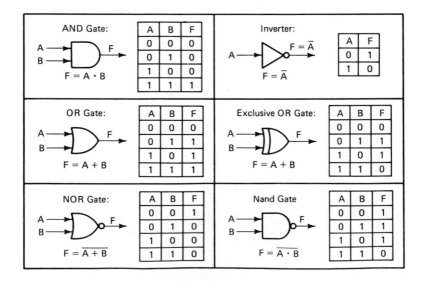

Figure 1. The basic logic gates and their truth tables.

It should be noted that A · B or A + B do *not* represent multi-plication or addition operations in the ordinary algebraic sense— rather they are AND and OR *operations* in the Boolean logic, or Boolean algebra sense. It is also worth mentioning De Morgan's theorems, which can be useful.

$$\overline{A \cdot B} = \overline{A} + \overline{B}$$ i.e.

and

$$\overline{A + B} = \overline{A} \cdot \overline{B}$$

(──o── indicates a NOT operation).

The two gates preceded by circles have no special names, they are simply equivalents. Thus AND/NOT ≡ NOT/OR and OR/NOT ≡ NOT/AND. The gates can have more than two inputs except for the inverter. The truth tables can be augmented accordingly.

Flip Flops, Latches, and Registers

Flip flops, latches, and registers are especially important in microprocessor work and microprocessor architecture.

There are S-R, T, J-K, and D Flip Flops. We will here single out a particularly important one, the *D (Data) flip flop* (the 7474 integrated circuit chip—See Appendix A).

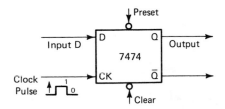

Note definition of a clock pulse: ⌐‾⌐

(The 7474 chip contains two such flip flops.) When Preset = 0 and Clear = 1, clock and D are overridden and Q = 1. When Clear = 0 and Preset = 1, clock and D are overridden and Q = 0. Preset = 0 and Clear = 0 produce undefined conditions. Only when Preset and Clear = 1 do D and clock inputs have an effect on the output Q. Thus

Preset	Clear	CK	D	Q
0	1	X	X	1
1	0	X	X	0

For Preset = Clear = 1

D	CK	Q
1	↑	1
0	↑	0
X	↟	Q_0

(See Ref. 10)

where X indicates either 0 or 1, ↑ indicates that the output Q assumes the value of the input *Data D only when a clock pulse ⌐ is inputted to the 7474 clock* and that the leading edge is responsible for making Q = D; ↟ indicates there is no such leading edge transition present, and Q_0 indicates that in that case Q *stays at the last value it assumed.* Thus a flip flop is in a sense a memory: data (1 or 0) is *clocked* in and the output remembers this data, i.e. retains it, as long as there are no further leading edge transitions (clock pulses). Any change at the input D will not alter the output Q until another clock pulse arrives.

    A *register* can be considered as a series of flip flops (in the 8080, generally 8 such flip flops) so that a byte can be retained, or stored, there. Thus

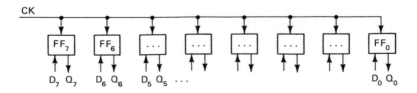

and $Q_i = D_i$ when a clock pulse is applied to the CK line. Thus $(271)_8 = (10\ 111\ 001)_2$ input to the D lines ($D_7 = 1$, $D_6 = 0$,

$D_5 = 1, \ldots$) would appear as stored values in the register ($Q_7 = 1$, $Q_6 = 0$, $Q_5 = 1, \ldots$) *after* a clock pulse were applied. Registers form an important part of the CPU (central processing unit—or the microprocessor) as we will see in the next chapter.

A special flip flop, *the latch* (IC 7475) is of great importance in microprocessor work, both internally and in external I/O (input/output) device interfacing (i.e., in talking to or controlling I/O devices from the microcomputer).

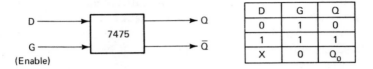

D	G	Q
0	1	0
1	1	1
X	0	Q_0

(Note the 7475 contains four such flip flops shown above—See Appendix A and Ref. 10.) Q_0 is the last value that Q acquired while G was 1 before going to 0.

It is of interest and importance to compare the output behavior of Q in the 7475 and 7474 flip flops when similar changing input data D is applied to both:

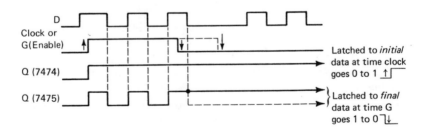

Figure 2. The 7474 D Flip Flop vs. the 7475 Latch.

These results are understood by noting the 7474 and 7475 truth tables. The 7475 latches to the *final* data appearing at the input while the 7474 latches to the *initial* data appearing at the input (by initial we mean at the time ⌐ appeared and by final we mean at the time ⌐ appeared).

These properties of the two flip flops will be used time and again thru-out the experiments, especially in data bus and address bus monitoring (Chap. 4) and in interfacing the microcomputer to output devices (Chap. 5). Clearly the 7475 is more receptive to following changes in its input data than is the 7474. As we shall see the 7475 is particularly useful when outputting data (a byte) from the microprocessor's accumulator (an 8 bit register) to an output device. It will be seen in the interfacing experiments how a certain program instruction (323) can be made to cause (A) (contents of the accumulator) to flow via the data bus (see Chap. 2) to an output device (the 7475−2 of them) *at the same time* that a pulse known as $\overline{Out}$ = ⊔* is applied (in inverted form $\overline{out}$ = ⊓) to G of the 7475's, thus *latching* this data byte (A) to the output Qi of the 8 flip flops in the two 7475's. Then as future instructions in the program are fetched and run over the data bus from memory to CPU for execution (see Chap. 2), they will *not* affect or change the latched outputs Q_7 . . . Q_0 on the 7475's because no further $\overline{\overline{out}}$ will have been generated by *those* instructions to make G = 1 on the 7475 enable. The 7475's have latched *only* the data that the program has told the microprocessor to output from A. They stay latched as long as G = 0 (i.e. no further $\overline{\overline{out}}$ generated). The 8 bits of latched data can, of course, be displayed on 8 LED's (light emitting diodes−on/off), as a decimal number on a numeric display (7 segment or matrix−more to be said about this in the experiments), or the 8 bits can control 8 traffic lights or different devices (on/off) according to the program's instructions which determined (A), or they can tell computers, CRT, teletype, and such devices to do certain things. This will be illustrated in the experiments. The 7474 (or 7476) on the other hand is useful in a powerful procedure known as single stepping, described later in the book (Chap. 4)−a procedure which allows us to examine a program in detail (debugging) and see its effects at each step, as well as to gain insight into data bus and address bus flow of instructional/data/address bytes. It and the 7476 J-K flip flop are useful because of their preset and clear inputs (e.g. turn a motor on or off) which the 7475 does not possess. The experiments will bring out these differences clearly.

The Tristate Gate

Up to this point all our gates had two, and only two, possible outputs, 1 (+5 volts) or 0 (ground). There are many registers and

*Fig. 11 and Chap. 5.

certainly many, many memory locations in the microcomputer and each contains 8-bit bytes (an instruction or data). These bytes have to flow from memory to register in the CPU, or vice versa, or from register to register. This occurs over a *"data bus"* (in the former case over the external CPU ↔ memory data bus, in the latter over the internal CPU data bus (see Chap. 2). If every memory location had its own data bus to every register, and every register its own data bus to every other register the internal microcomputer architecture would be hopeless as far as size, cost, and complexity. The tristate gate makes possible the microprocessor-microcomputer in the form we know it by allowing every memory location to *share* the *same single* external data bus with every register and all the internal CPU registers to share the same *single* internal data bus. It affords a way of keeping *all* memory locations and registers off the data bus except the single *source* memory location (or register) and the single *destination* memory location (or register) in question that are involved in a particular instruction. All the unwanted memory locations and registers (not needed for the fetch and execution of a *particular* instruction in the program) are kept in a *third state*, neither 1 nor 0, but in the high impedance state. This means no current drive is present at the output of the gate on to the data bus. *Only* the source byte and destination are on the data bus—the source sending its 1 or 0 to the destination while all the other parties are waiting on the line in the hi impedance state for their turn. If all were sending their 1's and 0's together chaos would result, not to mention possible chip burnout. Every register or memory location would be receiving bytes that were not intended for it. Likewise an *"input device"* waiting to input its data to the microprocessor's accumulator register via the data bus *must* be kept off the data bus in the high impedance state while data (instructions) are flowing back and forth between CPU and memory (Chap. 2) during the program's execution, until its turn in the program comes at which time it is forced off its tristate (hi impedance state) and puts out its byte on to the data bus (the "IN" instruction (333) does this by generating a pulse $\overline{\text{IN}} = \sqcup$* and this, as we shall see below, brings the tristate gate off the high impedance state momentarily). See National Semiconductor Hdbks (Ref. 12) on their tri-state chips.

The symbol for a tristate buffer (the 8093 in this case) is

---

*Fig. 11 and Chap. 5.

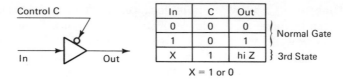

In	C	Out
0	0	0
1	0	1
X	1	hi Z

} Normal Gate

} 3rd State

X = 1 or 0

If we had

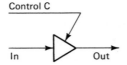

the above table would apply with $C = 0 \rightarrow 1$, $C = 1 \rightarrow 0$. The 8095 is a tri-state hex buffer (see Ref. 12) having 6 tri-state gates organized as follows (only 2 gates are shown—note that hi Z here occurs for $C = 0$; i.e. either or both DiS_1, $DiS_2 = 1$).

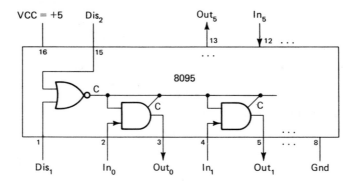

It is clear (see NOR Gate and AND Gate truth tables) that the truth table of the 8095 tristate buffer must be as shown in the following table (Ref. 12).

8095

Dis_1	Dis_2	C	In	Out
0	0	1	0	0
0	0	1	1	1
0	1	0	X	hi Z
1	0	0	X	hi Z
1	1	0	X	hi Z

} Normal two state behavior

} 3rd State: hi Z

X = 0 or 1

Thus, if we keep DiS_1 = 0 and make DiS_2 go ⊔ (e.g. $\overline{IN}$ pulse from the CPU—see Chap. 2) then as the above table shows (the encircled regions) the output will immediately put the input data on line and then go right back to its hiZ state from whence it came, staying off the data bus until it is again called into action by DiS_2 = ⊔. The programmed instruction "In" (333) will bring this about through the $\overline{IN}$ pulse generated in the CPU* and interfacing it with the 8095; i.e., to DiS_2 or to DiS_1 keeping the other low.

Register Transfer—an Example of Instruction Execution and the Need for Control Section Timing Signals. Concepts of the Macro-instruction, Micro-operation, Microcontrol, and the Microprogram.**

Suppose we wish to execute a "macro" instruction Mov $\overset{\frown}{C, B}$ ("move the contents of register B to register C"), which appears, for whatever reason, in the program. How does the microprocessor do this? We are getting a bit ahead of our story (see Chap. 2) but we have enough background at this point to see how this gets accomplished. There is a decoder in the microprocessor called the Instruction Decoder (ID) and when the macro-instruction $(110)_8$ = Mov $\overset{\frown}{C, B}$ is fetched from memory it goes over the data bus to the Instruction Register (IR) (see Fig. 10) for display (latching) to the ID which decodes $(110)_8$ and "tells" the control section to move (B) to (C) (( ) = "contents of"). The particular output line from the decoder (see next section) enabled by the 8 bit instruction activates the control-timing section in a way unique to that instruction. The control section (Chap. 2) now provides the necessary *timing pulses* (clocks) to implement this instruction. This is done as shown in the following figure (for simplicity we will assume each register shown contains just 2 bits; i.e., 2 flip flops). From our knowledge of the And gate/Or gate truth tables we see that the pulse ⊓ from the control section to the "Transfer B to Bus" line causes the bus to receive the contents B_1, B_2 of Reg. B when the pulse is 1. The control section *also* provides a clock pulse ⊓ to Reg. C's clock input via the "Transfer Bus to Reg. C." As these are D type flip flops the leading edge of the clock pulse causes Register C's flip flop outputs Q to mirror data B_1, B_2 waiting at the inputs (D) to those flip flops. Register transfer has been accomplished. The execution of all instructions is controlled

---

*Fig. 11 and Chap. 5.
**Ref. 28, Chap. 8.

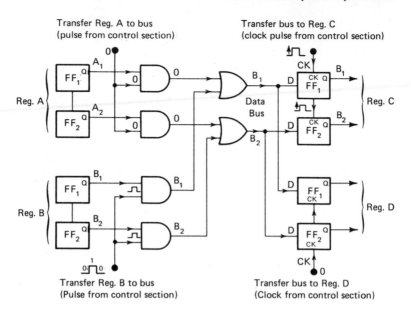

Figure 3. Controlled register to register transfer—how the instruction MOV C, B is executed. An example of microcontrol operations.

and accomplished, one way or another, in this fashion by the ID and control section. This control of register transfer is an example of what is known as *micro-operations*. The micro-operation control process is carried out under the direction of the *microprogram* buried in a ROM memory in the CPU's control section. The decoded macro-instruction from the ID initiates the pertinent part of the microprogram so that the micro-operations can be carried out under various control pulses thereby implementing (executing) that macro-instruction (see Ref. 28, Chap. 8). The instructions in the microprogram are referred to as *micro-instructions* and they control the generation of the control pulses at the right times to initiate the micro-operations necessary to affect source to destination register (macro) transfers in a program. It can be appreciated now how clock pulses and general *timing pulses* generated by the CPU's control and timing section, in collaboration with the microprocessor's clock generator, are the heart of the microprocessor. Gates, tristates, flip flops, register transfers, program counter (address latch), ID and IR, the Flag Flip Flops, the ALU (Arithmetic

Logic Unit), etc. (see Chap. 2 and Fig. 10) are all controlled to perform their functions at just the right times by the timing and control pulses emanating from the control section. For a 2 MHz clock (clock pulse widths 0.5μ) the timing between the various clock or timing pulses to the various internal registers, ALU, etc., of the CPU must be precise. There is very little room for error as one instruction after the other in the program flows from memory to CPU (fetch) for decoding, execution, and realization. As seen above, the clock pulses and timing control are particularly important during the instruction execution phase of the "machine cycle."

Decoders

Decoders form most important functions in microprocessor-microcomputer work. They are intimately tied up with how data/ instruction bytes are written into memory locations, one at a time, and later retrieved for decoding and execution, one at a time. They are also of the utmost importance in interfacing the microcomputer to the external Input or Output Device to micro-control it, accept its data or signals, or feed it data or control signals, particularly when several such I/O's exist. Then "device selecting" becomes necessary and the decoder does it. This will be a very important topic in the experiments on interfacing (Chap. 5) where these ideas will be developed and carried out practically.

Rather than go through every decoder (3 line to 8 line, BCD to decimal, etc.) we can bring out our points by discussing the 4-line to 16-line decoder (hexadecimal decoder) which will be used frequently in device selecting in our experiments. Nor will we discuss how the decoder is realized from the basic gates (see Refs. 1, 2, 3, and 4). It should be mentioned that the decoder is also used to select digits in numeric displays of all kinds.

The "Hexa" decoder* (IC 74154) has 4 inputs and 16 outputs (Appendix A).

*See Ref. 10

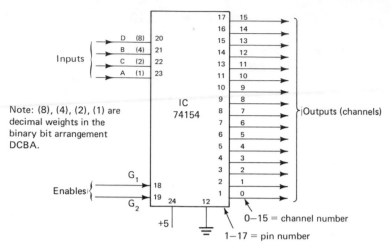

Figure 4. The hexadecimal 4 line to 16 line decoder.

The truth table for this chip follows (See Ref. 10).

◄── Input binary ──►						◄──────── Output channel number, decimal ────────►															
G_1	G_2	D	C	B	A	0	1	2	3	4	5	6	7	8	9	10	11	12	13	14	15
0	0	0	0	0	0	0	1	1	1	1	1	1	1	1	1	1	1	1	1	1	1
0	0	0	0	0	1	1	0	1	1	1	1	1	1	1	1	1	1	1	1	1	1
0	0	0	0	1	0	1	1	0	1	1	1	1	1	1	1	1	1	1	1	1	1
0	0	0	0	1	1	1	1	1	0	1	1	1	1	1	1	1	1	1	1	1	1
0	0	0	1	0	0	1	1	1	1	0	1	1	1	1	1	1	1	1	1	1	1
0	0	0	1	0	1	1	1	1	1	1	0	1	1	1	1	1	1	1	1	1	1
0	0	0	1	1	0	1	1	1	1	1	1	0	1	1	1	1	1	1	1	1	1
0	0	0	1	1	1	1	1	1	1	1	1	1	0	1	1	1	1	1	1	1	1
0	0	1	0	0	0	1	1	1	1	1	1	1	1	0	1	1	1	1	1	1	1
0	0	1	0	0	1	1	1	1	1	1	1	1	1	1	0	1	1	1	1	1	1
0	0	1	0	1	0	1	1	1	1	1	1	1	1	1	1	0	1	1	1	1	1
0	0	1	0	1	1	1	1	1	1	1	1	1	1	1	1	1	0	1	1	1	1
0	0	1	1	0	0	1	1	1	1	1	1	1	1	1	1	1	1	0	1	1	1
0	0	1	1	0	1	1	1	1	1	1	1	1	1	1	1	1	1	1	0	1	1
0	0	1	1	1	0	1	1	1	1	1	1	1	1	1	1	1	1	1	1	0	1
0	0	1	1	1	1	1	1	1	1	1	1	1	1	1	1	1	1	1	1	1	0
0	1	X	X	X	X	1	1	1	1	1	1	1	1	1	1	1	1	1	1	1	1
1	0	X	X	X	X	1	1	1	1	1	1	1	1	1	1	1	1	1	1	1	1
1	1	X	X	X	X	1	1	1	1	1	1	1	1	1	1	1	1	1	1	1	1

Figure 5. Truth table for the hexadecimal decoder (IC74154).

Note how the channel number that goes low (0) corresponds to the decimal value of the DCBA binary arrangement (8, 4, 2, 1) and that this occurs *only* when *both* G_1 and G_2 ("enables") are low. We have thus decoded the binary no. DCBA into its *unique* decimal equivalent as indicated by a 0 appearing on a *particular*, single output line. Note also how a "demultiplexer" can be realized: if $G_1 = $ ⎍⎍⎍⎍, for example, but $G_2 = 0$, and DCBA = 0111, then channel 7 and *only* channel 7's output will be ⎍⎍⎍⎍, exactly as G_1. Thus a varying bit pattern at the "input" G_1 can be *demultiplexed* on to any specific output line by *"selecting" that* line by means of the DCBA combination of bit values. Note also, if $G_1 = 0$ and $G_2 = 1$, so that every output line is 1, then when G_2 goes to 0 temporarily (i.e., $G_2 = $ ⎍ such as produced by an $\overline{\text{Out}}$ or $\overline{\text{In}}$ pulse from the microprocessor after an "output" or "input" instruction in the program is executed, as already mentioned, and to be discussed in more detail in Chap. 2 and in the interfacing experiments of Chap. 5), the particular channel determined by the DCBA combination will also go low ⎍. Thus if DCBA = 1001 and $G_1 = 0$, $G_2 = 1$, all outputs are 1, but if G_2 now goes to 0 and back to 1 (i.e., an $\overline{\text{Out}}$ or $\overline{\text{In}}$ pulse), channel 9's output will do exactly the same ⎍. Much use of this will be made in "device selecting" in connection with our interfacing experiments. It will be seen how this ⎍ output from a particular channel of the 74154 directed to a "strobe" or "enable" input of a particular output or input device having *that channel* as its *device number* (which device itself can be another IC chip used to control the *actual* device) will force *that* device to either latch the output data from the microprocessor (e.g., 7475's) or to input its data to the microprocessor (e.g., detristating an 8095). These points should be understood from the material presented on latches and tristates in this chapter. The same type ⎍ pulses at the decoder's output channel can be used to address (select) a particular memory location in order to store (write) or retrieve (read or fetch) data/ instructions when the decoder is used that way, as it must with all memory cells. In that case the input to the decoder would be the *address bus* lines and any address on it at a given moment will be decoded to ⎍ on *one, and only one,* output channel—and it is *that* channel that activates a particular memory cell or location to accept data/instruction from the *data bus* ("write" or "store") or to give back the byte to the data bus ("fetch," "retrieve," "read"). See Ref. 28, Chap. 2.

Encoders

Encoders are very important in microcomputer work. As discussed earlier in this chapter, we input bytes from the keyboard, say, in octal code, but the computer, internally, only understands binary numbers. Thus if we punch in an instruction or address (byte) such as $(271)_8$ on the keyboard, a device in the computer must take this information and convert it to 10 111 001 (machine language) for flow on to the 8-bit data bus to accumulator, registers, memory, or, in the case of the MMD-1, also to LED's for viewing. The encoder does this in a fashion opposite to the way the decoder worked. Thus, for example, IC 74148,* an 8-line to 3-line (4, 2, 1) encoder works in conjunction with the keyboard as shown here.

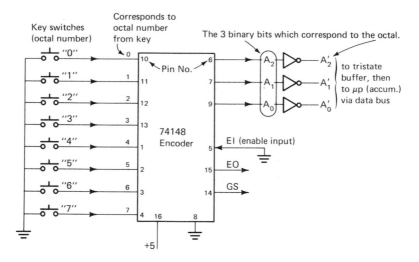

Figure 6.   The 74148 encoder (inverters after A_2, A_1, A_0 are not part of the encoder).

The truth table follows (the three inverters shown to the right of $A_2 A_1 A_0$ are *not* part of the encoder; we have put them there and present the truth table for $A_2' A_1' A_0'$ rather than $A_2 A_1 A_0$ in order to have 7↔111 rather than 000, etc.).

*See Appendix A.

← Octal input from particular key →								Binary ← Outputs →		
0	1	2	3	4	5	6	7	A'_2	A'_1	A'_0
X	X	X	X	X	X	X	0	1	1	1
X	X	X	X	X	X	0	1	1	1	0
X	X	X	X	X	0	1	1	1	0	1
X	X	X	X	0	1	1	1	1	0	0
X	X	X	0	1	1	1	1	0	1	1
X	X	0	1	1	1	1	1	0	1	0
X	0	1	1	1	1	1	1	0	0	1
0	1	1	1	1	1	1	1	0	0	0

Valid for EI = 0. Outputs GS and EO are then 0 and 1, respectively.

Figure 7. The 74148 8 line to 3 line octal priority encoder. Truth table for inverted outputs A'_2, A'_1, A'_0. Pressing of a key(s) causes 0 input(s) to the 74148.

Thus pressing the key for octal number 5 at the input of the 74148 grounds *that* input and according to the above table this will produce the three binary bits 101 at the outputs $A'_2A'_1A'_0$. These bits then flow to the data bus and accumulator (or LED's for viewing) as the binary representation of octal 5. In this way pressing 271 produces 010 111 001 in successive groups of bits which go to the respective groups of 3 lines (2 lines) on the 8-line data bus to the accumulator (or successive groups of 3 (2) LED's). We will use these facts again in Chap. 2 in discussing the writing into memory of a program via the keyboard in which octal keys are encoded into binary bits by means of the 74148 encoder so that an instruction (e.g. 11 000 011) is produced (stored in memory— and eventually fetched) by pressing the keys 3, 0, 3 in succession. Note that the 74148 is a priority encoder; i.e., if keys 3, 4, and 5 are simultaneously pressed, the highest 0 (5) takes priority (note X's in above table).

Chapter 2

Basis of Microprocessor-Microcomputer Architecture: Data Flow and Bus Structure

It is not the purpose, nor within the scope, of this book to present an in-depth study of the internal architecture[28] of the microprocessor-microcomputer with associated studies of timing, memories, control, CPU, etc. Our aim here is to present the essential points which will foster an intelligent understanding of the workings of the microprocessor-microcomputer in order to quickly and efficiently prepare for the wide-ranging experiments to be presented in the following chapters. The reader seeking additional information and discussion is referred to the references listed in Appendix E. Often we will employ "analogies" in explanations (e.g., memories: "addresses," "locations," "spilling" information back out, etc.). Yet these analogies describe well what is occurring. Except for a brief discussion of how a ROM (read-only memory) works, the reader is referred to the excellent references (1, 2, 3, 4, 21, 22, 28) for further detailed studies of memories: RAMs (Random Access Memory), ROMs, PROMs (Programmable Read-Only-Memory), etc. The same will be true in our discussion of the control section and the ALU (Arithmetic Logic Unit). But the explanations presented should give a good overall feel and understanding of what is going on inside the microprocessor-microcomputer. It is hoped that the reader will be stimulated to proceed further into the literature (e.g., the "Intel 8080 Micro-computer System User's Manual" Sept. 1975, and the texts on Digital Computer Design and Microprocessors-Microcomputers listed in Appendix E).

For purposes of concreteness and illustration we present our explanations (and later the experiments) taking the E & L Instruments Inc. MMD-1 8080 Microcomputer trainer as our model (see Appendix F for remarks on the 3rd generation chip, the Intel 8085 and its relation to the 8080). These explanations can be extrapolated to any 8080-based system with minor exceptions and modifications. The experiments presented in Chaps. 3 and most of 4 do not depend on our explicit use of the MMD-1. The experiments in Chaps. 3, 4, and 5 have been performed on the MMD-1 both because of the convenience it provides and the peda-gogical clarity it offers. The interfacing experiments in Chap. 5 can be done on other 8080-based systems if certain factors are con-sidered and adaptations and changes are made, if necessary. These are explicitly pointed out and discussed in Appendix H. No such changes are necessary if the 8080 microcomputer provides control signals (Chap. 5), device selects (Chap. 5), access to address and data bus, and a keyboard with encoder and bootstrap PROM to allow writing programs into RAM. We also wish to point out that while the experiments are presented in octal, as are the explana-tions in this chapter, they can all be done in hexadecimal if so desired. The 8080 instruction list in Appendix B is given both in octal and hexa and E & L Instruments Inc. has as add-on hexa keyboard ("HEX Key Pad") for the MMD-1.

2.1 BLOCK DIAGRAM OF AN 8080 MICROCOMPUTER—DATA FLOW AND ADDRESSING—DATA AND ADDRESS BUSSES—CPU AND MEMORY—I/O's.

The reader will be constantly referred to Figs. 8, 9, 10, 11, 12, and 13 in this chapter. Figure 8 is crucial and shows the overall relationship and interactions in a microcomputer among micro-processor (CPU), memory, and I/O devices—and the data flow therein. Figure 9 shows pin connection details for the 8080 micro-processor chip; Fig. 10 is a detailed block diagram of the contents of the 8080 microprocessor (CPU) and their interrelation to ad-dress and data busses; Fig. 11 shows memories, CPU, control bus, and relevant IC logic in the MMD-1 microcomputer trainer and their relation to the data and address busses; Fig. 12 shows the

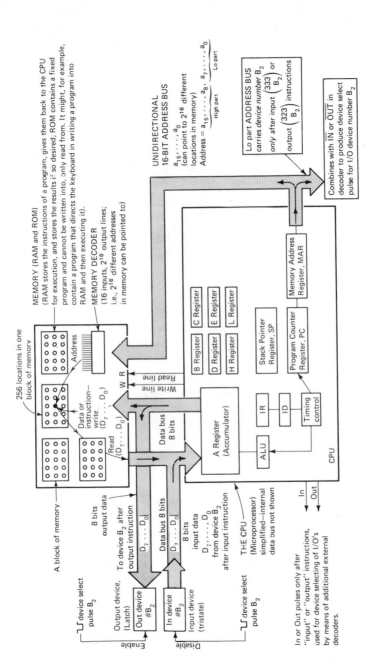

Figure 8. Basic block diagram of a microprocessor controlled microcomputer. IR and ID are instruction register and decoder. Each location in memory holds a word (byte) of 8 bits. The data bus (8 bits) is bi-directional.

three output ports 0, 1, and 2 (8 LED's at each port) and the one
input port 0 (the keyboard) inherent in the MMD-1, how they are
logically realized, and how they interact with one another and
with the data and address busses; and finally Fig. 13 shows the
face of the MMD-1 in block form with its functional regions.

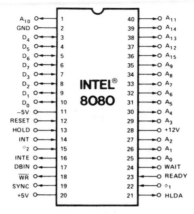

Figure 9. Pin Configuration of the 8080 (power, control, clock, address
bus, and data bus pins). Courtesy Intel Corp.

Of relevance at the moment are Figs. 8, 10, 12, and 13. As
Fig. 12 is brought into the discussion in this chapter we should be
in a fairly good position to understand much, but perhaps not all,
of it on the basis of the material presented in Chap. 1. The experiments, particularly those in Chap. 5 on interfacing and device selecting, should help clear up all questions pertaining to Figs. 11, 12
and the other figures as well. By that time we should also have a
much better appreciation of how the KEX program (Appendix C)
("Keyboard Executive Program" in the MMD-1-Prom IC 1702 in
memory block 0—see Figs. 11 and 13) works to store a program
punched in on the keyboard into RAM memory (block 3) and
then to have it executed. Such a PROM is called a *bootstrap loader*
(see Section 2.2). Programming experience with the experiments
presented in Chap. 3 and exposure to the 8080 set of instructions
will further help in this understanding. You should patiently keep
this in mind as explanations are given in this chapter. You should
be consulting the Intel 8080 instruction list (Appendix B) to
understand the discussions in Sections 2.1 and 2.2 as they relate
to writing in and execution of a program under direction of the
KEX bootstrap, which itself is a program composed of 8080 instructions.

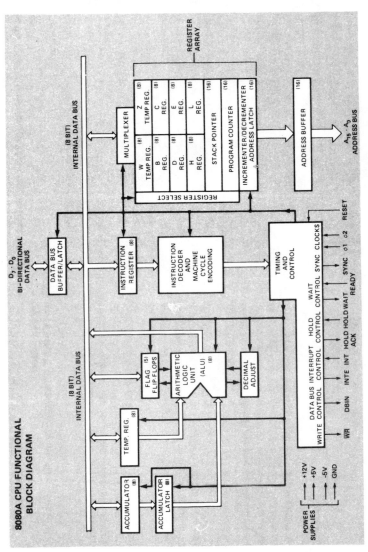

Figure 10. Internal structure of the 8080 microprocessor. CPU functional block diagram. (Courtesy of Intel Corp.)

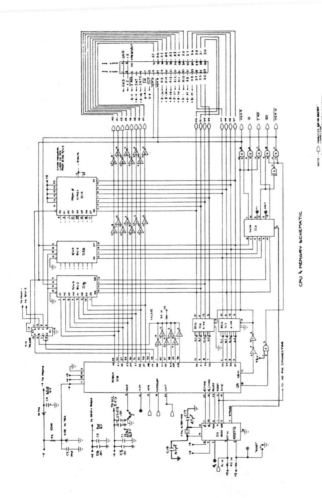

Figure 11. Memories/CPU—Address/Data Busses—Clock/Drivers/Control Bus: MMD-1 8080 Microcomputer (Courtesy E & L Instruments Inc).

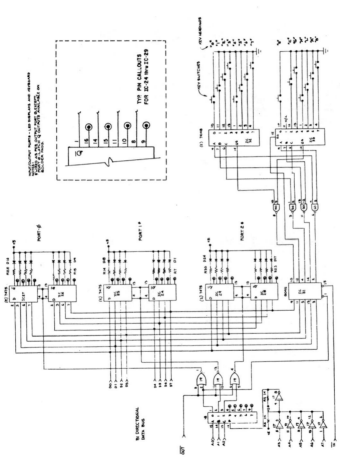

Figure 12. Keyboard (Input Port 0), Output Ports 0, 1, 2, Keyboard Encoder and Device Selects. MMD-1 (Courtesy E & L Instruments Inc).

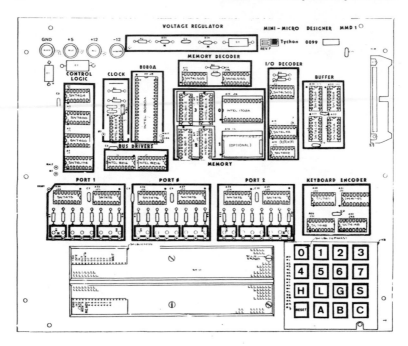

Figure 13. Face of MMD-1 in block form (Courtesy E & L Instruments Inc).

Referring to the CPU section in Fig. 8, the registers each can retain 8 bits (one byte) of information in their flip flops. The program counter (PC) and stack pointer (SP) are 16-bit registers. IR is the Instruction Register (8 bits), ALU the Arithmetic Logic Unit (to add, subtract, compare, do logical operations such as AND, OR), ID the Instruction Decoder (see also Fig. 10). The 8-bit instruction is latched by the IR. 2^8 different instructions are possible. The ID is an 8×256 decoder meaning that a given instruction $D_7 \ldots D_0$ input to it will cause *one* of 256 output lines Qi to go low where i is the decimal equivalent of the binary $D_7 \ldots D_0$. The line going low thus *identifies* the instruction to the control section and microprogram. The "W" line is the "write" line—its logic state allows an address, or location, in memory to receive and store a data or instruction byte sent to it from the CPU via the data bus when the address bus is pointing to that location via the memory decoder. The "R" line is the "read" line—its logic state allows a location or address in memory (the one pointed to by the address bus via the memory decoder) to empty its contents on to the data bus back to the CPU. This sends the stored byte back to the CPU via the bidirectional data bus. Decoders and control signals $\overline{MEMW}$ and $\overline{MEMR}$ generated by the microcomputer (Fig. 11) determine whether the W line to a particular memory goes low (write into memory, as when programming or when storing the results of a program execution) or whether the R line to a particular memory goes low (read from memory, as when fetching an instruction from memory during a program execution or when retrieving results stored in memory). (The relevant control signals $\overline{MEMW}$ and $\overline{MEMR}$ referred to above are generated from "status bits" (see Chap. 5, Section 2G). Until the subject of status bits and control signals are taken up in more detail in Chap. 5, we may say briefly here that status bits are signals that the CPU sends on to the data bus at the beginning of an instruction cycle and these bits tell us the nature of the instruction that will follow, i.e., whether it will write into memory, or read from memory, or write into an I/O, etc.) When we say that the location or address in memory that we are referring to is determined by the address bus pointing to it, we mean that the 16 bits $A_{15} \ldots A_8, A_7 \ldots A_0$ on the address bus determine a precise location address (a high part of the address $A_{15} \ldots A_8$ —the block number, and a low part of the address $A_7 \ldots A_0$ —the specific location in that block). It is the program counter, PC, under the direction of the control section, that puts this address on the address bus during the program's *fetch* (read) (see Fig. 8 and 10), while the keyboard, via the encoder, and the H, L registers in conjunction with a MOV M, C instruction (KEX program), puts the address on the address bus during the *programming in* (write). The "input device" in Fig. 8 may be the keyboard (device number 000 octal), another computer, paper tape, a measuring instrument feeding in its data or status (e.g., traffic sensors), a teletype (TTY), cassette tape, etc. The "output device" in Fig. 8 may be a CRT monitor, a printer, another computer, a device to be controlled, a bank of LED's or other numeric display, a TTY, a counter, an IC chip, etc., any of which are to receive information or instructions from the microcomputer for control purposes. Often the "isolated" I/O devices can be considered as extensions of the memory in that they are locations that must also be read from or written to. This is accomplished (see Chaps. 3, 5) by two, and only two, 8080 instructions: "output ⟨accumulator⟩ to device number B_2," or "input data from device number B_2 to the accumulator,"—both implemented via the data bus.*

---

*"Memory mapped I/O," not treated in this book, uses memory based instructions for I/O's to avoid the accumulator.

The data bus (Figs. 8, 10) consists of 8 lines each carrying a bit D_i of information, the totality forming an instruction (or data) byte D_7, D_6 ... D_0; e.g., $(11\ 011\ 101)_2 = (335)_8$. The data bits thus flow in parallel from CPU to memory or I/O device, or in reverse—the data bus is bidirectional. The address bus consists of 16 lines each containing a bit, A_i, the totality forming an "address" of a location in memory: A_{15}, A_{14}, ... A_0 —usually divided into a Hi part A_{15} ... A_8 and a Lo part A_7 ... A_0. This delineates a "block" in memory (the high part of the address) in which the various "houses" reside (the low part of the address). Note the importance of tristating buffers to keep all registers, memory, and I/O's off the common busses except the source and destination members relevant at the time they are called by the instruction in the program.

Each location in memory is capable of storing and retaining an instruction byte (and eventually giving it back); for example, 074 = 00 111 100 (which means, in the Intel 8080 instruction code, "increment the contents of the accumulator by 1"); the totality of instructions one after the other in logical order residing in various specific memory locations forms the "program" which when run or executed will control a process or device, or put out a numerical result, or make a decision, etc. The CPU recalls (fetches) these instructions from the various memory locations when the program is run and executes them according to what the ID finds out about that instruction. The result of the ID's decoding is to get the control section in the CPU to execute the instruction that it has decoded; i.e., identified. Thus a "Mov C, B" instruction $(110)_8$ already discussed in Chap. 1 (pp. 00—00) will be decoded by the ID as a "Move contents of register B to register C" and the timing and control section, responding to the *microprogram* stored in the CPU, will put out the necessary pulses and clock signals to effect this transfer (B)→C, precisely as explained in pp. 00—00. In this way a complete program is run and its instructions executed. The final results (numerical values, or bytes, producing control decisions) might be stored in a register, in the accumulator, in memory, or they might be output to a device (traffic lights, or measurement instruments) for control purposes, or have a device input its status or data to the microcomputer. Thus a result 10 101 111 might tell devices 0, 1, 2, 3, 5, and 7 to go on and devices 6 and 4 to go off.

The arched lines with arrows in Fig. 8 inside the memory are intended to show "how" a location in memory is "addressed" by the address bus/decoder combination. They also show "how" an

8-bit instruction or data byte gains access, via the data bus, to that address in memory. This is used for storage during the programming, or writing, into memory. During the execution of the program the address arc in memory still points to particular locations, one after the other under direction of the constantly incrementing PC—but the data/instruction arc is reversed as a given location empties its byte back to the CPU via the data bus for decoding and execution (this is the read or fetch cycle).

The way we address a location is simple: $A_{15} \ldots A_0$ are the bits on the address bus and they are divided into a high part and a low part:

$$10\ 111\ 011, \quad 00\ 101\ 110 \ = \ (273)_8 H, \quad (056)_8 L$$
$$\leftarrow Hi \rightarrow \qquad \leftarrow Lo \rightarrow$$

This is analogous to a house address in the form "124-21 Queens Boulevard"—the 124 might correspond to the block number and the 21 to the house in that block. For that reason we have shown the memory in Fig. 8 divided into blocks, with each block consisting of various locations (dots). Clearly

$$A_{15} \ldots A_8, \quad A_7 \ldots A_0$$
$$\leftarrow Hi \rightarrow \qquad \leftarrow Lo \rightarrow$$

shows 2^8 possible blocks (Hi addresses) and 2^8 possible locations (Lo addresses) in each block, the 2^8 *blocks* coming from all different possible combinations of $A_{15} \ldots A_8 H$ (i.e., 000 000 000 up to 11 111 111 which gives a total of 256 different blocks) and the 2^8 *locations* in a block coming from all different possible combinations of $A_7 \ldots A_0 L$ (i.e., 00 000 000 up to 11 111 111, again, 256 in number). Thus a total of $256 \times 256 = 65,536$ (64K) different locations can be addressed (if the memory is big enough to accommodate all those locations). This of course agrees with all possible different address combinations $A_{15} \ldots A_0$ that can exist in bit form on the address bus; i.e., 2^{16} different combinations. Because each location can store 8 bits (one byte, or one word) from the data bus, we say we have 65,536 bytes or 65,536 words or $65,536 \times 8$ bits, or $64K \times 8$-bit words. If we had a memory with only *one* block of capacity, the high address $A_{15} \ldots A_8$ would be a fixed number; e.g., $(000)_8$ or $(001)_8$, etc. and the low address would vary from $(000)_8$ to $(377)_8$ for a total of 256 different locations, maximum, in one block. We then say we have a memory capacity of 256 words, or 256 bytes, or 256×8 bits.

(This is indeed the case with two 8111 RAM IC memory chips or one 1702 PROM in the MMD-1).

We may think of the memory in another way.

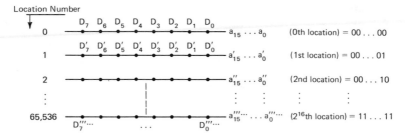

Figure 14.   Memory with 16 bit address bus and 8 bit data bus. 2^{16} locations each filled with 8 bits constituting an instruction. 2^8 different instructions.

Each location stores a data or instruction byte $\widehat{D_7 D_6}\ \widehat{D_5 D_4 D_3}$ $\widehat{D_2 D_1 D_0}$ (or word) that will subsequently be fetched (read) and sent to the CPU for execution when the program is run.

In the MMD-1 (see Fig. 13) there are four blocks of memory. Block 000 H (Hi address), block 001 H, block 002 H, and block 003 H. Block 000 is reserved for the IC 1702 Prom in which the KEX "bootstrap" program is written (Appendix C). It is a read-only memory which contains the program of instructions necessary to make the keyboard work properly with CPU and RAM memory; i.e., to insure during writing of the program, when certain keys are pressed, that a location in RAM memory is successfully addressed, that the data or instruction written in from the keyboard *gets to that location for storage*, and, in the case of the MMD-1, to have the hi address of the location displayed visibly on the 8 LED's of port 1, the lo address of the location displayed on the 8 LED's of port 0, and the instruction byte stored there displayed on the 8 LED's of port 2. It also insures that the program written in will be *executed* when other keys are pressed. Block 001 H is vacant but can accommodate another PROM. Block 002 is empty but can accommodate another RAM. Finally block 003 H is occupied by two 8111 IC memories (RAMS) comprising, together, 256 locations each capable of storing one byte when properly addressed and written into. Thus the capacity of block 000 is 000 H, 000 L to 377 L; that of block 001, if it were present, would be 001 H, 000 L to 377 L, and ditto for blocks 002 H and 003 H. As far as we are concerned, for the rest of this book (re: the MMD-1), we write into and read from, memory block 003 H only. We, of course, cannot write into 000 H which is the KEX PROM—it reads out only. The view of memory locations in the MMD-1 RAM that follows is the one we will stick to throughout the rest of the book.

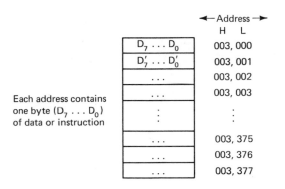

Figure 15. Memory locations in the 256 byte RAM—the situation in memory block 3 in the MMD-1.

2.2 HOW A PROGRAM IS WRITTEN INTO MEMORY AND EXECUTED: WHAT HAPPENS INSIDE THE MICROCOMPUTER (ADDRESS BYTE AND INSTRUCTION/DATA BYTE FLOW). THE KEYBOARD. BOOTSTRAPPING AND BOOTSTRAP LOADERS. THE "MACHINE CYCLE."

We will, for purposes of explanation, relate specifically to the MMD-1 microcomputer. We thus need only concern ourselves with memory block 003 H, where the read-write RAM resides, and into and from which instruction bytes will flow to the various locations (000 to 377) addressed. Note particularly in Fig. 13 the three ports: port 1 (left), port 0 (middle), port 2 (right)—each consisting of two 7475 latches (Chap. 1) and 8 LED's.

In what follows, the keyboard, keyboard encoder, and programmed "bootstrap" PROM are central in understanding the mechanism by which programs are written into RAM, and how their execution is started. We have used the KEX bootstrap (Keyboard Executive Program—Appendix C—courtesy Gernsback Publications) and the keyboard/encoder arrangement on the MMD-1 (Fig. 12, Chap. 2) to illustrate the bootstrapping of any program that we wish to write into RAM. However, the general principles, if not the specifics, are completely applicable to any other keyboard, encoder, and bootstrap PROM. Such dedicated PROMs are called *bootstrap loaders*.

The first step after power is turned on is to press the Reset Key. Pressing this key causes the CPU to place $A_{15} \ldots A_0 = 0$ in 0 on the address bus and into the program counter. This addresses block 000 H where the KEX bootstrap program is written into memory Prom IC 1702 A. Its purpose is to interact with the keyboard and make sure that each time a key is pressed certain things happen to insure the flow of a set of instructions into the correct address in memory, or to insure the execution of that program when another key (G) is pressed. This is referred to as *bootstrapping*. Briefly, pressing "Reset" causes KEX to load the H register in the CPU with 003 and the L register with 000 (see Appendix C). These 16 bits in the H, L register *pair* eventually reach the memory address register (MAR) and the *address bus*, which points to location 000 L in block 003 H. At this point we see LED's at port 1 indicate 000 000 011 = 003 and LED's at port 0 indicate 000. Port 2 will indicate some random data or bits that happen to be present in 003 H, 000 L after turn-on. The reason for the appearance of 003 and 000 at ports 1 and 0 will become clear in what follows. It is essential that you consult the 8080 instruction list (Appendix B) in all that follows, as well as App. C for KEX.

Suppose we now wish to write a program starting at, say, 172 L. Our first 8080 instruction to be entered there is, say, $(110)_8$ ("Move the contents of Register B into Register C": *Mnemonic*: "Mov C, B"). We first press 172 L on the keyboard and then 110 S. What happens? Consider first pressing 172. 1 gets encoded to 001, 7 to 111, and 2 to 010; each group is produced by the 74148 encoder (see Fig. 12 and Chap 1, p. 18). These binary bits flow to the 8095 IC (tristate buffer) shown in Fig. 12. After some programming experience with the experiments in Chap. 3, a study of the KEX program (Appendix C) will reveal how *each* key punch generates a pulse $\overline{IN} = \sqcup$ from the CPU in conjunction with the instruction $\begin{pmatrix} 333 \\ 000 \end{pmatrix}$ ("input keyboard data into the accumulator").

Figure 12 indicates that this $\overline{IN}$ pulse is applied to pin 15 (DIS_2) of the 8095, causing the successive binary bits waiting at the 8095 output to be "detristated" from their hi Z state (see Chap. 1, p. 10—on tristating). Thus (Fig. 12) the 001, 111, and 010 corresponding to 172 appear one after the other at the inputs to the latches (7475) of *each* port 0, 1, 2, as well as on the data bus going to the accumulator from which it is transferred to Reg. C to be saved (instruction 117 at location 130 in KEX). (See also Fig. 8, the "input device" there being the keyboard.) However, to this point *only* port 2 will show the 8 bits 01 111 010 corresponding to 172. This is so because the KEX program, detecting so far only numbers 172 from the keyboard, provides an instruction $\left(\begin{array}{c}323\\002\end{array}\right)$ ("output accumulator contents to port 2") *after* a MOV A, C = 171 instruction, generating another pulse from the CPU called $\overline{out}$ = ⊔, and this pulse is directed to port 2. See Fig. 12, particularly IC 19 whose inputs are $\overline{out}$ = ⊔ and an input from channel 2 of the 74L42 decoder. This latter input is also a pulse (called the *"device code pulse"*) and together with $\overline{out}$ = ⊔ produces a *"device select pulse"* ⊓ out of IC 19 which enables the two 7475's comprising *port 2* (pins 4, 13). This, of course, (Chap. 1) latches the $(172)_8$ bits input on the 7475's to port 2's LED's where they are displayed. ("Device selecting" and "device codes" are subjects which will concern us quite a bit in the experiments on interfacing in Chap. 5, so a complete understanding of them in the above context is not yet expected.) (Note that $A_2A_1A_0$ in Fig. 12 is the device code: $A_2A_1A_0 = (000)_2$, $(001)_2$, or $(010)_2$ for ports 0, 1, or 2 (i.e., $(000)_8$, $(001)_8$, $(002)_8$.) Thus at this point port 2 shows 01 111 010 and the accumulator and C registers contain 01 111 010.

We next press "L." The encoder and KEX generate $(011)_8$ = 00 001 001. It is "L's" code in KEX. The KEX program (Appendix C) stores this code in the accumulator at 355 and then tries to establish which key was pressed so that it will know what to subsequently do with the 172 waiting in register C. It does this by a *search-and-compare* routine using the "compare immediate" instruction $\left(\begin{array}{c}376\\011\end{array}\right)$, which does nothing more than subtract 011 from what's in A (the key code of the key pressed). If it is 0 then the "L" key was pressed and a JNZ ("jump if not zero") is ignored. 172 in C is transferred to L (Mov L, C = 151), then from L to A (Mov A, L = 175) and finally output from A to port 0, $\left(\begin{array}{c}323\\000\end{array}\right)$, where it is displayed. The latter instruction generates both $\overline{out}$ = ⊔ and a device code ⊔ pulse (the latter from channel 0 of the 74L42 IC in Fig. 12) which are combined in IC 19 to give a *device select pulse* ⊓ which goes to pins 4 and 13 of the 7475 latches at port 0 enabling them to latch the 172 coming from the accumulator via the data bus as a result of $\begin{pmatrix} 323 \\ 000 \end{pmatrix}$ instruction. Thus 172 = 01 111 010 now appears at *port 0*. This is the port that *always* exhibits the *Lo* part of the address at any given time in the programming sequence. (More on the 8080 instruction set in Chap. 3 and on device codes and selects in Chap. 5.)

To sum up when 1, 7, 2 are entered on the keyboard the resulting 8 bits are seen at port 2 and also reside in the accumulator and register C. When "L" is pressed 172 goes from C to the L register, then back to A and out to port 0. It disappears at port 2. (It is, however, still in the L register—register transfer does not destroy the data in the source register.) Thus at this point H = 003, L = 172 (a study of KEX will show that 003 appears at port 1 for the same basic reasons that 172 appears at port 0) and *this location in memory will be ready to receive data or an instruction as soon as the S key is pressed after the data or instruction are next entered on the keyboard.* See Figs. 16, 17.

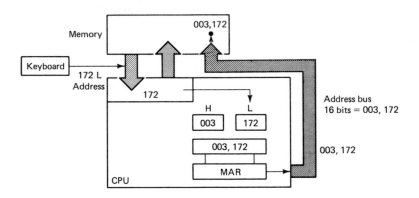

Figure 16. Accessing an address in memory via keyboard in order to write an instruction into RAM. The bits 003, 172 will be on the address bus as soon as key S is pressed (Fig. 17), for that will invoke the instruction 161: MOV M, C in KEX (M pointed to by the H, L register contents which this instruction dumps onto the address bus).

The next step is to write into location 003, 172 the instruction byte, in our example $(110)_8$. We press 1, it gets encoded to 001 and appears in the 8095 (Fig. 12). $\overline{\text{IN}} = $ ⊔ on pin 15, generated by the CPU at the direction of the KEX program when the key was punched, causes the 8095 to dump 001 on to the data bus to the accumulator and to the 7475's at port 2 where it is latched and exhibited (due to $\overline{\text{out}}$ from the CPU generated by the KEX program, and to the device code 002 from the 74L42). Likewise the next 001 in $(110)_8$ appears at port 2, and finally the 000. Again KEX transfers 110 to register C for saving—see instruction 117 at 130. Thus port 2 exhibits $(110)_8 = 01\ 001\ 000$ and $(110)_8$ resides in the accumulator and register C. *Pressing S* (110S) now causes something *different* to happen. The S key has its own KEX code which is generated by KEX and the 74148 (namely 013). The KEX program (Appendix C) stores the key code in A and searches and compares. When it concludes from its CPI $= \begin{pmatrix} 376 \\ 013 \end{pmatrix}$ (i.e., $\langle A \rangle = 013$) "compare" instruction that S has been pressed it follows up with a 161 instruction (MOV M, C). This instruction *transfers the 110 instruction in the accumulator* (by now in register C) *to the memory location 003 H, 172 L* being pointed to by the *address bus* (or in 8080 language, to "the location in memory being pointed to by (H), (L)"). The MOV M, C instruction places the contents of the H, L registers on the address bus and generates the necessary status bits* from which the control signal* $\overline{\text{MEMW}}$ (Figs. 11, 8) ⊔ is generated to cause the write (W) line to the RAM memory to go low. This *enables* the RAM to have C's data *written* into it, via the data bus, *at the location H, L present on the address bus.* KEX does something else after S is pressed and detected. It immediately follows with an instruction to *increment* the register pair H, L (i.e., "INX H" = 043). Thus 172 in L becomes 173 in L *and shows up immediately at port 0* (due to two instructions in KEX which transfers (L) to the accumulator (MOV A, L = 175), and then outputs (A) to port 0: $\begin{pmatrix} 323 \\ 000 \end{pmatrix}$). Thus the next location, 003 H, 173 L will be pointed to by the address bus the *next* time S is pressed. The situation is shown in Fig. 17 below.

We do not have to enter 173 L to get ready for our next instruction. We simply enter our next *instruction*, say 057 S ("complement the contents of Accum."). Then 174 L appears at port 0 and 003, 174 will be ready to receive *its* data or instruction next, and so on. In this way we enter our program and store it in memory at successive locations starting at 172 L.

If, for some reason, we wish to break the order of entering instructions and start programming at, say, 100 L (e.g., to enter

*Chap. 5, Section 5.2(G); Fig. 11 and Fig. 69.

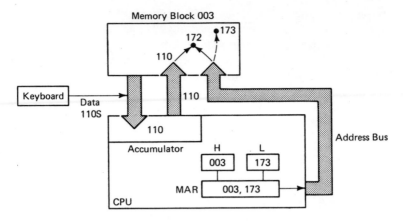

Figure 17. Writing an instruction into memory and incrementing the address bus. 003, 173 will be pointed to the next time the S key is pressed (another MOV M̂, Ĉ instruction does that). Pressing the S key the previous time caused L to increment by 1 to 173 as a result of 043 instruction: INX H (H, L pair) in KEX.

a subroutine), we would simply press 100 L on the keyboard; 100 would appear at port 0 and be contained in register L; we would then enter our instruction — — — S into memory. 101 L would immediately appear at port 0 and location 101 L in memory would be ready to accept the next instruction for the subroutine the next time S is pressed.

If we have more memory space available, we could store our program in higher memory blocks. We would simply start by pressing 030 H, for example, and the starting Lo address — — — L and then punch in the program as before, each — — — S causing the Lo address to increment by 1, but now in block 030 H.

We can very easily check our stored program. We would simply press 172 L—we would then observe 172 at port 0 and the data stored at that location would be revealed at port 2. Pressing S would reveal at port 2 the next instruction stored in 173 L (173 being shown at port 0); pressing S *again* would reveal at port 2 the instruction stored at 174 L, with 174 showing a port 0, etc. Thus we can "S" our way through successive memory locations and *S*ee the data *S*tored there. However, we must press a *particular* location (when it is not the next consecutive location in the program), if we wish to see the data stored there. A study of KEX shows how pressing S invokes Mov M̂, Ĉ, Mov Ĉ, M, Mov Â, Ĉ,

$\left(\begin{matrix}\text{Out}\\002\end{matrix}\right)$, Mov $\overparen{A, L}$, $\left(\begin{matrix}\text{Out}\\000\end{matrix}\right)$, Mov $\overparen{A, H}$, and $\left(\begin{matrix}\text{Out}\\001\end{matrix}\right)$ instructions to accomplish all this. Verify this.

Often, but not always (the writing of subroutines is a case in point), we start our main program at 003 H, 000 L, (pressing "Reset" gets us directly to KEX and then to 003 H, 000 L). We are then immediately ready to enter instructions one after the other. All we need to do in this case is key in an instruction, press S, key in the next one, press S, and so on, each press of S causing (L) to increment by 1, preparing the next address for the next instruction to be entered.

Since RAM's are "volatile" you cannot expect to turn off the power, turn it back on another time and find the program still stored in memory. It has been destroyed. ROM's, on the other hand, are non-volatile.

We are now ready to discuss what happens when we execute the program we have written into memory. If we stored the program starting at 003 H, 000 L, we simply press Reset, taking us back to 003 H, 000 L, and then G (Go). The program is now running and being executed. If it was stored starting at 003 H, 172 L we would press 172 L, thus assuring that location 003 H, 172 L will be pointed to by the address bus, and *then* press G. If the program was *already* running, or if a halt instruction had halted the computer run, you would first have to take it *out* of its run or halt *by pressing Reset, then* pressing 172 L, *then* G. This is a point to keep in mind. You cannot expect to run, or reprogram, if the computer is in a halt state (after instruction 166 is executed), or if it is already running. Reset brings it out of those states by pointing to 000, 000.

What happens when G is pressed? Refer to Fig. 8. For concreteness let's assume the following program has been written into memory.

Address	*Instruction*		*Mnemonic*
000L 001	$\left(\begin{matrix}076\\123\end{matrix}\right)$	——	MVI, A (move immediate byte to accum.)
002 003	$\left(\begin{matrix}323\\002\end{matrix}\right)$	——	out (A) to device 002 (here port 2)
004	166	——	HALT

Pressing G causes $(012)_8 = (00\ 001\ 010)$ to be encoded into the accumulator (a combination of the 74148 encoder action in Fig. 12 and KEX conversion of the encoder code from its own look-up table). KEX tests this number by its "search and compare" routine and when it finds that 012 is in the accumulator it concludes that G was pressed and it follows up with a PCHL = 351 instruction. PCHL (Intel 8080 Manual, Sept. 1975, pp. 4–12) moves ⟨H⟩ and ⟨L⟩ (the *starting* address in the program where we have already positioned ourselves) into the PC and then on to the address bus, thus pointing to, in this case, 003, 000, to *fetch* the instruction stored there. It is important to recognize that the status bits* associated with the PCHL instruction generate the necessary $\overline{\text{MEMR}}$ ⊐⌐ control signal* for the "read line," R, to memory (Figs. 8, 11) to go low, thereby enabling the memory at location H, L to *read out*. This is the antithesis of the situation when we were writing into memory, where Write instructions of the type Mov M̂, C created status bits* and subsequent control signals* which made the "write line" W go low, enabling the memory to be *written into*. In any event, instruction 076 is now *fetched* (read) from 000 L to the IR via the data bus. The IR latches 076 and exhibits it to the ID for identification and decoding. The result of this decoding is to recognize the instruction and prepare to implement it. The implementation is the responsibility of the timing and control section of the CPU in conjunction with the microprogram in the CPU which responds to what the ID has "told" it (see register transfer, Chap. 1). The microprogram will put out the necessary control pulses and timing signals to direct the actions between the specific source and destination pertinent to the macro-instruction that has been decoded by the ID. When 076 has been recognized and the PC has been incremented by 1 to 001 by the control section and placed on the address bus (as it always is during a *fetch*) the next byte (123) is fetched from memory position 001 via the data bus into the CPU. The fact that the *first byte* was 076 = MVI, A causes the CPU to recognize 123 as the *second* (companion) byte in the two byte instruction (here 076) and it transfers 123 to A (again the control section under microprogram direction implements the two byte instruction MVI, A in a manner similar to register transfer). PC has, meantime, been increased by 1 and location 002 in memory is addressed by the address bus. Its contents, 323, are fetched and read and recognized by the IR/ID

---

*Chap. 5, Section 5.2(G). Also Figs. 11, 69.

decoder as an "output to I/O" instruction.*   PC increases by 1 to 003 and location 003 dumps its byte (002) on to the data bus and is recognized by the CPU as the *companion byte* in the two byte instruction $\begin{pmatrix} 323 \\ 002 \end{pmatrix}$, i.e., as the address of the I/O port to which ⟨A⟩ is to be output.*   The execution of this two-byte instruction by the control section causes the data byte 123 presently in A to be output to port 2. The PC increases by 1 to 004 and location 004 L has its contents (166—a one byte instruction) fetched via the data bus into the IR/ID where it is identified and implemented (by the microprogram—control section): "halt the computer"—the CPU stops. Execution of the program should produce the visible result 123 at port 2.

And this is essentially the way all programs are executed: successive macro-instructions are fetched from addresses in memory pointed to by the address bus, the latter being constantly reloaded with the successive contents of the program counter. (The PC constantly increments the address by one during the program run, unless otherwise told by the control section in response to a particular instruction.) The fetched instruction flows to the IR in the CPU via, first, the external data bus (memory to CPU), then the internal (CPU) data bus. The ID examines the macro-instruction latched in the IR and, after decoding and identification, has the microprogram in the CPU direct the control and timing section to prepare for its execution by means of the proper pulses and clocks which will effect proper transfer from "source" to "destination." The control section increments the count in the PC during the fetch. The PC's contents then become the address on the address bus for the *next* location in memory whose stored byte will be fetched. In all of this the decoded instructions will have the microprogram generate the necessary status bits** from which control signals** are synthesized to allow memory and I/O read/write ⊔ where and when necessary. The following Fig. 18 summarizes the above. It shows how the clock pulses from the control section are vital in synchronizing the program counter with a fetch cycle and an execute cycle for each instruction in a typical microcomputer "machine cycle." We have shown the machine cycle as composed of 3 "states" (i.e., 3 clock pulses). It could consist of 4 or 5 states, depending on how many states are required for executing the

*Intel 8080 Manual, Sept. 1975, pp . 2-18.
**Chap. 5

machine cycle. An instruction might *need several machine cycles* for execution if, say, it were a *two- or three-byte instruction* (examples of these instructions will be given in the programs in Chap. 3). Additional machine cycles will be needed to fetch these additional bytes from memory. In addition, still "extra bytes" might be necessary to write other data into memory or I/O, or read back such data from memory or I/O *if the instruction calls for it*, Call, Ret, Push, Pop operations (Chap. 3), for example, must save or pop back "return addresses" or register contents, and the write into or read from memory (the "Stack") of these quantities via the data bus *becomes part of the instruction execution in the form of "extra bytes."* These extra machine cycles (see Chap. 4) are needed to accomplish these read/write–data/address bus transfers over and above the actual number of bytes in the instruction. *A new machine cycle is required each time the CPU has to access memory (fetch or otherwise) or an I/O port (to input or output data) during the program run.* You are referred to Fig. 35 in Chap. 4 and the Intel 8080 material reproduced there discussing machine cycles and state transitions. It should be carefully studied as it not only sheds further light on the relation between machine cycles and the flow of "extra bytes" on the one hand and the nature of the instruction, its fetch, and execution on the other hand, but will lead to an understanding of how single stepping (Chap. 4) can reveal the data and address flow on the busses during each machine cycle belonging to a given instruction, including the extra bytes.

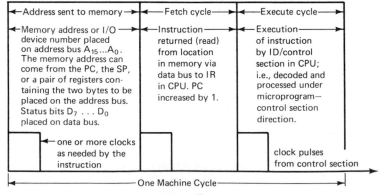

Figure 18. Events during a typical machine cycle in a program run (fetch-execution of an instruction). See also Fig. 2-5 Intel Manual Sept. 1975 and Fig. 35. Chapter 4. Several machine cycles may be needed to execute one instruction as in 2 or 3 byte instructions. Still extra machine cycles may be further required (Chapter 4).

Typical instructions require from 1 to 5 machine cycles for complete execution and the number of states (clock pulses) required can be anything from 4 to 18. For a 2 MHZ clock driving the 8080, a state would last 0.5 μs so, depending on the instruction, fetch and execution of a complete instruction can take anywhere from 2–9 μs. This is important to remember in estimating time delays or times for complete program execution in Chap 3. Details on machine cycles and the number of clock pulses required for every 8080 instruction are given in Chap. 4 of the "Intel 8080 Microcomputer System User's Manual," Sept. 1975.

A word on memories. This is an extensive subject and the reader is referred to Refs. 1, 2, 3, 4, 21, 22, 28. It is beyond the scope of this book to go into details. An explanation of how a simple ROM works, however, will give the reader a feeling for memory and its importance in the microcomputer. Figure 19 shows a simple ROM of the linear selection type.

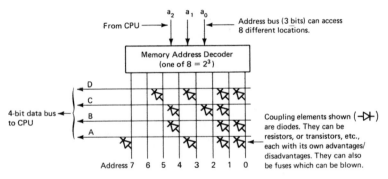

Figure 19. 3 bit address bus, 4 bit data bus. Read only memory (8 words each 4 bits).

It is clear that when $A_2 A_1 A_0$ = 000, or 001, or 002, . . . or 111 only address 0 is +5 volts, or address 1 is +5 volts, or . . . address 7 is +5 volts, respectively. This is the result of the 3-line to one of 8-line decoder. If we are addressing location 0, then the diode coupling elements ("written" in by us or the manufacturer, permanently, in accordance with the desired program we wish to store) cause DCBA to output the "instruction" byte 1011. As the PC increments $A_2 A_1 A_0$ = 001 and location 1 (now at 5 volts) causes the 1111 "instruction" stored there to emerge on the data bus. In this way, as the PC constantly increments inside the CPU, the "instructions" 1011, 1111, 0100, 1001, 0110, 1000, 0000, 0001 come out (fetched) one after the other for execution in the CPU.

It should be reiterated here that at this point we are assuming the microcomputer can and does generate the control signals ($\overline{\text{MEMR}}$, $\overline{\text{MEMW}}$, $\overline{\text{IN}}$, ($\overline{\text{I/OR}}$), $\overline{\text{Out}}$, ($\overline{\text{I/OW}}$), and $\overline{\text{IACK}}$ ($\overline{\text{INTA}}$)) that are essential if it is to successfully implement the writing in of a program, its execution, and the I/O interfacing necessary to communicate with I/O's under program control. They were briefly introduced in this chapter but cannot be completely understood until the matter of "status bits" with which they are intimately related is taken up in Chap. 5. Briefly they are signals that are generated by the microcomputer in response to the status bits associated with an instruction (or byte) fetched from ROM or RAM, and assure that the demands of the *machine cycle* (read or write) associated with *that (extra) byte or instruction (OP. Code)* will be carried out. When these control signals are correctly interfaced to memories or I/O's they will, at the appropriate times in the program run (ROM or RAM), ensure that the memories or I/O's can be written into or read from as dictated by the program and the nature of each machine cycle or by the I/O itself (as with interrupts). A good appreciation of microcomputer *interfacing* work depends on an understanding of status bits and control signals. The interfacing experiments in Chap. 5 and the theory in Section 5.2(G) will elucidate these matters.

Chapter 3

Software and Programming Experiments with the 8080 Instruction Set

3.1 INTRODUCTION

We are now ready to launch into the experiments. Chapters 1 and 2 should give us a good idea as to what happens, and why, within a microcomputer when a program is written into memory and then executed. The experiments start out simply and build in complexity and power in orderly, logical fashion as we progressively familiarize ourselves with the use and capabilities of the 8080 Instruction set (Appendix B). The experiments are divided into three chapters—one on software and programming alone (Chap. 3), one on single stepping which involves some hardware (Chap. 4), and one on the important subject of interfacing and device selecting which involves an intimate relationship among software, hardware, I/O's, and often single stepping (Chap. 5). Each chapter is broken down to fundamental experiments which increase in complexity as various subheadings and new subject matter are introduced. Where a new subject is introduced, the basic theory and discussion is presented first before the experiments are undertaken. Only that theory is presented which is relevant and essential to the subject and to the group of experiments presented illustrating that subject. You should consult at all times Appendix B (the Intel Instruction Set) and Appendix C (the KEX Program for MMD-1), as well as Appendix A for IC and display details.

The experiments will undoubtedly motivate you to try out your own variations on the software and interfacing experiments presented. You should be encouraged to do so everywhere you can, playing with as many different instructions or hardware versions as possible (even if your program is longer) in order to gain confidence and ability. We have tried to employ as wide a variety of instructions as possible, some very powerful ones. By trying alternative approaches and thinking up still other motivating experiments you will be gaining a thorough understanding of the 8080 and, ultimately, of microprocessors generally. At the end of the series of experiments in this book you should be in an excellent position to go on to more sophisticated and practical interfacing applications and studies involving, to name a few: CRT monitors, character generators, memory extensions, TTY, cassette recorders, modems, graphics, Priority Interrrupts, Programmable Peripheral Interfacing, controls of all kinds of processes from instrumentation to traffic, Debug Proms, electronic music, and so on. A second book on applications experiments will be forthcoming sometime in 1978.

Note that all experiments in Chaps. 3, 4, and 5 are programmed in octal code, but can be programmed in hexadecimal as well. The Instruction list for the 8080 in Appendix B is given in both octal and hexadecimal. E & L Instruments Inc. has an add-on keyboard ("HEX Key Pad") adapter for its MMD-1 which allows programming in either octal or hexadecimal.

Contents of a register or memory location will be denoted by e.g., ⟨B⟩ or (B) or ⟨M⟩ or (M), etc. throughout. The register or memory location itself is denoted simply by B or M etc.

3.2 SIMPLE PROGRAMS ILLUSTRATING THE 8080 INSTRUCTION SET AND ITS POSSIBILITIES

Experiment 3-2(a)   Demonstration that 377 + 1 = 000
                              and 000 − 1 = 377
                              (see Chap. 1, Sec. 1)

Load and execute the following program (A = accumulator, B_2 = second byte of two-byte instruction)

	Address	Instruction	Mnemonic
003	230	$\begin{pmatrix} 076 \\ 377 \end{pmatrix}$	MVI A, (B_2) (move immediate byte to A)
"	231		
"	232	074	INR A: (increment (A) by 1)
"	233	$\begin{pmatrix} 323 \\ 000 \end{pmatrix}$	out (B_2): (output (A) to port 0)
"	234		
"	235	075	DCR A: (decrement (A) by 1)
"	236	$\begin{pmatrix} 323 \\ 001 \end{pmatrix}$	out (B_2): (output (A) to port 1)
"	237		
"	240	166	HLT (halt)

Observe the results 000 at port 0 and 377 at port 1. Don't forget to start your run from 230L.

A variation of the above would be

230	$\begin{pmatrix} 076 \\ 377 \end{pmatrix}$
231	
232	074
233	$\begin{pmatrix} 323 \\ 001 \end{pmatrix}$
234	
235	166

and of course we again see 000 at port 1. But if we now replace 166 by (just Press 235 L and "S" in the following instructions from that point)

235	$\begin{pmatrix} 303 \\ 232 \\ 003 \end{pmatrix}$	——	JMP to B_2, B_3
236		——	Lo address $= 232 = B_2$
237		——	Hi address $= 003 = B_3$

we will see 377 at port 1. Why? 303 is an unconditional jump instruction (3 bytes) to go back to 003, 232 and redo the program from that point. We are clearly in a loop, for every time we come back down to 303 we are forced back to 232 where another increment of the accumulator occurs. The program is executed so fast that the successive increments at 232 appear one after the other at port 1. The eye cannot distinguish them.

Experiment 3-2(b)   A Program to Store Data Into Memory

000	$\begin{pmatrix} 076 \\ 333 \end{pmatrix}$	MOV I, A, (B_2)
001		(B_2)

002	$\begin{pmatrix} 062 \\ 100 \\ 003 \end{pmatrix}$	STA (B_2) (B_3) = store (A) direct into M
003		B_2 = Lo addressed by B_2, B_3; i.e.,
004		B_3 = Hi into location 003 H, 100 L

005	000 = NOP
006	000 = NOP (no operation)
007	000 = NOP
010	166 = Halt

Run the program, bring it out of halt by resetting, observe 333 in memory location 100 L. The two NOPs at 006 and 007 do nothing but consume time. They are useful in leaving blank spaces where programs can be easily modified. Thus, after running, re-program 006 and 007 to 323, 001, run and observe 333 at port 1. STA is a good way to modify the contents of a memory location "on the run", thereby exerting running control over another program.

Experiment 3-2(c)   Only Way to Examine a Register's Contents Is Through the Accumulator

The only output instruction available is $\begin{pmatrix} 323 \\ B_2 \end{pmatrix}$, and it means:

"output (A) to output device no. B_2" (here one of the three ports 0, 1, 2 on the MMD-1. In the interfacing experiments in Chap. 5 we will learn how to output (A) to any of a number of *other* ports outside the MMD-1.)

There is no instruction that allows us to "out (R) to port B_2" with the 8080 chip alone,* where R is a register other than the accumulator. Hence to demonstrate how to examine the contents of register D, for instance, we write the following program.

000	$\begin{pmatrix} 026 \\ 321 \end{pmatrix}$	MVI D, (B_2) (move immediate byte to D register)
001		
002	172	MOV $\overset{\frown}{A, D}$ (move contents of D to accumulator)
003	$\begin{pmatrix} 323 \\ 002 \end{pmatrix}$	output (A) to port 2
004		
005	$\begin{pmatrix} 303 \\ 000 \\ 003 \end{pmatrix}$	jump to 003 H, 000 L
006		
007		

*except by "memory mapped I/O," which we shall not discuss in this book. The next book on Applications will treat that subject.

We have placed the byte 321 into register D and then examined its contents at port 2. You should find 321 there. You can just as well run the program with a halt at 005. Try it. Try also

$$
\text{I}\begin{cases} 100 \\ 101 \\ 102 \end{cases} \quad \begin{pmatrix} 026 \\ 321 \end{pmatrix} \\ 166
$$

$$
\text{II}\begin{cases} 000 \\ 001 \\ 002 \\ 003 \end{cases} \quad \begin{matrix} 172 \\ \begin{pmatrix} 323 \\ 002 \end{pmatrix} \\ 166 \end{matrix}
$$

Run I, then II. Observe port 2. I stores a byte in D. II explores D for that byte.

Experiment 3-2(d)   The Need for a Time Delay Program (e.g., Programming a Counter)

Consider the following counter program. Run it.

000	$\begin{pmatrix} 076 \\ 000 \end{pmatrix}$	put 000 in A
001		
002	$\begin{pmatrix} 323 \\ 001 \end{pmatrix}$	out (A) to port 1
003		
004	074	INR A by 1

004

▓▓▓▓▓▓▓▓▓ ←————→ future time delay program here

005

005	$\begin{pmatrix} 303 \\ 002 \\ 003 \end{pmatrix}$	JMP to 003 H, 002 L
006		
007		

You should see 377 at port 1 because the INR A instructions are occurring so fast, as are the subsequent outputs to port 1 ($\sim$5 μs per instruction). We are almost instantly counting from $(000)_8$ to $(377)_8$ and then back over again. Hence all the LED's will *appear* to be constantly lit.

Here is an obvious case where we need a time delay program to slow down the intervals between successive 074 increments. A time delay program does nothing more than that—it wastes time doing nothing, going round and round in a *loop*(s) of instructions until the program tells it to get out of the loop(s) at a predetermined (programmed) time and go back to the main program, then to go back into the T.D. (time delay loop) again if we want to, then out of it, and so on. In this way we should be able to see 074 produce discrete, visible increments at port 1 as we count up from 000 to 377, then jump back down to 000, count up to 377 again, etc. Looking at the program, we see that writing a time delay routine in the shaded block region of the program (say 0.5 or 1 second in delay) would do the trick. Let us discuss a time delay program that can waste anywhere from ~ 0.03 millisecond to 9 or 10 minutes. We shall use this time delay program throughout the book with appropriate "timing bytes" inserted into the T.D. program to give us the desired time delay for a particular application. The program is *based* on the 10 ms debouncing time delay residing in KEX at 000, 277 (see Appendix C) and presented on p. 30 of E & L Instrument's MMD-1 Operating Manual (801-0082, REV. B 8/76), but is extended here to give flexibility for producing time delays from less than 0.01 second to over 550 seconds (note KEX resides in 000 H, ours in 003 H). We wish to acknowledge E & L Instruments Inc. and Gernsback Publications for their permission to use this part of the KEX program. The extended Time Delay Program is presented below and the explanation follows. (Note, we present it starting at address 100 for convenience only. The starting address can be altered to suit the programming needs of a particular experiment. Just be careful about the "jump to" addresses inserted into the JNZ instructions.) The time delay program and how it works follow.

003	100	305	Push B	These instructions* free
	101	325	Push D	registers (B,C), (D,E) (A
	102	365	Push PSW*	and the flags) in turn for use in the T.D. program. Their previous contents are saved in "the stack"* to be retrieved at the end of the time delay program.
	103	006	MVI B, B_2 move byte B_2 into register B.	
	104	B_2	timing byte B_2 (adjustable)	
	105	021	LXI D/E: Load register pair D,E with bytes B_3, B_2, respectively.	
	106	046	time byte E (adjustable) = B_2.	
Loop 2	107	D	time byte D (adjustable) (KEX takes D=001) = B_3.	

*See Sections 3-3 and 3-6.

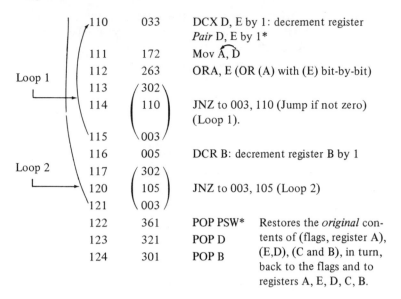

	110	033	DCX D, E by 1: decrement register *Pair* D, E by 1*
	111	172	Mov A, D
Loop 1	112	263	ORA, E (OR (A) with (E) bit-by-bit)
	113	302	
	114	110	JNZ to 003, 110 (Jump if not zero) (Loop 1).
	115	003	
	116	005	DCR B: decrement register B by 1
Loop 2	117	302	
	120	105	JNZ to 003, 105 (Loop 2)
	121	003	
	122	361	POP PSW* Restores the *original* con-
	123	321	POP D tents of (flags, register A),
	124	301	POP B (E,D), (C and B), in turn, back to the flags and to registers A, E, D, C, B.

The actual time delay resides between 103 and 121, as indicated. Why the instructions Push B, Push D, and Push PSW at 100, 101, 102, and the instructions POP PSW, POP D, and POP B at 122, 123, and 124? A *lot* more will be said about the Push and Pop instructions, and the "stack," further on in this chapter. But we can give good reasons here why they must be used by alluding generally to what Push and Pop instructions do. As we saw in Experiment 3-2(d), the time delay program must be inserted somewhere in the middle of the main program. Now our time delay program, spanning 103 to 121, uses registers B, D, and E, as well as the accumulator. It may well be that a particular program needs to use B, D, E and the accumulator registers *before* and *after* the time delay portion. The portion of the program *after* the T.D., to be successful, requires that the contents of registers B, D, E be exactly what they were *before* the T.D. (Indeed Experiment

---

*DCX D, E means E gets decremented by 1. Doing it enough times will eventually bring E to 000 and then to 377, at which point the borrow causes D to now decrement by 1. DCR E would only decrement E and *never* borrow from D.

*PSW = "processor status word" which is a 16 bit word consisting of ⟨A⟩ followed by the 8 bit "flag" word status. See more on flags in Section 7, this chapter, and pp. 4–13, Intel Manual, Sept. 1975.

3-2(d) does use A before and after the T.D., though not the B, D, E registers.) In that case it is absolutely necessary to save what was in B, D, E and A *somewhere* (in the "stack"—a portion of memory which we can assign for use—more on that later) before we enter the actual T.D. at 103 to 121 (hence the Push B, Push D, and Push PSW instructions—they accomplish this task). Then after the T.D. is completed it is essential that these contents be restored back to their former respective registers A, E, D, B (POP PSW, POP D, and POP B accomplish this). *Specifically*, as we shall see later in this chapter in some detail, "Push D" saves the register *pair* D and E (pushes their contents on to the stack in memory). Likewise "Push B" with respect to the register pair B, C, and "Push PSW" with respect to (A) and the (flag word). POP D pops the former contents of the *pair* E and D from the stack back to registers E and D, and similarly for "POP B" and "POP PSW"; i.e., POP PSW restores the former content of the flag word and A back to the flags and A, respectively. Thus Push's and POP's act on register *pairs*. Even if you need to save and restore the contents of one register, you must do so via a Push and POP on its concomittant *register pair* (A, flags; B, C; D, E; H, L). Note also that we POP in the *exact reverse* order that we push. This is very important as we shall discuss later. Your program won't work if you don't adhere to this. You may end up popping (D), (E) back to the B, C registers.

The balance of the program, after the T.D. is finished, can now continue to do its job with the registers containing the precise values they had before the time delay was entered, even though those registers were used and altered *during* the time delay program.

Let us analyze what happens during the time delay between 103 and 121. As an example take B_2 at 104 to be 003 and D at 107 to be 001 (as in the 10 ms KEX program). The instruction 033 at 110 decrements E by 1 to 045 and 172 at 111 moves 001 to A. 263 at 112 OR'S (A) = 001 with (E) = 045, the result (Chap. 1) being *not* zero. Hence JNZ returns us to 110 (via Loop 1) where 033 reduces E to 044, D *still being 001*. 263 therefore gives a result which is *still* not 0. Hence back to 110 via Loop 1. This goes on a total of $(046)_8 = (38)_{10}$ times till E = 000 and D = 001. One more time and E decrements to 377 (000 − 001 = 377, Chap. 1) in which case the ensuing borrow reduces D from 001 to 000 (*the DCX D, E instruction causes the borrow to be effective on D. Contrarily*, a *DCR E* instruction (035) would decrement E to 377 but the borrow would *not* affect D). At this point 172 puts

000 into A, but (A) OR'd with (E) = 377 is still not 000. So JNZ goes through 256 more motions in loop 1 till E decrements to 000 and finally the ORA, E instruction will OR (D) = 000 with (E) = 000 to yield 000. JNZ at 113 is ignored and we proceed to 116 where 005 instruction (DCR B) causes (B) to go from 003 to 002. The JNZ at 117 thus takes us back to 105 via *loop 2* and we start *all over again*. Then (B) goes from 002 to 001, and we go back to 105 again. Finally (B) = 000 and JNZ at 117 is ignored. We POP PSW, D, and B and are ready to get out of the time delay program. We have successfully produced time delay. How much? Look at Loop 1, the heart of the time delay. From Chap. 4, pp. 4–15, Intel 8080 Microcomputer Systems User's Manual (Sept. 1975) the instructions 033, 172, 263, and (302, B_2, B_3) consume 5, 5, 4, and 10 clock cycles respectively. The MMD-1 clock generator has been slowed to 750 kHz or 1.33 μs. Hence 24 $\times$ 1.33 μs $\times$ 294 $\simeq$ 10 ms. Where is the 294 from? We have had to decrement E 294 times ($046_8 = 38_{10}$ and $377_8 = 255_{10}$) to get *both* (D) and (E) back to 0 before we get out of *Loop 1* and move on to 116. *Thus inner Loop 1 with D = 001 takes 10 msec.* Multiply this, in this case, by B_2 = 003 and get 3 $\times$ 10 ms = 30 ms total time delay, where 3 = the number of times outer *Loop 2* must be traversed before we get out of it and move on to 122.

It is clear that if we increase all or some of the time bytes E at 106, D at 107, and B_2 at 104 we will increase our time delay proportionately (each increase in D by 1 causes another 256 transversals of inner Loop 1). Simple calculation or measurement yields the following approximate time delays in seconds for various timing bytes B_2 and D (keeping E at 046).

Table 3-1. Approximate time delays in seconds as a function of B_2 and D bytes for E = 046. Note: Maximum T.D. for D = B_2 = E = 377. In that case (T.D.) max $\sim$ 9 minutes. Minimum T.D. for D = 000, B_2 = E = 001. Then (T.D.) min $\sim$ 0.03 msec.

E = 046: Time Delay Program

D \ B_2	001	005	012	024	062	144	310	370
001	.01	.05	.1	.2	.5	1	2	2.5
015	.1	.5	1	2	5	10	20	25
032	.2	1	2	4	10	20	40	50

It is important to note that, whether you employ all or some of the Push and Pop instructions at 100, 101, 102 and 122, 123, 124 depends on whether registers B, D, E, and A (all or some of them) will be required in your program after the T.D. is finished (*and with the same content they had before the T.D. was entered*). If the answer is yes use that particular Push and Pop, if not don't use it (them) at the pertinent 100, 101, 102, 122, 123, or 124 addresses. You must thus examine your program before and after the T.D. for register deployment. To play safe, *if in doubt,* always use Push B, Push D, Push PSW at 100, 101, 102 and Pop PSW, Pop D, Pop B at 122, 123, 124. To repeat, we will use this T.D. program in various versions throughout this book.

You will also see later how $\begin{pmatrix} 006 \\ B_2 \end{pmatrix}$ at 103, 104 may have to be pulled out of the T.D. program and inserted in the main program just before the T.D. is entered. This will allow us to use the T.D. several times with different delays. More on this aspect in the examples that follow throughout the book.

The above table should prove helpful in choosing the length of time delay to fit your needs. This is a two-loop time delay program. Other 2-loop and 3-loop T.D. programs are given in the literature (see references Appendix E). By adding another look before 103 e.g. $\begin{matrix} 016 \\ C_2 \end{matrix}$ with proper 015 and JNZ instructions you can achieve a *35 hour t.d.* (C=B=D=E=377).

Getting back to Experiment 3-2(d) let us insert the above time delay program just after 004 in that program. (Take $B_2 = 144$, D = 001, E = 046 for a 1 second T.D. Speed it up or slow it down if you like.) The Program is presented below.

Run the experiment and observe the discrete counting pattern at port 1; for example, 00000001, 00000010, 00000011, 00000100, . . . , up to 11111111 and then back to 00000000, etc. Try various timing bytes ($B_2 = 062$ and D = 001) at 007 and 012 and observe the count at port 1. (See Table 3-1.) Observe that the experiment does not work without the Push and Pop instructions. Try it with NOP's (000) at either 005 or 025 or at both places. You can add $\begin{pmatrix} 323 \\ 000 \end{pmatrix}$ and $\begin{pmatrix} 323 \\ 002 \end{pmatrix}$ instructions after 003L and before 004L and get counting at all three ports.

Can you think of a program that will allow counting at the three ports, each at different speeds?

000	$\begin{pmatrix} 076 \\ 000 \end{pmatrix}$	
001		
002	$\begin{pmatrix} 323 \\ 001 \end{pmatrix}$	(A) to port 1
003		

	004	074	INR A
	005	365	Push PSW (the only Push needed for this program since only A is involved before and after the T.D.)
	006	(006	MVI B
	007	144) =	B_2 (See Table 3-1)
	010	(021	LXI D/E
	011	046	
	012	001) =	D (See Table 3-1)
	013	033	DCX D,E
Time	014	172	Mov A,D
Delay	015	263	ORA, E
	016	(302	
	017	013	JNZ
	020	003)	
	021	005	DCR B
	022	(302	
	023	010	JNZ
	024	003)	
	025	361	Pop PSW
	026	(303	
	027	002	JMP
	030	003)	to 003 H, 002 L

Experiment 3-2(e)   **Some Experiments on Storing Data Into And Retrieving Data From Memory—The Instructions Mov M,R and Mov R,M (M = memory location pointed to by the H, L pair, and R is any register, including the accumulator).**

(i) — *The Basic Mechanics*

000	(001	LXI B,* (B_2) (B_3) Load immediate 2 bytes into Register *Pair* B,C
001	111	— (B_2) into Reg C
002	222)	— (B_3) into Reg B
003	(041	LXI H,* (B_2) (B_3) load immediate 2 bytes into Register *Pair* H,L
004	100	— into L
005	003)	— into H } *Memory Pointer*; i.e., will point to address 003H, 100L via address bus

*Sometimes written as LXI B,C and LXI H,L.

006	160	Mov M̂,B (Move (B) to M pointed to by (H), (L); i.e., to 003 H, 100L)
007	176	Mov Â,M (Move (M) to A;M pointed to by (H), (L); i.e., from 003H, 100L)
010	$\left(\begin{array}{c}323\\001\end{array}\right)$	out (A) to port 1
011		
012	043	INXH Increment H,L *Pair* by 1*
013	161	Mov M̂,C (Move (C) to M pointed to by H, L; i.e., to 003H, 101L)
014	176	Move A,M (Move $M_{003,101}$ to A).
015	$\left(\begin{array}{c}323\\002\end{array}\right)$	
016		out (A) to port 2
017	166	HALT

Run the program and then examine the contents of 100L and 101L. They should contain the bytes 222 and 111, respectively, *as should ports 1 and 2, respectively*. Replace the program starting at 017L by

017	$\left(\begin{array}{c}303\\012\\003\end{array}\right)$	
020		JMP back to 003H, 012 L
021		

Preload locations, for example, 100L up to 110L with any kind of data you like (garbage). Run the new program. What do you expect to happen?

Examine the contents of 100L on up in memory, and also 000L on up. Explain the results.

You might vary the program as shown here.

000	$\left(\begin{array}{c}076\\222\end{array}\right)$	MVI, A
001		
002	$\left(\begin{array}{c}041\\100\\003\end{array}\right)$	LXI, H
003		—— to L
004		—— to H

---

*INX H (also written as INX H,L) increments L by 1. Doing it enough times brings L to 377 and then to 000 at which point the carry spills over into the H register incrementing it by 1—in our case from 003 to 004 if enough INX H were applied. INR L, on the other hand, increments *only* L and in going from 377 to 000 the carry would not affect H.

005	167	Mov M̂,A
006	074	INR A
007	043	INX H
010	167	Mov M̂,A
011	053	DCX H
012	176	Mov Â,M
013	⎛ 323 ⎞	(A) → port 0
014	⎝ 000 ⎠	
015	043	INX H
016	176	Mov Â,M
017	⎛ 323 ⎞	(A) → port 1
020	⎝ 001 ⎠	
021	166	Halt

Results. You should see 222 at port 0 and 223 at port 1; 222 at 100L and 223 at 101L.

(ii) Simulation of the transfer of a program from cassette tape into memory and then running it on the microcomputer. The program that follows simulates what happens when a program of instruction bits is to be transferred from tape to memory and then run on the microcomputer. Programs in principle similar to this are provided and must be employed whenever programs stored on tape are to be transferred to and used in a microcomputer.

200L	⎛ 041 ⎞	LXI H ⎫
201	⎜ 000 ⎟ — L Reg	⎬ Initializes the memory pointer H, L
202	⎝ 003 ⎠ — H Reg	⎭
203	⎛ 076 ⎞	Mov I, A
204	⎝ 076 ⎠	
205	167	Mov M̂,A where M is location pointed to by H, L = 003, 000
206	043	INX H
207	⎛ 076 ⎞	Mov I, A
210	⎝ 111 ⎠	
211	167	Mov M̂,A
212	043	INX H
213	⎛ 076 ⎞	Mov I, A
214	⎝ 323 ⎠	
215	167	Mov M̂,A

216	043	INX H
217	(076	Mov I, A
220	000)	
221	167	Mov M͡,A
222	043	INX H
223	(076	Mov I, A
224	166)	
225	167	Mov M͡,A
226	166	HLT

Run the program from 200L. Then examine the *contents* of 000L up to 004L. Then reset and press G. Explain what you see and why. We have transferred a program from "tape" to 003H, 000L–004L. The program to affect this transfer is written into memory starting at 200L. All the 076 instructions simulate movement of data into the accumulator from tape whence they are stored in memory (000 to 004 here).

(iii) Moving programs around in memory. The following transformation program* can be useful in moving programs around in memory, or from one memory block to another. The program to be moved (the *source*) is:

003	200	(076		202	(323
	201	111)		203	001)
				204	166

The transformation program is

003	300	(026	MVI, D
	301	005) =	size of block; i.e., size of source program above
	302	(041	LXI H
	303	200)	— Reg. L beginning address of data to be
	304	003)	— Reg. H moved; i.e., the *source address*

*This program is due to Mr. Ron Katz, EE senior at Pratt Institute, present affiliation Bell Telephone Laboratories.

305	⎛011⎞	LXI B	
306	⎜000⎟ — Reg. C	beginning address of *destination* where we wish program to finally
307	⎝003⎠ — Reg. B	reside
310	176	Mov A̅,M̅ (M pointed to by H,L)
311	002	STAX B =Store (A) in memory location pointed to by B,C
312	025	DCR D by 1
313	⎛302⎞	
314	⎜317⎟	JNZ: Jump if not 0 to 317L
315	⎝003⎠	
316	166	Halt
317	003	INX B,C by 1
320	043	INX H,L by 1
321	⎛303⎞	
322	⎜310⎟	JMP to 003, 310
323	⎝003⎠	

Press reset. Then G. What do you observe? Press 200L, then G. What do you observe? Now press 300L then G. Examine the contents of locations 000L to 004L. Finally press reset and then G. What do you observe? We have transferred the program originally residing at 200L to 204L to 000L to 004L. The program at 200L is, of course, still there, as you can easily determine either by examining contents at 200L to 204L or running the program at 200L and observing the results. If we had memory space and wished to transfer the program to block 030H, say, then the instruction at 307 would be 030.

Experiment 3-2(f)   Some simple calculation and arithmetic programs

(i)   Multiply 9 × 5 (binary multiplication)

000	⎛006⎞	MVI, B	
001	⎝010⎠→	9 − 1 = 8 decimal = B = number of times we add 005 to itself
002	⎛076⎞	MVI,A	
003	⎝005⎠ = Multiplicand	

004	$\begin{pmatrix} 306 \\ 005 \end{pmatrix} =$	ADI, B_2 = add immediate to Register A and store in A
005		B_2
006	005	DCR B by 1
007	$\begin{pmatrix} 302 \\ 004 \\ 003 \end{pmatrix}$	
010		JNZ
011		
012	$\begin{pmatrix} 323 \\ 000 \end{pmatrix}$	Out (A) to port 0
013		
014	166	

We should see the binary result $9 \times 5 = 45 = 00101101$ at port 0 (055 octal). We have approached the problem by adding 005 = 00000101 8 times to itself.

(ii)   Add A + B + C (binary addition)

000	$\begin{pmatrix} 076 \\ A \end{pmatrix} \to$	MVI to Accumulator
001		A in octal form
002	$\begin{pmatrix} 306 \\ B \end{pmatrix} \to$	ADI,B_2: add immediate byte to (A) and store in A
003		B in octal form
004	$\begin{pmatrix} 306 \\ C \end{pmatrix}$	
005		
006	$\begin{pmatrix} 323 \\ 000 \end{pmatrix}$	out (A) = result to port 0
007		
010	166	

Take several examples; e.g., $(2 + 3 + 32)_{10} = \overset{A}{(002)_8} + \overset{B}{(003)_8}$
$+ \overset{C}{(040)_8}$ and observe $(00100101)_2 = (045)_8 = (37)_{10}$. Or $(100$
$+ 64 + 32)_{10} = \overset{A}{(144)_8} + \overset{B}{(100)_8} + \overset{C}{(040)_8} = (196)_{10} = (304)_8$,
so in this case we should see 11000100 at port 0.

3.3   MORE ADVANCED PROGRAMS—THE NEED FOR A STACK AND SUBROUTINES.

(A)   Examples of "Software for Hardware".

Experiment 3-3(a)   A Monostable Multivibtator (one-shot); A Pulse Generator

The beauty of the microprocessor-microcomputer is its ability to "software" many design problems that were formerly total hardware problems. Therein lies much of its power. An example of this is the program below to software a monostable multivibrator. The result will appear at port 0 where pins are available to tap off the pulse ⌐Ⴑ_w if one desires.

Monostable Multivibrator

000	(076	MVI A
001	000)	
002	074	INR A←
003	(323	(A) → pt. 0
004	000)	
005	365	Push PSW
006	(006	MVI B
007	B₂)	= On time byte
		B₂ = 144 (1 sec)
010	(021	
011	046	LXI D/E
012	001)	= D
013	033	= DCX D,E
014	172	= Mov A,D
015	263	= ORA,E
016	(302	
017	013	JNZ
020	003)	
021	005	DCR B
022	(302	
023	010	JNZ
024	003)	
025	361	POP PSW
026	075	DCR A
027	(323	(A) → pt. 0
030	000)	
031	166	

Left margin bracket (013–024): Time Delay. Experiment 3-2(d)

Making a Pulse Generator out of the Monostable Multivibrator

031	365	Push PSW
032	(006	
033	B₂′)	Off time byte B₂′ = 144 (1 sec)
034	(021	
035	046	
036	001)	
037	033	
040	172	
041	263	
042	(302	
043	037	
044	003)	
045	005	
046	(302	
047	034	
050	003)	
051	361	POP PSW
052	(303	
053	002	JMP
054	003)	to 003H, 002L

Right margin bracket: Time Delay. Experiment 3-2(d)

Notice that only Push PSW and Pop PSW are here needed, as the program before the T.D. at 005 and after the T.D. at 026 involves only manipulations with A. T_w can be varied by varying the on-time byte B_2 at 007. Rerun with $B_2 = 370$, $D = 001$; then $B_2 = 144$, $D = 015$; then $B_2 = 024$, $D = 001$, etc. (see Table 3-1). Again note how the Push/Pop instructions are vital. Replace any one of them with NOP and the experiment will not work.

To produce a pulse generator from the monostable we simply replace the Halt at 031 by the program on the other side of the page, which is nothing more than an identical time delay with, this time, an off-time byte B_2' at 033. This T.D. ends in a jump back to 003H, 002L where INRA occurs. Studying this program shows that the first time we pass INR A a 1 is output at port 0 and an LED stays lit for ~1 second. It then goes off due to DCR A at 026 and stays off for 1 s as we go through the second T.D. at at 031. But the JMP at 052 back to 002 causes port 0 to go on again for 1 s, then off again for 1 s, as we go through the second T.D. once again. This repeats over and over again. Thus a square wave generator has been produced. For variable duty cycle we need only play around with the timing bytes B_2 at 007 and B_2' at 033. Doing so should give

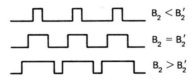

Try $B_2 = B_2' = 144$; $B_2 = 310$, $B_2' = 144$; $B_2 = 144$, $B_2' = 310$. (Table 3-1.)

An interesting facet of this experiment is brought out if we interchange the 074 and 075 instructions at 002 and 026. We will then see 8 pulse generators instead of 1 at port 0. OR simply insert 377 at 001. Try it. Why so? You can also output to all *three* ports after 074 and after 075 and get 24 pulse generators. Also try the following: 4 pulse generators $(D_7 D_6 D_5 D_4)$ out of phase with 4 other generators $(D_3 D_2 D_1 D_0)$; i.e., place $\begin{pmatrix} 076 \\ 360 \end{pmatrix}$ at $\begin{pmatrix} 000 \\ 001 \end{pmatrix}$, $\begin{pmatrix} 076 \\ 017 \end{pmatrix}$ at $\begin{pmatrix} 026 \\ 027 \end{pmatrix}$, NOP at 002, and $\begin{pmatrix} 303 \\ 000 \\ 003 \end{pmatrix}$ at the end. Try different timing bytes at 007 and 034. Then try $\begin{pmatrix} 076 \\ 252 \end{pmatrix}$ at $\begin{pmatrix} 000 \\ 001 \end{pmatrix}$ and $\begin{pmatrix} 076 \\ 125 \end{pmatrix}$ at $\begin{pmatrix} 026 \\ 027 \end{pmatrix}$. The program is now one address longer so watch out in labeling your JNZ's in the second time delay. Try the above by using simply the complement instruction 057 at 026 and a NOP at 002.

(B) The Need for a Subroutine. How a Subroutine is implemented By Use of the "CALL" and "RETURN" Instructions together with the concept of the "STACK"

The pulse generator example in the last experiment used two time delay programs (basically identical) in the main program. We will see examples later where time delay programs might have to be written into a program many times. This is bad because it is using up valuable memory space (in our case we are limited to 256 locations) just for time delays (not to mention the increased possibilities for errors programming them in over and over). It is conceivable that many cases can arise where little or no space would be left for the main program. Clearly a technique is needed whereby the time delay program or other program which has to be frequently used, can be written *once* (as a subroutine) and this subroutine called for from the main program as many times as we need it to implement our total program. Thus we want a situation that e.g. can be depicted as shown on page 64.

We have here introduced two new instructions, the 3-byte instruction $\begin{pmatrix} 315 \\ B_2 \\ B_3 \end{pmatrix}$ which means "<u>Call</u> the subroutine located at B_3H, B_2 L, and remember the address in the main program just below where the call originated "(007L or 035L in the example shown above)", and the one-byte Instruction RET=311 which means "<u>Return</u> to the place just below where the last call was made in the main program (here 007L or 035L) when the subroutine is finished up." Clearly a call could never operate successfully if no Ret instruction were placed at the end of the subroutine. Without the Ret instruction we'd never get back to finishing up the main program. It is clear that if the above could be implemented we could use the subroutine over and over again just by calling it as many times as necessary in the main program. Since

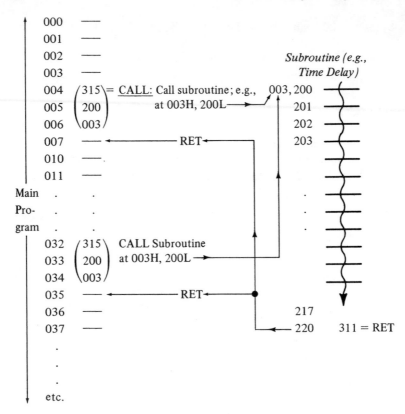

the Call instruction is 3 bytes and the Ret is 1 byte it is surely advantageous to take the subroutine approach as the subroutine will almost surely be longer than 4 bytes so that a net saving of memory space will accrue as compared to writing the subroutine many times into the main program.

The question is, of course, how does the microcomputer remember that it has to come back to 003H, 007L after the first call was made, and to 003H, 035L after the second call was made, etc.?

The answer is through a part of memory called "the Stack" where the return addresses from the program counter (003H, 007L or 003H, 035L) are temporarily stored and saved at the time the call was made, until the subroutine is finished, at which time the stack supplies those return addresses back to the program counter as a result of the Ret instruction. It must be stressed here (see Chap. 2) that the program counter (PC) plays a vital role. It controls the order in which a program is executed. It is the 16-bit register in the CPU which contains the address of the *next* instruction to be executed. Thus

PCH	PcL
B_3	B_2

PC Register

means the next instruction to be executed in the program is located at address B_3H,B_2L. Normally, of course, as a program is run, PC increments by 1 after each instruction is executed (the control section—Chap. 2—does this). This causes the address bus to point to the immediately neighboring location in memory so that *successive* instructions in successive addresses in the program are fetched and executed. But there are important exceptions to this situation. We have to look at the PC in a broader sense: It is the 16-bit register that contains the Hi and Lo address of the *next* instruction in the program to be executed. The next instruction does not necessarily have to be the instruction in the *next* successive memory location. In a program as follows

```
000    ——
001    ——
002    ——
003    ——
004    / 303 \
005    ( 002 )  =   Jump to 003H, 002L
006    \ 003 /
007    ——
008    ——
```

the control section forces the PCL to take on the successive contents 000, 001, 002, 003, 004, 005, 006, 007, 002, 003, 004, ...

The same would be true for a JNZ $\begin{pmatrix} 302 \\ 002 \\ 003 \end{pmatrix}$ instruction if it were placed at 004 if zero were *not* the result of the previous logic or arithmetic operation. We have already encountered the conditional 302 and unconditional 303 jumps in several of our previous programs. The first Call $\begin{pmatrix} 315 \\ 200 \\ 003 \end{pmatrix}$ will do the same thing. After the ID decodes it the control section responds by causing the PC to be loaded with 003H, 200L forcing the program to jump to the instruction at 003H,200L where the subroutine to be executed is loaded. Thus, in the diagram shown (PCL) would take on the successive values 000, 001, 002, 003, 004, 005, 006, 007, 200, 201, 202, . . . , 220, 221, 007, 010, 011, . . . , 032, 033, 034, 035, 200, 201, 202, . . . , 220, 221, 035, 036, 037, . . . and the program would be executed precisely in this order as the address bus would take on these successive addresses from the PC (to which it is buffered) and point to those successive locations in memory for each fetch of an instruction back to CPU via the data bus for subsequent execution. (However, before PCL = 007 can fetch the instruction at 007, it is superseded by PCL = 002 (or in the case of the Call by PCL = 200) due to the Jump instruction (or Call instruction).)

The question still remains: How does the PC get loaded with the "return address" 003H,007L after the subroutine is finished and a RET instruction encountered at 220, and then again with the next return address 003H,035L after the subroutine is used again with the call at 032 and the RET again encountered at 220?

There is a 16-bit register (see Fig. 10 Chap. 2) called the "Stack Pointer." Its contents B_3, B_2 are the specific address B_3H, B_2L of a location in memory. The 3-byte instruction

$$\begin{pmatrix} 061 \\ 300 \\ 003 \end{pmatrix} = \begin{pmatrix} \text{LXI S.P.} \\ B_2 \\ B_3 \end{pmatrix} = \quad \text{(Load the Stack Pointer Register with the immediate 2 bytes)}$$

causes the S.P. register to be loaded as shown in the drawing here.

B_3 (Hi)	B_2 (Lo)
003	300

SP Register

It mean that a specific place (003H,300L) in memory is being *pointed* to (not being loaded, just being pointed to). In reality this location will be pointed to only if (SP) are dumped on to the address bus, which they will be in connection with certain instructions (Call, Ret, Push, etc).

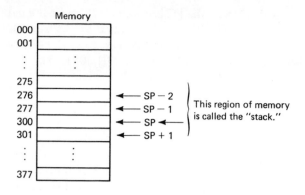

Figure 20. The stack. SP = 003, 300 is here arbitrary.

Now the exact Intel 8080 description of the call instruction $\begin{pmatrix} 315 \\ B_2 \\ B_3 \end{pmatrix}$

$= \begin{pmatrix} 315 \\ 200 \\ 003 \end{pmatrix}$ *just* before the address 003,007 in our mock main program is*

definition of
Call B_2, B_3
With SP
Pointing
to 003, 300.

$\left\{ \begin{array}{l} (SP-1)=277 \longleftarrow \text{(PCH) of } next \text{ instruction} \\ \qquad\qquad\qquad \text{after the call; i.e., 003 here} \\ (SP-2)=276 \longleftarrow \text{(PCL) of } next \text{ instruction} \\ \qquad\qquad\qquad \text{after the call; i.e., 007 here} \\ SP \longleftarrow \qquad\quad SP-2; \text{ i.e., 276 here} \\ PC \longleftarrow \qquad\quad (B_3), (B_2); \text{ i.e.; 003H, 200L} \\ \qquad\qquad\qquad \text{here—the location of the sub-} \\ \qquad\qquad\qquad \text{routine} \end{array} \right.$ $\left.\begin{array}{l} \text{"}\underline{\text{Push}}\text{"} \\ \text{PC} \\ \text{(Return} \\ \text{Address).} \end{array}\right\}$

Thus when the Call $\begin{pmatrix} 315 \\ 200 \\ 003 \end{pmatrix}$, before 003H,007L in the main program, is encountered 003 gets placed into memory location $SP-1 = 277$; 007 gets placed into memory location $SP-2 = 276$ (by means

*Intel 8080 Microcomputer System User's Manual, Sept. 1975, pp. 4—11.

of a flow of data from the PC inside the CPU over the data bus to the memory locations 277 and 276—see Fig. 8, Chap. 2); the S.P. changes from 300 to 276; *and* the PC gets loaded with the address of the subroutine to be called; i.e., 003H,200L. The situation in the *"stack"* after the Call is shown in Fig. 21.

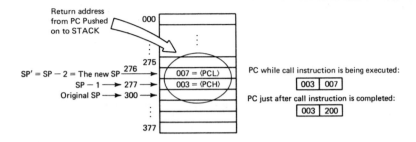

Figure 21. Details of the stack after execution of the Call. ⟨PC⟩ during and after execution of Call.

We say that the (PC) has been *"pushed"* on to the stack. Indeed it has, and it is saved there as the *return address* to where the RET instruction at the end of the subroutine must get us back in the main program. The (PC) are no longer 003,007 but 003,200, forcing the program to jump from 003,006 to 003,200 where the subroutine is located and is then executed.

When we are finished with the subroutine we encounter the instruction RET=311. The exact Intel 8080 definition of this instruction is the following:*

$$
\begin{array}{ll}
\text{definition} & \text{PCL} \quad \leftarrow \quad (M_{SP'}); \text{i.e., here 007 with SP}'=276 \\
\\
\text{of RET} & \text{PCH} \quad \leftarrow \quad (M_{SP'+1}); \text{i.e., here 003 with SP}'+1=277 \\
\\
& \text{SP} \quad \leftarrow \quad \text{SP}'+2; \text{i.e., here 300}
\end{array}
$$

The stack situation is now depicted as shown in Fig. 22.

Because the PC (and address bus) contain 003H,007L, as a result of the POP from the stack, the program control is turned back to 003H,007L which is exactly where we want to go to pick up the main program again from the point where the call was made. And the next time we put out a call 315 at 003H,032L we go through exactly the same process: 003 gets saved (pushed) in address 277,

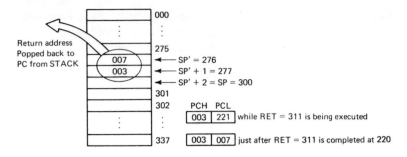

Figure 22. The stack after execution of the Return. ⟨PC⟩ during and after execution of Ret.

035 gets saved (pushed) in address 276, PC gets loaded with 003,200, the program control goes over to the subroutine at 003H,200L, and finally when the RET is again met at 220 in the subroutine, 035 gets popped from 276L back to PCL and 003 gets popped from 277 back to PCH. The PC then takes us back to 003H,035L to continue with the main program.

In the MMD-1 it is not necessary to load the S.P. with an LXI

$$SP, \ B_2 B_3 \ = \begin{pmatrix} 061 \\ B_2 \\ B_3 \end{pmatrix}$$ instruction. KEX (Appendix C) does that for

us upon RESET after turn-on. It loads the SP. with 004H,000L. We do not care that 004H,000L does not exist as memory space in the MMD-1 because all that plays a role in pushing and popping to save and restore (PC) are the locations SP−1 and SP−2; and SP−1 = 004,000−1 = 003,377 (Chap. 1) while SP−2 = 003,376; i.e., the very last 2 places in memory become reserved for the first of what can be several stack operations involving, perhaps, pushes and pops of other kinds in which a register's contents, or the "flags," can be saved in the stack and then popped—more on that later. If, however, for some reason or another, we do wish to use a *specific* region of memory for pushing and popping type stack operations we can do so simply by employing the instruction

$$\begin{pmatrix} 061 \\ B_2 \\ B_3 \end{pmatrix}$$ early in the *main* program in which case SP will point to

$B_3 H, B_2 L$.

The best way to illustrate the use of the CALL, RET, and stack in connection with a subroutine is to redo the pulse generator program of Experiment 3-3(a).

Experiment 3-3(b)   **The Pulse Generator Redone Using Time Delay As a Subroutine and Employing CALL and RET Instructions**

000	⎛076⎞	MVI, A
001	⎝000⎠	
002	⎛323⎞	out (A)
003	⎝000⎠	port 0
004	⎛006⎞	MVI, B
005	⎝310⎠	B=off time byte
		(2 sec)
006	⎛315⎞	
007	⎜100⎟	Call Sub
		at 003H,100L
010	⎝003⎠	
011	⎛006⎞	MVI, B
012	⎝144⎠	B'=on time byte
		(1 sec)
013	074	INR A by 1
014	⎛323⎞	
015	⎝000⎠	
016	⎛315⎞	Call
017	⎜100⎟	
020	⎝003⎠	
021	⎛303⎞	JMP
022	⎜000⎟	
023	⎝003⎠	

The Time Delay Routine*

Call ⟶	003,100	365	Push PSW
			[only (A) need
			be saved]
	101	⎛021⎞	
	102	⎜046⎟	LXI D/E
	103	⎝001⎠	
	104	033	DCX D,E
	105	172	Mov A͡,D

*See Experiment 3-2(d) and Table 3-1.

106	263	OR A,E
107	/ 302 \	
110	(104)	JNZ
111	\ 003 /	
112	005	DCR B
113	/ 302 \	
114	(101)	
115	\ 003 /	
116	361	POP PSW
117	311	RET

Study the program carefully in relation to Experiment 3-3(a). Note that $\left(\begin{array}{c}006\\B\end{array}\right)$ and $\left(\begin{array}{c}006\\B'\end{array}\right)$ have been pulled out of the T.D. routine and inserted in the main program at 004 and 011, respectively. This allows for variable on/off times (duty cycle). Observe the results. Again vary the off and on time bytes B and B' at 005 and 012 using Table 3-1 and observe. Note that there are 45 steps in the original program of Experiment 3-3(a) and 36 steps here using CALL RET/subroutine concepts. We shall see in future programs that the savings in memory space become *considerable* for other types of problems. Again, note the importance of Push/POP. Try running without them in the program.

It should be remarked that one of the attractive and important facets of the microcomputer is that it is small, and in many cases of "dedicated control" application does not need large amounts of memory space. This, of course, is one of the factors that makes it cheap and small, but also imposes on us the need for skillful programming to make most efficient use of the limited memory space. *The stack, CALL and RET, the concepts of Push and Pop (to be further exploited later), and the repeated use of the subroutine then become essential tools.*

Experiment 3-3(c)   Calling a Time Delay Subroutine in KEX

A perusal of the KEX Prom Program (Appendix C) reveals a T.D. routine located at 000H,277L. This routine is the 10 ms time delay [discussed in Experiment 3-2(d)], the purpose of which is to make sure the key that was released is "debounced"— see Experiment 5-2(i), Chap 5. In other words, it makes no further multiple contacts that would "confuse" the encoder, so that a 172S instruction might become a 1111111 . . . 77777 . . . 2222 . . . "instruction." A study of the following program making use of the KEX subroutine at 000H,277L will show a 2.5 second T.D.* $(10 \text{ ms} \times (370)_8 = 10 \text{ ms} \times (248)_{10})$.

003	000	$\left(\begin{matrix}006\\370\end{matrix}\right) =$	MVI B
	001		Time Byte
	002	$\left(\begin{matrix}315\\277\\000\end{matrix}\right)$	Call 10 msec T.D.
	003		KEX Subroutine
	004		at 000H,277L
			(See Appendix C)
	005	005	DCR B by ← Ret
	006	$\left(\begin{matrix}302\\002\\003\end{matrix}\right)$	
	007		JNZ to 003H,002L
	010		
	011	$\left(\begin{matrix}076\\377\end{matrix}\right)$	MVI, A
	012		
	013	$\left(\begin{matrix}323\\000\end{matrix}\right)$	out (A) = 11111111
	014		to port 0
	015	166	HLT

Run the program and observe what happens.

Experiment 3-3(d)   How to Examine the Instructions or Program in a ROM (e.g., KEX) Using a T.D. Program.

003	000	$\left(\begin{matrix}006\\016\end{matrix}\right) =$	MVI, B
	001		14_{10} (length of Program to be examined within KEX)
	002	$\left(\begin{matrix}041\\277\\000\end{matrix}\right)$	
	003		LXI H,L
	004		Start of ROM Program we wish to examine

*MMD-1 Operating Manual 801-0082 Rev B 8/76−p. 23 (Courtesy of E & L Instruments Inc. and Gernsback Publications).

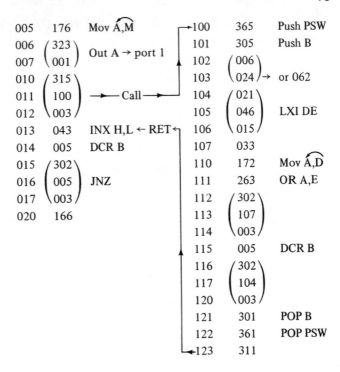

005	176	Mov A͡,M
006	(323	Out A → port 1
007	001)	
010	(315	
011	100	——Call——
012	003)	
013	043	INX H,L ← RET←
014	005	DCR B
015	(302	
016	005	JNZ
017	003)	
020	166	

→100	365	Push PSW
101	305	Push B
102	(006	
103	024)	→ or 062
104	(021	
105	046	LXI DE
106	015)	
107	033	
110	172	Mov A͡,D
111	263	OR A,E
112	(302	
113	107	
114	003)	
115	005	DCR B
116	(302	
117	104	
120	003)	
121	301	POP B
122	361	POP PSW
←123	311	

Observe the read-out at port 1 of the part of the program in KEX from 000,277 to 000,314. Modify the program to read out Lo address as well.

Experiment 3-3(e)   Sequential Turning on of Output Ports for Programmable Times, then Off, in Sequence, etc.*

This experiment** has practical implications in plants where many machines or motors have to be turned on and closed at the start and end of the day. The large power factor, when all are turned on or off together, is uneconomical. The following program* is designed to turn on the motors one after another for a

---

*See Experiment 5-2(f) where this experiment is interfaced to control ports (machines) outside the MMD-1.
**Suggested by Mr. Wm. Dawson and Mr. Larry Curran, U. S. M. Corp.

definite period, and then turn them off one after another for another definite period.

000	227	Clear A
001	⎛ 323 ⎞	
002	⎝ 001 ⎠	Ports 1 and 0
003	⎛ 323 ⎞	go off
004	⎝ 000 ⎠	
005	⎛ 006 ⎞	Ports 1, 0 off 5 sec
006	⎝ 062 ⎠ →	Time byte for 5 sec
007	⎛ 315 ⎞	
010	⎜ 100 ⎟ →	Call → to 100
011	⎝ 003 ⎠	
012	074 ←	Ret ←
013	⎛ 323 ⎞	Port 1 goes on
014	⎝ 001 ⎠	
015	⎛ 006 ⎞	
016	⎝ 012 ⎠ →	Time byte for 1 sec
017	⎛ 315 ⎞	
020	⎜ 100 ⎟ →	Call → to 100
021	⎝ 003 ⎠	
022	⎛ 323 ⎞	Port 0 goes on 1 sec Later ← Ret
023	⎝ 000 ⎠	
024	⎛ 006 ⎞	Ports 0 & 1 stay *on* 5 sec.
025	⎝ 062 ⎠	
026	⎛ 315 ⎞	
027	⎜ 100 ⎟ →	Call →
030	⎝ 003 ⎠	
031	227 ←	Ret ←
032	⎛ 323 ⎞	Port 1 goes off
033	⎝ 001 ⎠	
034	⎛ 006 ⎞	
035	⎝ 012 ⎠ →	Time byte for 1 sec
036	⎛ 315 ⎞	
037	⎜ 100 ⎟ →	Call →
040	⎝ 003 ⎠	
041	⎛ 323 ⎞	Port 0 goes off 1 sec Later ← Ret ←
042	⎝ 000 ⎠	
043	⎛ 303 ⎞	
044	⎜ 005 ⎟	JMP
045	⎝ 003 ⎠	

Time Delay (Experiment 3-2(d) and Table 3-1)

100	365	Push PSW
101	021	LXI D,E
102	046	Time Bytes
103	015	
104	033	
105	172	
106	263	
107	302	
110	104	JNZ
111	003	
112	005	
113	302	
114	101	JNZ
115	003	
116	361	POP PSW
117	311	Ret

Try varying time bytes at 006, 016, 025, etc. (see Table 3-1).

3-4 CONTROL OVER AUDIO-VISUAL DISPLAYS. THE ROTATION INSTRUCTION.

In the next four experiments, microcomputer software control over an audio-visual display is demonstrated. The visual part is displayed at one or more of the ports 0, 1, or 2 of MMD-1 and the audio aspect is implemented easily: a TIP 29 (A7525) transistor is mounted with its three leads B,C,E on the SK-10 socket of the MMD-1, together with an 8Ω = U-261 speaker as in Fig. 23*.

It is recommended that the set-up be wired on the microcomputer interface socket and employed in the following four experiments. As the complexity of these experiments is developed, you should try your own programs to implement other displays. In every case the use of CALL and RET instructions together with a subroutine is indispensable as time delays are needed over and over again.

*Digital Directions (Courtesy E & L Instruments Inc.), Jan. 1977, p. 9

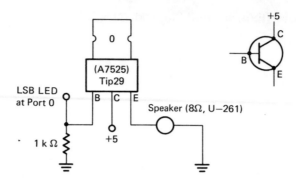

Figure 23. Audio set-up in experiments 3-4a, 4b, 4c, 4d.

Experiment 3-4(a)   One-Port Display—Without Reflections— Use of Rotation Instruction.

The following program makes repeated use of a time delay subroutine. Run it, observe the results at port 0, and then analyze why you are seeing what you are seeing.

000	$\left(\begin{array}{c}076\\B\end{array}\right)=$	MVI A
001		pattern byte
002	$\left(\begin{array}{c}315\\100\\003\end{array}\right)\rightarrow$	Call Subroutine
003		at 003H,100L
004		
005	$\left(\begin{array}{c}323\\000\end{array}\right)$	out (A) to Port 0
006		
007	017	RRC=Rotate (A) one bit to right
010	$\left(\begin{array}{c}303\\002\\003\end{array}\right)$	JMP
011		
012		

Time Delay Subroutine*

100	365	Push PSW
101	$\left(\begin{array}{c}006\\B'\end{array}\right)=$	MVI B
102		Timing byte

*See Experiment 3-2(d), Table 3-1.

103	⎛021⎞	
104	⎜046⎟	LXI D/E
105	⎝001⎠	
106	033	DCX D/E
107	172	Mov A͡,D
110	263	OR A,E
111	⎛302⎞	
112	⎜106⎟	JNZ
113	⎝003⎠	
114	005	DCR B
115	⎛302⎞	
116	⎜103⎟	JNZ
117	⎝003⎠	
120	361	POP PSW
121	311	RET

The operator 017 = RRC is crucial. Its 8080 definition is*

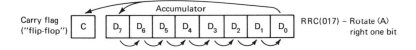

Each bit in the accumulator is shifted one position to the right and the LSB (least significant bit) is moved to the MSB (most significant bit) *and* to the carry flip flop. Compare this with the three other rotation* instructions.

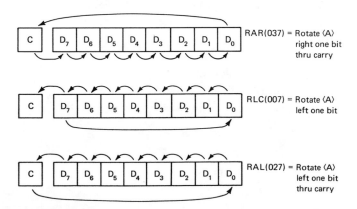

*Intel Corp "8080 Microcomputer Systems User's Manual," Sept. 1975, pp. 4–10.

Modify the program to have all three ports participate in the display. Also run the above experiment with 007=RLC in the program at 007L. Place B=200,300,340, . . . , 001,003,007, . . . in turn at 001L and run each pattern for timing bytes B'=144, 062, 024, 012, 005, and 001, in turn, at 102L. Try other patterns using B=140, 120, etc. Microcomputer software control of the audio-visual display is evident. Again note the importance of the Push/ POP instructions. Try running with NOP's in their place (000).

Experiment 3-4(b)   Two-Port Displays (same or opposite directions)—No Reflections.

An extension of the last program follows. Note that since we are now using D and E registers in the main program we can use LXI H/L in the T.D. program to avoid using Push D and POP D instructions.

000	$\left(\begin{array}{c}036\\ B\end{array}\right)=$	MVI E
001		Pattern Byte for Port 0
002	$\left(\begin{array}{c}026\\ B'\end{array}\right)=$	MVI D
003		Pattern Byte for Port 1
004	$\left(\begin{array}{c}315\\ 100\\ 003\end{array}\right)$	
005		Call time delay Subroutine $\rightarrow$
006		
007	173	Mov $\widehat{A,E}$ ← RET ←
010	017 (B'')	Rot. (A) Right one bit = RRC
011	137	Mov $\widehat{E,A}$ (Saves (A) in Register E)
012	$\left(\begin{array}{c}323\\ 000\end{array}\right)$	(E)=pattern byte for Port 0
013		
014	172	Mov $\widehat{A,D}$
015	007 (B''')	RCL=Rotate (A) left one bit
016	127	Mov $\widehat{D,A}$ (Saves (A) in Register D)
017	$\left(\begin{array}{c}323\\ 001\end{array}\right)$	(D)=Pattern byte for Port 1
020		
021	$\left(\begin{array}{c}303\\ 004\\ 003\end{array}\right)$	JMP
022		
023		

Time Delay Program*

100	365	Push PSW
101	006	MVI B
102	B* =	Time Byte
103	041	LXI H/L
104	046	L,H Time Bytes
105	001	
106	053	DCX H,L
107	174	Mov A,H
110	265	OR A,L
111	302	
112	106	JNZ
113	003	
114	005	DCR B
115	302	
116	103	JNZ
117	003	
120	361	POP PSW
121	311	RET

Run the program under the conditions shown in the table that follows and observe your results at ports 0 and 1.

Port 1	Port 0	B	B′	B″	B‴
←	→	200	001	017	007
		300	003	017	007
→	→	200	200	017	017
		300	300	017	017
←	←	001	001	007	007
		003	003	007	007
→	←	001	200	007	017
		003	300	007	017

Try also various time bytes B* at 102L such as 062, 024, 012, 005, and 001.

*See Experiment 3-2(d) and Table 3-1.

Again microcomputer software control over the audio-visual display is demonstrated. Note how the program does not work if you omit the Push PSW and/or POP PSW instructions. Try it with NOP's (000) at either 100 or 120 or at both.

Experiment 3-4(c)   Two-Port Displays with Reflections From the MSB and LSB.

A more complex development of the last two programs is given below. Bytes and registers are associated with the ports as follows:

This description relates to the program given below. The program merits careful study, particularly the back and forth transfer of (D) and (E) to and from A, then rotation, then storage of (A) back into D and E, . . . , interspersed with outputs of (A) to ports 0 and 1. Also note carefully the role of the "masking" bytes at 022L and at 047L. In conjunction with ANI,B_2 and JNZ instructions they produce the reflections from the MSB and LSB. [More on "masking" in Experiment 3-5(c).]

	000	⎛036⎞	MVI, E
	001	⎝ B ⎠	Display Byte Port 0 (take B=200)
	002	⎛026⎞	MVI, D
Before	003	⎝ B′ ⎠	Display Byte Port 1 (take B′=001)
Reflection	004	⎛315⎞	
	005	⎜100⎟	Call T.D. Routine →
	006	⎝003⎠	at 003H,100L
	007	173	Mov A͡,E ← RET ←
	010	017 =	B″ Rot.RT.(RRC)
	011	137	Mov E͡,A
	012	⎛323⎞	out
	013	⎝000⎠	Port 0
	014	172	Mov A͡,D

	015	007 =	B''' Rot. Left, (RCL)
	016	127	Mov D͡,A
	017	(323	out Port 1
	020	001)	
	021	(346)*	ANI B_2, (A) (AND B_2 with (A))
	022	201)=	Mask byte to cause LSB & MSB reflections
	023	(302	
	024	031	JNZ: LSB or MSB reached
	025	003)	
	026	(303	
	027	004	JMP: LSB or MSB not reached
	030	003)	
After	031	(315	
Reflection	032	100	CALL →
	033	003)	
	034	173	Mov A͡,E ← RET
	035	007 =	B̄'' (Rot. Left)
	036	137	Mov E͡,A
	037	(323	Out Port 0
	040	000)	
	041	172	Mov A͡,D
	042	017 =	B̄''' (Rot RT.)
	043	127	Mov D͡,A
	044	(323	Out Port 1
	045	001)	
	046	(346)*	ANI B_2 with (A)
	047	201)=	mask byte to cause end reflections
	050	(302	
	051	004	JNZ
	052	003)	
	053	(303	
to 031	054	031	JMP
↑	055	003)	

*See Experiment 3-5(c).

T.D. Exactly as in Experiment 3-4(b)

100	365	Push PSW
101	(006)	
102	(B*)	Time Byte
103	041	LXI H/L
,	,	,
,	,	,
,	,	,
,	,	,
,	,	,
,	,	,
,	,	,
120	361	POP PSW
121	311	RET

It is suggested you try

1) B=003, B'=003
   $\underline{B''=007}$, $\underline{B'''=007}$
   $\overline{B''}=017$, $\overline{B'''}=017$

2) B=300, B'=003
   $\underline{B''=017}$, $\underline{B'''=007}$
   $\overline{B''}=007$, $\overline{B'''}=017$

3) B=340, B'=007
   $\underline{B''=007}$, $\underline{B'''=007}$
   $\overline{B''}=017$, $\overline{B'''}=017$, etc.,
   and B*=144, 062,
   024, 012, 005, 001.

Note the difference between Experiment 3-4(a), 4(b) on the one hand and Experiment 3-4(c) on the other. In 4(c) reflections from the ends are produced, whereas 4(a) and 4(b) are characterized by the patterns going back abruptly to the same end from which they started and then repeating. Again note the importance of Push/POP.

Experiment 3-4(d)   "Full Scan" Display.

The following program with slight modification is presented here coutesy Mr. E. Spruck, USM Corp. Try it. The time delay is the same as presented in Experiment 3-4(b). Take time byte B* there equal to 005, 012, or 024 and observe. Explain the result in terms of RAL (027) thru carry and the saving of ⟨A⟩ in various registers.

000	$\left(\begin{array}{c}036\\001\end{array}\right)$	MVI, E
001		
002	$\left(\begin{array}{c}026\\000\end{array}\right)$	MVI, D
003		
004	$\left(\begin{array}{c}016\\000\end{array}\right)$	MVI, C
005		
006	$\left(\begin{array}{c}315\\100\\003\end{array}\right)$	Call Time Delay
007		
010		
011	173	Mov A, E
012	027	RAL Thru Carry
013	137	Mov E, A
014	$\left(\begin{array}{c}323\\002\end{array}\right)$	Out Port 2
015		
016	172	Mov A, D
017	027	RAL
020	127	Mov D, A
021	$\left(\begin{array}{c}323\\000\end{array}\right)$	Out Port 0
022		
023	171	Mov A, C
024	027	RAL
025	117	Mov C, A
026	$\left(\begin{array}{c}323\\001\end{array}\right)$	Out Port 1
027		
030	$\left(\begin{array}{c}303\\006\\003\end{array}\right)$	JMP.
031		
032		

3.5 USE OF "COMPARE" INSTRUCTION AND "MASKING" TECHNIQUES IN SOFTWARE CONTROL—COUNTING OR STEPPING TO A PREDETERMINED BYTE—UP/DOWN COUNTER (SEQUENCERS). SAWTOOTH AND TRIANGULAR STEPPING AND WAVEFORMS. RING COUNTER.

Experiment 3-5(a) Binary Counting to a Specified Byte. (Use of CMP,r Instruction; Time Delay with Call and Ret.); Sequencer.

The "Compare" Instruction 27S (S=7 for accumulator, S=0, 1, 2, 3, 4, 5 for Registers B, C, D, E, H, L, respectively) has the following 8080 Intel definition:* *"CMP, r (Compare Register): (A) — (r):*

The contents of register r are subtracted from those of the accumulator. The accumulator remains unchanged. The condition flags (flip flops) are set as a result of the subtraction. The Z flag is set to 1 if (A)=(r). The CY flag is set to 1 if (A) < (r)". The contents of accumulator and register r remain unchanged. (Note: Z flag = 1 indicates that the result of the arithmetic operation (A) — (r) is zero; CY flip flop (flag) = 1 if (A) — (r) causes a borrow out of the MSB; i.e., if (A) < (r). Thus CY=1 indicates a negative result for (A) — (r). See Sec. 7 in this chapter on the five "flags").

The following program to count up to a predetermined byte and then halt will show the power of this control instruction.

000	⎛ 076 ⎞	MVI, A
001	⎝ B ⎠ =	Starting Byte. Count starts here.
002	⎛ 323 ⎞	(A) → Port 0
003	⎝ 000 ⎠	
004	⎛ 315 ⎞	
005	⎜ 100 ⎟	Call →
006	⎝ 003 ⎠	
007	⎛ 016 ⎞	MVI, C
010	⎝ B* ⎠ =	Count Stops here—upper limit
011	271	CMP C: (A) — (C)
012	⎛ 302 ⎞	
013	⎜ 050 ⎟	JNZ
014	⎝ 003 ⎠	

*Intel Corp "8080 Microcomputer Systems User's Manual," Sept. 1975, pp. 4–9.

015	166	Halt
050	074	INR A
051	⎛ 303 ⎞	
052	⎜ 002 ⎟	JMP
053	⎝ 003 ⎠	

1 sec T.D. Program (B'=144) Exactly as in Experiment 3-4(a)

100	365	Push PSW
101	⎛ 006 ⎞	
102	⎝ B' ⎠	Time Byte
103	⎛ 021 ⎞	LXI D/E
104	⎜ 046 ⎟	E,D Time Bytes
105	⎝ 001 ⎠	
106	033	DCX D,E
107	172	Mov A͡,D
110	263	OR A,E
111	⎛ 302 ⎞	
112	⎜ 106 ⎟	JNZ
113	⎝ 003 ⎠	
114	005	DCR B
115	⎛ 302 ⎞	
116	⎜ 103 ⎟	JNZ
117	⎝ 003 ⎠	
120	361	POP PSW
121	311	

Run the program and observe Port 0. You will see binary counting in increments of 1 at Port 0 from Byte B at 001 up to the value of Byte B* at 010. The counting then stops. Try the experiment with various values of B and B*; for example, B=004, B*=010; B=000, B*=011; etc. Again note the program won't work without Push/ Pops in the TD program.

To make a repetitive *sequencer*, modify the above program as follows:

015	⎛ 303 ⎞
016	⎜ 000 ⎟
017	⎝ 003 ⎠

Port 0 should show counting from B to B*, then immediately repeat from B to B*, etc. This program will be most useful in microcomputer software control of a multiplexer-demultiplexer interfacing experiment designed to send many parallel bits serially over one wire (multiplex) and then redistribute the bits from serial form to parallel form (demultiplex). (Computers work with parallel bits, transmission from computer to computer or terminal to terminal is best accomplished via serial form; i.e., telephone lines.) See Experiment 3-5(d) this section.

Save the program for the next experiment. In the above experiment if you input the counting bits to a Digital to Analog converter the output voltage would be a sawtooth waveshape.

Experiment 3-5(b)   Up/Down Binary Sequencer

This is an important experiment and is an extension of the previous experiment. Modify the previous program by adding on the following:

015	075	DCR (A)
016	$\begin{pmatrix} 323 \\ 000 \end{pmatrix}$	(A) → Port 0
017		
020	$\begin{pmatrix} 315 \\ 100 \\ 003 \end{pmatrix}$	CALL →
021		
022		
023	$\begin{pmatrix} 016 \\ B \end{pmatrix}$	← RET ←
024		Lower Limit of Count (same as at 001)
025	271	CMP C: (A) − (C)
026	$\begin{pmatrix} 302 \\ 015 \\ 003 \end{pmatrix}$	JNZ
027		
030		
031	$\begin{pmatrix} 303 \\ 050 \\ 003 \end{pmatrix}$	JMP to 050 Experiment 3-5(a)
032		
033		

Run the program with different bytes B* at 010 and B at 024. See how port 0 counts up to byte B* and then back down to B, then back up, etc.

This software controlled up/down sequencer or counter can be used to drive the address bus up and down in a Prom to retrieve stored data in symmetric fashion (a sine wave musical tone). The available terminals at Port 0 of the MMD-1 can be used to drive $A_7 \ldots A_0$ address bus into the Prom. Thus

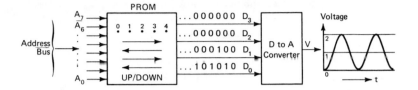

In this illustration we would have counting from address 0 to address 4 and back down as follows:

A_2	A_1	A_0
0	0	0
0	0	1
0	1	0
0	1	1
1	0	0
0	1	1
0	1	0
0	0	1
0	0	0
0	0	1

etc., with data output on the data $(D_3 D_2 D_1 D_0)$ bus shown above (representing the stored bits in addresses 0, 1 . . . 4). (See Ref. 9, p. 62.)

If you inputted the counting bits directly to a DAC, the output voltage would be a triangular waveform.

Experiment 3-5(c) Stepping Left or Right to a Predetermined Point Using "Masking": Ring Counter or Timing Slot Generator

The masking technique is another powerful software control tool. It is based, for example, on the "logical And" operation

$$\text{ANI, } (B_2) = \binom{346}{B_2} = \text{AND Immediate byte with (A)}$$

The Intel Sept. 1975 Microcomputer Systems User's Manual, p. 4–9, defines ANI, (B_2) as "the content of (B_2), the second byte of the instruction, is logically anded (*bit-by-bit*) with the contents of the accumulator and the results are placed in the accumulator. The CY and AC flags are cleared." (Recall that $1 \cdot 0 = 0 \cdot 1 = 0 \cdot 0 = 0$, $1 \cdot 1 = 1$—Chap. 1.) ANI was used in experiment 3-4(C).

This operation is referred to as masking because, for example,

$$
\begin{array}{ll}
\text{Data in A:} \underline{\hspace{2cm}} & \text{XX XXX XXX} \\
\text{Masking Byte } B_2 \underline{\hspace{1cm}} & \text{00 100 000} \\
\hline
\text{ANI Result} \underline{\hspace{1.5cm}} & \text{00 X00 000} = B_2 \cdot A
\end{array}
$$

In other words, all the bits in A are masked out (to 0) except the one corresponding to the position where the bit "1" in B_2 is located. *That bit in A is exposed, the others masked.* Its power is demonstrated in the program that follows.

000	(076)	MVI,A
001	(B)	starting Byte
002	(315)	Call →
003	(100)	T.D.
004	(003)	
005	(323)	← RET
006	(000)	out (A) to Port 0
007	117	Mov C,A (Save (A) in C)
010	(346)	ANI (B) with (A) and store in A.
011	(B′)	Stop byte
012	(312)	
013	(016)	JZ (if (A) is not zero proceed to 015 and halt)
014	(003)	
015	166	Halt
016	171	Mov A,C
017	007	RLC=Rot. (A) one bit left
020	(303)	
021	(002)	JMP to 002
022	(003)	

Time Delay Program [Experiment 3-4(a)]

100	365	Push PSW
101	(006)	
102	(144)	Time Byte

$$103 \quad \begin{pmatrix} 021 \\ , \\ , \end{pmatrix}$$

120	361	POP PSW
121	311	RET

Note that B and B' each contain no more than one bit, which is 1. Try various start and stop bytes B and B'; e.g., B=001 or 002, etc. and B'=040 or 004, etc. The 1 in each B' case indicates the stop position for the last of the RLC rotations. Note that if B'=00100000=040 for example, then ANI, $(B_2) = \begin{pmatrix} 346 \\ B_2 \end{pmatrix}$ will produce 000 in A *always*, unless the successive RLC's cause (A) itself to finally become 00100000 at which time ANI, (B_2) produces 00100000 (property of the And operation—Chap. 1). In the latter case a non-zero result has been produced and it resides in A. In that case the JZ instruction at 012 is ignored and we proceed to 015 and Halt—the successive RLC's at port 0 stop at 00100000. Note, also, what happens if you choose B'=000. Explain it. The same experiment could be programmed using the compare instruction CMP,r=27S, with the same time delay subroutine Try it.

007	$\begin{pmatrix} 016 \\ B' \end{pmatrix} =$	MVI C, (B_2)
010		Stop byte
011	271	(A) − (C) evaluation and comparison
012	$\begin{pmatrix} 312 \\ 050 \\ 003 \end{pmatrix}$	JZ to 050
013		
014		
015	007	RLC (or RRC)
016	$\begin{pmatrix} 303 \\ 002 \\ 003 \end{pmatrix}$	JMP to 002
017		
020		
050	166 =	Halt

Try the experiment with stop bytes containing *two or more 1's*; e.g., set B'=030 at 010. Run it. Explain the result. Again note the importance of Push/Pop in this time delay program. Try also with B=003 at 001.

Reprogram so that the bit repeatedly starts over from B after reaching B'. Take B = 001 and B' = 040, for example. You now have a Ring Counter or Timing Slot Generator. Two such counters and a comparator can be used in keyboard scanning to determine row and column of key pressed. This information can address the corresponding location in a ROM from which the code assigned to that key can be read out (see Ref. 36, p. 276).

Experiment 3-5(d)   Microcomputer Software Control of Channel Select Sequencing in a Multiplexer-Demultiplexer System

Strictly speaking this experiment belongs in Chap. 5 on interfacing, but its software control aspect is directly related to Experiment 3-5(a) on sequencers. Hence we are presenting it here. The wiring and interfacing are straightforward. The reader is advised to consult Chap. 1 on the 74154 hexadecoder chip and its use, not only as decoder, but as demultiplexer. It is also suggested that he consult Ref. 10, Texas Instruments TTL Data Book, pp. 7-158, 7-171 for truth tables and pin connections of the 74150 multiplexer and 74154 chips, respectively (see also Appendix A).

The idea in this experiment is to transmit parallel bits of data from a source (transmitter) to a destination (receiver) *via one wire in serial form* and then reconstruct the parallel arrangement of the bits at the receiver end. The 74150 chip serves to *multiplex* the bits of parallel data (in our experiment 8 bits), one after the other, into serial form on to its output line and the 74154 chip then takes the incoming serial bits and sequentially distributes (*de-multiplexes*) them on to its output lines into parallel form (Chap. 1), reproducing the parallel input at the output. Channel "selects" are employed both at the multiplexer to choose successive input lines and at the demultiplexer to choose successive output lines. Because we want to have output lines correspond to input lines, bit-for-bit, the channel selection should be sequenced at the multiplexer and demultiplexer in *synchronized* fashion. If we are talking about 16 input and output lines (16 bits) then the tied input/output sequencer selects must contain 4 bits, which together with common ground and output line constitute 6 wires vs. *direct* transmission over 16 wires at long distances. Hence the economic advantage of multiplex-demultiplex systems—albeit at a sacrifice in speed (sequencing the 16 lines). We shall, for the sake of simplicity, illustrate the experiment with 8 input/output bits. The circuitry and wiring are presented in Fig. 24:

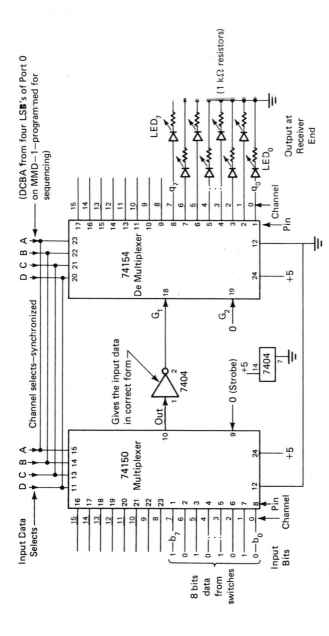

Figure 24. Microcomputer control of multiplexer-demultiplexer channel sequencing.

DCBA (the data selects) serve to pick out that input channel of the 74150 (0 to 15) corresponding to the decimal value of the binary number DCBA=8, 4, 2, 1. That Channel's data will be output to pin 10. The *same* DCBA on the 74154 serves to direct the incoming data at pin 18 (G_1) to that output channel picked by its decimal value. Thus if DCBA=0110=6, then channel 6's data at pin 2 of 74150 will emerge at pin 10 and be directed to channel 6 (i.e., pin 7) of the 74154 output. The sequencing is done precisely with the microcomputer program of Experiment 3-5(a), with B=000 and B*=007 to cover the 8 bits at channels 0 thru 7 of the 74150. If we tie the four LSB's of Port 0 of the MMD-1 to DCBA at either pins 11, 13, 14, 15 of the 74150, or pins 20, 21, 22, 23 of the 74154, we should observe each LED at output channel i of the 74154 (i=0, 1, 2, . . . 7) reflect, in turn, (spaced one time delay apart) the exact data bit present at the same input channel i to the 74150. Try it with Input Data b_0 . . . b_7 = 01010101 maintained at pins 8 through 1 of the 74150 and observe these bits appear sequentially as 01010101 at q_0 . . . q_7 of the 74154 (pins 1 through 8). Try the experiment with different input bytes and observe the corresponding output bytes appear at the LED's. Clearly the frequency with which the channels are sequenced must be 16 X the rate at which *new* data is appearing at the input. Vary the T.D. [byte B' in Experiment 3-5(a)].

Note that the input bytes are *not* latched at the output; i.e., a 0 appears and then goes to 1 *after* that channel was selected. How can you *latch* the input data at the output? One way, of course, is to use 7475's with their enable G driven by a ⊓ pulse from an inverter connected to the outputs of *another* sequenced 74154 used as a decoder. See Chap. 1 and more on device selecting in Chap. 5. Try it now, or later after you go through Chap. 5.

Note that the microcomputer software controls the sequencing operation that normally would be accomplished by digital random logic—in this case by a clock (555 timer) followed by a 7490 or 7493 counter. It is not only easy to program the sequencing *rate* with the microcomputer but also the sequencing steps by correct programming [we can, for example, sequence from channels 3 to 7 and back, etc.—see Experiments 3-5(a), 5(b)].

3-6   THE STACK (continued): ITS REAL POWER: CALL, RET, POP, AND PUSH INSTRUCTIONS RELATED TO THE USE OF SUBROUTINES

We have used the PUSH/POP instructions in all our time delay programs thus far. We now explain the basis for these instructions and why they do what they do. We follow up with detailed experiments on PUSH/POP in contexts other than merely time delay routines.

The idea of the stack and the employment of the Call and RET in subroutines, whereby the stack saves the address of the instruction immediately following the position of the Call in the main program has already been discussed [see section 3.3B)].

The question arises: If the stack can save the return address by means of Push (PCH) and Push (PCL) onto the stack and then retrieve it by popping (PCL) and (PCH) back from the stack to the PC so that the main program can continue in orderly fashion after the subroutine is used, then can the contents of other registers be saved elsewhere in the stack as well? It would be nice, for example, to have the contents of registers, if they are being used in the main program, pushed on to the stack for saving, thus freeing them to do work in the subroutine. Then when their employment in the subroutine is ended, have the stack pop the register's former contents back to those registers so as to proceed with the execution of the main program. This becomes exceedingly important when one considers that the number of registers in a microcomputer is limited; they can quickly become deployed in a program, and very well could be needed for use in the subroutine. The capability and adaptability of the microcomputer would be greatly enhanced if the contents of the B, C; D, E; H, L; A registers, and flags (all or some of them), could be temporarily saved on the stack before subroutines are executed, and retrieved from the stack after the subroutine is over.

A)   Review of Call, Ret; Push(PC), Pop(PC), SP, the Stack.

The extension of this concept from the notion of Push (PC) and POP (PC), already discussed, is not hard to realize. Before doing this, let us review the Call and Ret instructions and how the return address is pushed on to, and later popped from, the stack.

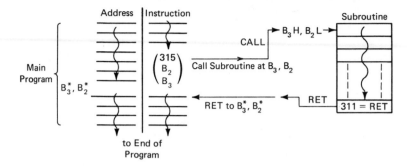

$B_3 H, B_2 L$ is address of subroutine. $B_3^* H$, $B_2^* L$ is address of the next instruction following the call instruction (i.e., the return address). We save B_3^*, B_2^* in the stack, somewhere down in memory, near a place determined by the stack pointer. The latter is determined by the instruction, inserted early in the main program, called "Load the Stack Pointer." For example

$$\begin{pmatrix} \text{LXI S.P.} \\ 200 \\ 003 \end{pmatrix} = \begin{pmatrix} 061 \\ 200 \\ 003 \end{pmatrix}$$

which fills the stack pointer register with

Hi	Lo
003	200

SP

and causes the SP to "point" to 003H,200L. When the Call (=315) is reached in the run of the main program, the Instruction Register (IR) in the CPU displays it to the Instruction Decoder (ID), which identifies it and lets the control section know that it is a "Call." The control section (see Chap. 2) then implements the following transfers:

$M_{SP-1} \leftarrow (PCH) = B_3^*$ } the next address, after the Call, is *pushed*
$M_{SP-2} \leftarrow (PCL) = B_2^*$ } on to the stack from the PC.
$SP' \leftarrow SP-2$
$PC \leftarrow B_3, B_2$ } program jumps to the subroutine at B_3, B_2.

Thus

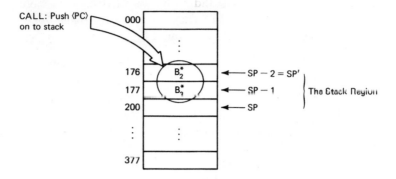

When the Ret (=311) instruction is reached at the end of the sub-routine (and the latter must *always* be terminated with a Ret instruction) the control section in the CPU effects the following transfers:

$$PCL \leftarrow (M_{SP'}) = B_2^* \quad \left.\begin{array}{l} \text{next address after} \\ \text{Call popped back} \\ \text{to PC from stack} \end{array}\right\}$$
$$PCH \leftarrow (M_{SP'+1}) = B_3^*$$
$$SP \quad \leftarrow SP'+2$$

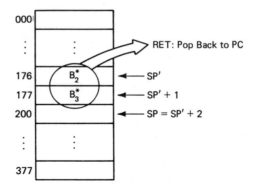

so that the return address B_3^*H, B_2^*L is popped from the stack back to the PC, and program control is transferred back to just after where the call originated in the main program.

B) Extension to: Push rp, Pop rp, Push PSW, Pop PSW

We are now ready to see how registers, which have been loaded with data or instructions in the main program, can be freed to do work in a subroutine by saving their contents in the stack till the subroutine is just about over. At that point we retrieve (pop) those contents from the stack and place them back in the original registers so they can continue with execution of the main program as if nothing happened.

In the above "rp" stands for "register pair" and "PSW" for "Processor Status Word." There are 3 register "pairs": register pair B (B and C), register Pair D (D and E), and register pair H (H and L). B, D, and H are, respectively, the Hi registers of each register pair and C, E, and L the respective Lo registers. A register pair is equivalent to two 8-bit registers or one 16-bit register. The "Processor Status Word" is composed of 16 bits, namely the contents of the accumulator register and the contents of the 5 flags (flip flops) together with three other arbitrary bits (see Section 3-7 for discussion of flags). Thus, PSW =

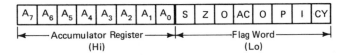

where S, Z, Ac, P, CY are the 5 flag (flip flop) bits which will be explained, defined, and interpreted, with experiments, in section 3-7 which follows. These flags describe the status of Sign, Zero, Auxiliary Carry, Parity, and Carry as a result of the last arithmetic or logical operation carried out by the CPU.

8080 Definition:
Push rp* (305: Push B pair; 325: Push D pair; 345: Push H pair)

$$M_{SP-1} \leftarrow (rph) = (\text{Hi part of the register pair rp})$$
$$M_{SP-2} \leftarrow (rpl) = (\text{Lo part of the register pair rp})$$
$$SP' \leftarrow SP-2 \quad (rp = SP \text{ not permitted})$$

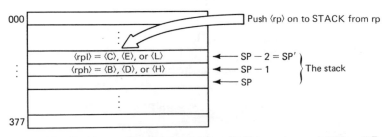

Figure 25. Pushing a register pair's contents ⟨rp⟩ on to the stack (BC or DE or HL).

8080 Definition:
Pop rp* (301 = Pop B pair; 321 = Pop D pair; 341 = Pop H pair)

$rpl \leftarrow (M_{SP})$
$rph \leftarrow (M_{SP+1})$
$SP' \leftarrow SP+2$

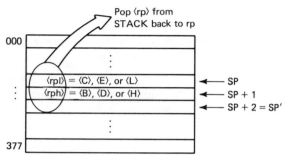

Figure 26. Popping the former contents back to the register pair.

8080 Definition Push PSW* = 365

$M_{SP-1} \leftarrow (A)$
$M_{SP-2} \leftarrow$ Flag word (S,Z,0,AC,0,P,1,CY)
$SP' \leftarrow SP-2$

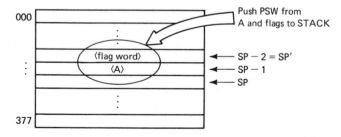

Figure 27. Pushing ⟨A⟩ and flags on to the stack, i.e., push PSW.

8080 Definition Pop PSW* = 361

flag word (status) $\leftarrow (M_{SP'})$
accumulator $\longleftarrow (M_{SP'+1})$
SP $\longleftarrow$ SP'+2

*Intel 8080 Microcomputer Systems User's Manual, Sept. 1975, pp. 4–13.

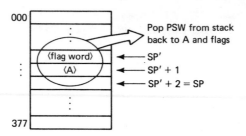

Figure 28. Popping former contents of PSW back to A and the flags.

The PSW is certainly very important, for it describes a lot about the "status" of the microprocessor at any given moment in the program run; i.e., (A) & the (flags). We can save this status by a Push operation on the stack, freeing A and flags for duty during a subroutine, and then restore to A and the flags their original contents after the subroutine is over as if nothing happened. The main program can thus be resumed. The question is: which register do we push? Do we push, for example, PSW? This depends on which register(s) are occupied with data or instructions necessary to the main program, and whether they will be needed in the subroutine. If the answer to *both* parts is "yes," then that register pair must be pushed at the very beginning of the subroutine and popped at the very end of the subroutine, freeing that rp for use in the subroutine and subsequently retrieving their original data just before the subroutine is completed. If in doubt about an rp always Push and Pop that rp. The trouble we can get into if we do not use a Push and Pop when needed should be clear. Suppose, for example, register D is loaded with certain data in the main program before a call to a subroutine is put out. This data is needed later on in the main program to interact with another instruction down the line. If we blithely use it in the subroutine, filling it up with data, we will certainly lose the original contents of D and hence ruin the results to be expected when the main program execution is resumed. It becomes, in this case, essential to save (Push) and restore (Pop) the original contents of D. Clearly the Push D=325 and Pop D=321 instructions must be written, respectively, at the beginning and end of the subroutine.

Supposing *all* register pairs BC, DE, HL are occupied in the main program. We wish to free them, as well as the PSW, for use in the subroutine and at the end of the subroutine restore their former contents to continue the main program. The subroutine program would look as follows (note that no particular order of pushing is demanded, but the order of popping *must* be the exact reverse of the order of pushing, as the succeeding diagrams will show):

Main Program:

———
———
———

$$\begin{pmatrix} 315 \\ B_2 = \text{e.g., } 100 \\ B_3 = \text{e.g., } 003 \end{pmatrix} \rightarrow \text{Call at 003, 100}$$

B_3^*, B_2^* ——— $\leftarrow$ Ret

———
———
———
———

To End

Subroutine:

003, 100 $\left.\begin{array}{l} 325 = \text{Push D,E.} \\ 305 = \text{Push B,C.} \\ 365 = \text{Push PSW} \\ 345 = \text{Push H,L} \end{array}\right\}$ Contents saved on stack

$\left.\begin{array}{l} — \\ — \\ — \\ — \\ — \\ — \\ — \\ — \end{array}\right\}$ Main instructions of the subroutine in which all kinds of things with B, C, D, E, H, L, A, and the flags can be done.

End of subroutine:

___

___

341 = Pop H, L ⎫
361 = Pop PSW ⎪
301 = Pop B, C ⎬ Contents restored to registers and flags
321 = Pop D, E ⎪
311 = Ret to main program at B_3^*, B_2^*

Thus, looking at the stack, taking $\begin{pmatrix} \text{LXI SP=061} \\ 300 \\ 003 \end{pmatrix}$ for example, we

have

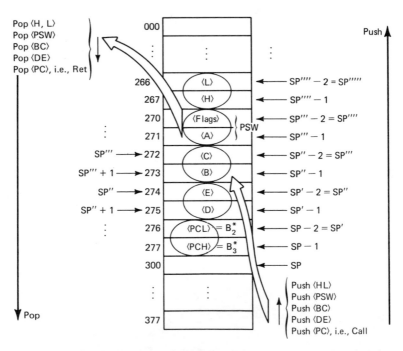

Figure 29. Stack structure and contents relative to the subroutine given in the example above.

Note the order of popping must be the reverse of the order of pushing (Last In during Push = First Out during Pop—"LiFo").

Thus, in this example (L), (H) are the first to be restored, (PSW) the next, (C), (B) the next, and so on.

If only one register pair will be needed during the subroutine and it is occupied in the main program, then *only* that register pair must be pushed and popped. If no register pair will be needed in the subroutine then none need be pushed and popped even if occupied in the main program. If none are occupied, but any or all will be needed in the subroutine, then again none need to be pushed or popped.

We shall illustrate the use of push and pop in subroutine work with experiments. We strongly recommend that you come back to these experiments and single step them after you have read Chap. 4 on single stepping and done the experiments there. Single stepping will show beautifully the flow of pushed and popped register, flag, and return address data from CPU for storage in the memory stack, and back from memory stack to the registers, flags, and PC in the CPU. (Be sure to replace a 166 instruction at the end of a program by a Jump $\begin{pmatrix} 303 \\ 000 \\ 003 \end{pmatrix}$ for reasons to be explained in Chap. 4—single stepping will not work otherwise).

Experiment 3-6(a)   Use of Push and Pop in a Subroutine

This experiment will show how the contents of accumulator and register D can be saved so that A and D can be used in any fashion we like in a subroutine. They will then have the original contents restored to them and exhibited in the main program, and they will be totally unaffected by what happened to them in their subroutine employment.

Though, as has been pointed out, there is no need to load the stack pointer with the MMD-1 (Reset automatically takes us to SP=004H,000L), we shall do so in this example.

$$
\begin{array}{ll}
000 & \left(\begin{array}{l} 061 \\ 300 \\ 003 \end{array} \right. \quad \text{LXI SP, } (B_2) (B_3) \\
001 & \\
002 & \left. \right\rangle \text{Stack Pointer Bytes} \\
003 & \left(\begin{array}{l} 021 \\ 111 \\ 222 \end{array} \right. \quad \text{LXI D, } (B_2) (B_3) \\
004 & \rightarrow \text{ E Reg Byte} \\
005 & \rightarrow \text{ D Reg Byte}
\end{array}
$$

006	$\left(\begin{array}{c}076\\333\end{array}\right)$	MVI, A
007		
010	$\left(\begin{array}{c}041\\377\\000\end{array}\right)$	LXI H, (B$_2$) (B$_3$)
011		→ L Reg Byte
012		→ H Reg Byte
013	$\left(\begin{array}{c}315\\100\\003\end{array}\right)$	
014		Call →
015		
016	$\left(\begin{array}{c}323\\001\end{array}\right)$	out (A) to Port 1 ← Ret
017		
020	172	Mov $\overset{\frown}{A,D}$
021	$\left(\begin{array}{c}323\\000\end{array}\right)$	out (A) to Port 0
022		
023	166	Halt

Subroutine

003,100	365	Push PSW
101	325	Push D
102	$\left(\begin{array}{c}026\\123\end{array}\right)$	MVI, D
103		
014	172	Mov $\overset{\frown}{A,D}$
105	$\left(\begin{array}{c}323\\002\end{array}\right)$	
106		(A) → Port 2
107	321	Pop D
110	361	Pop PSW
111	311	Ret

If you observe 333 at port 1, 222 at port 0, and 123 at port 2, then the push and pop instructions did what they were supposed to do. In other words, we freed (D) from 222 it had in the main program, saved it in the stack (Push D), loaded it with 123 in the subroutine, transferred it to A, whose 333 contents in the main program were saved on the stack (Push PSW), and then outputted 123 to port 2 in the subroutine, popped 222 and 333 back to D (Pop D) and A (Pop PSW) respectively, and then outputted (A) = 333 to Port 1 and finally moved (D) = 222 to A and then to port 0. The situation in the stack can be depicted as shown in Fig. 30.

If, *after* the program run, we examine locations 272, 273, 274, 275, 276, and 277, we will find the following stored data:

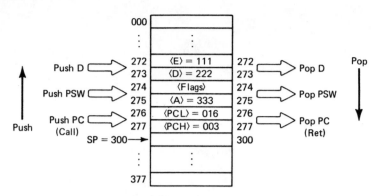

Figure 30. Stack contents relative to experiment 3-6(a).

111,222, flags (=?), 333, 016, 003 in that order, confirming the existence and effects of the Call, Push PSW, and Push D operations (remember that register transfer, or memory to register transfer— as during the Pops—does not destroy the contents of the source register or memory location). The ? on flags will be answered in Section 3-7.

Experiment 3-6(b)   Use of Push and Pop in a Main Routine

This experiment shows how Pushes and Pops can also be used in the main program.

000	/001\	LXI, B
001	(111)→	C Reg Byte
002	\222/ →	B Reg Byte
003	/ 076 \	MVI, A
004	(333)	
005	/061\	
006	(300)	LXI SP
007	\003/	
010	305	Push B
011	365	Push PSW
012	(006)	MVI, B
013	\ 377 /	
014	170	Mov A͡,B
015	(323)	(A) → Port 1 (377)
016	\ 001 /	
017	361	Pop PSW

020	301	Pop B
021	$\begin{pmatrix} 323 \\ 000 \end{pmatrix}$	(A) → Port 0 (333)
022		
023	170	Mov $\widehat{A,B}$
024	$\begin{pmatrix} 323 \\ 002 \end{pmatrix}$	(A) → Port 2 (222)
025		
026	166	Halt

We should see 377 at Port 1 from the MVI,B instruction, 333 at Port 0 from the original MVI,A instruction and the Push PSW which saved it, and finally 222 at Port 2 from the original LXI,B instruction and the Push B which saved it. Note

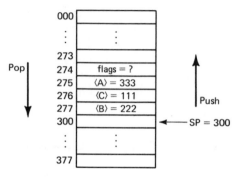

Figure 31. Stack for experiment 3-6(b).

After the program is run, examination of memory locations 277, 276, and 275 should reveal 222, 111, 333 respectively, thus confirming the Push B and Push PSW operations.

Experiment 3-6(c)   Use of a Pop Alone (Popping of Pre-stored Information from Memory)

000	$\begin{pmatrix} 061 \\ 276 \\ 003 \end{pmatrix}$	LXI SP.
001		← SP
002		
003	361	POP PSW
004	$\begin{pmatrix} 323 \\ 000 \end{pmatrix}$	out Port 0
005		
006	166	

Prestored   } 276—anything
Information } 277—333

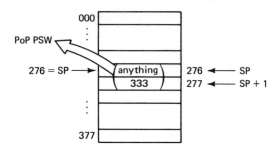

Figure 32. Stack for experiment 3-6(c).

Running the program, we should see 333 at Port 0 because we have popped pre-stored information from SP=276 and SP+1=277 to the flags and to A, respectively, by means of the Pop PSW instruction. (Remember: POP PSW means $M_{SP}{\to}$Flag word and $M_{SP+1}{\to}$A). 333 should still be observed at 277L after the run. This confirms the nature of the POP PSW operation. More on the flags in section 7.

Experiment 3-6(d)   A Program with Push, Pop, Call, and Return for Future Use in Single Stepping

The following program will be most instructive and should be done after single stepping is taken up in the next chapter. Single stepping through it will reveal all the intricacies involved with Pop, Push, Call, Ret, and Out, In and allow us to see the effect of each instruction, particularly as it pertains to outputting data at a port. Running it full speed will obliterate the results because each port is used here several times to output all kinds of different data. Single stepping will reveal the individual outputs to the ports in turn as they occur in the program. Don't expect to see much if you run it full speed now. The program has no purpose other than instructional with respect to Out, Push, Pop, Call, and Ret as revealed by single stepping. Draw the stack and follow the program carefully.

$$
\begin{array}{ll}
\begin{array}{l} 000 \\ 001 \\ 002 \end{array}
\left(\begin{array}{l} 061 \\ 300 \\ 003 \end{array} \right)
& \text{LXI SP}
\end{array}
$$

003	$\begin{pmatrix} 041 \\ 100 \\ 177 \end{pmatrix}$	LXI H
004		
005		
006	$\begin{pmatrix} 076 \\ 333 \end{pmatrix}$	
007		
010	$\begin{pmatrix} 323 \\ 000 \end{pmatrix}$	Out
011		
012	174	Mov $\widehat{A,H}$
013	$\begin{pmatrix} 323 \\ 001 \end{pmatrix}$	Out
014		
015	175	Mov $\widehat{A,L}$
016	$\begin{pmatrix} 323 \\ 002 \end{pmatrix}$	Out
017		
020	$\begin{pmatrix} 315 \\ 200 \\ 003 \end{pmatrix}$	Call →
021		
022		
023	000	← RET
024	$\begin{pmatrix} 303 \\ 000 \\ 003 \end{pmatrix}$	
025		
026		

Subroutine

200	365	Push PSW
201	345	Push H
202	174	Mov $\widehat{A,H}$
203	$\begin{pmatrix} 323 \\ 000 \end{pmatrix}$	Out
204		
205	175	Mov $\widehat{A,L}$
206	$\begin{pmatrix} 323 \\ 000 \end{pmatrix}$	Out
207		
210	$\begin{pmatrix} 041 \\ 111 \\ 166 \end{pmatrix}$	LXI H
211		
212		
213	174	Mov $\widehat{A,H}$
214	$\begin{pmatrix} 323 \\ 000 \end{pmatrix}$	Out
215		
216	175	Mov $\widehat{A,L}$
217	$\begin{pmatrix} 323 \\ 000 \end{pmatrix}$	Out
220		

221	⎛ 021 ⎞	
222	⎜ 273 ⎟	LXI D
223	⎝ 003 ⎠	
224	032	LDAX D
225	⎛ 323 ⎞	Out
226	⎝ 000 ⎠	
227	⎛ 021 ⎞	
230	⎜ 272 ⎟	LXI D
231	⎝ 003 ⎠	
232	032	LDAX D
233	⎛ 323 ⎞	Out
234	⎝ 000 ⎠	
235	341	Pop H
236	361	Pop PSW
237	174	Mov A,H
240	⎛ 323 ⎞	Out
241	⎝ 000 ⎠	
242	175	Mov A,L
243	⎛ 323 ⎞	Out
244	⎝ 001 ⎠	
245	311	→ RET to 023

Experiment 3-6(e) Pushing With and Without an LXI SP Instruction in RAM—Top of RAM Reserved for KEX Stack Operations.

Run the following program:

000	⎛ 061 ⎞	
001	⎜ 300 ⎟	LXI SP
002	⎝ 003 ⎠	
003	⎛ 021 ⎞	
004	⎜ 111 ⎟	LXI D, E
005	⎝ 222 ⎠	
006	325	Push D, E
007	166	HALT

Reset and examine memory locations 277 and 276 (SP—1, SP—2). They should, of course, contain 222 and 111, respectively. Examine also locations 376 and 377. You will observe 113 and 000, respectively. Now turn the power off, back on, and reprogram as follows:

$$
\begin{array}{cc}
000 & \left.\begin{array}{c} 021 \\ 111 \\ 222 \end{array}\right) \\
001 & \\
002 & \\
003 & 325 \\
004 & 166.
\end{array}
$$

Remember that in turning the power on, we will be taken to 000H, 000L upon Resetting before programming. This puts us in KEX at PROM 000H. The first instruction there takes us to 000, 070 where the SP gets loaded with 004, 000, unlike the first program above which, when run, sets SP at 003, 300 and therefore places (D) and (E) into 277, 276. Since the SP in the second program is set by KEX, any push (e.g., 325) instruction should, one might think, load SP—1 at 003, 377 with (D) = 222 and SP—2 = 376 with (E) = 111. Instead, however, after running the program, *resetting*, and examining locations 377 and 376 we again find 000 and 113, respectively. (277 and 276 will now hold some random, turn-on, data.) The reason is simple: in resetting after running the program, we are again back in KEX at 000, 000 and the run through KEX again sets SP = 004, 000 and reveals, also, a push first occurring at 000, 110 due to a Call there. This Call pushes PCH = 000, PCL = 113 (the return address) on to SP—1 = 377 and SP—2 = 376, in RAM 003, respectively (i.e., SP—1 = 003, 377), obliterating the 222 and 111 placed there by push D in our program run. This is what we mean when we say that the top of memory 377, 376 . . . is "reserved for KEX": it takes priority for storing registers used by KEX whenever Reset is pressed thereby forcing a *KEX* program run. This does *not* mean that a push D, for example, and later a POP D in our program will not work if you do *not* load the SP with an LXI SP instruction. It will work: (D) and (E) will be stored at 377, 376 and later restored to D and E *during* the program run. But after pressing Reset to determine what's at 377, 376 you will *not* see (D) and (E), as you did at 277, 276 in the first program run, because Reset causes a run through KEX and the Call at 000, 110 pushes 000 and 113 into 377, 376 as the *last* information to be stored there. Note also that after Reset, running through KEX also reveals other pushes: push PSW, push D, and push H at 277, 300, and 347 and they will load 375, 374, etc. with (A), (flags), (D), (E), etc. as determined by the details of the KEX program. Examine those locations and try to account for what you see. This is tricky because you will get different answers depending on whether you press 370*L*, then 371*L* . . . or whether you press 370L and then *S* your way up to 377 to examine the contents. KEX distinguishes between an S or an L key and loads accumulator and registers accordingly (encoder codes) so that Push PSW, push D, push H will give different results for the two cases in *some* of the locations between 370 and 377. But in any event, if you did several pushes in the second program above without setting SP, you would *not* find the corresponding register contents at 377 . . . 370 after running and *resetting* but rather contents as determined by KEX.

Writing a program into the top of R/W RAM 003 will, therefore, not work because KEX will push registers into that area reserved for its stack, destroying the very program you write in. Thus, for example, try writing and executing the following program:

$$
\begin{array}{cc}
003, 373 & \left(\begin{array}{c} 076 \\ 111 \end{array}\right) \\
374 & \\
375 & \left(\begin{array}{c} 323 \\ 000 \end{array}\right) \\
376 & \\
377 & 166
\end{array}
$$

There is no problem writing the program in, but the moment you press 373*L* just before striking G you are back to "point A" (000, 076) in KEX (see "Point D"; i.e., 000, 134 thru 143 in KEX) and this takes you to the "Call KBRD" routine at 000, 110 which jumps to 000, 315 leaving PCH = 000, PCL = 113 (return address) pushed on to the stack at 000, 377 and 376 (as KEX has already set SP to 004, 000), thus destroying the program. Try executing the above. You will get nowhere. Examine the contents of 373 to 377 *either* after writing the program in or after execution. What do you see at, say, 376 and 377? Try writing the program at 003, 360. Can it be executed successfully?

While we are on the subject of KEX, the following experiment, in conjunction with a study of Appendix C, should prove revealing as to some of KEX's "mysteries."

Experiment 3-6(f)   A KEX "Mystery."

Turn on your microcomputer and program in the following:

$$\begin{matrix} 000 \\ 001 \end{matrix} \left(\begin{matrix} 323 \\ 000 \end{matrix}\right) \quad \langle A \rangle \rightarrow \text{Port } 0.$$

$$002 \qquad 166$$

Press "G" and observe port 0. Turn off the power, turn back on, reprogram, run and again observe port 0. Reprogram with ports 001 and 002 at location 001. In every case, no matter how many times you do this experiment you will *always* see 012 at the port. Remember that the *last* key pressed before running a program is always "G." A study of "KBRD" starting at 000, 315 in KEX shows that when G is pressed its *encoder code* 373 (see Fig. 12, MMD-1 Schematic—the 74148 encoders) is stored in the accumulator. A mask operation at 345, an ADI 360 at 352, a Mov L, A at 354, and a Mov A, M at 355 fetches the contents of *location* 360 + 013 = 373 and places them into A. The contents of location 373 are 012 corresponding to the *KEX* (not *encoder*) code for "G." Hence the *last* quantity in A *just after* G is pressed will be 012 and the above program outputs it to a port, unless, of course, the program itself supersedes "G" by placing its own value into A (i.e., $\left(\begin{matrix} 076 \\ B_2 \end{matrix}\right)$).

3-7   THE 5 FLAGS AND CONDITIONAL JUMPS, CALLS, AND RETURNS*

In the experiments performed so far we have frequently encountered *conditional* instructions such as JNZ = $(302, B_2, B_3)$ which means "jump to address B_3 H, B_2 L and continue the program there *if* the 8-bit result of the previous arithmetic or logic operation was *not* zero, otherwise ignore this instruction and proceed as usual." (i.e., jump if the *zero* flip flop = logic 0). This is opposed to the *unconditional* jump instruction JMP = $(303, B_2, B_3)$ which says "jump to address B_3 H, B_2 L and continue the program there." It can be appreciated that the conditional instruction

---

*Intel 8080 Microcomputer Systems User's Manual, Sept. 1975, pp. 4–11, 12, 13.

is one of the most powerful tools in the microprocessor's instruction repertoire as it is the basis of a control decision. Its use in a program will allow the microprocessor to decide whether a traffic light should turn green or not, whether a device should at a given moment stop or start, whether data should be output to or input from a device (teletype, CRT monitor, or cassette tape), whether a time delay is finished or not, whether a lock should be opened or not, and a host of other decision making control possibilities. We have particularly seen its power, so far, in Experiments 3-5(a), (b), (c), and (d) where a count or bit movement was controlled by the microprocessor in such a way with the JNZ instruction (in conjunction with the CMP, r or ANI, B instructions) that the process stopped just *where* and *when* we wanted it to.

There are other conditional jump instructions which can, and many times have to, be used in a program if the microprocessor is to make a decision controlling a process or event on the basis of the information fed to it from the input device, which then becomes the output device when the control decision is made. We now want to explain the basis of those instructions and how they are to be used. We are referring to decision making instructions such as the following (see Intel Ref.).

JNZ $\begin{pmatrix} 302 \\ B_2 \\ B_3 \end{pmatrix}$ Jump to address B_3H, B_2L if the result of the last arithmetic or logic operation is not zero and continue with program from there. Otherwise proceed straight ahead in the program (i.e., jump only if *zero* flip flop = logic 0)

JZ $\begin{pmatrix} 312 \\ B_2 \\ B_3 \end{pmatrix}$ Jump to address B_3H, B_2L if the result of the last arithmetic or logical operation is zero, and continue with program from there. Otherwise proceed straight ahead in the program (i.e., jump if *zero* flip flop = logic 1)

JNC $\begin{pmatrix} 322 \\ B_2 \\ B_3 \end{pmatrix}$ Jump to address B_3H, B_2L if the result of the last arithmetic or logical operation produced no carry out of the MSB (most significant bit) (i.e., jump if *carry* flip flop = logic 0)

JC $\begin{pmatrix} 332 \\ B_2 \\ B_3 \end{pmatrix}$ Jump to address B_3H, B_2L if the result of the last arithmetic or logical operation produced a carry out of the MSB (i.e., jump if *carry* flip flop = logic 1)

JPO $\begin{pmatrix} 342 \\ B_2 \\ B_3 \end{pmatrix}$ Jump to address B_3H, B_2L if the result of the last arithmetic or logic instruction produced (O) odd parity (odd number of ones in the 8-bit result) (i.e., jump if *parity* flip flop = logic 0)

JPE $\begin{pmatrix} 352 \\ B_2 \\ B_3 \end{pmatrix}$ Jump to address B_3H, B_2L if the result of the last arithmetic or logic operation produced (E) even parity (even number of ones in the 8-bit result) (i.e., jump if *parity* flip flop = logic 1)

JP $\begin{pmatrix} 362 \\ B_2 \\ B_3 \end{pmatrix}$ Jump to address B_3H, B_2L if the result of the last arithmetic or logic operation produced D_7 (MSB) = 0 (i.e., jump if *sign* flip flop = logic 0)

JM $\begin{pmatrix} 372 \\ B_2 \\ B_3 \end{pmatrix}$ Jump to address B_3H, B_2L if the result of the last arithmetic or logic operation produced D_7 (MSB) = 1 (i.e., jump if *sign* flip flop = logic 1).

Note in *each* case that to jump or not to jump is determined by an 8-bit result of *the last arithmetic or logical operation* [which sets (to 1) or resets (to 0) a relevant flag (or flip flop)]. In each of the above instructions if the specified condition is true, $(PC) \leftarrow B_3 B_2$ and control passes to address B_3H, B_2L in the program.

How does the microprocessor know whether the preceding result was or was not zero, or whether it did or did not produce a carry out of the MSB, or whether the result was of even or odd parity, or whether the MSB was 1 or 0? The answer is: through a set of 5 *flip flops* (each called a "flag") which reside in the microprocessor chip (see Fig. 10, Chap. 2).

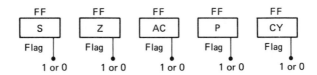

Figure 33. The flag flip-flops: sign, zero, auxiliary carry, parity, carry.

The status of each of these flags (whether a 1 or a 0) depends on the result of the immediately preceding logic or arithmetic operation(s) that were performed in the ALU on the data stored in memory, or in the accumulator, or in the registers.

Thus, if the MSB produced by the immediately preceding arithmetic or logic operation was 0, the S flip flop (flag) becomes 0; if it was 1, the S flag is set to 1. If the result of the preceding arithmetic or logic operation was zero, the Z "flag" is set to 1; if not, the Z flag is 0 (reset). If the preceding arithmetic or logic operation produced a result that had even parity, the P flip flop ("flag") is set to 1; if odd, the flag is 0. If the preceding arithmetic or logic operation produced an 8-bit result that had a carry emerge from the MSB, the CY flag (or C flag) is set to 1; otherwise it is 0. If there is a carry out of bit 4 (b_3) into bit 5 (b_4) as a result of the last arithmetic or logic operation, then the AC flag is set to 1; otherwise it is set to 0. (The AC flag is not used much except in decimal adjust operations where it is very important. More on that in later experiments.) The ALU together with the control section obviously are paramount in setting or resetting the flag flip flops. Finally a flag *word** is formed to convey the overall situation in the 5 flip flops.

D_7	D_6	D_5	D_4	D_3	D_2	D_1	D_0
S	Z	0	AC	0	P	I	CY

where S=0 (MSB=0), S=1 (MSB=1); Z=0 (non zero result), Z=1 (zero result); AC=0 (no carry out of bit 4), =1 (Carry out of bit 4); P=0 (odd parity result), =1 (even parity result); CY=0 (no carry out of MSB), =1 (carry out of MSB).

The 1 and two zeroes are put in arbitrarily. Thus, if the MSB were 0, and there was a zero result, with no carry produced out of bit 4, a carry out of MSB and the parity were even, the flag word would be 01000111.

An important quantity is the *processor status word*, "PSW", which is a 16-bit word consisting of the contents of A as the MSByte and the flag word as the LSByte.

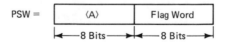

PSW reveals the current status of the microprocessor with respect to (A) and flags. We have already illustrated PSW in experiments in section 3-6 on Push PSW, Pop PSW and we will use PSW again in the experiments in this section.

Let's return to our JNZ, JZ, JNC, JC, JPO, JPE, JP and JM instructions. When an instruction such as $\begin{pmatrix} JC \\ B_2 \\ B_3 \end{pmatrix}$ is met in the program, the control section under command of the Instruction

*Intel Manual, Sept. 1975, pp. 4–13.

Decoder (ID) immediately *tests* one of the 5 flags (Fig. 10, Chap. 2), in particular here, the CY flag. If CY is set to 1, this means there is a carry, $(B_3, B_2) \rightarrow PC$, and the program would jump to $B_3 H, B_2 L$. If, however, the control section found the CY flag to be 0, a no carry would be indicated and the program would go straight on, ignoring $\begin{pmatrix} JC \\ B_2 \\ B_3 \end{pmatrix}$: $PC \rightarrow PC + 1$.

Or, as another example: If we had an instruction $\begin{pmatrix} JNZ \\ B_2 \\ B_3 \end{pmatrix}$ in the program, the control section would test the Z flag and if it found $Z=1$, indicating the result of the last operation was zero, the instruction would be ignored $(PC \rightarrow PC+1)$. But if we had used $\begin{pmatrix} JZ \\ B_2 \\ B_3 \end{pmatrix}$ as the conditional jump instruction, the program would indeed jump to $B_3 H$, $B_2 L$ $(B_3, B_2 \rightarrow PC)$. Or if we had an instruction $\begin{pmatrix} JP \\ B_2 \\ B_3 \end{pmatrix}$, the control section would test the S flag and if it found S flag=0 (indicating MSB=0), the program would jump to $B_3 H$, $B_2 L$. But if it found the S flag = 1 (indicating MSB=1), the program would ignore this instruction and proceed straight ahead.

You are urged to use as many different kinds of conditional jump instructions in your decision making programs in order to gain mastery and confidence in their use. Often one of several conditional jump instructions can be used to do the required task and produce the same end result.

The following experiment should help you gain that confidence.

Experiment 3-7(a) Testing Conditional Jump Instructions and Verifying That They Occur When They Are Supposed to

000	⎛ 061 ⎞	LXI SP
001	⎜ 300 ⎟	
002	⎝ 003 ⎠	

003	361	Pop PSW: ⟨300 in stack⟩ to Flags and ⟨301 in stack⟩ to A

004	⎛ JNZ (302) or JZ (312) ⎞	
	JNC (322) or JC (332)	Various conditional jumps
	JPO (342) or JPE (352)	to 003H,000L
	JP (362) or JM (372)	
005	000	
006	⎝ 003 ⎠	

007	⎛ 323 ⎞	out (A) to Port 1
010	⎝ 001 ⎠	
011	166	Halt

300	——	*Flag Byte F* ⎫ see instruction at 003
301	127	*accum Byte A* ⎭

Recall that a) F = Flag Byte =

S	Z	O	AC	O	P	I	CY

D_7 -------------------- D_0

and that b) the LXI SP together with the pop instruction produces the following situation in the stack:

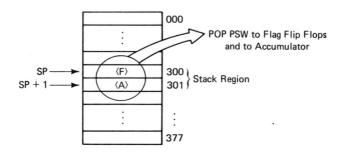

In *all* the pop instructions, be they Pop rp or Pop PSW types, ⟨M$_{SP}$⟩ [here 300] goes to rl (low register—here the flags) and ⟨M$_{SP+1}$⟩ [here (301)] goes to rh (high register—here the accumulator). See Section 3-6. Note also that we load 301L and 300L with anything *we* want.

The idea in this experiment is to observe when a jump occurs by noting the output at Port 1. If there is output of 127 at Port 1, then we have *not* jumped back to 003H,000L as required by the conditional instruction in 004L,005L, and 006L. In other words if the condition for the jump is met, we go back to 000 and keep looping between 000L and 006L and observe no output at Port 1 except the usual 003H. If, however, the condition for the jump is *not* met, we ignore it and go to 007 and then to halt, thereby seeing the byte 127 at Port 1. Thus the presence or absence of 127 at Port 1 should tell us whether the condition for the jump to occur was met or not, and thus whether the jump did or did not occur.

Do the experiment by comparing the results produced at Port 1 when JNZ and then JZ are used at 004 (with flag words 002 (no zero) and then 102 (a zero) stored at 300L in each case); then when JNC and JC are used at 004 (with flag words 002 (no carry) and then 003 (carry) stored at 300L in each case); then when JPO and JPE are used at 004 (with flag words 002 (odd parity) and then 006 (even parity) stored at 300L in each case); and finally when JP and JM are used at 004 (with flag words 002 (MSB=0) and then 202 (MSB=1) at 300L in each case).

Do the jumps occur where they are supposed to? You have stored the *simulated* flag word at 300L and then popped it into the flags themselves by means of the POP PSW instruction. The output at Port 1 will tell if the jump instruction was obeyed or ignored in relation to the contents of the flags you have chosen.

Experiment 3-7(b)   Experiment to Determine Flag Status After an Arithmetic Operation

000	⎧ 061 ⎫	
001	⎨ 200 ⎬	
002	⎩ 003 ⎭	
003	⎛ 006 ⎞	MVI, B
004	⎝ 337 ⎠	
005	⎛ 076 ⎞	MVI, A
006	⎝ 200 ⎠	
007	200	Add (B) to (A) and store in A
010	365	Push PSW; i.e., (A) to 177L and (flags) to 176L
011	166	Halt

Run and then examine the contents of 177L and 176L. In accordance with the addition 337 + 200 in this program, (A) in location 177L should read $(137)_8$ and the flag word in 176L

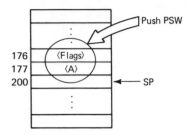

should read 00000111 indicating MSB=0 (S=0), a non zero result (Z=0), no auxiliary carry (AC=0), even parity in the answer in A (P=1), and carry out of MSB (C=1).

It is instructive to rerun the program using 001 instead of 200 at address 006. What do you now observe for (A) at 177L and the flag word in 176L? Interpret the flag word you observe and its meaning as far as sign, whether the result is 0, whether there was an auxiliary carry, whether the parity in (A) is even or odd, and whether there was a carry out of MSB. Does it make sense? Remember: *S tests whether* $D_7 = 1$ *or 0.*

Another interesting case would be to insert 377 at 004L and 001 at 006L. Examine (A) at 177L and flag word at 176L. The flag word should read 01010111 indicating MSB=0, a zero result in (A), an auxiliary carry during the arithmetic addition operation, an even parity [all zeros in (A)], and a carry out of MSB during the addition.

Finally try 222−111 and see 111 at 177 and 002 at 176. Why? Then try 111−222 and see 267 at 177 and 227 at 176. Why? Use the pertinent subtraction instruction (SuI, for example).

There are in addition to conditional jumps, conditional calls and returns. Thus

$$\begin{pmatrix} 304 \\ B_2 \\ B_3 \end{pmatrix} = \text{CNZ} = \text{Call if not zero}$$

$$\begin{pmatrix} 314 \\ - \\ - \end{pmatrix} = \text{CZ}$$

$$\begin{pmatrix} 324 \\ - \\ - \end{pmatrix} = \text{CNC}$$

$$\begin{pmatrix} 334 \\ - \\ - \end{pmatrix} = \text{CC}$$

$$\begin{pmatrix} 344 \\ - \\ - \end{pmatrix} = \text{CPO}$$

$$\begin{pmatrix} 354 \\ - \\ - \end{pmatrix} = \text{CPE}$$

$$\begin{pmatrix} 364 \\ - \\ - \end{pmatrix} = \text{CP}$$

$$\begin{pmatrix} 374 \\ - \\ - \end{pmatrix} = \text{CM}$$

$$\begin{pmatrix} 315 \\ - \\ - \end{pmatrix} = \text{unconditional Call}$$

```
300  =  RNZ = Return if not zero
310  =  RZ
320  =  RNC
330  =  RC
340  =  RPO
350  =  RPE
360  =  RP
370  =  RM
311  =  RET (unconditional)
```

Several experiments are presented below to illustrate their use:

Experiment 3-7(c)   Using a Conditional Call

000	$\begin{pmatrix} 076 \\ 001 \end{pmatrix}$	MVI, A
001		
002	074	INR A by 1
003	$\begin{pmatrix} 314 \\ 100 \\ 003 \end{pmatrix}$	CZ
004		
005		
006	$\begin{pmatrix} 076 \\ 111 \end{pmatrix}$	← Ret
007		
010	$\begin{pmatrix} 323 \\ 001 \end{pmatrix}$	
011		
012	166	

Subroutine

```
003,100   ⎛076⎞
    101   ⎝333⎠
    102   ⎛323⎞
    103   ⎝000⎠
    104    311  =  RET
```

Run the program as is. We should see 111 at Port 1 but *not* 333 at Port 0. Now rerun the program with 075 (DCR A by 1) inserted at 002L. You will now see 111 at Port 1 *and* 333 at Port 0 indicating the condition (zero) for the call was met and the subroutine was called.

Experiment 3-7(d)   Using a Conditional Return

```
000   ⎛076⎞
001   ⎝111⎠
002   ⎛323⎞
003   ⎝001⎠
004   ⎛315⎞
005   ⎜100⎟   Call
006   ⎝003⎠
007    166
```

Subroutine

```
003,100   ⎛076⎞
    101   ⎝200⎠
    102   ⎛306⎞         ADI, B₂ to Reg A
    103   ⎝200⎠
    104    320          (RNC) = Ret. if no carry.
    105   ⎛076⎞
    106   ⎝333⎠
    107   ⎛323⎞
    110   ⎝000⎠
    111    311  =  Uncond. Ret.
```

As the program stands, we have a carry in the arithmetic operation just before RNC. Hence, the RNC is ignored and we proceed down to 311 and return there. We should see 111 at Port 1 *and* 333 at Port 0. If we modify the program at 103L and insert the byte 100 there, there will *be no carry* and RNC will be obeyed. In that case, we should see 111 at Port 1 but *not* 333 at Port 0.

Experiment 3-7(e)   Dangers With The JM and JP Conditional Jump Instructions.

JP(362: "Jump on Plus") and JM (372: "Jump on Minus") do nothing of the sort. They are 3-byte conditional jump instructions which depend on the outcome of *testing* D_7 *(MSB)* after an arithmetic or logical operation. If the result of the last arithmetic or logical operation yields an MSB=1, that result is interpreted as negative (S=1); if the MSB=0, it is interpreted as positive (S=0). JM would thus jump if D_7=1 and JP would jump if D_7=0. 350 − 150 would be interpreted as *negative* (result=200, D_7=1)! You can get into one heck of a lot of trouble in programming control decisions based on these instructions as the following program will show. One wishes that Intel had "mnemonic'd" the instructions 362 and 372 as JD_7^0 and JD_7^1, respectively, instead of JP and JM. The importance of the instructions is illustrated in the KEX "KBRD" subroutine starting at 000, 315 (Appendix C) where JM and JP are used, *after an arithmetic or logical operation,* to test for D_7=1 or 0. When a key is pressed (Fig. 12) D_7=1 as a result of the 74148 keyboard encoder arrangement, otherwise D_7=0, so that after ORA, A, which changes nothing, JM and JP can test as to whether a key on the MMD-1 has been pressed or not, a *prerequisite* to debouncing, code storage, and search/compare as to *which* key was pressed. But JM and JP have nothing to do with the actual *sign* of the quantity D_7 ... D_0, as one might be tempted to think (*except in 7 bit arithmetic!*)

The following program will demonstrate the above remarks.

003, 000	(076	MVI, A	
001	350)	A	
002	(326	SuI	} ⟨A⟩ − ⟨B⟩
003	150)	B	
004	(332		
005	020	JC (A < B)	
006	003)		

$$
\begin{array}{lll}
007 & \left(\begin{array}{c} 312 \\ 030 \\ 003 \end{array}\right) & \text{JZ (A = B)} \\
010 & & \\
011 & & \\
012 & \left(\begin{array}{c} 076 \\ 111 \end{array}\right) & \text{(A} > \text{B)} \\
013 & & \\
014 & \left(\begin{array}{c} 323 \\ 001 \end{array}\right) & \text{Port 1 (A} > \text{B): 111} \\
015 & & \\
016 & 166 & \text{Halt} \\
020 & \left(\begin{array}{c} 076 \\ 222 \end{array}\right) & \text{(A} < \text{B)} \\
021 & & \\
022 & \left(\begin{array}{c} 323 \\ 000 \end{array}\right) & \text{Port 0 (A} < \text{B): 222} \\
023 & & \\
024 & 166 & \text{Halt} \\
030 & \left(\begin{array}{c} 076 \\ 333 \end{array}\right) & \text{(A = B)} \\
031 & & \\
032 & \left(\begin{array}{c} 323 \\ 002 \end{array}\right) & \text{Port 2: (A = B): 333} \\
033 & & \\
034 & 166 & \text{Halt}
\end{array}
$$

Run the program and observe 111 at port 1 indicating $A > B$. Now place 150 at 001 and 350 at 003. Run and observe 222 at port 0 $(A < B)$. Place 150 at both 001 and 003. Run and observe 333 at port 2 $(A = B)$. All is as it should be. Now change the instruction at 004 to 372 (JM). Again place 350 at 001 and 150 at 003. Run and observe 222 at port 0 $(A < B)$—rather preposterous if you interpret JM as indicating a minus sign. All it indicates is that $350 - 150$ gives 200 with $D_7 = 1$. Now place 150 at 001 and 350 at 003. This time $\langle A \rangle - \langle B \rangle$ is negative and it *does* produce $D_7 = 1$ (try the arithmetic) so the jump to 020 with output of 222 to port 0 is indeed justified. Finally place 150 at both 001 and 003. Subtraction now gives $D_7 = 0$ and a zero product result so we go to 007 and to 030 where 333 is output to port 2. With JM still at 004 try $A = 000$ and $B = 377$. $A - B$ gives $D_7 = 0$ (do the arithmetic) which could erroneously be interpreted as positive and port 1 will yield 111 to indicate that. You can amuse yourself by playing with other A, B combinations with JM still at 004. Try $A = 000$ with $B = 200$ and 300 and explain your results at ports 0 and 1. SuI for *both* choices of B yields negatives, yet for $B = 300$ port 1 lights while for $B = 200$ port 0 lights indicating a positive and then negative result, respectively. Or try $A = 111$; $B = 222, 333$. In every case, after you try the test with JM, replace with JC = 332 at 004 and see how *JC followed by JZ is foolproof.*

Then why the mnemonics JM and JP? The answer is that they apply to *7 bit* arithmetic, in which case $\langle A \rangle - \langle B \rangle$ *will* produce $D_7 = 1$ (carry into *MSB* D_7) indicating $\langle A \rangle < \langle B \rangle$ (*Minus*), or $D_7 = 0$ indicating $\langle A \rangle \geqslant \langle B \rangle$ (*Positive*). Devise a program similar to the above which will prove that in 7 bit arithmetic if $\langle A \rangle \geqslant \langle B \rangle$, JP works ($D_7 = 0$ for $\langle A \rangle - \langle B \rangle$) while if $\langle A \rangle < \langle B \rangle$ JM works ($D_7 = 1$ for $\langle A \rangle - \langle B \rangle$).

3-8 THE MYSTERIES OF THE DECIMAL ADJUST OPERATOR (DAA=047) AND BCD ADDITION

A tricky arithmetic instruction that is used often in BCD arithmetic (additions and subtractions) is the "Decimal Adjust the Accumulator" = DAA=047. Decimal arithmetic is still popular in the world as we know it and Binary Coded Decimal is then used in the computer in which binary numbers are used to represent decimal numbers: i.e., $97 \equiv (1001)\ (0111)$. But adjustments are then necessary to obtain correct results. We discuss DAA here, with experiments, because there is much to be learned from it concerning binary and BCD arithmetic, and also to gain familiarity and confidence in its use in those very important cases when it must be used.

Its definition follows:* *DAA*: the 8-bit number *in the accumulator* is adjusted to form *two 4-bit BCD digits* by the following process:

1. If the value of the four LSB's in A is > 9, *or* if the AC flag is set (i.e., there is a carry out of the fourth bit to the fifth bit in the last operation), then 0110 ($=6_{10}$) is added to (A)–(to the 4 *LSB's*).
2. If the value of the four MSB's in A is *now* > 9, *or* if the CY flag is set (indicating there was a carry out of the MSB in the last operation), then 0110 ($=6_{10}$) is added to the 4 *MSB's* of A.

As we shall see soon, if we did not make this adjustment, the 8080 could not produce the correct BCD result. It would produce the correct *binary* result. The adjustment converts the correct binary result to the correct BCD result. Computers work in binary, not BCD.

The best way to understand this is through the examples in the experiments which follow. Recourse will be made time and again

*Intel "8080 Microcomputer Systems User's Manual," Sept. 1975, pp. 4–8.

to the above definition in which the procedure for the DAA is given. The experiments will show that when two *BCD numbers* are added the ALU in the CPU adds them in pure *binary* fashion. *Only if a DAA is then* applied in the program will the *binary* answer be converted to the correct *BCD* answer, *representing the decimal sum of two decimal numbers, coded in BCD.* If no DAA is applied a binary answer results whose decimal equivalent is *not* the true decimal answer.

Experiment 3-8(a)   Adding Two Binary or BCD Numbers with and without Decimal Adjust

Program (a)

$$
\begin{array}{lll}
000 & \left(\begin{array}{c}076\\005\end{array}\right) & \text{MVI, I}\\[2ex]
001 & & \\[1ex]
002 & \left(\begin{array}{c}306\\010\end{array}\right) & \text{ADI } (B_2) \text{ to } (A)\\[2ex]
003 & & \\[1ex]
004 & \left(\begin{array}{c}323\\000\end{array}\right) & (A) \to \text{Port 0}\\[2ex]
005 & & \\[1ex]
006 & 166 &
\end{array}
$$

Program (b)

$$
\begin{array}{l}
\left(\begin{array}{c}076\\005\end{array}\right)\\[2ex]
\left(\begin{array}{c}306\\010\end{array}\right)\\[2ex]
047 = \text{DAA}\\[1ex]
\left(\begin{array}{c}323\\000\end{array}\right)\\[2ex]
166
\end{array}
$$

In Program (a) we have

$$
\begin{array}{rl}
00000101 = & (5)_{10}\\
+\ 00001000 = & (8)_{10}\\
\hline
00001101 = & (13)_{10} = \text{correct } \textit{binary} \text{ result.}
\end{array}
$$

Observe this result at Port 0. In Program (b) we have

$$
\begin{array}{l}
00000101 = (5)_{10} \\
+\,00001000 = (8)_{10} \\
\hline
00001101 \qquad > 9 \text{ (four LSB's)} \\
0110 \;\text{(DAA)} \\
\hline
(0001)(0011) = (1)_{10}(3)_{10} = 13. = \text{correct } BCD \text{ result.}
\end{array}
$$

Observe (0001) (0011) at Post 0. This is the *BCD* equivalent of 13. In the above case the *binary* for 5_{10} and for 8_{10} are the *same* as the *BCD* for 05 and for 08. Hence DAA worked to give the correct BCD answer 13. Not so in program (a) of the next experiment. *In other words, the two numbers to be added must already be in BCD before the DAA is applied if we are to realize the correct BCD sum.*

Experiment 3-8(b)   Adding Two Binary or Two BCD Numbers with and without DAA (cont'd)

Program (a)

$$
\begin{array}{ll}
000 & \left(\begin{array}{l} 076 \\ 031_8 \end{array}\right) \quad = 00011001 = (25)_{10} \text{ in } binary \\
001 & \\
002 & \left(\begin{array}{l} 306 \\ 070_8 \end{array}\right) \quad \begin{array}{l}\text{ADI } (B_2) \text{ to } (A) \\ = 00111000 = (56)_{10} \text{ in } binary\end{array} \\
003 & \\
004 & \left(\begin{array}{l} 323 \\ 000 \end{array}\right) \\
005 & \\
006 & 166
\end{array}
$$

Program (b)

$$
\begin{array}{ll}
000 & \left(\begin{array}{l} 076 \\ 045_8 \end{array}\right) \quad = (0010)\,(0101) = (25)_{10} \text{ in } BCD \\
001 & \\
002 & \left(\begin{array}{l} 306 \\ 126_8 \end{array}\right) \quad = (0101)\,(0110) = (56)_{10} \text{ in } BCD \\
003 & \\
004 & \left(\begin{array}{l} 323 \\ 000 \end{array}\right) \\
005 & \\
006 & 166
\end{array}
$$

Program (c)

$$
\begin{array}{ll}
000 \\
001
\end{array}
\left(
\begin{array}{l}
076 \\
045_8
\end{array}
\right) = (25)_{10} \text{ in } BCD \text{ i.e., } (0010)\,(0101) = (045)_8
$$

$$
\begin{array}{ll}
002 \\
003
\end{array}
\left(
\begin{array}{l}
306 \\
126_8
\end{array}
\right) = (56)_{10} \text{ in } BCD \text{ i.e., } (0101)\,(0110) = (126)_8
$$

$$
004 \quad 047 \quad = \text{DAA}
$$

$$
\begin{array}{ll}
005 \\
006
\end{array}
\left(
\begin{array}{l}
323 \\
000
\end{array}
\right)
$$

$$
007 \quad 166
$$

Running program (a) we should find

$$
\begin{array}{l}
00011001 = (25)_{10} \text{ in binary} \\
+\ 00111000 = (56)_{10} \text{ in binary} \\
\hline
01010001 = (81)_{10} \text{ in } binary \\
\qquad\qquad = \text{correct result at Port 0}
\end{array}
$$

Now place 047 after location 003 in program (a). Do you get (1000) (0001) = 81 in BCD at Port 0? You will *not* because 25 and 56 were *not* expressed in BCD to begin with. Running the program in (b) we should find

$$
\begin{array}{l}
(0010)\,(0101) = (25)_{10} \text{ in BCD} \\
+\ (0101)\,(0110) = (56)_{10} \text{ in BCD} \\
\hline
0111 \quad 1011 \neq 81 \text{ } either \text{ } in \text{ } binary \text{ } or \text{ } in \text{ } BCD.
\end{array}
$$

Running the program (c) gives *correct* results in BCD at Port 0:

$$
\begin{array}{l}
(0010)\,(0101) = (25)_{10} \text{ BCD} \\
+\ (0101)\,(0110) = (56)_{10} \text{ BCD} \\
\hline
0111 \quad 1011 > 9 \\
\qquad\quad 0110 \text{ (DAA)} \\
\hline
(1000)\,(0001) = (81)_{10} \text{ BCD at Port 0.}
\end{array}
$$

Thus, DAA takes the binary result in the accumulator and adjusts it to its correct BCD value: (1000) (0001) = 81. *But,* the two numbers to be added *must* be in *BCD* to begin with. In Experiment 3-8(a), program (b), the binary and BCD representations of the two numbers to be added *happened* to be the same.

Experiment 3-8(c)   More on DAA

Consider the following experiment* in which we wish to add two binary numbers stored in two different places in memory, decimal adjust the result, and then store this result in another place in memory. We wish to see if the stored results agree with the DAA operation. Study the program carefully.

000	⎛021⎞	LXI, D
001	⎜100⎟ →	in Reg E
002	⎝003⎠ →	in Reg D
003	⎛041⎞	LXI H
004	⎜110⎟ →	Reg L
005	⎝003⎠ →	Reg H
006	⎛001⎞	LXI B
007	⎜120⎟ →	Reg C
010	⎝003⎠ →	Reg B
011	257	Clear A and the carry flag (XRA with A)
012	032	LDAX, D (load A with the contents from the memory location pointed to by D pair; i.e., from location 003H, 100L)
013	216	ADC M (add the carry bit and the contents of the location M pointed to by the H pair; i.e., contents of the location 003H,110L, to the contents of A and store in A)
014	047	DAA Dec. Adjust
015	002	STAX B (store (A) into memory location M pointed to by B pair; i.e., by 003H,120L)
016	043	INX (HL) by 1
017	023	INX (DE) by 1
020	003	INX (BC) by 1
021	⎛076⎞	MVI, A
022	⎝110⎠	
023	273	CMP, E; i.e., evaluate (A) − (E)
024	⎛302⎞	
025	⎜011⎟	JNZ. Go to 027 when (E) = 110 is reached
026	⎝003⎠	
027	166	Halt.

*The program presented is based on the assembly language version on p. 15, Intel 8080 Microcomputer Systems Manual, Jan. 1975.

Load the following data into memory (we will be adding the data in the left column to the data in the right column, byte-for-byte, and then store the decimal-adjusted result in memory locations 120 up to 127).

100	335	110	375
101	236	111	375
102	364	112	365
103	366	113	375
104	017	114	117
105	222	115	313
106	013	116	027
107	112	117	356

When you run this experiment you should find the following results in stored locations 120L through 127L:

120	100
121	001
122	111
123	131
124	144
125	303
126	050
127	236

That these are the results to be expected can be verified for two cases.

Case 1: $(120) \stackrel{?}{=} (100) + (110)$

$$
\begin{array}{r}
1101\ 1101 = (335)_8 \\
+\ 1111\ 1101 = (375)_8 \\
\hline
11101\ 1010 \\
11 \leftarrow \text{DAA} > 9 \\
\hline
1110\ 0000 \\
> 9\ \text{DAA} \rightarrow 11 \\
\hline
0100\ 0000 = 01000000 = (100)_8\ :\ \text{see}\ (120).
\end{array}
$$

Case 2: $(125) \overset{?}{=} (105) + (115)$

$$1001\ 0010 = (222)_8$$
$$+\ 1100\ 1011 = (313)_8$$
$$\overline{1\ 0101\ 1101}$$
$$11 \leftarrow DAA > 9$$
$$\overline{0110\ 0011}$$
Carry DAA $\rightarrow 11$
$$\overline{1100\ 0011 = 11000011 = (303)_8 : \text{see } (125).}$$

See the definition of DAA at beginning of section 3-8 to understand the above steps. It all works like a charm.

Experiment 3-8(d)   Addition of Two 4-digit BCD Numbers*

The following experiment should show the real power of the DAA when two decimal numbers, coded in BCD form, are added. Study the program very carefully.

	000	/021\	LXI, D
	001	(100)→	Reg E Byte
	002	\003/→	Reg D Byte
	003	/041\	LXI, H
	004	(110)→	Reg L Byte
	005	\003/→	Reg H Byte
	006	/001\	LXI, B
	007	(120)→	Reg C Byte
	010	\003/→	Reg B Byte
	011	257	Clear A and CY Flag. (XRA with A)
Add (100)	012	032	LDAX, D (load A from M pointed to by D,E)
to (110)	013	216	ADC, M (add (M) pointed to by H,L to (A), and carry, and store in A)
and store	014	047	(or 000) DAA (or NOP)–Dec. Adjust (or not)
in 120	015	002	STAX, B (Store (A) in M pointed to by B,C)
	016	043	INX H,L
	017	023	INX D,E
	020	003	INX B,C

*See assembly language version on p. 15, Intel 8080 Microcomputer Systems Manual, Jan. 1975.

Add (101) to (111) and store in 121	021	032	LDAX, D
	022	216	ADC, M
	023	047	(or 000) DAA (or NOP)
	024	002	STAX, B
	025	043	INX H,L
	026	023	INX D,E
	027	003	INX B,C
Add (102) to (112) and store in 122	030	032	LDAX, D
	031	216	ADC, M
	032	047	DAA
	033	002	STAX, B
	034	166	Halt.

The two numbers to be added are stored in 100 to 102 and 110 to 112, respectively, and the result is stored in 120 to 122. Calculate the exercise that follows *first* before running it in the program.

$$11\ 11$$
$$7{,}489 \quad \text{decimal}$$
$$6{,}579 \quad \text{decimal}$$
$$\overline{14{,}068 \quad \text{decimal}}$$

In BCD language this would be treated as follows:

```
11 11                      CY      AC
 7,489 =  (0111) (0100)|(1000)|(1001)
+ 6,579 = +(0110) (0101)|(0111)|(1001)
                       └1     └1
14,068      1101┐ 1010   0000   0010       See definition of the
                │  11(>9) 11(CY) 11←(AC)   DAA procedure at the
            └1                             beginning of section 8.
            1110   0000   0110   1000
            11(>9)
           1 0100
          ═══════════════════════════
            1   4      0      6      8
```

Result is 14,068 dec.—as it should be.

To run the program, *load* locations in memory as follows:

$100 : 211_8 \ (=(1000)\,(1001) = (89)\ \text{BCD}$
$101 : 164_8 \ (=(0111)\,(0100) = (74)\ \text{BCD}$
$102 : 000_8 \ (=(0000)\,(0000) = (00)\ \text{BCD}$

$110 : 171_8 \ (=(0111)\,(1001) = (79)\ \text{BCD}$
$111 : 145_8 \ (=(0110)\,(0101) = (65)\ \text{BCD}$
$112 : 000_8 \ (=(0000)\,(0000) = (00)\ \text{BCD}$

Run the program. You should see the answer stored in memory location 120, 121, and 122.

$120 : (0110)\,(1000) = (68)\ \text{BCD}$
$121 : (0100)\,(0000) = (40)\ \text{BCD}$ or a final result of *014,068 dec.*
$122 : (0000)\,(0001) = (01)\ \text{BCD}$

Rerun the program with NOP's at 014L and 023L instead of DAA. Convince yourself that you get *wrong* BCD answers. Try another example on your own. Add 9481 and 1249 in BCD form to get 10,730 as your BCD answer; i.e., (120) : (0011) (0000) = (30) BCD; (121) = (0000) (0111) = (07) BCD; (122) : (0000) (0001) = (01) BCD.

Experiment 3-8(e)

Experiment 3-2(f)i: (9 × 5) with DAA: Answer appears in BCD.

Reprogram Experiment 3-2(f)i so that the answer 45_{10} appears at the 8 LED's of Port 0 in BCD form; i.e., 0100 0101 instead of 00101101 in binary. To do this merely follow $\binom{306}{005}$ by 047 (DAA) and then proceed with the rest of the program.

Experiment 3-8(f)   A 16 Digit Decimal (BCD)
Subtraction Routine*

The following program should be clear.* We shall calculate $R = m - S$ (m = menuhend, S = subtrahend) m will be placed in memory from 300 thru 307, each location holding two digits, *each expressed in BCD*. Likewise S in BCD will be placed in memory from 310–317. (The lowest two digits of m will be stored in 300, those of S in 310.) The result, R, will be stored in 300 thru 307. Registers D, E are loaded with the hi–lo address of the memory location holding the two LSD's of m, likewise for registers H, L with respect to the memory location holding the two LSD's of S (thus in our case D, E = 003, 300 and H, L = 003, 310). The program is written around 10's complement subtraction arithmetic.*

000	⎛021⎞	LXI D, E
001	⎜300⎟	(location of two LSD's of m)
002	⎝003⎠	
003	⎛041⎞	LXI H, L
004	⎜310⎟	(location of two LSD's of S)
005	⎝003⎠	
006	067	STC (Set carry to 1)
007	⎛016⎞	MVI, C
010	⎝010⎠	Loops 8 times (8 locations, 16 digits)
011	⎛076⎞	MVI, A
012	⎝231⎠	99 decimal (BCD) placed in A.
013	⎛316⎞	ACI
014	⎝000⎠	add carry and 000 to ⟨A⟩ and store in A.
015	226	Sub M. ⟨A⟩ − M = ⟨A⟩ − S and store in A.
		(M pointed to by H, L.)
016	353	XCHG. D, E ↔ H, L
017	206	ADD M. ⟨A⟩ + ⟨M⟩ = ⟨A⟩ + m and store in A.
		(M pointed to by D, E.)
020	047	DAA
021	167	Mov M, A: Store ⟨A⟩ in M pointed to by D, E
022	353	XCHG. D, E ↔ H, L

*Based on the Assembly Language version suggested on p. 15 of Intel Microcomputer System Manual, Jan. 1975. See also Ref. 28 pp. 252, 53, 54, and Chap. 9, pp. 326–332.

023	023	INX D, E
024	043	INX H, L
025	015	DCR C by 1
026	302	
027	011	JNZ to 011
030	003	
031	166	HALT.

As a start take the following 8 digit example.

$$R = m - S = 45{,}319{,}617 - 31{,}403{,}128 = 13{,}916{,}489.$$

Store as follows:

Location	m(BCD)	m(Octal)	Location	S (BCD)	S (Octal)
300	17	027	310	28	050
301	96	226	311	31	061
302	31	061	312	40	100
303	45	105	313	31	061
304	00	000	314	00	000
305	00	000	315	00	000
306	00	000	316	00	000
307	00	000	317	00	000

Run the program and examine locations 300 on up. You will find

```
300 : 89 (BCD)   ↑
301 : 64
302 : 91              13,916,489.
303 : 13
304 : 00         |
      .    .
      .    .
      .    .
```

Try with other *m* and S digits up to 16 digits maximum. Extend the program to more than 16 BCD digits. If you subtract e.g., 25−35 you will read in locations 300, 301, etc. the BCD number 90 which is valid if there were more digits to come. If there weren't more digits what would you have to do in the program to read out −10?

Experiment 3-9   A Binary Multiplication Program* (16 Bits × 8 Bits) With Examples.

A study of this program reveals all the subtleties and intricacies of binary multiplication. It is, in essence, based on the way multiplication is usually carried out in a computer.

$$
\begin{array}{r}
1011 \\
1101 \\
\hline
0000 \ \text{(initializes partial products)} \\
1011 \\
1011 \\
1011 \\
\hline
10001111
\end{array}
$$

We see shifts left of each partial product *relative* to the partial product below, and then, of course, partial additions of the partial products with further shifts left, etc. If the multiplier bit is 0 there is another shift left before partial addition.

The program also illustrates the use of still further powerful 8080 instructions such as DAD,H = 051 and DAD,D = 031 as explained below.

In this program, the accumulator A contains the 8-bit multiplier (MR), and register pair D,E contains the 16-bit multiplicand (MD). Register pair H,L contains the partial products. The final 24-bit answer will appear as the final (A), (H), and (L) in that order at Ports 1, 0, and 2, respectively.

Careful study should be made of the instruction explanations below, which are more detailed than usual so as to help in understanding the mechanics of the multiplication process. Further, it is

---

*This program, with added features, is based on the Assembly Language version suggested on p. 15 of the Intel Microcomputer System Manual, Jan. 1975. See also Ref. 28, pp. 204−208, and Chap. 9; pp. 332−335. Also Ref. 36, pp. 344−350.

suggested you take the above numerical example and, on paper, apply the program below to it step-by-step, seeing what each instruction does to the numbers and how the answer is finally arrived at by build-up of the appropriate numbers in registers A, H, L, D, and E. The program follows.

000	$\begin{pmatrix} 076 \\ MR \end{pmatrix}$	MVI, A
001		= Multiplier byte into A ≡ MR (8 bits)
002	$\begin{pmatrix} 021 \\ E \\ D \end{pmatrix}$	LXI, D
003		D,E = Multiplicand ≡ MD (16 bits)
004		
005	$\begin{pmatrix} 041 \\ 000 \\ 000 \end{pmatrix}$	LXI, H
006		Initializes partial products to 0 in L and H.
007		HL will hold partial products.
010	$\begin{pmatrix} 006 \\ 010 \end{pmatrix}$	MVI, B
011		= (8) dec. for B control loop (number of multiplier bits).
012	051	= DAD, H (add HL) to (HL) and store in HL. This has the effect of doubling (HL); i.e., shifting the partial product one bit left and into the carry flag as overflow.)
013	027	= RAL (Rotate (A) 1 bit thru carry).
014	$\begin{pmatrix} 322 \\ 022 \\ 003 \end{pmatrix}$	
015		JNC. If there is a carry go to 017, otherwise to 022 (i.e., test whether multiplier bit is a 1 or 0).
016		
017	031	DAD,D: add (DE) to (HL) and store in HL; i.e., add multiplicand (D,E) to partial product *if* carry=1 and store the new partial product in HL. The carry flag is affected by what happens in H,L after the addition. It is set if there is a carry out of the double precision add.
020	$\begin{pmatrix} 316 \\ 000 \end{pmatrix}$	= ACI: Add carry from DAD,D operation and the immediate byte to (A) and store in A.
021		
022	005	DCR, B (decrement B by 1)
023	$\begin{pmatrix} 302 \\ 012 \\ 003 \end{pmatrix}$	
024		JNZ
025		
026	$\begin{pmatrix} 323 \\ 001 \end{pmatrix}$	MS byte of answer (in A) goes to Port 1.
027		

030	174	Mov A͡,H
031	⎛ 323	Middle significant byte of answer goes to Port 0
032	⎝ 000 ⎠	
033	175	Mov A͡,L
034	⎛ 323	LS byte of answer goes to Port 2
035	⎝ 002 ⎠	
036	166	Halt

Try the following examples, multiplying them out on paper first and comparing with the results at Ports 1, 0, and 2•when the program is run.

(1)   10110110 (MD) = 000, 266 in D, E.
     X 10100001 (MR) = 241 in A

(2) 1000000000000000 (MD) = 200, 000 in D, E.
     X   10000001 (MR) = 201 in A

(3) 1000000100100101 (MD) = 201, 045 in D, E.
     X   10000101 (MR) = 205 in A

(4)   00001011 (MD) = 000, 013 in D, E.
     X 00001101 (MR) = 015 in A

Experiment 3-10 An 8 Bit Binary to Two Digit BCD Conversion Routine.*

Place any binary byte whose decimal value is less than $(100)_{10}$ in the accumulator at location 015, 016 (start of a *subroutine*) and observe port 1. Thus 01011101 = $(135)_8$ = $(93)_{10}$ placed at 016 will produce BCD = (1001) (0011) = $(93)_{10}$ at port 1. Try other entries.

Binary Entry:	015	⎛ 076 ⎞	
	016	⎝ A ⎠	binary byte in accumulator
	017	305	Push B

*Courtesy E & L Instruments Inc. and Mr. Dan Lasley, Memphis State University, Memphis, Tenn.

	020	$\begin{pmatrix} 016 \\ 000 \end{pmatrix}$	Clear Reg. C
	021		
$\langle A \rangle \geqslant (10)_{10}$?	022	$\begin{pmatrix} 376 \\ 012 \end{pmatrix}$	CMP I
	023		$\langle A \rangle - (10)_{10}$
			$\langle A \rangle$ unchanged
	024	$\begin{pmatrix} 332 \\ 035 \\ 003 \end{pmatrix}$	JC to
	025		"Save Remainder"
	026		if $\langle A \rangle < (10)_{10}$
	027	003	INX B, C (C will hold quotient)
	030	$\begin{pmatrix} 326 \\ 012 \end{pmatrix}$	SUI, B_2: $\langle A \rangle - (10)_{10}$
	031		and store in A
	032	$\begin{pmatrix} 303 \\ 022 \\ 003 \end{pmatrix}$	JMP to check
	033		
	034		if $\langle A \rangle \geqslant (10)_{10}$
Save Remainder:	035	107	Mov B, A (saves remainder)
	036	171	Mov A, C (number of subtractions before $\langle A \rangle \leqslant 10$)
	037	207	ADD A, store in A.
	040	207	Multiply by 16 to
	041	207	Shift Quotient Left,
	042	207	then add remainder to get BCD.
BCD value:	043	200	ADD B to A, store in A.
	044	301	POP B
Output BCD:	045	$\begin{pmatrix} 323 \\ 001 \end{pmatrix}$	$\langle BCD \rangle \rightarrow$ Port 1
	046		
	047	166	Halt.

Experiment 3-11: Copying a PROM or ROM Into RAM— A Memory Block Transfer Program.

There are times when writing the program that resides in a PROM into a read-write memory (RAM) is necessary. One such example relates to *editing* in which just a few instructions in the PROM may need to be changed. To do so *directly* on the PROM would require erasing the *whole* PROM, since one cannot erase just a few words with ultra violet light. In that case, the desired new program, *all* of it, would have to be written into RAM and this program then used to "cut" the PROM. It would be more convenient to *transfer* the PROM program into RAM, edit the instructions at the few desired places in the RAM, and then transfer the edited RAM directly into the original, erased PROM or into a new PROM, saving the original. In this indirect method the need to key the whole desired program into RAM before transferring to PROM would be obviated. Aside from editing the need for copying a PROM into RAM for any of various purposes can arise from time to time.

The memory block transfer program to accomplish this was presented in Experiment 3-2(e), part iii. It is general and will transfer a program residing in *any* memory block (ROM or RAM) with high *source* address octal $S_1 S_2 S_3$ to any other (RAM) memory block with high *destination* address octal $D_1 D_2 D_3$. We repeat the program here and then apply it to transferring the MMD-1 PROM KEX program at $S_1 S_2 S_3 = 000$ Hi into the RAM at $D_1 D_2 D_3 = 003$ Hi. We write the transfer program itself in RAM 003H starting at address 300L, thus leaving 000 to 277 in RAM 003H free to store part of the KEX (or any other memory's) program. In that case block size $D = (300)_8$ locations. If we had another RAM at 002H we could have the transfer program residing in 003H transfer the entire 256 PROM program in block 000H into the 256 word RAM at 002H. In that case $S_1 S_2 S_3 = 000$ and $D_1 D_2 D_3 = 002$ with block size $D = 000$ (to conform with 256 decrements needed to transfer 256 locations). The transfer program itself could, clearly, be written in any RAM other than 003H if such a RAM (hi address $X_1 X_2 X_3$) were available. The memory transfer program follows:

Hi $X_1 X_2 X_3$, 300	$\begin{pmatrix} 026 \\ D \end{pmatrix}$	MVI, D	
301		$D = $ Block size: number of locations in source program to be moved to destination RAM. ($D = 000$ for 256 locations.)	
302	$\begin{pmatrix} 041 \\ B_2 \\ B_3 \end{pmatrix}$	LXI H,L	
303			
304		*Source address:* $B_3 = S_1 S_2 S_3$ Hi address $B_2 =$ Starting Lo address in source.	
305	$\begin{pmatrix} 001 \\ B_2' \\ B_3' \end{pmatrix}$	LXI B,C	
306			
307		*Destination address:* $B_3' = D_1 D_2 D_3$ Hi address $B_2' =$ starting Lo address in destination	

Next Word:	310	176	Mov $\widehat{A,M}$, M pointed to by B_3, B_2 in H,L registers
	311	002	STAX B, store $\langle A \rangle$ in memory addressed by B_3', B_2' in B,C registers
	312	025	DCR D
	313	302	
	314	317	JNZ
	315	$X_1 X_2 X_3$	
	316	Halt	
Next Address:	317	003	INX B,C
	320	043	INX H,L
	321	303	
	322	310	JMP to "next word."
	323	$X_1 X_2 X_3$	

With $X_1 X_2 X_3 = 003$, $D = 300$, $B_3 = 000$, $B_2 = 000$, $B_3' = 003$ and $B_2' = 000$ run the program and examine the contents of the RAM (003) from 000 to 277. They should match, location for location, with the contents of the KEX PROM from 000 to 277. The transfer program itself, of course, remains intact. If you wish to reproduce just a portion of PROM, such as the 10 msec. time delay residing at 000, 277 through 000, 314, you would take $B_3 = 000$, $B_2 = 277$ with $D = 016$ and B_2' remaining at 000 in RAM; or if you wished to store the limited part of the PROM in a specific area in RAM, you could, for example, choose $B_3' = 003$ and $B_2' = 200$. The portion of KEX from 000, 277 to 314 will then lie in 003 between 200 and 215. Try it and see if this is so. If you write the transfer program at other than 300L, remember to change jump addresses at 314, 322 accordingly.

Experiment 3-12   A Simple 8 Bit by 8 Bit Binary Division Routine.

$$\frac{N}{D} = Q + \frac{R}{D}$$

Ports 1, 0, 2 will exhibit, respectively, the denominator, quotient, and remainder, all in binary form. The following routine is based on successive subtractions of D from N till the remainder is less than D in which case the next subtraction produces a carry which leads to jumping to the routine to output Q and R.

000	$\begin{pmatrix} 026 \\ D \end{pmatrix}$	MVI, D
001		Denominator D
002	172	$\overset{\frown}{A, D}$
003	$\begin{pmatrix} 323 \\ 001 \end{pmatrix}$	D → Port 1
004		
005	$\begin{pmatrix} 076 \\ N \end{pmatrix}$	Numerator N
006		
007	$\begin{pmatrix} 016 \\ 377 \end{pmatrix}$	C keeps track of Q
010		
011	014	INR C (= no. subtractions before neg. remainder results)
012	222	$\langle A \rangle - \langle D \rangle \to A$
013	$\begin{pmatrix} 322 \\ 011 \\ 003 \end{pmatrix}$	JNC
014		
015		
016	202	(neg. remainder. Place R = $\langle A \rangle + \langle D \rangle$ in A).
017	$\begin{pmatrix} 323 \\ 002 \end{pmatrix}$	R → Port 2
020		
021	171	$\overset{\frown}{A, C}$
022	$\begin{pmatrix} 323 \\ 000 \end{pmatrix}$	Q → Port 0
023		
024	166	

Try with $\dfrac{020}{003} = \dfrac{16}{3}, \dfrac{313}{101} = \dfrac{203}{65}, \dfrac{377}{002} = \dfrac{255}{2}, \dfrac{200}{074} = \dfrac{128}{60}, \dfrac{200}{300} = \dfrac{128}{192}$, etc. Study and analyze your results. (Note: See ref. 28 for extensive treatment of arithmetic algorithms).

Experiment 3-13 Simple Example Illustrating Fetching f(x) From Look-up Tables. Call "KBRD" In KEX (See App. C and K).

A study of KEX at 000, 315 shows the presence of routine "KBRD." Briefly this routine goes into a wait loop and through a series of JM and JP instructions (Experiment 3-7(e)) checks whether a key has been pressed and released ($D_7 = 1$ when key is pressed, 0 when released). When it detects that a key has been pressed JM and JP bring the routine out of its wait loop (after a debounce routine at 000, 277) into the part of the routine which stores the KEX code of the key pressed into the accumulator. The routine then returns to the main program to the point just after where the call to "KBRD" was made. In the context of this experiment the key pressed might represent the argument x of a function. We wish to find the value of the function for that x from a "look-up table" stored in memory. We shall illustrate this with a simple program in which, for example, eight values of x (000, 001, . . . 007) can be pressed in from the keyboard to the accumulator (corresponding to the codes of keys "0," "1," . . . "7") and the corresponding functions of x (here taken to be arbitrary values which might represent sin x, cos x, log x, or whatever) are stored in memory locations 200, 201, . . . 207. They are then retrieved for display at port 0 for any given x key pressed. Run the program, press keys "0" . . . "7" and see the "function" displayed at port 000. (Study "KBRD" in KEX, Appendix C. See also the encoder in Fig. 12).

000	⎛ 315 ⎞	Call "KBRD." Stores KEX code x
001	⎜ 315 ⎟	of key pressed into A.
002	⎝ 000 ⎠	
003	⎛ 306 ⎞	
004	⎝ 200 ⎠	Add 200 to x, store in A.
005	157	Mov L, A. Stores location of f(x) in A.
006	⎛ 046 ⎞	
007	⎝ 003 ⎠	MVI, H
010	176	Mov A, M. Fetches function at location pointed to by H, L, i.e., corresponding to x.
011	⎛ 323 ⎞	
012	⎝ 000 ⎠	
013	⎛ 303 ⎞	
014	⎜ 000 ⎟	
015	⎝ 003 ⎠	

x		f(x)	
000	200	377	
001	201	277	
002	202	177	"By using "call KBRD" together with STA
003	203	000	(062) you can implement keyboard control over
004	204	111	a device (e.g. a one-shot multivibrator or a
005	205	222	demultiplexer) while the program is running.
006	206	333	Devise several such experiments. See App. F of
007	207	077	"Applications" book by Boyet and Katz and also App. K here)".

Chapter 4

Single Stepping and Its Importance—Experiments

4-1 INTRODUCTION: THEORY AND INTERFACING-IMPLEMENTATION. ANALYSIS OF "MACHINE CYCLES."

When a program is run, the final results, be they numerical or control logic bits, are accomplished and evident within microseconds. Thus, a 50 instruction program at, say, 7 clocks per instruction, for a 2MHz clock, takes 175 μs (or 455 μs for the MMD-1). There is no way of checking what the program is doing at *each* of its steps, where a mistake in the program is occurring, if any, whether our flow chart chosen is the one that does the job, and if not, where it breaks down, where the interfacing to an I/O('s) might be faulty, and whether allowance has been made for factors and parameters in the problem that we may not have thought about. No enlightenment is shed on what is really happening inside the microcomputer with respect to addressing, address byte flow on the address bus, instruction or data flow on the data bus, execution of instructions, register transfers, the influence of status bits (Chap. 5), stack operations, the existence of the "extra bytes," where and how in the program I/O's are interacted with, and so on.

"Single stepping" is the technique to provide answers to all the above questions. It slows down the program execution to any time frame *we* choose by forcing the CPU to "wait" before each fetch and execution. We can then see at a glance the fetch and execution (machine cycles*) of every single instruction located in every single memory address of the program. Each address-fetched data byte pair belonging to an instruction (it might be multiple-byte) is played back to us. So are any "extra" address-data byte pairs if they are involved in the execution of the instruction. Data flow to or from an I/O (input, output instructions) or data flow to or from memory (the Stack as in Call, Push, and Pop instructions) are examples of these *"extra bytes"* necessary for complete instruction execution. We will see them in the experiments. The program is run in "slow" motion so that 175 μs becomes seconds, minutes, or however long we wish. Single step slows down the "heartbeat" of the system (i.e., the time *between* machine cycles) so that the effect of each machine cycle associated with an instruction on the flow of data (be it the fetch cycle, or the output of data from the accumulator to a port, or from a port into the accumulator, or the flow from CPU to or from memory, or indirectly the transfer of data between registers) can be seen and studied during the program run. Insight is shed on the internal memory $\leftrightarrow$ CPU $\leftrightarrow$ I/O interactions and relationships. *It is a powerful method for debugging a program and the interfacing.*

The purpose of this chapter is to explain the basis for single stepping, show it can be implemented, have a single stepping circuit wired up for future use in the interfacing experiments in Chap. 5, and present experiments of various kinds which will show its power. This will not only pinpoint programming details, but also reveal what is going on inside the microcomputer's data and address busses during a particular instruction's machine cycle(s)— notably with respect to instructions of the type $\left(\begin{smallmatrix} \text{out} \\ B_2 \end{smallmatrix}\right) = \left(\begin{smallmatrix} 323 \\ B_2 \end{smallmatrix}\right)$, $\left(\begin{smallmatrix} \text{IN} \\ B_2 \end{smallmatrix}\right) = \left(\begin{smallmatrix} 333 \\ B_2 \end{smallmatrix}\right)$, Call, Ret, Push, Pop, RSTN, STA, SHLD, Mov $\widehat{\text{M, r}}$ XTHL, etc. in which *"extra bytes"* appear on the address and data buses. It is recommended that after this chapter is concluded you single step through some of the more intricate programs of Chap. 3 [for example, the "display" experiments—Experiments 3-4(a), (b), (c), and (d)], to gain understanding and mastery of the tech-

---

*Chap. 2, Section 2.2

nique as it relates to programs employing a wide range of instructions. See also Experiment 3-6(d).

We present first a circuit for single stepping and then discuss what it does and how (see Refs. below** for other possible circuits).

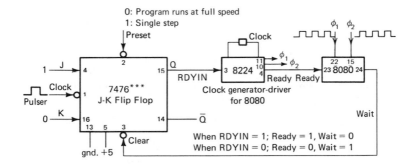

Figure 34. A logic interfacing circuit for single stepping. Note: In normal full speed operation where single stepping is not needed, chip 7476 is not present and RDYIN is kept high, so that Ready = 1, Wait = 0. See Fig. 11 and Fig. 35.

It should be noted that these connections to and from the 7476 JK flip flop are readily available on the MMD-1 at its SK-10 Bus socket (see "Ready" and "Wait" to the left on the SK-10 board). In any other 8080 based system "Ready" must be taken as pin 3 (input) of the 8224 (or equivalent) clock generator/driver (i.e., "RDY IN"), and "Wait" is pin 24 (output) of the 8080 chip. Before explaining the circuit, recall that the 7476 truth table (Ref. 10) is

	Preset	Clear	Clock	J	K	Q	$\overline{Q}$	
→	0	1	X	X	X	1	0	←
→	1	0	X	X	X	0	1	←
	1	1	⊓	0	0	Q_0	$\overline{Q}_0$	Latch
→	1	1	⊓	1	0	1	0	←
	1	1	⊓	0	1	0	1	
	1	1	⊓	1	1	$\overline{Q}$	Q	Toggle

**Ref. 20, pp. 11–42, and Ref. 25, p. 132.
***Single stepping is possible using the 7474, 7476 or any flip flop that has Preset, Clear, and Clock inputs.

The pertinent entries for single stepping are as indicated (arrows). We shall come back to this shortly.

The following material is reproduced, courtesy Intel Corp, from their Microcomputer Systems User's Manual, Sept. 1975 (pp. 2–4, 2–5, 2–8, 2–10) and should prove most helpful in understanding address and data bus flow during the various states of a machine cycle as it pertains to the explanation of single stepping with the circuit of Fig. 34. This explanation follows directly after the reproduced material.

Machine Cycle Identification:

With the exception of the DAD instruction, there is just one consideration that determines how many machine cycles are required in any given instruction cycle: the number of times that the processor must reference a memory address or an addressable peripheral device, in order to fetch and execute the instruction. Like many processors, the 8080 is so constructed that it can transmit only one address per machine cycle. Thus, if the fetch and execution of an instruction requires two memory references, then the instruction cycle associated with that instruction consists of two machine cycles. If five such references are called for, then the instruction cycle contains five machine cycles.

Every instruction cycle has at least one reference to memory, during which the instruction is fetched. An instruction cycle must always have a fetch, even if the execution of the instruction requires no further references to memory. The first machine cycle in every instruction cycle is therefore a FETCH. Beyond that, there are no fast rules. It depends on the kind of instruction that is fetched.

Consider some examples. The add-register (ADD r) instruction is an instruction that requires only a single machine cycle (FETCH) for its completion. In this one-byte instruction, the contents of one of the CPU's six general purpose registers is added to the existing contents of the accumulator. Since all the information necessary to execute the command is contained in the eight bits of the instruction code, only one memory reference is necessary. Three states are used to extract the instruction from memory, and one additional state is used to accomplish the desired addition. The entire instruction cycle thus requires only one machine cycle that consists of four states, or four periods of the external clock.

Suppose now, however, that we wish to add the contents of a specific memory location to the existing contents of the accumulator (ADD M). Although this is quite similar in principle to the example just cited, several additional steps will be used. An extra machine cycle will be used, in order to address the desired memory location.

The actual sequence is as follows. First the processor extracts from memory the one-byte instruction word addressed by its program counter. This takes three states. The eight-bit instruction word obtained during the FETCH machine cycle is deposited in the CPU's instruction register and used to direct activities during the remainder of the instruction cycle. Next, the processor sends out, as an address, the contents of its H and L registers. The eight-bit data word returned during this MEMORY READ machine cycle is placed in a temporary register inside the 8080 CPU. By now three more clock periods (states) have elapsed. In the seventh and final state, the contents of the temporary regis-

ter are added to those of the accumulator. Two machine cycles, consisting of seven states in all, complete the "ADD M" instruction cycle.

At the opposite extreme is the save H and L registers (SHLD) instruction, which requires five machine cycles. During an "SHLD" instruction cycle, the contents of the processor's H and L registers are deposited in two sequentially adjacent memory locations; the destination is indicated by two address bytes which are stored in the two memory locations immediately following the operation code byte. The following sequence of events occurs:

(1) A FETCH machine cycle, consisting of four states. During the first three states of this machine cycle, the processor fetches the instruction indicated by its program counter. The program counter is then incremented. The fourth state is used for internal instruction decoding.

(2) A MEMORY READ machine cycle, consisting of three states. During this machine cycle, the byte indicated by the program counter is read from memory and placed in the processor's Z register. The program counter is incremented again.

(3) Another MEMORY READ machine cycle, consisting of three states, in which the byte indicated by the processor's program counter is read from memory and placed in the W register. The program counter is incremented, in anticipation of the next instruction fetch.

(4) A MEMORY WRITE machine cycle, of three states, in which the contents of the L register are transferred to the memory location pointed to by the present contents of the W and Z registers. The state following the transfer is used to increment the W,Z register pair so that it indicates the next memory location to receive data.

(5) A MEMORY WRITE machine cycle, of three states, in which the contents of the H register are transferred to the new memory location pointed to by the W,Z register pair.

In summary, the "SHLD" instruction cycle contains five machine cycles and takes 16 states to execute.

Most instructions fall somewhere between the extremes typified by the "ADD r" and the "SHLD" instructions. The input (INP) and the output (OUT) instructions, for example, require three machine cycles: a FETCH, to obtain the instruction; a MEMORY READ, to obtain the address of the object peripheral; and an INPUT or an OUTPUT machine cycle, to complete the transfer.

While no one instruction cycle will consist of more then five machine cycles, the following ten different types of machine cycles may occur within an instruction cycle:

(1) FETCH (M1)

(2) MEMORY READ

(3) MEMORY WRITE

(4) STACK READ

(5) STACK WRITE

(6) INPUT

(7) OUTPUT

(8) INTERRUPT

(9) HALT

(10) HALT • INTERRUPT

The machine cycles that actually do occur in a particular instruction cycle depend upon the kind of instruction, with the overriding stipulation that the first machine cycle in any instruction cycle is always a FETCH.

The processor identifies the machine cycle in progress by transmitting an eight-bit status word during the first state of every machine cycle. Updated status information is presented on the 8080's data lines (D_0-D_7), during the SYNC interval. This data should be saved in latches, and used to develop control signals for external circuitry. Table 2-1 shows how the positive-true status information is distributed on the processor's data bus.

Status signals are provided principally for the control of external circuitry. Simplicity of interface, rather than machine cycle identification, dictates the logical definition of individual status bits. You will therefore observe that certain processor machine cycles are uniquely identified by a single status bit, but that others are not. The M_1 status bit (D_6), for example, unambiguously identifies a FETCH machine cycle. A STACK READ, on the other hand, is indicated by the coincidence of STACK and MEMR signals. Machine cycle identification data is also valuable in the test and de-bugging phases of system development. Table 2-1 lists the status bit outputs for each type of machine cycle.

State Transition Sequence:

Every machine cycle within an instruction cycle consists of three to five active states (referred to as T_1, T_2, T_3, T_4, T_5 or T_W). The actual number of states depends upon the instruction being executed, and on the particular machine cycle within the greater instruction cycle. The state transition diagram in Figure 2-4 shows how the 8080 proceeds from state to state in the course of a machine cycle. The diagram also shows how the READY, HOLD, and INTERRUPT lines are sampled during the machine cycle, and how the conditions on these lines may modify the

basic transition sequence. In the present discussion, we are concerned only with the basic sequence and with the READY function. The HOLD and INTERRUPT functions will be discussed later.

The 8080 CPU does not directly indicate its internal state by transmitting a "state control" output during each state; instead, the 8080 supplies direct control output (INTE, HLDA, DBIN, $\overline{WR}$ and WAIT) for use by external circuitry.

Recall that the 8080 passes through at least three states in every machine cycle, with each state defined by successive low-to-high transitions of the ϕ_1 clock. Figure 2-5 shows the timing relationships in a typical FETCH machine cycle. Events that occur in each state are referenced to transitions of the ϕ_1 and ϕ_2 clock pulses.

The SYNC signal identifies the first state (T_1) in every machine cycle. As shown in Figure 2-5, the SYNC signal is related to the leading edge of the ϕ_2 clock. There is a delay (t_{DC}) between the low-to-high transition of ϕ_2 and the positive-going edge of the SYNC pulse. There also is a corresponding delay (also t_{DC}) between the next ϕ_2 pulse and the falling edge of the SYNC signal. Status information is displayed on D_0-D_7 during the same ϕ_2 to ϕ_2 interval. Switching of the status signals is likewise controlled by ϕ_2.

The rising edge of ϕ_2 during T_1 also loads the processor's address lines (A_0-A_{15}). These lines become stable within a brief delay (t_{DA}) of the ϕ_2 clocking pulse, and they remain stable until the first ϕ_2 pulse after state T_3. This gives the processor ample time to read the data returned from memory.

Once the processor has sent an address to memory, there is an opportunity for the memory to request a WAIT. This it does by pulling the processor's READY line low, prior to the "Ready set-up" interval (t_{RS}) which occurs during the ϕ_2 pulse within state T_2 or T_W. As long as the READY line remains low, the processor will idle, giving the memory time to respond to the addressed data request. Refer to Figure 2-5.

The processor responds to a wait request by entering an alternative state (T_W) at the end of T_2, rather than proceeding directly to the T_3 state. Entry into the T_W state is indicated by a WAIT signal from the processor, acknowledging the memory's request. A low-to-high transition on the WAIT line is triggered by the rising edge of the ϕ_1 clock and occurs within a brief delay (t_{DC}) of the actual entry into the T_W state.

A wait period may be of indefinite duration. The processor remains in the waiting condition until its READY line again goes high. A READY indication **must** precede the falling edge of the ϕ_2 clock by a specified interval (t_{RS}), in order to guarantee an exit from the T_W state. The cycle may then proceed, beginning with the rising edge of the next ϕ_1 clock. A WAIT interval will therefore consist of an integral number of T_W states and will always be a multiple of the clock period.

The events that take place during the T_3 state are determined by the kind of machine cycle in progress. In a FETCH machine cycle, the processor interprets the data on its data bus as an instruction. During a MEMORY READ or a STACK READ, data on this bus is interpreted as a data word. The processor outputs data on this bus during a MEMORY WRITE machine cycle. During I/O operations, the processor may either transmit or receive data, depending on whether an OUTPUT or an INPUT operation is involved.

Figure 2-6 illustrates the timing that is characteristic of a data input operation. As shown, the low-to-high transition of ϕ_2 during T_2 clears status information from the processor's data lines, preparing these lines for the receipt of incoming data. The data presented to the processor must have stabilized prior to both the "ϕ_1—data set-up" interval (t_{DS1}), that precedes the falling edge of the ϕ_1 pulse defining state T_3, and the "ϕ_2—data set-up" interval (t_{DS2}), that precedes the rising edge of ϕ_2 in state T_3. This same

data must remain stable during the "data hold" interval (t_{DH}) that occurs following the rising edge of the ϕ_2 pulse. Data placed on these lines by memory or by other external devices will be sampled during T_3.

During the input of data to the processor, the 8080 generates a DBIN signal which should be used externally to enable the transfer. Machine cycles in which DBIN is available include: FETCH, MEMORY READ, STACK READ, and INTERRUPT. DBIN is initiated by the rising edge of ϕ_2 during state T2 and terminated by the corresponding edge of ϕ_2 during T3. Any T_W phases intervening between T_2 and T_3 will therefore extend DBIN by one or more clock periods.

Figure 2-7 shows the timing of a machine cycle in which the processor outputs data. Output data may be destined either for memory or for peripherals. The rising edge of ϕ_2 within state T_2 clears status information from the CPU's data lines, and loads in the data which is to be output to external devices. This substitution takes place within the

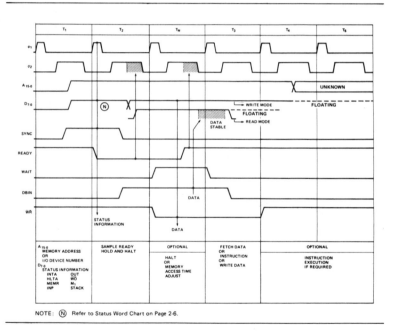

NOTE: (N) Refer to Status Word Chart on Page 2-6.

Figure 35. 8080 machine cycle, $T_i \equiv$ "state." An instruction may have several machine cycles.

"data output delay" interval (t_{DD}) following the ϕ_2 clock's leading edge. Data on the bus remains stable throughout the remainder of the machine cycle, until replaced by updated status information in the subsequent T_1 state. Observe that a READY signal is necessary for completion of an OUTPUT machine cycle. Unless such an indication is present, the processor enters the T_W state, following the T_2 state. Data on the output lines remains stable in the interim, and the processing cycle will not proceed until the READY line again goes high.

The 8080 CPU generates a $\overline{WR}$ output for the synchronization of external transfers, during those machine cycles in which the processor outputs data. These include MEMORY WRITE, STACK WRITE, and OUTPUT. The negative-going leading edge of $\overline{WR}$ is referenced to the rising edge of the first ϕ_1 clock pulse following T_2, and occurs within a brief delay (t_{DC}) of that event. $\overline{WR}$ remains low until re-triggered by the leading edge of ϕ_1 during the state following T_3. Note that any T_W states intervening between T_2 and T_3 of the output machine cycle will necessarily extend $\overline{WR}$, in much the same way that DBIN is affected during data input operations.

All processor machine cycles consist of at least three states: T_1, T_2, and T_3 as just described. If the processor has to wait for a response from the peripheral or memory with which it is communicating, then the machine cycle may also contain one or more T_W states. During the three basic states, data is transferred to or from the processor.

After the T_3 state, however, it becomes difficult to generalize. T_4 and T_5 states are available, if the execution of a particular instruction requires them. But not all machine cycles make use of these states. It depends upon the kind of instruction being executed, and on the particular machine cycle within the instruction cycle. The processor will terminate any machine cycle as soon as its processing activities are completed, rather than proceeding through the T_4 and T_5 states every time. Thus the 8080 may exit a machine cycle following the T_3, the T_4, or the T_5 state and proceed directly to the T_1 state of the next machine cycle.

STATE	ASSOCIATED ACTIVITIES
T_1	A memory address or I/O device number is placed on the Address Bus (A_{15-0}); status information is placed on Data Bus (D_{7-0}).
T_2	The CPU samples the READY and HOLD inputs and checks for halt instruction.
TW (optional)	Processor enters wait state if READY is low or if HALT instruction has been executed.
T3	An instruction byte (FETCH machine cycle), data byte (MEMORY READ, STACK READ) or interrupt instruction (INTERRUPT machine cycle) is input to the CPU from the Data Bus; or a data byte (MEMORY WRITE, STACK WRITE or OUTPUT machine cycle) is output onto the data bus.
T4 T5 (optional)	States T_4 and T_5 are available if the execution of a particular instruction requires them; if not, the CPU may skip one or both of them. T_4 and T_5 are only used for internal processor operations.

To quote the Intel Manual*: "*During T_1 (PC) is sent to the address bus*, SYNC is true, and the data bus contains the *status information*** (status bits) pertaining to the cycle (instruction) that is currently being initiated. T_1 *is always followed by another state T_2, during which the condition of the Ready, Hold, and Halt acknowledge signals are tested. If Ready is true, T_3 can be entered: otherwise the CPU will go into the wait state (T_w) and stay there for as long as Ready is false.* . . . *During T_3 the data coming from memory is available on the data bus and is transferred into the Instruction Register* . . . the Instruction Decoder and control sec-

* Courtesy Intel Corp. (Jan. 1975, p. 3)

**See Chap. 5, Sec. 5-2(G) and Experiment 5-2(l). Also Chaps. 2 and 3, Intel User's Manual, Sept. 1975.

tions then generate the basic signals to control the internal data
transfers, the timing, and the machine cycle requirements of the
new instructions" (emphasis is author's). The above is at the heart
of the fetch and execute portions of the machine cycle. (See also
Chap. 2.) Note particularly the table correlating "associated activities" with "state," and Fig. 35. They are crucial in understanding
machine cycles and their relation to execution of an instruction
as well as in the understanding of single stepping which follows.

Referring to Figs. 34, 35 and the 7476 truth table, suppose the
program is running at full speed (Preset = 0, Q = Ready = 1, Wait
= 0). Even though Preset and Clear are both 0, Q remains at 1
since Preset = 0 occurred first—the program continues to run. If
now Preset is made 1, Clear = 0 wins and Q → 0. Then Ready = 0
and we are in the Wait state, T_w (Fig. 35) and stay there *indefinitely*. No instructions are fetched from memory or executed.
*Shortly after Ready went to 0, Wait went to 1 and stays at 1
indefinitely*. So now Preset = Clear = 1 with Q = 0 on the 7476.
Whenever we decide to pulse the 7476 clock Q will go to 1 (since
J = 1, K = 0—see truth table). When we do so, we come out of
the Wait state because now Ready = Q = 1 causing T_3 (Fig. 35)
to be entered. The clock pulses ϕ_1, ϕ_2 now take us through T_3
(and T_4, T_5 if necessary). *Thus the machine cycle gets completed.*
But by now Wait has become 0 (Fig. 35) and this clears the output Q of the 7476 back to 0. (During all this time Preset remains
at 1.) Hence we are back to another indefinite wait state until we
pulse the 7476 clock for a run through the next machine cycle.
Memory or I/O address data appears on the address bus during T_1
and a data (fetched) byte from memory appears on the data bus
during T_3 of the machine cycle. It is these bytes we wish to latch
and display. It is *most important* to understand that there will be
at least N number of machine cycles where N is the number of
bytes comprising the particular instruction. For *each* of those
machine cycles the relevant byte belonging to the instruction is
fetched from its address in memory and flows to the CPU via the
data bus to play its part in the ultimate execution of the instruction under control section direction. There may well be more
machine cycles necessary to execute the instruction than there are
bytes in the instruction. The address and data byte flow during
those extra machine cycles are referred to as "extra bytes." An
example is the Call instruction $\begin{pmatrix} 315 \\ B_2 \\ B_3 \end{pmatrix}$. Its *fourth* machine cycle is

needed to place ⟨PCH⟩–upper part of the return address–on to the stack in memory, and its *fifth* machine cycle is also needed to place ⟨PCL⟩–lower part of the return address–on to the stack. The extra machine cycles involve the addresses SP–1 and SP–2 appearing on the address bus together with ⟨PCH⟩ and ⟨PCL⟩ appearing on the data bus during the fourth and fifth machine

cycles, respectively. A three byte instruction such as $\begin{pmatrix} \text{LXI H,L} \\ B_2 \\ B_3 \end{pmatrix}$

will *not* involve extra bytes–three fetch machine cycles for the 3 bytes comprising the instruction are all that are necessary. But any time you have instructions like Call, RET, Push, Pop, Mov r͡, M,

Mov M͡, r, $\begin{pmatrix} 323 \\ B_2 \end{pmatrix}$, $\begin{pmatrix} 333 \\ B_2 \end{pmatrix}$, STA, SHLD, etc., extra bytes above the

number of bytes in the instruction will be needed to read or write from or into the stack, or read or write from or into memory, or read or write from or into an I/O. The data flow on the data bus associated with these read or write operatings during the extra bytes will *also occur during T_3 of those extra machine cycles*, and naturally the pertinent stack, or memory, or I/O addresses will be placed on the address bus *during T_1 of those extra machine cycles*. These extra address and data bytes can also be latched, as we shall see. It is clear that the extra bytes are necessary for certain instructions if they are to be executed successfully. A one byte instruction such as Mov M͡, r will clearly require one extra byte, a three byte instruction such as (STA B_2, B_3) will require one extra byte, a 3 byte instruction such as (SHLD B_2, B_3) will require two extra bytes (see Experiment 4-2(g)), while the one byte instruction Mov A͡, B will not require any extra bytes. Remember that only the *first* fetch takes the data byte (OP. code of the instruction) to the IR/ID for decoding.

The latch arrangement to capture and display address and data bytes associated with a specific machine cycle is taken up below, where address and data bus monitor details are given. Note that you must first run the program at full speed (Preset = 0, Q = 1, Ready = 1, 7476 clock overridden). The reason for this is to make sure the PC and the address bus keep incrementing by one to point to the next address in memory from which a byte belonging to an instruction can be fetched. If we did not first set Preset = 0, press Reset and then G, we would never be able to single step no matter how many pulses we applied to the 7476 clock. In that case we would never reach the PCHL instruction at 175 in KEX and so the

PC would never be loaded with the H, L address of the first instruction nor would read ($\overline{\text{MEMR}}$) control signals be generated for RAM read-out. The program would never get executed. PCHL guarantees the generation of read signals through the status bits it puts out together with the hardware of Fig. 11. Without such $\overline{\text{MEMR}}$ signals the program of machine cycles simply would not get played back from RAM. The procedure, therefore, is to set Preset = 0 (full speed), press Reset, then G. The program runs. Then Preset is made 1 causing Q = Ready = 0 (because during the run Ready was 1 and Wait = Clear was 0). This produces a Wait state with Wait = 1. We are now ready to apply single stepping pulses to execute each machine cycle. Of course we don't know where in the program we will be at the moment we make Preset go from 0 to 1. But that doesn't matter because subsequent pulses on the 7476 clock will take us, step-by-step through the entire program and eventually bring us back to the first address/instruction in the program, unless we find ourselves in time delay loops—which brings up two points. To single step successfully, you can never end a program with a Halt (166) instruction. The reason is simple: The Halt instruction takes the (PC) off the address bus so that we have no way of addressing the next memory location with its instruction. Hence, all the pulses applied to the 7476 making Q = Ready = 1 will be of no avail. You must end your program in a $\begin{pmatrix} 303 \\ 000 \\ 003 \end{pmatrix}$ JMP back to the beginning and loop the program continuously *so that it never stops when run at full speed.* The other point is never to attempt to single step a program with a time delay loop(s) in it—you'll never get out of it. It might take literally thousands of pulses to get out of the loops we have been using in the time delay programs of Chap. 3.

Latching the contents of the address bus (address byte) and those of the data bus (data byte) during a machine cycle for visible read-out is now discussed: (displays other than the HP 5082-7300 4×7 matrix numeric display shown below will work. We like the HP5082-7300 because it has the driver/decoder/latch built in, whereas other displays might require wiring up separate latch/decoder/driver chips). The need for a latch is clear: We want to capture the *last* data (address or data byte) appearing on the address or data bus during the machine cycle. The machine cycle lasts perhaps 5 or 10 clocks* or several μs, and this is too fleeting

*Intel Manual, Sept. 1975, pp. 4–15.

for the address or data bytes coming over the buses to be observed on the display unless they are latched—see IC 7475 in Chap. 1). Consider.

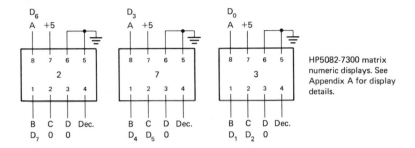

Figure 36. Data bus monitor, Pin 5 is "Enable."

The data (instruction) byte being monitored is $D_7D_6D_5D_4D_3D_2D_1D_0$ in octal form. These bits are taken from the SK-10 socket access to the data bus on the MMD-1 and wired to each matrix display in the fashion indicated above. Pin 6 is always at ground. Pin 7 is kept at +5 volts. Pin 5 is the "Enable." It must be kept at ground to enable the built-in latch. Keeping it high disables the latch.

The above interfacing is readily understood if we keep in mind that DCBA = 8, 4, 2, 1 will give an octal number if D is kept 0 and that D_7D_6, the MS octal digit, is equivalent to $00D_7D_6$ thus requiring *both* D and C to be zero. The above arrangement thus provides an octal read-out of the data byte appearing on the data bus during a machine cycle after the 7476's clock is pulsed. In similar fashion the address monitor is realized.

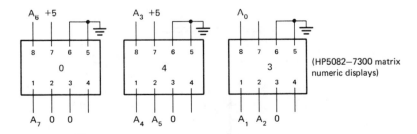

Figure 37. Address bus monitor.

The A_7A_6 . . . A_0 bits are taken from the MMD-1's SK-10 bus socket access to the address bus. The address byte, launched from either a register pair or the (PC) on to the address bus just after the 7476 is pulsed and the program embarks on a machine cycle, is thus latched and made visible for read-out. Or it might be an "extra" address bus byte associated with I/O or Call or Push, etc. instructions.

You can also employ 7-segment displays (Appendix A) as address and data bus monitors for single stepping. However, unlike the HP5082-7300 matrix displays which have built-in latches (to capture and hold the *last* data on the bus before a "wait" period) *and* BCD decoder-drivers to convert DCBA to decimal (or octal if D=0), the 7-segment display needs a 7447 or 7448 BCD to 7-segment decoder-driver chip (Appendix A).

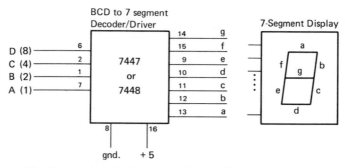

Figure 38. Connections for 7 segment display. Pins numbers for a, b, . . . on display are given by manufacturers.

Note: Pull up resistors are needed depending on the type of 7-segment display used. See, for example, the wiring in Experiment 5-2(k).

The truth table for the 7447 and 7448 is (see Ref. 10)

Dec	D	C	B	A	a	b	c	d	e	f	g
0	0	0	0	0	1	1	1	1	1	1	0
1	0	0	0	1	0	1	1	0	0	0	0
2	0	0	1	0	1	1	0	1	1	0	1
3	0	0	1	1	1	1	1	1	0	0	1
4	0	1	0	0	0	1	1	0	0	1	1
5	0	1	0	1	1	0	1	1	0	1	1
6	0	1	1	0	0	0	1	1	1	1	1
7	0	1	1	1	1	1	1	0	0	0	0
8	1	0	0	0	1	1	1	1	1	1	1
9	1	0	0	1	1	1	1	0	0	1	1
15	1	1	1	1	0	0	0	0	0	0	0

Figure 39. 7447/48 Decoder/driver truth table (BCD to 7 segment).

When using the 7-segment display with the decoder-driver as a monitor for the 8080 data or address busses in single stepping work, no 7475 latch is necessary because the 8080 microprocessor itself has a data bus buffer/latch as well as an address bus latch/ buffer incorporated into it (see Chap. 2, Fig. 10)—and they capture and hold the *last* data flowing on the data and address busses just before the "wait" sets in. Note: E & L Instruments Inc. markets their "Outboard" LR-4 which consists of a decoder-driver (7447) chip mounted with a single 7-segment display with pull-up resistor on board. They also market their "outboard" LR-50 which is a pulser-single step circuit that incorporates the features of the single step circuit shown in Fig. 34; i.e., a 7474 chip, terminals to be connected to "ready" and "wait" on the 8080 chip via the SK-10 socket on the MMD-1, a manual "clock" pulser, and additionally an internal clock (555 timer chip), which can serve as an internal pulser of adjustable rate. (Remember that single stepping can be done with either the 7474 or 7476 or any chip that has a Preset, a Clear, and a clock.) If using the E & L Instruments Inc. LR-4 and LR-50 outboards for single stepping, remember that we want *octal* read-outs of the instruction and address bytes and this necessitates that D & C be kept 0 on the MS digit and D be kept 0 on the other two digits. The LR-4's mount on the SK-10 socket board as shown here.

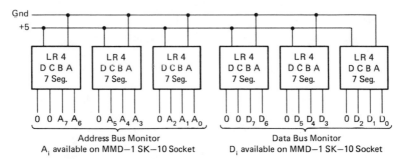

Figure 40. Data and address bus monitors using LR 4 7-segment displays. (E & L Instruments Inc.)

The LR-50 single stepper/pulser also mounts on the SK-10 socket board (see Fig. 41).

And so pulsing away, we see the machine cycle address and data bytes associated with a whole program appear one after the other at the monitors. Further, we can observe many of the program's actions and effects individually; for example, output from the accumulator to a port will be effected only

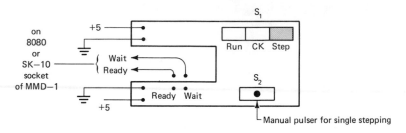

Figure 41. LR 50 single stepping outboard (E & L Instruments, Inc).

after certain points are reached in the single stepping procedure. Consider that after an $\begin{pmatrix} \text{out} \\ B_2 \end{pmatrix} = \begin{pmatrix} 323 \\ B_2 \end{pmatrix}$ instruction, (A) appears at port B_2. Of course, the contents of A depend on the previous instruction; e.g., RAL, or DCR, or INR, or DAA. In this way a slow motion version of, for example, a software controlled sequencer or counter can be observed at every output stage of the software control. Running the program at full speed would not permit us to observe the individual address bytes or the instruction bytes, or the individual effects of each instruction on the I/O device or port (the latter could be observed at full speed only if there were a time delay loop in the program at the right place(s)). The display of individual outputs, or lack of it, as we single step is most helpful in interface debugging. We can pinpoint just where in the program either programming or interfacing went awry.

We will be making much use of single stepping in Chap. 5 on interfacing. It is suggested you keep the single step circuit and displays permanently wired up on the interface socket. It is also suggested that after the experiments on single stepping presented below are performed, observed, and understood, you go back to Chap. 3 and single step through various programs presented there. We also ask you to pay particular attention to the "extra bytes" that will appear as you single step through *particular* instructions in the programs offered. They will be quite revealing as to what's going on inside the microcomputer and should be analyzed in the context of all the previous discussion. *A detailed study of the particular instruction used is essential. For that you are urged to consult pp. 2–16 thru 2–19 and Chap. 4 of Intel Sept. 1975 8080 User's Manual.* (See Appendix I: "The 8080 micro-operation 'Legalisms'").

4-2 EXPERIMENTS

Experiment 4-2(a)   Single Stepping with $\left(\dfrac{323}{B_2}\right)$ Instructions in the Program. What it Reveals.

Consider:

000	$\left(\begin{array}{c}076\\001\end{array}\right.$	MVI, A
001	$\left.001\right)$	
002	007	(or 027) RAL (or RLC)
003	000	(NOP)
004	$\left(\begin{array}{c}323\\001\end{array}\right.$	out Port 1
005	$\left.001\right)$	
006	000	NOP
007	$\left(\begin{array}{c}323\\000\end{array}\right.$	out Port 0
010	$\left.000\right)$	
011	000	NOP
012	$\left(\begin{array}{c}323\\002\end{array}\right.$	out Port 2
013	$\left.002\right)$	
014	000	
015	$\left(\begin{array}{c}303\\002\\003\end{array}\right.$	JMP to 002
016	002	
017	$\left.003\right)$	

In single stepping this program you must remember that the 8080 instruction $\left(\dfrac{323}{B_2}\right)$ means*: *(A) is put on the data bus for transmission to port (device) B_2; B_2 itself is transmitted to the address bus; and $\overline{out} = $ ⊔ is immediately produced.* Single step it and, in the context of what was just said, observe the "extra device address and data bytes" on the address and data bus monitors just after the $\left(\dfrac{323}{001}\right)$, $\left(\dfrac{323}{000}\right)$, and $\left(\dfrac{323}{002}\right)$ instructions are passed in

---

*Intel Manual, Sept. 1975, pp. 4−14, 2−6, 5−14, 2−18. $\overline{Out} = $ ⊔ is the output control signal available on the SK-10 socket or from an 8228 type system controller (see Chap. 5, Sec. 5-2(G) and Appendix A).

the program. Notice also how the bits at each output port are affected in turn *after* the RAL (or RLC) instruction is passed as we single step through and return to make another pass through the program. If you run this program at full speed, you will see 377 at each port (the rotations are occurring so fast that each LED is effectively lit all the time). Only single stepping reveals the individual actions produced by the individual RAL instructions at each port. We have slowed down the program run to any time scale we wish. The relevancy to program and interface debugging should be clear.

Note also that if you disconnect each display "Enable" from ground and take $\overline{out}$ = ⊔ from the SK-10 socket and wire it to pin 5 (enable) on each of the six HP matrix displays, and then single step the program, the monitors will be *disabled* until $\overline{out}$ = ⊔ *is produced just after each* $\left(\dfrac{323}{B_2} \right)$ *instruction is passed,* which *then enables each display. At that same time* B_2 *(=device number for the output port) is on the address bus, (A) is on the data bus and* $\overline{out}$ = ⊔ *enables the display to latch* B_2 *on to the address bus monitor* and $\langle A \rangle$ *on to the data bus monitor. Hence, you should see something like the following* sequence of address and data bus monitor readings as you single step. (Your observations will be different from those presented here depending on *where* you pulled out of the full-speed run after setting Preset to 1 from its previous value of 0.)

Address Monitor	*Data Monitor*
002	010
001	020
000	020
002	020
001	040
000	040
002	040
001	100
000	100
002	100
001	200
.	.
.	.
.	.

It is confirmed that the port (device) number B_2 appears on the address bus, (A) on the data bus, and that $\overline{out} = \sqcup$ was generated—all just after $a\begin{pmatrix} 323 \\ B_2 \end{pmatrix}$ instruction. Observe the three ports carefully as you single step. You have latched I/O port numbers and the data going to them. (This is *not* single stepping.)

While you are at it, with display enables on both address and data bus monitors tied to $\overline{out}$ and with Preset = 0 for full speed, press Reset and simply enter arbitrary data ("S" key), or a meaningful program, as you like, starting at 003, 000 and ending at, say, 010. What do you see on the address and data bus monitors as you do so? Reset and "S" your way through the data you have written in. What do you now see? In each case you will see *002* on the address bus monitor and the data you wrote in and later retrieved on the data bus monitor after each press of "S" (both when writing and retrieving). An analysis of why this occurs will shed a lot of light on the KEX bootstrap (Appendix C) which controls the keyboard. When you Reset (to 000, 000) KEX soon takes you to 000, 315 ("KBRD") which puts you in a wait loop till a key is pressed. When a key number (data) is entered, KEX comes out of the wait loop and, with this key code data in the accumulator, returns to 000, 113 where the data is eventually transferred to register C from A (see address 000, 130 in KEX) and stored. Two more key entries repeat the "KBRD" routine and enter the full 8 bits of data or instruction in register C. But note that after each key press the instruction at 000, 131 in KEX jumps back to 000, 105 where the data in C is moved to A and *outputted to port 002*. The $\begin{pmatrix} 323 \\ 002 \end{pmatrix}$ instruction there allows the data bus monitor to capture this data on the data bus in view of $\overline{out}$ generated by it which enables the latch in the display. We, therefore, see each piece of data from a key press displayed on the data bus monitor. KEX then goes back to "KBRD" when the call at 000, 110 is reached. No more $\overline{out}$'s are generated in "KBRD's" wait loop till the "S" key is next pressed, taking us back to 000, 113 with S's code 013 in A. Mov M, C at 000, 163 puts the instruction/data into memory pointed to by H, L. INX H, L increments L by 1 and we go back to 000, 076 where the data in the next memory address is eventually put out to the display and to port 2 via the data bus (see addresses 105, 106, 107 in KEX). This is the *last* $\overline{out}$ before we go back to "KBRD." Hence the data bus monitor continually captures the data flowing on the data bus (after every $\overline{out}$ at 106, 107 generated by a key press), but *device code 002* is continually put out on to the *address bus* at 106, 107 due to $\binom{323}{002}$; the $\overline{out}$ on the address bus monitor enable allows the latter to capture 002. Since it is always the *last* $\overline{out}$ before the wait loop in "KBRD," we *always* see 002 latched to the address bus monitor.

Likewise, resetting and pressing S to read through the program would *always* end up at 105, 106, 107 $\binom{323}{002}$ in KEX which puts the data in memory (Mov $\overset{\frown}{C, M}$ at 116) on to the data bus (to C and then A). $\overline{Out}$ then enables the monitor display to capture this data. Since $\binom{323}{002}$ at 107 also puts 002 on to the Hi and Lo parts of the address bus we would expect $\overline{out}$ = ⊔ to allow the address monitor display to latch 002 from the address bus, which it does. KEX then goes into "KBRD" to wait for the next "S" to be pressed.

To get a valid latched address as you "S" through your program, you would have to display port 0's eight LED's on a numeric display. Port 0 is influenced solely by Mov $\overset{\frown}{A, L}$ and $\binom{out}{000}$ at 102, 103, 104 in KEX, and L certainly increases by 1 for every INX H at 164. Thus if we take the 8 bits $b_7 \ldots b_0$ from the MMD-1's port 000 stand-off terminals and feed them to BA, CBA, CBA of the octal address bus monitor, with the strobe of the latter kept to Lo or tied to $\overline{Out}$ and with the data bus monitor tied to $D_7 \ldots D_0$ on the data bus, with its strobe tied to $\overline{out}$, we will see octal address and data being written into memory or read back from memory as we press the S key. Do not confuse this with single stepping where the address and data bus monitors are tied to $A_7 \ldots A_0$ and $D_7 \ldots D_0$, respectively, with strobes on *both* being kept low, *always*. In that case the *last* address and fetched data on the two busses will be latched, respectively, by the monitors during each pulsed machine cycle as their enables are *always* low. Extra bytes (port or memory addresses with I/O or R/W memory data) will *also* be exhibited (see Experiment 4-2(d)).

Reconnect each enable (pin 5) on the HP matrix display address and data bus display monitors to ground. Leave them that way for the rest of your single stepping experiments. We now wish to employ single stepping in more general programs and instructions in order to analyze program execution in more detail.

Experiment 4-2(b) Single Stepping a Binary Addition Program

$$
\begin{array}{ll}
\begin{array}{l} 000 \\ 001 \end{array} & \left. \begin{array}{l} 076 \\ 000 \end{array} \right) \\[8pt]
\begin{array}{l} 002 \\ 003 \end{array} & \left. \begin{array}{l} 306 \\ 222 \end{array} \right) \quad \text{ADI, } B_2 \text{ to (A)} \\[8pt]
\begin{array}{l} 004 \\ 005 \end{array} & \left. \begin{array}{l} 306 \\ 111 \end{array} \right) \quad \text{ADI, } B_2 \text{ to (A)} \\[8pt]
\begin{array}{l} 006 \\ 007 \end{array} & \left. \begin{array}{l} 323 \\ 000 \end{array} \right) \quad \text{out (A) to Port 0} \\[8pt]
\begin{array}{l} 010 \\ 011 \\ 012 \end{array} & \left. \begin{array}{l} 303 \\ 002 \\ 003 \end{array} \right) \quad \text{JMP to 002}
\end{array}
$$

Run at full speed. Note that Port 0 lights up to 377 as it must. Now single step. Notice the bits at Port 0 *just after* the $\binom{323}{B_2}$ instruction and compare it with the "extra byte" = (A) appearing on the data bus monitor at that time. They should, of course, be the same. (The address bus monitor will read the extra byte 000 at that point.) Loop through several times and convince yourself that each successive addition of 222 and 111 to the previous value of (A) gives the correct binary output at Port 0 and that the corresponding (A) byte is latched on to the data bus monitor from the data bus.

In experiments 2(a) and 2(b) you might try ending the program with a Halt 166 instead of a jump back. See if you then can single step through the program.

Experiment 4-2(c) Single Stepping with Various Types of Instructions in the Program

The purpose again is to keep an eye out for any "extra" single stepping bytes. Try the following:

$$
\begin{array}{ll}
\begin{array}{l} 000 \\ 001 \\ 002 \end{array} & \left. \begin{array}{l} 061 \\ 200 \\ 003 \end{array} \right) \quad \text{LXI, SP}
\end{array}
$$

003	(026	MVI, D
004	(111	
005	172	Mov A,D
006	(006	MVI, B
007	(002	
010	005	DCR B
011	(302	
012	(010	JNZ
013	(003	
014	(323	(A) to Port 0
015	(000	
016	(303	
017	(000	JMP to 000
020	(003	

003 (026) MVI, D
004 (111)
005   172   Mov A͡,D
006 (006) MVI, B
007 (002)
010   005   DCR B ⎤
011 (302)   ⎬ a two pass time delay loop
012 (010) JNZ   ⎦
013 (003)
014 (323) (A) to Port 0
015 (000)
016 (303)
017 (000) JMP to 000
020 (003)

You should see only one extra byte 000,111 just after address 015 is passed in the single stepping. All the other addresses and instruction bytes are revealed on the monitors during the single stepping in usual fashion with no "extra bytes." Try other programs of your own with other instructions of various kinds, the aim being to observe the passage of extra bytes.

Experiment 4-2(d)   Single Stepping a Program with Calls, Ret, Pops, Pushes (Single Stepping Through the Stack)

The real beauty and power of single stepping are brought out when Calls, Returns, Pops, Pushes, Restarts (RST), as well as input or output (333, 323) instructions are employed in a program.

000 (061) LXI, SP
001 (200)
002 (003)
003 (026) MVI, D
004 (111)
005 (315) Call →
006 (100)
007 (003)

010	172	Mov $\widehat{A,D}$ ← Ret
011	$\begin{pmatrix} 323 \\ 001 \end{pmatrix}$	(A) to Port 1
012		
013	$\begin{pmatrix} 303 \\ 000 \\ 003 \end{pmatrix}$	
014		
015		

Subroutine

100	325	Push D
101	$\begin{pmatrix} 026 \\ 222 \end{pmatrix}$	MVI, D
102		
103	172	Mov $\widehat{A,D}$
104	$\begin{pmatrix} 323 \\ 001 \end{pmatrix}$	(A) to Port 1
105		
106	321	Pop D
107	311	Ret

Run at full speed and then observe the stack at locations 177, 176, 175, and 174. Note the stack structure of this program after the Call and the Push D are executed. Also observe 333 at port 1. Why?

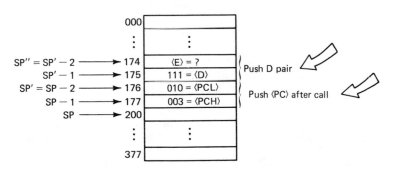

Figure 42. The stack relative to Expt. 4-2(d).

Now single step the above program and keep an eye on port 1. Note how it changes at the appropriate times. The results should be revealing, and perhaps, at first, puzzling. You

will find *extra bytes* (+) appear just after (007, 003)—namely $\binom{177,003}{176,010}^+$, followed by (100, 325) (the first address, instruction in the called subroutine), followed by $\binom{175,111}{174,(E)=?}^+$ followed by (101,026). . . . Then after (105,001) you will see (001,222)$^+$ followed by (106,321), followed by $\binom{174,(E)=?}{175,111}^+$, followed by (107,311), followed by $\binom{176,010}{177,003}^+$, followed by (010,172), ...
Then, after (012,001), you will see (001,111)$^+$; then (013,303); (014,000); (015,003); (000,061); (001,200); and a repeat of all the above as we continue single stepping through the program a second time.

The key to understanding these results requires careful study of the Call, Push, Pop, and Ret instructions described in section 3-6 of Chap. 3 as well as the Out instruction described earlier in this chapter (see also pp. 4-11, 4-12, 4-13, 4-14, 2-16, 17, 18 and 19, Intel Manual, Sept. 1975). See also Fig. 42.

Thus, (1): $\begin{pmatrix} 315 \\ 100 \\ 003 \end{pmatrix}$ = Call means that 003 flows from PC to $M_{SP-1} = 177$ and 010 flows from PC to $M_{SP-2} = 176$ (i.e., a Push of (PC) = return address on to the stack). Since PC lies in the CPU and the stack is in memory this data must flow via the data bus— hence 003 and 010 are latched by the data bus monitor. Since 003 flows to 177 and 010 to 176, these memory locations must be pointed to by the address bus (the stack pointer is involved here— see p. 2-18, Intel 8080 Manual and Fig. 8, Chap. 2). Hence, the address bus monitor captures 177 and 176; thus the $\binom{177,003}{176,010}^+$ extra bytes. (See also Appendix I.)

(2): 325 = Push D means (D) = 111 goes to $M_{SP-1} = 175$ and (E)=? goes to $M_{SP-2} = 174$. Since D,E registers lie in the CPU this data can get to the memory stack only via the data bus. The address bus must access 175 and 174 in order for the data to get there (Intel Manual, p. 2-18). Hence, the extra bytes $\binom{175,111}{174,(E)}^+$ are latched by the monitors. (See Appendix I).

(3): $\binom{323}{001}$ = output (A) to Port 1. This instruction appears at address 104. It implements [see Experiment 4-2(a)] (A) = 222 → Port 1 *via the data bus* with device code 001 appearing on the address bus. Hence the extra byte (001,222)$^+$ just after address 105 in the program.

(4): 321 = Pop D means (E)=? goes from M_{SP}=174 to register E and (D)=111 goes from M_{SP+1}=175 to register D. Again the data bus monitor will latch this data which is coming from memory to the CPU via the data bus. The address bus must access these SP memory locations and so the address monitor latches those addresses (p. 2-18, Intel Manual). Hence, the extra bytes $\binom{174,(E)}{175,111}^+$.

(5): 311 = Ret means that (PC) is popped from the stack back to the program counter so that (PC) = 003,010 i.e., the return address previously pushed on to the stack by the Call instruction is retrieved. Hence, 010 flows from 176 to PCL and 003 from 177 to PCH. Again this flow of data from memory stack to CPU can only occur over the data bus while the address data to access the relevant stack locations flow on the address bus and they, too, get latched (p. 2-18, Intel Manual). Hence, the extra bytes $\binom{176,010}{177,003}^+$.

(6): $\binom{323}{001}$ at address 011 outputs (A) = 111 to port 1 and places address (device code) 001 on the address bus. Hence, the extra byte (000,111) appears on data and address busses.

The same behavior would be exhibited by Push B, Push H, Push PSW, Pop B, Pop H, Pop PSW if they were in the program. It should be mentioned that in this manner all conditional calls and returns (e.g., CNZ, CZ, . . . ; RNZ, RZ, . . .) will exhibit the same extra bytes if they were part of a program, provided the conditions were met (try a program using CZ = 314 as an example). So will RSTN* = 3N7 (N=0, 1, 2, . . . , 7) which is nothing more *than a specialized call to a specific location in memory:*

$$M_{SP-1} \leftarrow (PCH)$$

$$M_{SP-2} \leftarrow (PCL)$$

$$SP' \leftarrow SP-2$$

PC $\leftarrow$ 000,0N0 i.e., *call the subroutine at 000,0N0.*

A word on RST N=3N7. It calls a subroutine that lies at (000,0N0) in KEX of the MMD-1. If we study the KEX program (see Appendix C), we find that RST0=307 takes us to 000,000, which contains a jump instruction to 000,070, *which in turn is*

---

*Intel 8080 User's Manual, Sept. 1975, p. 4-12.

the start of the main KEX program. Likewise, RST 7=377 takes us to 000,070. In other words, for the MMD-1, RST0 and RST7 will get us nowhere but into the heart of KEX program from which there can be no return to the RAM (003H) where we wish to write our *subroutine. If we use RST1, RST2, or . . . RST6, we call 000,010; or 000,020 . . . and these locations* in KEX are reserved for genuine restarts (calls) and vectored interrupts. In these cases RSTN takes us to 000,0N0 where the KEX program dictates $\begin{pmatrix} 303 \\ 0N0 \\ 003 \end{pmatrix}$ (jump) taking us to the RAM at 003,0N0 where we can indeed write our subroutine. Naturally, this subroutine must be terminated in a RET=311 instruction to get us back to the main program just after the point where the RSTN was executed. More on the use of restarts in Chap. 5, where we consider jamming interrupts using the 3N7 instruction. There, 3N7 will not be in the program but rather be waiting on a tri-stated (interrupt port) buffer on the data bus.

Experiment 4-2(e)   Single Stepping a Program Containing RSTN =3N7 Instruction With and Without RET.

(1)

000	$\begin{pmatrix} 076 \\ 367 \end{pmatrix}$	
001		
002	367 =	RST6 (go to 000,060 in KEX and then to 003,060 in RAM)
003	$\begin{pmatrix} 323 \\ 000 \end{pmatrix}$	(A) → Port 0
004		
005	$\begin{pmatrix} 303 \\ 000 \\ 003 \end{pmatrix}$	
006		
007		
060	222	
061	222	
.	.	
.	.	
.	.	
067	222	Put "garbage" into the subroutine
070	222	
.	.	
.	.	
077	222	

Single stepping this program will not take us to 060,222 but rather into the KEX "jungle" because no return was provided from the subroutine.

(2) *Same program as above, only RET=311 is programmed at, say, 003H,065L*

Single stepping now reveals the following results:

003	000	$\left(\begin{array}{c}076\\367\end{array}\right)$	
	001		
	002	367 =	RST6
	377	003	Extra bytes with return address
	376	003	stored in stack at 377 and 376; i.e., Push (PC) on to stack due to RST instruction.
KEX: 000	060	$\left(\begin{array}{c}303\\060\\003\end{array}\right)$	"Extra bytes" (i.e., the KEX program at 000,060)
000	061		
000	062		
RAM: 003	060	222	
	061	222	
	062	222	
	063	222	
	064	222	
	065	311	
	376	003	Extra bytes due to RET (Pop (PC))
	377	003	
	003	$\left(\begin{array}{c}323\\000\end{array}\right)$	
	004		
	000	367	Extra byte due to "out" instruction.
	005	$\left(\begin{array}{c}303\\000\\003\end{array}\right)$	
	006		
	007		
	000	$\left(\begin{array}{c}076\\367\end{array}\right)$	
	001		
	002	367	
	377	003	
	376	003	
KEX: 000	060	303	

⋮   ⋮

All goes well now because we have provided a RET instruction with the RST6.

(3) *Same Program, But Now:*

$$
\begin{array}{ll}
000 & \left(\begin{matrix} 076 \\ 377 \end{matrix}\right) \\
001 & \\
002 & 377 \quad = \quad \text{RST7 (go to 000,070).}
\end{array}
$$

003	070	222
003	071	222
003	072	222
003	073	222
003	074	222

If we provide no return, single stepping reveals that we are surely in KEX; i.e., 377=RST7 goes to 000,070, which is the beginning of the main KEX Program. There is no jump to 003,070 provided there as was the case at 000,060 in the last experiment, where KEX took us to 003,060. If we supply a RET 311 at say 003,074, we still can't get out of KEX because we are mired down in the main part of the KEX program after 000,070.

The moral of the story with the MMD-1 is this: Don't use RST0 (307) or RST7 (377). And if you use RSTN (N=1, 2, . . . , 6), be sure to use a Ret=311 instruction at the end of the sub-routine called.

You are reminded to single step through Experiment 3-6(d) in Chap. 3, and any other program in the experiments of Chap. 3. Wherever possible, employ single stepping in the interfacing experiments of Chap. 5.

Experiment 4-2(f)   Single Stepping by Pure Programming Using Output Ports as Address and Data Bus Monitors.

Consider a sample program.

$$\begin{array}{ll} 000 & \left(\begin{array}{c} 076 \\ 111 \end{array}\right) \\ 001 & \\ 002 & \left(\begin{array}{c} 323 \\ 000 \end{array}\right) \\ 003 & \\ 004 & 166. \end{array}$$

We wish to single step through this program, using Port 000 as address monitor and port 002 as the instruction/data monitor. The following program, with time delay, will allow us to do this. However, "extra bytes" will not be seen in this purely software method of single stepping.

176	(016	MVI, C
177	(005	= length of program
200	(041	
201	(000	LXI, H/L
202	(003	
203	176	Mov A͡,M
204	(323	
205	(002	data monitor
206	175	Mov A͡,L
207	(323	
210	(000	address monitor
211	043	INX H
212	(315	
213	(300	CALL →
214	(003	
215	015	DCR C
216	(302	
217	(203	JNZ
220	(003	
221	166	

Time Delay*

300	365	Push PSW
301	345	Push H

*See Experiment 3-2(d).

302	$\begin{pmatrix} 006 \\ 310 \end{pmatrix}$	
303		Time Byte (2 sec)
304	$\begin{pmatrix} 021 \\ 046 \\ 001 \end{pmatrix}$	
305		LXI D/E
306		
307	033	
310	172	
311	263	
312	$\begin{pmatrix} 302 \\ 307 \\ 003 \end{pmatrix}$	
313		
314		
315	005	
316	$\begin{pmatrix} 302 \\ 304 \\ 003 \end{pmatrix}$	
317		
320		
321	341	Pop H
322	361	Pop PSW
323	311	Ret

Observe the results at Ports 0 and 2. Are Push H and Pop H really needed? How about Push/Pop PSW? Try and see.

Experiment 4-2(g) Single Stepping with STA (062), SHLD (042), Mov M͡, A (167), XTHL (343), LDA (072), LHLD (052), STAX rp, etc. Instructions.

Single step the following programs and observe the extra bytes. Extend the experiment to LDA, LHLD, MVI, M, ADD, M (206), STAX rp, etc. instructions.

(i): *STA B_2, B_3:*

000	$\begin{pmatrix} 076 \\ 111 \end{pmatrix}$	
001		
002	$\begin{pmatrix} 062 \\ 100 \\ 003 \end{pmatrix}$	
003		STA B_2, B_3: $\langle A \rangle \rightarrow$ 003, 100 in memory.
004		
005	$\begin{pmatrix} 303 \\ 000 \\ 003 \end{pmatrix}$	
006		
007		

Observe the extra byte 100, 111 after 004. Examine memory location 003, 100 after the run.

(ii): *SHLD B₂, B₃:*

$$
\begin{array}{ll}
\begin{array}{l} 000 \\ 001 \\ 002 \end{array}
\left(\begin{array}{l} 041 \\ 111 \\ 222 \end{array} \right) & \text{LXI H, L.}
\end{array}
$$

$$
\begin{array}{ll}
\begin{array}{l} 003 \\ 004 \\ 005 \end{array}
\left(\begin{array}{l} 042 \\ 200 \\ 003 \end{array} \right) &
\begin{array}{l} \text{SHLD } B_2, B_3 : \langle L \rangle \rightarrow 003, 200 \\ \phantom{\text{SHLD } B_2, B_3 :} \langle H \rangle \rightarrow 003, 201. \end{array}
\end{array}
$$

$$
\begin{array}{l} 006 \\ 007 \\ 010 \end{array}
\left(\begin{array}{l} 303 \\ 000 \\ 003 \end{array} \right)
$$

Observe the extra bytes 200, 111; 201, 222 after 005. Examine memory locations 200, 201 after the run.

(iii): *Mov M̂, A*

$$
\begin{array}{ll}
\begin{array}{l} 000 \\ 001 \\ 002 \end{array}
\left(\begin{array}{l} 041 \\ 100 \\ 003 \end{array} \right) & \text{LXI H, L}
\end{array}
$$

$$
\begin{array}{l} 003 \\ 004 \end{array}
\left(\begin{array}{l} 076 \\ 111 \end{array} \right)
$$

$$
\begin{array}{ll}
005 & 167 & \text{Mov } \widehat{M, A} : \langle A \rangle \rightarrow 003, 100
\end{array}
$$

$$
\begin{array}{l} 006 \\ 007 \\ 010 \end{array}
\left(\begin{array}{l} 303 \\ 000 \\ 003 \end{array} \right)
$$

Observe the extra byte 100, 111 after 005. Examine location 003, 100 after the run. *Exercise*: Try with a Mov Â,M instruction.

(iiii): *XTHL*

This instruction executes $\langle L \rangle \leftrightarrow \langle M_{SP} \rangle$ and $\langle H \rangle \leftrightarrow \langle M_{SP+1} \rangle$.

$$
\begin{array}{ll}
\begin{array}{l} 000 \\ 001 \\ 002 \end{array}
\left(\begin{array}{l} 061 \\ 300 \\ 003 \end{array} \right) & \text{LXI SP}
\end{array}
$$

003   ⎛ 041 ⎞
004   ⎜ 111 ⎟   LXI H, L
005   ⎝ 222 ⎠

006   343   XTHL $\langle L \rangle \leftrightarrow \langle M_{300} \rangle$. $\langle H \rangle \leftrightarrow \langle M_{301} \rangle$.

007   ⎛ 303 ⎞
010   ⎜ 006 ⎟
011   ⎝ 003 ⎠

300   000

301   377

Observe the four extra bytes in the order 300, 111; 301, 222; 301, 377; 300, 000 all after 006. Continue the single stepping and next time after 006 you will observe 300, 000; 301, 377; 301, 222; 300, 111 in that order. Once more around and you will observe 300, 111; 301, 222; 301, 377; 300, 000 after 006, etc., confirming the nature of XTHL very clearly and convincingly.

Try other experiments with LDA (072), LHLD (052), MVI M, ADD, M, STAX rp, etc. instructions.

Software single stepping programs have been devised in which pulsing and circuits of the type in Fig. 34 are circumvented. They require additional Monitor PROMs (for Example, E & L Instrument Inc. KEX L/D and Monitor Proms). In that approach each press of "S" executes another *instruction in its entirety*. You do not see machine cycle bytes (except the *first* byte of a multibyte instruction). You can, however, observe the effect of that instruction's execution on each and every register and flag word in the CPU by simply pressing a key denoting that register *after* having pressed the "Monitor" key. Extra bytes, however, are not disclosed.

In all the single step experiments in this chapter you are urged to read carefully the complete description of the pertinent instruction employed as presented in Chap. 4 of the Intel 8080 User's Manual, Sept. 1975. That will allow you to appreciate the fact that "normal" and "extra" address and data bus bytes are seen whenever a memory address or an I/O must be referenced (pointed to) to carry out that machine cycle as part of the overall instruction execution. Single stepping helps to understand microcomputer architecture. Consult also pp. 2-16 thru 2-19 of the same Intel manual and Appendix I in this book.

Chapter 5

Interfacing Experiments: Controlling Input/Output Devices with a Microprocessor-Microcomputer; The Need For Device Select Pulses, Latching, and Tri-Stating; Data Acquisition, Storage, Read-Out; Status Bits; Interrupt Jamming; Control Signal Generation.

5-1. INTRODUCTION

Here "to control" means controlling a device(s) or process(es) in the most general sense; i.e., to program the microcomputer for the purpose of *decision-making* with regard to the device(s) or process(es) to be controlled *and* to interface with the output (or input) device(s) so that it may accept data, status bits, or control bits from the microcomputer (or so that the input device(s) may input their data or status or requests to the microcomputer for processing, control, and decision making). The device(s) can be just about anything: a counter, another computer, a motor, a TTY, a CRT, traffic lights, a microwave oven, a data transmission system, a point-of-sale terminal, a ventillating system, a gas pump, an appliance, a measuring instrument, another IC chip controlling a device, a bar (liquid state) mixer, a test set, an ignition timing system for optimum firing time and fuel consumption, a navigation controller, a video game, automation devices of every kind, etc. The number of devices or processes being program-controlled by microprocessor, microcontrollers, and microcomputers is increasing by leaps and bounds almost daily. Manufacturing process control is a large area, as are test sets, measuring instruments, machinery, and end products. Among the powerful advantages that the microcomputer-microprocessor offers, and which will help to propel it into every facet of our lives and into every conceivable device or process, are its low cost (and still going down as of this writing) and the fact that it can substitute software (decision-making programs that take into account changing conditions, which the controlling and controlled device must face) for hardware, thus eliminating to a large degree the need for switches, springs, relays, levers, and all kinds of transducers, as well as reducing enormously the number of circuit connections. The latter feature, of course, makes the microcomputer most attractive in that its reliability is better than that of the hard-wired systems and devices it is replacing. *The microprocessor will be used in any device or system in which electronics is to be found.*

The problem with which we concern ourselves in this chapter is of two parts: (a) to "interface" the microcomputer to the I/O (Input/Output) device we are trying to control; i.e., how does the microcomputer impose its decision-making program and its results on that device?, and (b) to present experiments illustrating typical ways by which "devices" are interfaced to the microcomputer and controlled by it—"devices" being an IC chip (which then actually controls the physical device of interest), or a set of LED displays (traffic lights or instrument-status—on/off—bits), or a "motor," or a matrix or 7-segment display, or another "computer," etc. A complete understanding of the software techniques studied in Chap. 3 and the single stepping-machine cycle discussion in Chap. 4 are essential.

The best way to introduce this most important practical subject is through specific experiments. These experiments will show the intimate relationships between microprocessor software and the interfacing hardware (integrated circuits and peripherals) necessary to accomplish the job of I/O device control—control in the sense of *what, how much,* and *when.* The software-digital logic hardware relationship is the essence of the problem of interfacing the microcomputer to the outside world. The experiments will give some idea of the real power of the microprocessor/microcomputer, in particular how a change in instruction in one or two places in the program (rather than a change in device hardware) can totally change the performance of the device or system being controlled. They will indicate how the microprocessor is ideally suited to the continually changing external conditions faced by the device and can make immediate new decisions as these changing conditions are fed back from the device to the microprocessor, *thus affecting immediate optimal control at any given moment.* (*Warning:* programmers and software people must cope with digital logic, interfacing, and the inner workings of a microprocessor (Chaps. 1, 2); digital logic and hardware people must face up to programming and software. As long as the microprocessor-microcomputer's mission is the optimal control of a device or process the marriage between software and hardware will be a necessary ingredient to its understanding, mastery, and use.)

We are presenting these experiments around the E & L Instruments Inc. 8080 MMD-1 trainer as our point of reference. They can, however, be performed on any 8080 based system if 1) the data and address busses are accessible, 2) there is a keyboard, encoder, and bootstrap PROM to write programs into RAM via the busses, 3) decoded addresses are available, and 4) control signals $\overline{\text{Out}}$, $\overline{\text{IN}}$, $\overline{\text{IACK}}$ ($\overline{\text{INTA}}$), $\overline{\text{MEMR}}$, and $\overline{\text{MEMW}}$ are available. If not, consult Appendix H for the few modifications that may be needed. Octal is used throughout, but the experiments are equally valid if the programming is done in hexadecimal.

The recent Intel 8085 microprocessor uses the same instruction set as the 8080. The reader is urged to consult the 8085 manual (see also Appendix F). Modifications necessary with the 8085 for these 8080 experiments will be taken up in detail in a second book on *Applications Experiments** to appear in the near future. They are relatively simple modifications involving only an address latch (8212) and a decoder (8205) to generate the control signals for standard (8080) memories and I/O's (see Appendix H).

5-2. THE EXPERIMENTS

I/O device control is built around three very powerful 8080 instructions: $\begin{pmatrix} 323 \\ B_2 \end{pmatrix}$ = output (A) from the microprocessor to output device number (B_2); $\begin{pmatrix} 333 \\ B_2 \end{pmatrix}$ = input data from input device number (B_2) to the accumulator of the microprocessor; and Restart (RST) = 3N7 (to be discussed later in the experiment on interrupt requests and jamming).

---

*"Applications Experiments with an 8080/8085 Microprocessor–Microcontroller" by Boyet and Katz.

It is important that we give the *detailed* descriptions*[†] of $\begin{pmatrix} 323 \\ B_2 \end{pmatrix}$ and $\begin{pmatrix} 333 \\ B_2 \end{pmatrix}$ here.

$\begin{pmatrix} 323 \\ B_2 \end{pmatrix}$:

(A) are put on the data bus for transmission to output device number (B_2). During the third machine cycle of this instruction (B_2) appears on the low part of the address bus (as an "extra" byte), (A) appears on the data bus (extra byte) on its way to device B_2, and the CPU[†] produces an $\overline{Out}$ pulse $= \sqcup\!\sqcap$ (½ μs wide), available at the SK-10 socket of the MMD-1. (The output device is thus like any one of a number of memory locations or addresses and *the address bus points to it just after the 323 instruction is encountered in the program and executed*, at which time $A_7 \ldots A_0$ $= (B_2) = B_7 \ldots B_0$). Note also that B_2 is placed on $A_{15} \ldots A_8$*.

$\begin{pmatrix} 333 \\ B_2 \end{pmatrix}$:

Input device number (B_2) puts its data on the data bus, which then goes to the accumulator. During the third machine cycle of this instruction B_2 appears on the low part of the address bus (extra byte), the data moves on the data bus from device B_2 to A (extra byte) and the CPU[†] produces an $\overline{In}$ pulse $= \sqcup\!\sqcap$ (½ μs wide), available at the SK-10 bus socket of the MMD-1. (The input device is just like another memory location and the address bus points to it so that $A_7 \ldots A_0 = (B_2) = B_7 \ldots B_0$, *just after the 333 instruction is encountered in the program and executed.)* Also $B_2 = A_{15} \ldots A_8$*.

It will be extremely helpful throughout all interfacing experiments with an 8080 chip to keep in mind the following diagrams, which embody and reflect the above descriptions of $\begin{pmatrix} 323 \\ B_2 \end{pmatrix}$ *and* $\begin{pmatrix} 333 \\ B_2 \end{pmatrix}$.

---

*Intel 8080 Manual, Sept. 1975, pp. 4-14, 2-6, 5-14, *2-18*.
[†]The generation of $\overline{In}$, $\overline{Out}$ $= \sqcup\!\sqcap$ pulses (and other control signals as well) is arranged by Nanding certain "status bits" with 8080 output control signals—See Section 5.2(G) this chapter. Also Fig. 11 and Fig. 69.

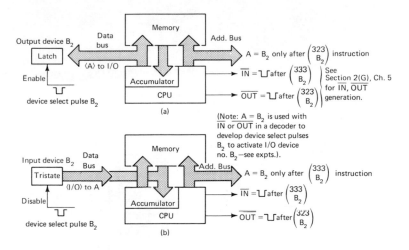

Figure 43. Address and data byte flow after 8080 output/input instructions.

Let us now see how these instructions, and their consequences can be used in interfacing the microcomputer to external devices for the purpose of control or data/information exchange. We shall first treat the *outputting* of *control* or *information* bytes to an output device B_2 [section 5-2(A) and 5-2(B)]. Inputting *information, or status, or requests* from an *input* device will be treated in section 5-2(D). Refer to Appendix A for the necessary pin connections on the relevant IC's.

5-2(A)   Outputting Control signals from the Microcomputer to an I/O Device

Experiment 5-2(a)   **Simple Example of Controlling an Output Device (Counter)—One External Device— Device Select Pulse Not Required—$\overline{Out}$ Pulse Sufficient**

(i) Problem: Direct a counter to clear itself every N seconds (N programmable), then resume the count, clear again, . . . , etc.

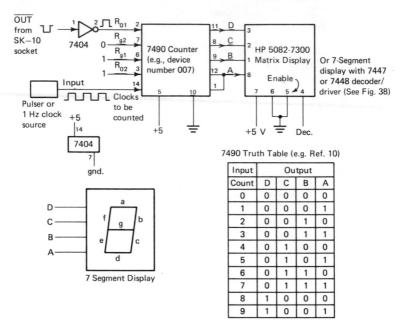

Figure 44. Clearing a counter—Expt. 5-2(a).

To understand this experiment, we present here the truth table for the IC 7490 counter chip (see Ref. 10).

7490 (Reset — Count Function Table)

	Pin 2	Pin 3	Pin 6	Pin 7	Pin 11	Pin 8	Pin 9	Pin 12	
	Ro_1	Ro_2	Rg_1	Rg_2	D	C	B	A	
	← Reset Inputs →				← Output Count →				
clears	1	1	0	X	0	0	0	0	clears
	1	1	X	0	0	0	0	0	
	X	X	1	1	1	0	0	1	
	X	0	X	0	← Counts →				
counts	0	X	0	X	← Counts →				counts
	0	X	X	0	← Counts →				
	X	0	0	X	← Counts →				

Note that the 7490 clears for $R_{01} = R_{02} = 1$, $R_{g1} = X$, $R_{g2} = 0$, and that it counts for $R_{01} = 0$, $R_{02} = X$, $R_{g1} = X$, $R_{g2} = 0$. Hence the circuit diagram shown in Fig. 44 with the 7490 pins maintained at the logic levels indicated will produce a clear every time an $\overline{\overline{out}}$ is generated ($\overline{\overline{out}} = \sqcap = R_{01}$) and resume the count when $\overline{out}$ is again zero ($\overline{\text{out}}$ comes back to 1). This is so because $R_{02}=1$, $R_{g2}=0$, $R_{g1}=1$ do not change. Since $\overline{\text{out}}$ is generated only after a $\left(\dfrac{323}{B_2}\right)$ instruction in the program is encountered (we have arbitrarily designated the counter as device 007), the counter will clear at that time.

The following program will force the counter to count for N seconds, then to clear almost instantaneously (in ~13 μs for a $\left(\dfrac{323}{B_2}\right)$ instruction with the 8080 MMD-1), then to resume the count, then to clear, etc. N is, of course, determined by the time delay routine—its duration is governed by the B_2 byte at 101L in the program.

Wire up the circuitry, run the program, and observe the results. Vary the B_2 byte and observe the results.

000	$\left(\begin{array}{c}323\\007\end{array}\right)$	microcomputer generates $\overline{\text{out}} = \sqcup\!\!\!\sqcap$ to clear the counter (device 007)
001		
002	$\left(\begin{array}{c}315\\100\\003\end{array}\right)$	Call →
003		
004		
005	$\left(\begin{array}{c}303\\000\\003\end{array}\right)$	JMP ← Ret
006		
007		

Time Delay Subroutine* during which counter counts for N secs.

100	$\left(\begin{array}{c}006\\B_2\end{array}\right)$	MVI B, B_2 / Time Byte
101		
102	$\left(\begin{array}{c}021\\046\\015\end{array}\right)$	LXI D/E
103		
104		
105	033	DCX D,E
106	172	Mov $\overarc{\text{A,D}}$
107	263	ORA, E

*See Experiment 3-2(d) and Table 3-1. With D=015 and E=046, as shown here, $B_2=$ 012, 024, 062, 144 produce delays of N = 1, 2, 5, 10 secs. respectively.

110	⎛ 302 ⎞	
111	⎜ 105 ⎟	JNZ
112	⎝ 003 ⎠	
113	005	DCR B
114	⎛ 302 ⎞	
115	⎜ 102 ⎟	
116	⎝ 003 ⎠	
117	311	Ret

Note that no Pushes and Pops are needed in the T.D. as the main program does not use registers B, D, and A. Note also that the time delays may vary from MMD-1 to MMD-1 depending on the exact clock frequency for each unit.

Note that no device select is required because our output device of interest (external to the MMD-1 which has its own device-selected "output" ports 0, 1, 2) is the *counter* whose device number is $007 \neq 001$, or 000, or 002. Thus, when $\overline{out}$ is generated after $\binom{323}{007}$ it affects *only* device 007 and *not* 001, 000, or 002. The latter are affected only by device *select* pulses, not by simple $\overline{out}$ pulses as in this experiment (See Experiment 5-2(f) and section 5-2(C) where generation of *device selects* for ports 000, 001, 002 and for other external ports are discussed and implemented, and where the distinction between $\overline{out}$ pulses and "device select" pulses is made clear). Try the experiment with $B_2 = 012, 024, 062, 100, 120,$ and 144 and observe when the counter clears in each case. Save the circuit for the next experiment.

(ii)   This control program is a variation of the previous experiment. Here we count for N seconds and then clear the counter permanently. The circuitry is exactly the same as in Experiment 5-2(a)i.

000	⎛ 323 ⎞	generates $\overline{out} = \sqcup$ to clear device 007 counter at the
		outset.
001	⎝ 007 ⎠	
002	⎛ 315 ⎞	
003	⎜ 100 ⎟	Call →
004	⎝ 003 ⎠	
005	⎛ 323 ⎞	← Ret.
006	⎝ 007 ⎠	

$$
\begin{array}{l}
007 \\
010 \\
011
\end{array}
\left(
\begin{array}{l}
303 \\
005 \\
003
\end{array}
\right)
$$

Same T.D. Subroutine as in Experiment 5-2(a)i

$$
\left.
\begin{array}{ll}
100 & \left(\begin{array}{l}006\\ B_2\end{array}\right) \\
101 \\
\vdots & \vdots \\
117 & 311
\end{array}
\right\}
\begin{array}{l}
\text{N second time delay during which counter counts,} \\
\text{after which it is permanently cleared}
\end{array}
$$

The wait loop starting at 005 through 011, and back, causes the counter to be pinned down in a cleared state; i.e., $\left(\begin{array}{l}323\\007\end{array}\right)$ generates $\overline{\text{out}}$ after $\overline{\text{out}}$ to R_{01} of the 7490, *thus keeping it cleared.* Try with B_2 = 012, 024, 062, 100, 120, and 144 and observe the results in each case.

(iii) Control Problem: The Counter is to run for N seconds, then clear for N' seconds, then run for N seconds, etc.

The circuitry is exactly the same as before.

This experiment will again demonstrate how programming with a microcomputer can easily accomplish with software what normally might be a complicated hardware job. The program follows.

000	$\left(\begin{array}{l}323\\007\end{array}\right)$	clears 7490 on ⊔ = $\overline{\text{out}}$
001		
002	$\left(\begin{array}{l}315\\100\\003\end{array}\right)$	Call →
003		
004		
005	$\left(\begin{array}{l}006\\B_2'\end{array}\right)$	MVI B, B_2' ← Ret
006		Time Byte N' (B_2') during which counter is cleared.
007	$\left(\begin{array}{l}021\\046\\015\end{array}\right)$	LXI D/E
010		
011		
012	$\left(\begin{array}{l}323\\007\end{array}\right)$	clears 7490 on ⊔ = $\overline{\text{out}}$
013		

Counter is cleared for N'(B_2') seconds ↓ to 025

014	033	DXC D,E
015	172	Mov A,D
016	263	OR A,E
017	⎛ 302 ⎞	
020	⎜ 012 ⎟	JNZ
021	⎝ 003 ⎠	
022	005	DCRB
023	⎛ 302 ⎞	
024	⎜ 007 ⎟	JNZ to 007
025	⎝ 003 ⎠	
026	⎛ 303 ⎞	
027	⎜ 000 ⎟	JMP
030	⎝ 003 ⎠	

See Experiment 5-2(a)i for T.D. routine:
counter counts for N seconds

100	⎛ 006 ⎞	MVI B, B_2
101	⎝ B_2 ⎠	Time Byte $N(B_2)$ during which counter counts
.	.	
.	.	
.	.	
117	311	RET

Note carefully that from 005L to 025 L we have a replica of the subroutine T.D. at 100L with the exception that $\binom{323}{007}$ is inserted at 012L. Its repetitive appearance there pins the counter down to clear for $N'(B_2')$ seconds after which a JMP to 003,000 and then to 100L allows the counter to count for $N(B_2)$ seconds.

Do the experiment with $B_2=062$ and $B_2'=024$, then $B_2=024$ and $B_2'=062$, etc. and observe the results. Note that Table 3-1 will not quite apply to the T.D. $N'(B_2')$ from 005L to 025L because of the insertion of $\binom{323}{007}$ at 012 which takes 10 cycles. The *inner loop* 1 has thus been increased by 10/24, and the outer loop some also, so the N'T.D. is increased by >40%. Bear this in mind in using Table 3-1 for the 005L to 025L time delay.

Experiment 5-2(b)   The Need for "Device Selecting".
Control Signals

Problem: We now have two counters. We desire one counter to clear at a certain time and the other counter to clear at a specified later time (N seconds later). (Generation of device select pulses— non-absolute selecting with one hexadecimal decoder.)

The reader will surely see how this problem can be generalized to changing two (or more) different traffic lights, or starting and stopping two or more different fans, motors, or measuring devices, and so on.

Let us try the same approach employed in Experiment 5-2(a)i; i.e., each counter counts for N seconds and is then cleared before each one, separately, resumes counting.

000	$\begin{pmatrix} 323 \\ 007 \end{pmatrix}$	generates $\overline{\text{out}} = $ ⊔ for device 007 to clear
001		
002	$\begin{pmatrix} 315 \\ 100 \\ 003 \end{pmatrix}$	Call →
003		
004		
005	$\begin{pmatrix} 323 \\ 006 \end{pmatrix}$	generates $\overline{\text{out}} = $ ⊔ for device 006 to clear ← Ret
006		
007	$\begin{pmatrix} 315 \\ 100 \\ 003 \end{pmatrix}$	Call →
010		
011		
012	$\begin{pmatrix} 303 \\ 000 \\ 003 \end{pmatrix}$	← Ret ←
013		
014		

Time Delay* N Seconds During Which Both Counters Count.

100	$\begin{pmatrix} 006 \\ B_2 \end{pmatrix}$	MVI B, B_2
101		Time Byte
102	$\begin{pmatrix} 021 \\ . \end{pmatrix}$	
.	.	
.	.	
.	.	
117	311	Ret

*See Experiment 5-2(a)i.

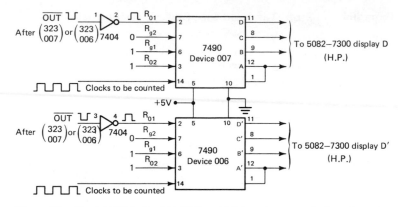

Figure 45. Expt. 5-2(b). Devices 006 and 007 are here *not* device selected. They are distinct from the device selected ports 0, 1, 2 on the MMD-1.

The problem cannot be solved with the interfacing as shown, simply because an $\overline{\text{out}}$ pulse ⊔ is generated for *both* devices at R_{01} each time $\binom{323}{007}$ is passed in the program and again for *both* devices each time $\binom{323}{006}$ is passed in the program. Thus, both counters will stop counting at the same time and then resume their counts at the same time. We have to come up with a way of "selecting" *which* device we want to clear and *when* we want each to clear, independent of the other, and this necessitates the generation of *"Device Select Pulses."*

Generation of Device Select Pulses: One way of generating device select pulses is through use of the 74154 Hexa 4- to 16-line decoder. This chip was introduced in Chap. 1 and its truth table and pin connections were presented in Section 1-2 there. Consider it again here.

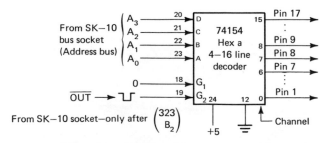

Figure 46. 74154 used for device selecting.

$G_1=0$. If $G_2=1$, then *every* output pin is Hi regardless of what happens at pins 20, 21, 22, 23 (Chap. 1). If $G_2=0$, then every output pin is Hi *except* the pin whose channel number corresponds to the *decimal* value of $(A_3 A_2 A_1 A_0)$ (=DCBA). *That* pin goes Lo.

Thus if $G_1=G_2=0$, then $A_3 A_2 A_1 A_0 = 1111$ produces 0 at pin 17 only; $= 1000$ produces 0 at pin 9 only; $= 0111$ produces 0 at pin 8 only; $= 0110$ produces 0 at pin 7 only; and so on. What is important to remember is that $\begin{pmatrix} 323 \\ B_2 \end{pmatrix}$ causes B_2 to appear on the address bus and $\overline{\text{out}}$ to be generated. If we take $\overline{\text{Out}} = \underline{\Box}$ from the SK-10 socket and wire it to pin 19 (G_2), then, since after the $\begin{pmatrix} 323 \\ 007 \end{pmatrix}$ instruction *007 is temporarily placed on the address BUS* $(A_3 A_2 A_1 A_0 = 0111)$ *and* $\overline{\text{Out}} = \underline{\Box}$ is generated for G_2, a Lo is temporarily produced at pin 8. Thus the output at pin 8, and *only* at pin 8 (channel 7), will do the following:

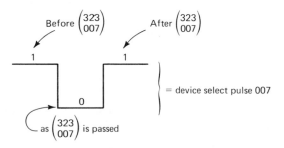

Likewise, *only* after $\begin{pmatrix} 323 \\ 006 \end{pmatrix}$ is passed in the program, $(A_3 A_2 A_1 A_0 = 0110$ and $G_2=0$ due to $\overline{\text{Out}} = \underline{\Box}$ generated), will pin 7 (channel 6) go to 0. See diagram below.

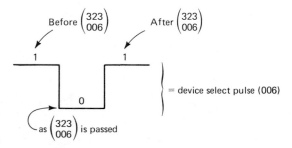

No other pin will be 0 at that time.

Clearly if pin 8 is inverted and then tied to R_{01} of device 007 (one of the 7490 counters) and if pin 7 is inverted and then tied to

R_{01} of device 006 (the other counter), each will be cleared at different times: Clearing for device 007 will occur *only* after $\begin{pmatrix} 323 \\ 007 \end{pmatrix}$ is passed in the program and clearing for device 006 will occur *only* after $\begin{pmatrix} 323 \\ 006 \end{pmatrix}$ is passed in the program N seconds later.

Note carefully that this method is not *absolute* device selecting. If we had many devices and one of them had to be labeled as device number $B_2 = 107$ or 207 or 307 or 027, etc. then in *each* of these cases $A_3 A_2 A_1 A_0 = 0111$ so that *those* devices, as well as device 007, would be controlled at the same time after $\begin{pmatrix} 323 \\ B_2 \end{pmatrix}$ was passed in the program—contrary to our desire to have *only* device 007 controlled at that time. This will be remedied by *absolute* device selecting covered in Experiment 5-2(f) and section 5-2(C) later on. Thus, one hexa decoder 74154 allows *16* different device selects for devices 000 to 017 i.e., $\begin{pmatrix} 323 \\ B_2 \end{pmatrix}$, B_2 = 000 to 017 , corresponding to $A_3 A_2 A_1 A_0$ from 0000 to 1111.

The interfacing must proceed as shown in Fig. 47.

Wire it up and run the program. Observe the displays. Vary the time byte B_2 at 101L. The instruction $\begin{pmatrix} 323 \\ 007 \end{pmatrix}$ will clear device (007) and *only* device (007). An N-second time delay ensues during which device 007 *and* device (006) count together. Then instruction $\begin{pmatrix} 323 \\ 006 \end{pmatrix}$ is encountered and it clears device (006) and *only* device (006), after which the N-second time delay is again entered and both counters count. $\begin{pmatrix} 323 \\ 007 \end{pmatrix}$ appears again after we get out of this time delay and so device (007) is again cleared, and so on. The key to the problem was the generation of device select pulses at, in this case, pins 7 and 8 of the 74154, at *different times*, and then having each device select pulse routed to separate device enables or disables to control each one independently of the other.

We can device select 256 different devices by means of instructions $\begin{pmatrix} 323 \\ 000 \end{pmatrix}$ for device 0 up to $\begin{pmatrix} 323 \\ 377 \end{pmatrix}$ for device number 255. The Hexa decoder shown can do up to 16 of them by itself (already a good number). Cascading methods and other approaches to device selecting (Refs. 19, 20) can readily yield the 256 different device select pulses needed when many devices are involved.

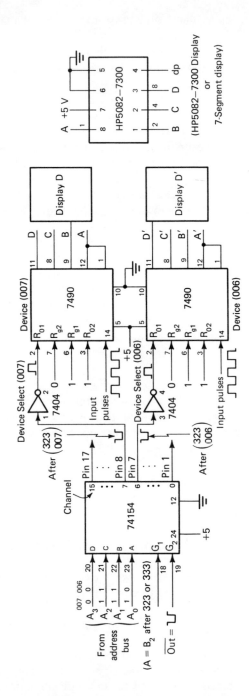

Figure 47. Expt. 5-2(b) with device selects.

This interfacing experiment and its solution should make it apparent that

(a) device select pulses are necessary when more than one external device is involved, unlike Experiment 5-2(a)i, ii, and iii where $\overline{out}$ was sufficient for one device;

(b) the device select pulses can be put to any use in *device control*: clear a counter, or a register or a latch, or make a device accept data (7475 latch for example—more on that later), or turn a motor on or off (see next experiment) or turn traffic lights on or off, or detristate an I/O holding input data, etc.;

(c) the control of the device resides in the program which can readily be changed to meet changing conditions; hardware interfacing and device select logic are equally important in order for the microcomputer to communicate with the device;

(d) a single 74154 hexadecimal decoder causes no confusion in device control so long as no more than 16 devices are to be selected (from $B_2 = 000$ to 017 with $A_3 A_2 A_1 A_0 = 0000$ to 1111). For more than 16 devices, selection can be extended by, for example, using another hexadecimal decoder in cascade—256 device selects possible.

Experiment 5-2(c)   It is desired to turn a machine or device on for a certain time, then off for another period of time. Software control of two external devices.

We can just as well be talking about a motor, a relay, a measuring instrument, a test set, or any of a number of devices. The principle is the same: device selecting is necessary. We may be talking about *one* actual device such as a motor, but the fact that we want it *on* and then *off* puts it in the class of a device select problem. (Here on/off corresponds to two external devices even though one physical device is being controlled. This will be evident in Fig. 48.)

The circuit is shown in Fig. 48, the program then presented, and the problem discussed.

The TTL level at Q can be boosted by a buffer in order to operate a relay (one of the optically isolated solid state relay type) so as to control the ac power required to turn a machine or other

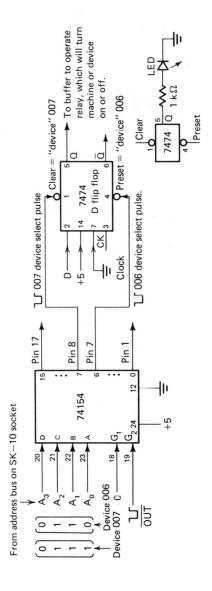

Figure 48. On/Off time control of a machine (Expt. 5-2(c)).

heavy duty device on or off. If you do not have these items you can still do the experiment and content yourself with observing the on period ($Q=1$) and the off period ($Q=0$) with an LED or probe at pin 5 of the 7474. Remember that the part of the truth table for the 7474 (see Chap. 1, Section 1-2) which pertains here is

Preset	Clear	Clock	D	Q
0	1	X	X	1
1	0	X	X	0
1	1	⌁	X	Q_0

Q_0 = latched to last value.

The two "devices" here are pins 1 (clear) and 4 (preset) on the 7474 chip. The preset sets $Q=1$ when device select ⊔ 006 from pin 7 of the Hexa arrives at pin 4 of the 7474. This will turn the machine or device on. The clear will set $Q=0$ and turn the machine or device off when device select ⊔ 007 from pin 8 of the Hexa arrives at pin 1 of the 7474.

000	$\left(\begin{array}{c}323\\006\end{array}\right)$*	generates pulse that turns machine on
001		
002	$\left(\begin{array}{c}006\\B_2\end{array}\right)=$	MVI B, B_2
003		"Machine on" time byte
004	$\left(\begin{array}{c}315\\100\\003\end{array}\right)$	Call (T.D. "Machine on") →
005		
006		
007	$\left(\begin{array}{c}323\\007\end{array}\right)$**	generates pulse that turns machine off ← Ret
010		
011	$\left(\begin{array}{c}006\\B_2'\end{array}\right)$	"Machine off" time byte
012		
013	$\left(\begin{array}{c}315\\100\\003\end{array}\right)$	Call (T.D. "Machine off") →
014		
015		
016	$\left(\begin{array}{c}303\\000\\003\end{array}\right)$	← Ret.
017		
020		

*$\overline{\text{Out}}$ = ⊔ is generated for pin 19 of 74154, 006 goes on address bus to Hexa input ($A_3 A_2 A_1 A_0 = 0110$), device select pulse ⊔ from 74154 at pin 7 is generated to "Preset" (pin 4 of 7474—device select 006) turning machine on.

**$\overline{\text{out}}$ = ⊔ is generated for pin 19 of 74154, 007 goes on address bus to Hexa input ($A_3 A_2 A_1 A_0 = 0111$), device select pulse ⊔ from 74154 at pin 8 is generated to "Clear" (pin 1 of 7474—device select 007) turning machine off.

Time Delay (See Experiment 5-2(a)i) (Machine on or off).

100	⎛021⎞	
101	⎜046⎟	LXI D/E
102	⎝015⎠	
103	033	DCX D/E
104	172	Mov A,D
105	263	OR A,E
106	⎛302⎞	
107	⎜103⎟	JNZ
110	⎝003⎠	
111	005	DCR B
112	⎛302⎞	
113	⎜100⎟	JNZ
114	⎝003⎠	
115	311	Ret

Start by taking $B_2 = 062$ and $B_2' = 024$. Then vary them. (See Table 3-1). Use a probe or LED with $1K\Omega$ resistor to observe pin 5 of the 7474. If in Fig. 48 (inset) you branch from $\overline{Q}$ and then into another resistor and LED, you will realize a programmable blinking light system.[*] Again, we take our device numbers 006,007 distinct from the internal "output" devices 001,000,002 on the MMD-1. This, of course, is not necessary. If you are willing to have port 001, 000, or 002 on the MMD-1 exhibit (possibly irrelevant) accumulator data then you could certainly use device numbers 000, 001, for example, instead of 006, 007. In that case you would use pins 1 and 2 of the 74154.

Simultaneous turning on of two instruments, but turn-off at different times, might be necessary. This might be the case in photoconductivity—fluorescence experiments where the flashing on of a lamp must occur simultaneously with a multichannel analyzer going on. This can be realized with two 7474 flip flops in which the $\left(\dfrac{323}{006}\right)$ device select is applied to Presets of both flip flops while the $\left(\dfrac{323}{007}\right)$ device select is applied to the Clear of one flip flop and a $\left(\dfrac{323}{010}\right)$ device select (after another time delay Call is introduced into the program) is applied to the other flip flop.[**]

---

[*]Suggested by Messrs. Hietbrink and Martin (IBM).
[**]Suggested by Dr. Steve Garoff of Exxon Research and Engineering.

5-2(B) Outputting Data from a Microcomputer to an I/O Device

You are urged to re-read carefully the exact description of the $\begin{pmatrix} 323 \\ B_2 \end{pmatrix}$ = output (A) instruction at the beginning of section 2 of this chapter. In this instruction three ingredients are evident: (A) is put on the data bus for transmission to device number B_2. B_2 appears on the Lo part of the address bus; and the MMD-1 microcomputer produces an $\overline{out}$ = ⊔̄ signal (½ μs wide). In the experiments in section 5-2(A), *control* through device selecting was the main aim and *two* of the above ingredients were employed to generate device selects (the use of $\overline{Out}$, and in the case of more than one device, the use of B_2 on the address bus). In this section we are still interested in one of several devices, but we now wish to output *data* to the device, so that the first ingredient [(A) → device B_2] is utilized as well as the other two. (A) might represent 8 bits of data that will control 8 different devices (for example, one to go on, another to go off, etc.). Or the output device might be a bank of 8 LED's to display the state (A) of the microcomputer (as is the case with ports 0, 1, 2 of the MMD-1 itself). Or (A) is to feed another computer needing this information, etc. (see also Fig. 43).

Experiment 5-2(d)   Output the Accumulator Byte to a Single Device (8 LED's or other Display). Simple Calculator. Code Conversion. Display of Look-up Table Data. (Device Select not needed.)

000	$\begin{pmatrix} 076 \\ 252 \end{pmatrix}$	
001		
002	$\begin{pmatrix} 323 \\ 001 \end{pmatrix}$	(A) goes to data bus on way to device 001 (latches)
003		and $\overline{out}$ = ⊔̄ is generated to latch ⟨A⟩.
004	166	

(Just for your information, 252 is a byte much used in traffic control experiments in the "blinking" part of the "nighttime routine." It is used with an RCL = 007 instruction to constantly rotate (A) left; i.e., 10101010.)

We wish to output (A)=252 *via the data bus* to device 004, which is composed of two 7475 latches. *They are used to latch $\langle A \rangle$ from the data bus* to a group of 8 LED's. See Fig. 49. This means we must wire up $D_7 D_6 \ldots D_0$ (the data bus bits) available at the SK-10 bus socket on the MMD-1 to the correct inputs of the two 7475 latches (each can handle only 4 bits) and then wire up the 7475 outputs to the 8 LED's or other display. The reader is referred to section 1-2 of Chap. 1 to review the properties of the important 7475 IC latch. They are repeated here: it contains 4 flip flops, each comprised of one D input, a Q (and $\overline{Q}$) output, and a G input Enable (Disable)—4 bits total. The truth table is

D	G	Q
0	1	0
1	1	1
X	0	Q_0

Q_0 = last value of Q, before G became 0. Clearly G= ⎍ is needed to latch the last value Q=D that occurred while G was 1. The interfacing is shown in Fig. 49.

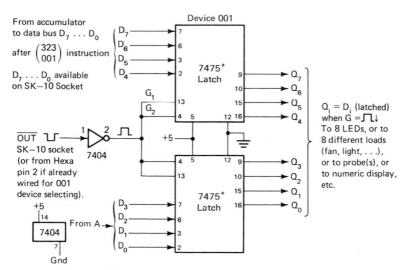

Figure 49. Expt. 5-2(d): $\langle A \rangle$ to Port 1. *The IC's can also be either 74174's or 74175's.

If you are using a numeric display to observe the output *octally*, don't forget to make the connections as follows:

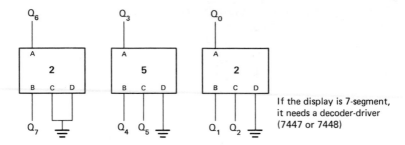

If the display is 7-segment, it needs a decoder-driver (7447 or 7448)

$\overline{\overline{Out}}$ is generated by inverting $\overline{out}$ from the SK-10 socket through a 7404 IC. You can use device select 001 from the HEXA if convenient, otherwise $\overline{out}$ is all that is necessary.

Wire up and run the program. You should see 252 at the LED's or Display or Probe. If you now disconnect $\overline{out}$ from G on the 7475's, you will not see 252 at the display when you rerun the program, and surely without the 7475's the LED's will not yield 252. Latching is necessary and this requires the correct enable pulse $\overline{out}$ = $\sqcap$ on G of the 7475's *at the same time that (A) is placed on the data bus*, so that Q_i will latch at the value D_i. These two occurrences, of course, take place *just after* $\begin{pmatrix} 323 \\ 001 \end{pmatrix}$ *is passed in the program.* If there were no 7475's and we tried to tie the LED's *directly* to the data bus, we would see nothing (or a bit of everything) on the LED's as the program is run. This would happen because during the run each fetch from memory produces *another* data byte on the data bus and their rapid succession (in matters of μs) would not permit the LED's to follow the changing bytes, much less hold on to the byte (A) which appears for a fleeting moment on the data bus just after $\begin{pmatrix} 323 \\ 001 \end{pmatrix}$ is passed. The 7475's, enabled by $\overline{out}$ at the time that (A) is on the data bus, and then disabled *immediately*, latch (A) to the display "permanently." No $\overline{out}$ is being generated by any *other* instructions as they are fetched from memory on to the data bus and executed, and hence the 7475's do not latch any of those instruction bytes.

It is suggested that you try different bytes at 001 and explore the results on the display, LED's, or Probe. Also go back to the multiplication (9 × 5) example in Experiment 3-2(f), program it using $\begin{pmatrix} 323 \\ 000 \end{pmatrix}$ for outputting , and you should see 00101101 = $(45)_{10}$ at port 0 *on the MMD-1 and* octal $(055)_8$ $(=(45)_{10})$ *on your octal display* (or simply 00101101 on your LED's or Probe).

If you add a decimal adjust instruction 047 in the right place in the multiplication program and rewire, you should see the decimal (BCD) number 45. Try it. Thus a calculator:*

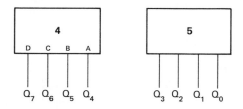

Then multiply, for example, $4 \times 9 = 36$ or $5 \times 10 = 50$. In the latter case place 004 at 001 and 020 (10_{10} = BCD) at 003 and 005 with 047 at 006. You should see 0101000 = BCD 50 at port 0.

It is also suggested that you replace 166 at 004 by $\begin{pmatrix} 303 \\ 001 \\ 003 \end{pmatrix}$ and write 227 at 000 and 074 at 001. *Single step this program* and notice how the LED's or other display latch *new* accumulator data each time after $\begin{pmatrix} 323 \\ 001 \end{pmatrix}$ is passed (when G = ⊓). If you take the very pulse you use to single step and apply it to G, the LED's or display should assume the same values as are on the data bus monitor at each step—the instruction bytes. Thus, you have constructed *another* single step data bus monitor (the 7475's and display or LED's).

Another interesting aspect to this experiment would involve the application to fetching and displaying data from look-up tables stored in memory, or to code conversion. Consider the following program (see KEX "KBRD" subroutine at 000, 315 in Appendix C, where pressing a key "0," "1," . . . "7" etc. has the effect of placing KEX key codes 000, 001, . . . 007 etc. into the accumulator before returning to the main program—pressing H, L, G, . . . C stores 010, 011, 012, . . . 017 in A; we wish to *change* these codes by means of a look-up table):

---

*Construct a program to add, for example, $39_{BCD}=(071)_8$ and $18_{BCD}=(030)_8$ using a NOP and then a DAA just after $\begin{pmatrix} \text{ADI} \\ \text{B}_2 \end{pmatrix} = \begin{pmatrix} 306 \\ 030 \end{pmatrix}$. Observe port 0 on the MMD-1 and your BCD display (and octal display if still connected) in each case. You should observe (51) BCD with a NOP and (57) BCD with the DAA. Compare with your decimal adjust arithmetic on paper (Ch. 3).

000	/315\	
001	(315)	Call "KBRD." Waits. Press Key: places key code in A.
002	\000/	
003	/046\	
004	\003/	MVI, H
005	/306\	
006	\100/	ADI to A: 100 + KEX key code and store in A.
007	157	Mov L, A
010	176	Mov A, M (pointed to by H, L) i.e., fetches from look-up table.
011	/323\	Port 0 or other display shows value stored in look-up
012	\000/	table at address H, L i.e., our *new* key code.
013	/303\	
014	(000)	JMP.
015	\003/	

Look-up Table For Code Conversion (arbitrary):

100	200	Our code for Key "0"—different from KEX codes just for illustration.
101	201	Key "1"
102	202	Key "2"
103	203	Key "3"
104	204	Key "4"
105	205	Key "5"
106	206	Key "6"
107	207	Key "7"
110	210	Key "H"
111	211	Key "L"
112	212	Key "G"
113	213	Key "S"
114	214	-----
115	215	Key "A"
116	216	Key "B"
117	217	Key "C"

Running the program and pressing the various keys will show how the KEX key codes have been *converted* to other key codes fetched from a stored look-up table. Obviously any other code representation of the keys is possible—just store the desired codes starting at 100. Your interfaced display, as well as the LED's on the MMD-1 at port 0, will show these codes at the time the various keys are pressed. Obviously the look-up table could contain data or information other than key codes. In that case the keys are used to retrieve various kinds of stored information (telephone directory) for display. (Note: another way to interface would be to tap $D_7 \ldots D_0$ from stand-off terminals available at port 0 and wire them to three 7-segment/7447 decoder driven or three HP 5082-7300 matrix displays to get octal read-out. In that case 7475's are not needed as in Fig. 49 because port 0 has its own 7475's and the $\begin{pmatrix} 323 \\ 000 \end{pmatrix}$ device select 000 = $\sqcap$ from the 7442/7402 decoder combination (Fig. 12) is applied to those 7475's enables—pins 4 and 13).

Experiment 5-2(e) Outputting Different Accumulator Data to Two Different Devices (Device Selects Needed). Memory Address-Data Read-out.

This is basically the same experiment as the previous one but since we are interested in outputting *different* data to two *different* devices, device select pulses are required (see Fig. 50).

000	$\begin{pmatrix} 076 \end{pmatrix}$	
001	$\begin{pmatrix} 111 \end{pmatrix}$ = (A)	
002	$\begin{pmatrix} 323 \end{pmatrix}$	$\overline{out}$ and 004 on address bus cause hexa to generate
003	$\begin{pmatrix} 004 \end{pmatrix}$	device *select* pulse 004 $\sqcup$* which enables 7475's to latch (A) from the data bus

004	$\begin{pmatrix} 076 \end{pmatrix}$	
005	$\begin{pmatrix} 222 \end{pmatrix}$ = (A)'	
006	$\begin{pmatrix} 323 \end{pmatrix}$	$\overline{out}$ and 005 on address bus cause hexa to generate
007	$\begin{pmatrix} 005 \end{pmatrix}$	device select pulse 005 $\sqcup$* which enables the other 7475's to latch (A)' from data bus
010	166	

The device selects (when inverted) clearly perform the *separate* enables at G and G', thus allowing 111 to be seen at the LED's comprising device 004 (the Lower 7475's) and 222 to be seen at the LED's comprising device 005 (the upper 7475's).

If we merely inverted $\overline{out}$ from the SK-10 socket and then placed $\overline{out}$ directly on G and G' of *each* 7475 pair as in the pre-

---

*Inverted device selects enable the 7475's.

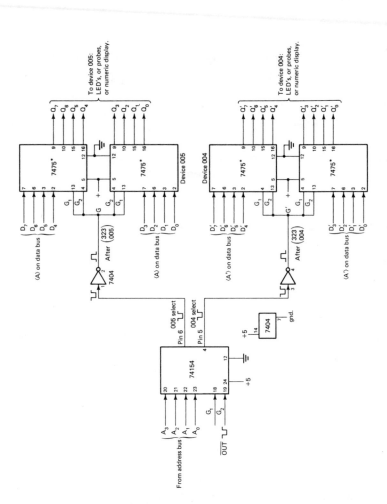

Figure 50. Data output to different devices (Expt. 5-2(e)). (*IC's 74175 or 74174 can be used as latches).

ceding experiment then $\begin{pmatrix} 323 \\ 004 \end{pmatrix}$ would put (A)=*111* on *both* pairs of 7475's and $\begin{pmatrix} 323 \\ 005 \end{pmatrix}$ would put (A)'=*222* on *both* pairs of 7475's a moment later and we would see *333* as a sort of "steady state" on *both* sets of LED's instead of the desired 111 on one set and 222 on the other. Try it. Hence the need for the device selecting shown.

Again, it is instructive to replace 166 at 010 by $\begin{pmatrix} 303 \\ 001 \\ 003 \end{pmatrix}$; 076 at 000 by 227; 111 at 001 by 074; 076 at 004 by 000 (NOP); 222 at 005 by 074; and then single step through the program. The respective sets of LED's will take on their appropriate values only after the $\begin{pmatrix} 323 \\ 004 \end{pmatrix}$ and $\begin{pmatrix} 323 \\ 005 \end{pmatrix}$ instructions when *new* accumulator data is latched by the 7475's. Single stepping here allows you to really see how (A) from a microcomputer gets to the correct output devices if the proper device select pulses are used on the enables of the latches comprising the respective output devices.

Using three 7-segment displays with decoder drivers as in Experiment 5-2(d), each connected appropriately to the stand-off terminals with their own 7475 latches at port 0 of the MMD-1 ($D_7, D_6 \rightarrow$ B, A; $D_5, D_4, D_3 \rightarrow$ C, B, A; $D_2, D_1, D_0 \rightarrow$ CBA, all D's are 0 and highest C is 0), and three other such displays driven by $D_7 \ldots D_0$ latched from the data bus by a pair of 7475's (as in Fig. 49, with device select $002 = \sqcap$ from pin 4 of IC 19 (Fig. 12) driving the 7475 enables (pins 4, 13)), we should see octal readout of address and data on the displays as we "S" through memory (either ROM or RAM). Try it. (*Consult addresses 105, 106, 107, and 163 through 167 in KEX to understand this and the need for latching of $D_7 \ldots D_0$ as well as the need for device select 002.*) It certainly makes program debugging much easier with octal rather than binary read-outs of address and instruction.

5-2(C) Absolute Device Selecting (Device Code Pulses vs. Absolute Device Select Pulses)

On top of the MMD-1 (see Fig. 12, Chap. 2 and Appendix A), you will notice IC 7442 (A18), a 4-line to 10-line decoder.

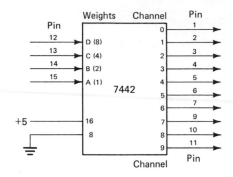

Channels 3, 4, 5, 6, and 7 are available as terminals on the MMD-1 board next to the chip itself. As we shall see, these pins (called device codes 003, 004, 005, 006, 007) can be used with OR gates to generate device select pulses more simply than the 74154 Hexa decoder that has been employed throughout the interfacing experiments thus far—less wiring will be required. Further, these generated device selects will be absolute device selects in that device 107, for example, will not conflict or be confused with device 007. In this way 5 absolute device select pulses will be available as compared to the 16 non-absolute device selects that can be made available from the 74154 Hexa.

The truth table for the 7442 follows (see Ref. 10).

	BCD In				Decimal Out (channel)									
DEC	D	C	B	A	0	1	2	3	4	5	6	7	8	9
0	0	0	0	0	0	1	1	1	1	1	1	1	1	1
1	0	0	0	1	1	0	1	1	1	1	1	1	1	1
2	0	0	1	0	1	1	0	1	1	1	1	1	1	1
3	0	0	1	1	1	1	1	0	1	1	1	1	1	1
4	0	1	0	0	1	1	1	1	0	1	1	1	1	1
5	0	1	0	1	1	1	1	1	1	0	1	1	1	1
6	0	1	1	0	1	1	1	1	1	1	0	1	1	1
7	0	1	1	1	1	1	1	1	1	1	1	0	1	1
8	1	0	0	0	1	1	1	1	1	1	1	1	0	1
9	1	0	0	1	1	1	1	1	1	1	1	1	1	0
>9	>1	0	0	1	1	1	1	1	1	1	1	1	1	1

Invalid → (rows 8, 9, >9)

It is easily made into a 3-line to 8-line decoder. Merely set D=0 and you see how the truth table is confined to the region inside the heavy lines—CBA going from 000 to 111.

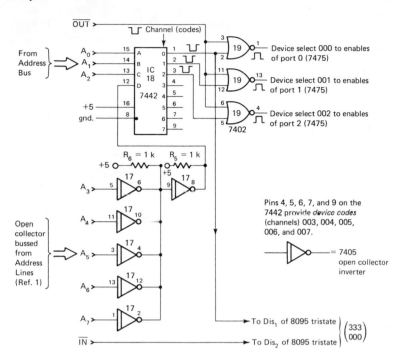

Figure 51. Absolute *Device Selects* 000, 001, 002 at 7402 and *Device Codes* 000, 001, 002, 003, 004, 005, 006, 007 available at 7442 decoder on MMD-1. Obtained by making 7442 a 3 line to 8 line decoder (holding D = 0). D = 1 when *any* of $A_7 \ldots A_3 = 1$. D = 0 only when *all* of $A_7 \ldots A_3 = 0$. See discussion below. (Courtesy E & L Instruments Inc: MMD-1 Operating Manual p. 33—see also Fig. 12).

Note that A_3, A_4, A_5, A_6, A_7 are open collector bussed so that for D to be 0 to effect a 3-line to 8-line decoder, *only* device numbers 003, 004, 005, 006, 007 (aside from 000, 001, and 002) can be used, in which cases $A_3 = A_4 = A_5 = A_6 = A_7 = 0$ and hence D=0. The NOR gates shown are A19 (IC7402) on the top of the MMD-1 board next to the 7442. The outputs of channels 0, 1, and 2 are wired up to them, together with $\overline{\text{Out}}$. Thus, instructions $\begin{pmatrix} 323 \\ 000 \end{pmatrix}$, or $\begin{pmatrix} 323 \\ 001 \end{pmatrix}$, or $\begin{pmatrix} 323 \\ 002 \end{pmatrix}$ which appear constantly in the KEX program as it interacts with pressing of keys will cause

1) bytes 000 or 001 or 002 to temporarily appear on the address bus for which $A_2 A_1 A_0 = 000, 001, 010$ in these cases.

2) The appearance of ⊔ *device codes* at channels 0, 1, or 2, as the case may be (see 7442 truth table for CBA = $A_2 A_1 A_0 = 000, 001, 010$).

3) And finally the generation of $\overline{out}$ = ⊔ for each case.

When $\overline{out}$ and device codes ⊔ at either channels 0, 1, or 2 are NORed together, we get the respective *positive device select* pulses ⌐ shown (000, 001, 002). These go to the enables (G) (pins 4/13) of the respective 7475's at each port 0, 1, or 2 of the MMD-1 which allows data from the data bus to the 7475's to be latched and exhibited at the respective LED's (see Fig. 12, Chap. 2). This is how the KEX bootstrap program (Appendix C) together with the interfacing shown in Fig. 51 generates the Hi address at port 1, the Lo address at port 0, and data at port 2 (see discussion in Chap. 2 and above). In this way internal device selects for ports 0, 1, 2 of the MMD-1 are provided.

What concerns us most here are channels 3, 4, 5, 6, and 7 (pins 4, 5, 6, 7, and 9) of the 7442 in Fig. 51. These are the *device codes* which will be converted into *negative* absolute *device select pulses.* If we employ device numbers 003, 004, 005, 006, or 007 with a 323 or 333 output or input instruction, *then these address bytes appear temporarily on the address bus just after a* $\left(\begin{smallmatrix}333\\B_2\end{smallmatrix}\right)$ *or* $\left(\begin{smallmatrix}323\\B_2\end{smallmatrix}\right)$ *operation and* $A_2 A_1 A_0$ *equals 011, 100, 101, 110, or 111,* respectively. The 7442 truth table shows that in these cases channel 3= ⊔, or channel 4= ⊔, or channel 5= ⊔, or channel 6= ⊔, or channel 7= ⊔ ($A_2 A_1 A_0$ =CBA). These ⊔ pulses at the various channels of the 7442 are *device codes* (not *selects*). A device *select* pulse 003, or 004, or 005, or 006, or 007 is now easily logically constructed. Suppose we wish to create the negative device select pulse 004=⊔. Proceed as follows:

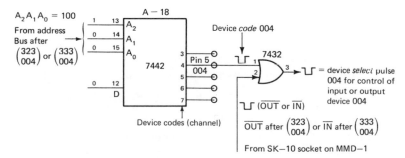

Figure 52. Generation of device select pulse from device code.

In the same way the other device select pulses 003, 005, 006, or 007 can be generated.

The question may be asked: Why can't we simply use channel 4 (in Fig. 52) *alone* as our device select pulse without having to wire up the OR gate with $\overline{out}$ or $\overline{in}$? The answer is that if we did so and our program were of the following nature,

$$
\begin{array}{cc}
000 & \text{---} \\
001 & \left(\begin{array}{c} 323 \\ 004 \end{array} \right) \\
002 & \\
003 & \text{---} \\
004 & \text{---} \\
005 & \text{---} \\
. & . \\
. & . \\
. & . \\
\end{array}
$$

then device 004 (a counter, a latch, or whatever) would be activated twice: once after $\left(\begin{array}{c} 323 \\ 004 \end{array} \right)$ is passed in the program run, and *again* when *address* 004 is passed in the program run. In *each* case, 004 would appear on the address bus $(A_2 A_1 A_0 = 100)$. This would produce ⊔ at pin 5 (channel 4) of the 7442. Device 004 would then be activated at a time when we didn't want it activated and the control process would be faulty. This is avoided by ORing device *code* 004= ⊔ with $\overline{out}$ or $\overline{in}$, in which case device *select* 004= ⊔ appears *uniquely* after $\left(\begin{array}{c} 323 \\ 004 \end{array} \right)$ or $\left(\begin{array}{c} 333 \\ 004 \end{array} \right)$ is passed in the program.

It is suggested that any of the previous experiments requiring device selects (2 or more devices present) be redone using the device codes 003 to 007 available on the MMD-1 face together with 7432 OR gates. For example, try the machine on-off experiment [Experiment 5-2(c)], or the experiment outputting different accumulator data to two different devices [Experiment 5-2(e)] — replacing the Hexa decoder device selector with the 7442 device codes available on the MMD-1. In the latter experiment use device codes 004 and 005 at the 7442 on the MMD-1 face and NOR them with $\overline{out}$ to produce device select pulses 004 and 005 for G' of one set of 7475's and G for the other set, respectively. In the former experiment use device codes 006 and 007 to produce the device select pulses and wire them to preset and clear of the 7474 flip flop, respectively.

It must be stressed that this is absolute device selecting in the following sense: In the case of the Hexa 74154 decoder, $\left(\dfrac{323}{B_2}\right)$ or $\left(\dfrac{333}{B_2}\right)$ with $B_2 = 003$ would produce a device select pulse at channel 3 of the Hexa but so would $B_2 = 103, 203, 023,$ Or 303, etc. at the *same* channel, for in *each* of these cases $A_3 A_2 A_1 A_0$ into the 74154 would equal 0011. Whereas in the case of the 7442 3−8-line decoder wired as shown in Fig. 51, $B_2 = 103$ or 203 or 023 etc. would produce $D = 1$ at pin 12 of the 7442. In each of these cases one (or more in other cases) of the quantities $A_7 \ldots A_3$ would be 1 and the open collector bussing of these quantities together, as shown in Fig. 51, would produce $D = 1$. This makes the 7442 a 4−10-line decoder for which the truth tables shows that *no* device select code ⊔ is generated (i.e., $DCBA = 1011 = 11_{10}$ in this case). Similarly, a device number 004 would not conflict with device number 104 or 204 because in the former case $A_7 \ldots A_3 = 0$, $D = 0$ and a device select is generated at channel 4. In the latter two cases one of $A_7 \ldots A_3 = 1$, so that $D = 1$ and *no* device select code is generated from the 7442 for $DCBA = 1100$ (see truth table). Even $DCBA = 1000$ cannot generate a device code because there is no channel 8 in Fig. 51.

Absolute device selecting is the preferred method used to avoid confusion among "competing" devices, *including the keyboard and encoder which is device 000 on the MMD-1* for *all* input instructions of the form $\left(\dfrac{333}{000}\right)$ occurring in the KEX bootstrap program. (See 000, 315 in KEX.) The latter occurs whenever we press a key to send data or instructions via data bus to CPU and then to memory (programming in), or to key in addresses via the data bus to CPU registers and from registers to the address bus (Mov M̂, C). The experiments on *inputting* to the microcomputer will show the need for *absolute* device selects.

Experiment 5-2(f)   Sequential Turning Two Machines On and Off for Definite Time Periods. Programming and Interfacing Using 4 Absolute Device Selects. [See Experiment 3-3(e)] (A Power Control Problem).

We have done this experiment in purely software fashion using ports 0 and 1 of the MMD-1 [see Experiment 3-3(e)]. We now wish to modify and *interface* that program to several *outside* ports; i.e., to machines or motors existing outside the MMD-1. We shall do so using the "clears" and "presets" available on the 7474 D flip flop, and shall absolute device select the "clears" and the "presets" using the device codes available on the MMD-1 together with $\overline{out}$ and the 7432 OR gate. We are here concerned with two "motors" Q_A and Q_B—hence 4 device selects: a clear and preset on each.

The interfacing is simple [recall the 7474 IC contains two flip flops, each with a clear and preset (see Appendix A)].

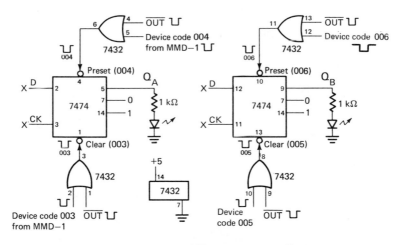

Figure 53. Interfacing for Expt. 5-2(f). Sequential ON/OFF. Use of absolute device selects.

Note that the experiment could just as well be performed using the 74154 Hexadecimal Decoder in which we would use pins 7, 6, 5, and 4 for device selects 006, 005, 004, and 003 going to pins 10, 13, 4, and 1, respectively, of the 7474. [In the program that follows see Table 3-1 and Time Delay in Experiment 3-2(d); see also Experiment 3-3(e).]

000	$\left(\begin{array}{c} 323 \\ 003 \end{array} \right)$	device select 003 turns motor A off
001		
002	$\left(\begin{array}{c} 323 \\ 005 \end{array} \right)$	device select 005 turns motor B off
003		
004	$\left(\begin{array}{c} 006 \\ 062 \end{array} \right)$	Q_A and Q_B stay *off* 5 seconds
005		
006	$\left(\begin{array}{c} 315 \\ 100 \\ 003 \end{array} \right)$	Call →
007		
010		
011	$\left(\begin{array}{c} 323 \\ 004 \end{array} \right)$	device select 004 turns Q_A on ← Ret ←
012		
013	$\left(\begin{array}{c} 006 \\ 012 \end{array} \right)$	Time Byte for 1 second
014		
015	$\left(\begin{array}{c} 315 \\ 100 \\ 003 \end{array} \right)$	Call →
016		
017		
020	$\left(\begin{array}{c} 323 \\ 006 \end{array} \right)$	device select 006 turns Q_B on 1 second later ← Ret
021		
022	$\left(\begin{array}{c} 006 \\ 062 \end{array} \right)$	Q_A and Q_B stay *on* 5 seconds
023		
024	$\left(\begin{array}{c} 315 \\ 100 \\ 003 \end{array} \right)$	Call →
025		
026		
027	$\left(\begin{array}{c} 323 \\ 003 \end{array} \right)$	device select 003 turns Q_A off ← Ret
030		
031	$\left(\begin{array}{c} 006 \\ 012 \end{array} \right)$	Time Byte for 1 second
032		
033	$\left(\begin{array}{c} 315 \\ 100 \\ 003 \end{array} \right)$	Call →
034		
035		
036	$\left(\begin{array}{c} 323 \\ 005 \end{array} \right)$	device select 005 turns Q_B off 1 second later ← Ret ←
037		

040	⎛ 303 ⎞	
041	⎜ 004 ⎟	JMP
042	⎝ 003 ⎠	

Time Delay (Experiment 3-2(d), Table 3-1)

100	⎛ 021 ⎞	LXI
101	⎜ 046 ⎟	D, E
102	⎝ 015 ⎠	Time Bytes
103	033	
104	172	
105	263	
106	⎛ 302 ⎞	
107	⎜ 103 ⎟	JNZ
110	⎝ 003 ⎠	
111	005	
112	⎛ 302 ⎞	
113	⎜ 100 ⎟	JNZ
114	⎝ 003 ⎠	
115	311	Ret.

Run the experiment with various sequential times at 014 and 032 and various on/off times at 023, 005. See Table 3-1.

Note that the time delay needs no Push or Pop instructions because in this purely control experiment neither the D/E nor accumulator registers are being used in the main program.

5-2(D)   Inputting Data From an Input Device(s) Via Tristate Buffers to a Microcomputer

We are now concerned with inputting data from an input device to the microcomputer via its microprocessor. Examples are: an instrument's data measurement, or a sensor's findings (e.g., the number of cars at an intersection, or the size of a component being produced, etc.) , a keyboard code or message, each to be either stored in memory, or re-routed, or processed for control and decision making. This can be accomplished with the 8080 microprocessor only by sending the input device data to the accumulator of the microprocessor via the data bus (see Fig. 43). From there we can route it into memory for storage (experiments in Chap 3), or back out via the data bus to another output device(s) [see Experiments 5-2(d), 2 (e)] (one can see here the basis for data acquisition (logging) and read-out; this will be treated later in this chapter as a separate experiment); or a special program (subroutine) might treat this inputted data and make decisions to determine control over the input device based on the nature of this data. As was the case with outputting control signals or data, device select pulses will be necessary whenever there are two or more input devices involved. This time the keyboard on the MMD-1, which is device 000, has to be considered as another input device since it may be competing with the input device of interest to gain access to the accumulator via the same data bus. Hence, the need for tristating to keep all but the input device of interest off the data bus and the need for device selecting to de-tristate *that particular input device* at the time we wish it to input its data to the accumulator. It should be clear that a complication exists now that was not present with the experiments on the outputting of data to output devices. Namely, the input device is holding the data to be fed into the accumulator and it can only feed the data via the data bus. If its data were on the data bus at all times it would surely interfere with the instruction bytes which are being fetched from memory to CPU, also via the data bus, as the program is being run. This would confuse the accumulator and instruction register—all operations in the program which store data in, or transfer or fetch data to the IR or accumulator would fail as the accumulator tries to latch the input device's data in competition with these operations. The program could not be successfully executed (what is the result of a simultaneous 1 and 0 on a particular bit of the data bus?). The problem is solved by tristating in which the input device with its data is held in the Hi impedance state *off* the data bus (see Chap. 1, section 1-2 and Ref. 1, p. 40–42). A tristate buffer (e.g., the 8212 or 8095 or 8097) is used. The program "tells" it to come off its hi Z state at the desired moment and place its input data on the data bus for transmission to the accumulator. The program tells it to do so by means of a *unique* instruction already discussed at the beginning of section 5-2—the input $\left(\genfrac{}{}{0pt}{}{323}{B_2} \right)$ instruction. At the moment this instruction is fetched and executed, no other instruction or data byte is being fetched from memory to CPU via the data bus so the input device, *if de-tristated,* can send its data in to the accumulator as the third or "extra" byte without competition. Interfacing is required to accomplish this task. To understand how the input device is de-tristated at the moment we want its data to enter A, recall that the $\begin{pmatrix} 333 \\ B_2 \end{pmatrix}$ input instruction, when executed, does three things:*

1) It causes device number B_2 to input its data on to the data bus to the accumulator (the extra byte)—*if the device has been de-tristated.*

2) It causes B_2 to appear temporarily on the lo part of the address bus (the extra byte) (and on the hi part as well).

3) It causes an $\overline{\text{In}}$ pulse ⊔ to be generated from the CPU (see Fig. 11, Chap. 2 $\overline{\text{In}}$ appears on the SK-10 bus socket of the MMD-1).

It is precisely the $\overline{\text{In}}$ pulse which must be converted into a device select pulse either using the hexadecimal decoder method already discussed and employed or, preferably, the absolute decoding procedure using the device codes 003 to 007 available on the face of the MMD-1 [see Section 5-2(C)]; *the device select pulse is then used to de-tristate the 8095 tristate buffer which is holding the data to be input* (see Experiment 5-2(g) below). This is accomplished by applying the device select pulse to DIS_2 of the 8095 (see below)—the data is then sent in from the 8095 to the accumulator via the data bus at that moment. This will occur *only* after $\begin{pmatrix} 333 \\ B_2 \end{pmatrix}$ is encountered in the program at which time $\overline{\text{In}}$ is generated. These remarks are based on the truth table of the 8095 tristate buffer (Chap. 1, section 1-2 and Experiment 5-2(g) Figs. 54, 55 below].

Experiment 5-2(g)   Inputting Data From 4 Logic Switches Via an 8095 Tristate Buffer Into the Accumulator and Outputting Same to an Output Port**

Device selecting is needed because there are two devices: the keyboard (device 000) and the logic switches/buffer. We shall take our output port to be one of the three MMD-1 ports available 000, 001, 002.

---

*Intel 8080 Manual, Sept. 1975, pp. 4-14, 2-6, 5-14, *2-18.*
**See also experiments 5-3(c), (d) for further input control experiments.

$$\begin{matrix} 000 \\ 001 \end{matrix} \begin{pmatrix} 333 \\ 003 \end{pmatrix}$$ generates $\overline{\text{In}} = \text{⊔}$ and device code 003 for use in device selecting; ⟨device 003⟩ → A

$$\begin{matrix} 002 \\ 003 \end{matrix} \begin{pmatrix} 323 \\ 001 \end{pmatrix}$$ output (A) to Port 1

$$\begin{matrix} 004 \\ 005 \\ 006 \end{matrix} \begin{pmatrix} 303 \\ 000 \\ 003 \end{pmatrix}$$

The nature of the program indicates that we are using the microcomputer as a *controller* and *distributor* of data from one input device to another output device—to a display. Remember that KEX (Appendix C) puts out many $\overline{\text{In}}$ pulses, so that if we used $\overline{\text{In}}$ alone to de-tristate the 8095 buffer in the circuit shown below, it would send in its data to the accumulator all the time we were writing in our program. The conflict on the data bus between key byte and input device data byte would mess up the very program we are trying to write. Hence, device selecting is needed to pick out *one* of the two devices present here to input its data when we want it. Device select 000 is accomplished inside the MMD-1 for uniquely selecting the keyboard when we write in our program (with the aid of KEX), and device select 003 will, in this experiment, be reserved for the logic switches/buffer as the input device of interest to us. The simplest way to generate absolute device select 003 is to make use of the NOR gate in the 8095 itself. Noring device code 003 from pin 4 of the 7442 on the face of the MMD-1 with $\overline{\text{IN}}$ from SK-10 socket (both available after $\begin{pmatrix} 333 \\ 003 \end{pmatrix}$) will produce device *select* 003   at the control *output* of the 8095, allowing data to be inputted to the CPU and stored. (See Fig. 55.)

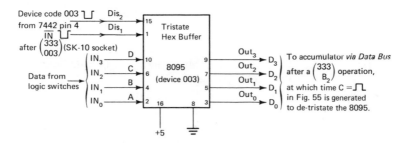

Figure 54. Expt. 5-2(g): Inputting data to microcomputer. Device *select* 003 is generated within the 8095 (see Nor gate in Fig. 55).

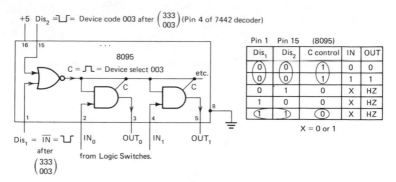

Figure 55. Pin connections and Truth Table for 8095 Tristate Buffer—Expt. 5-2(g).

The circled areas in the truth table for the 8095 show the conditions under which we want the 8095 to operate in this experiment. They indicate how the device *select* pulse 003 (C) ⌐⌐ after the 8095 NOR gate does indeed take us out of the hi Z tristate condition at which time $Out_i = In_i$ (from the switches) is placed directly on the data bus for transmission to the accumulator.

Take any suitable combination of IN_3, IN_2, IN_1, and IN_0 from the logic switches (DCBA=1111 or 0000, etc.) and note the equivalent output at port 1. Note that bits 7, 6, 5, and 4 are high as they were kept floating in this experiment. Input data is here comprised only of bits 3, 2, 1, 0. Changing the input data switches while the program is running should be immediately reflected at output port 1. The microprocessor has thus controlled the inputting of data from an input device, through a combination of programming and interfacing, as well as the outputting of this data to another device.

This is a good experiment to single step. Change the input data freely as you do so and observe port 1. You may want to redo the program to include the possibility of also storing into memory the data which you input and output. Try it and check the memory location after the run.

See experiments 5-3(c), (d) for further input control experiments.

Experiment 5-2(h) Successive Inputting of Data from Two Input Devices to CPU, then to Memory, then to Output Devices. Elements of Data Acquisition and Multiplexing of Input Devices

Here two device select pulses are required for de-tristating in turn each 8095 tristate buffer associated with each input device in order to get the different input data on to the *same* data bus, *one after the other.* In this experiment we use 4 logic switches as the input data waiting on one 8095 chip, and 4 other logic switches as the input data waiting on another 8095 chip. See the last experiment for the 8095 truth table. Again absolute device selects are needed and realized most simply from the device codes (say 003 and 004 in this experiment) available at IC18 (the 7442) on the MMD-1, together with $\overline{\text{IN}}$ from the SK-10 socket. Again use is made of the NOR gate in the 8095 (Fig. 55) to generate device select 003 = C = ⎍ from the above signals. C then detristates the 8095. (See Fig. 56.)

000	(333)	Input data from device 003 to A and generate $\overline{\text{IN}}$= ⎍
001	(003)	and device code 003 for device selecting to buffer 003
002	(323)	
003	(001)	out (A) to port 1
004	(041)	LXI H (Storage location 003, 200 for data from
		device 003)
005	(200)	
006	(003)	
007	167	Mov M,A (M at 003,200)
010	043	INX H, L by 1
011	(333)	Input data from device 004 to A and generate $\overline{\text{IN}}$= ⎍
012	(004)	and device code 004 for device selecting to buffer 004
013	(323)	
014	(002)	out (A) to port 2
015	167	Mov M,A (M at 003,201)
016	(303)	
017	(000)	JMP
020	(003)	

Take DCBA=1111 as data on device 004 and D'C'B'A'=0000 as data on device 003. Run the program at full speed. You should observe 1111 at port 2 and 0000 at port 1. Changing the data switches should be immediately reflected in corresponding changes at the output ports 2 and 1, respectively. Notice the most significant "nibbles" ($D_7 D_6 D_5 D_4$) at ports 2 and 1. Can you explain why they are what they are?

After running the program and inputting the data you should examine the contents of memory locations 200L and 201L. They

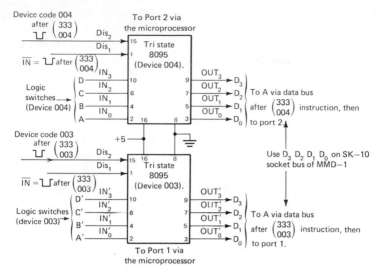

Figure 56. Successive inputting of data to microcomputer from several input
devices. Expt. 5-2(h). (See Figs. 51, 52 for device codes.) Device
selects 003 and 004 are generated within the 8095 (see Nor gate
in Fig. 55). Device codes 003 and 004 are taken from pins 4 and
5 of 7442 decoder.

should contain the exact data you inputted from the logic switches.
This experiment contains the elements of data acquisition, be it
from an inputting test device or instrument, or from an inputting
cassette tape or TTY, etc. What would happen if you placed LXI H
immediately *before* "Input from device 3" and jumped back from
020 to 003? Data acquisition? Try it with time delays in the proper place. *Hint*: You need another INX. Change the switch data
during the time delay and then examine the pertinent memory
locations to see if the relevant data has been stored.

It is most instructive to single step through the program and
observe ports 1 and 2. As you do so, note your results on the address and data bus numeric display monitors as well as at the ports
2 and 1 of the MMD-1. With DCBA=1111 and $D'C'B'A'$=0000, as
examples, you should see the following extra bytes: 003,360 after
001L; 001,360 after 003L; 004,377 after 012 L; and 002,377
after 014L. Observe ports 1 and 2 as you change the input switch
data to devices 003 and 004 while continuing the single stepping.
Account for these extra bytes.

You have acquired data from two input devices by means of
microprocessor program/interfacing control. The acquired data
was then redistributed to two other output devices (ports 1 and 2)

and simultaneously stored in memory. If the two output devices were one and the same ports and you inserted a time delay routine between 010 and 011 and again between 015 and 016, you would have the microcomputer functioning as a *multiplexer* of several input devices onto one output device. The time delays are needed to change the data at input ports 003 and 004 before outputting to the port and storage in the next memory locations.

Tristate buffer latches form an important part of internal microcomputer design (see Fig. 10, Chap. 2), as well as in interfacing the microcomputer to outside I/O devices. They keep data from all registers or memory addresses not pertinent to a particular instruction in the program off the data or address busses, *except* the *one* source and destination register or memory address (or device) that are involved in the fetch and execution of a particular instruction (or in the transfer of I/O data) in the program. The data bus buffer/latch and the address bus buffer/latch of the 8080 CPU are important examples (Fig. 10, Chap. 2).

5-2(E)   Interrupt Requests and Jamming

In this section we discuss the following very important situation: the microcomputer is engaged in its normal routine while one or more standby (input) devices are waiting a moment of *their* choosing to input their data or status into the microcomputer for processing, for storage, for outputting to other devices, or for a control decision request. This requires that the standby device(s) make an "interrupt request" asking the microcomputer to cease further execution of its *main program* and instead go to a service subroutine which has been programmed to accept data or status bits or a character from the input devices (traffic sensors, or temperature or flow sensors, or TTY or cassette tape) and execute or process them for some desired purpose (usually control) as dictated by the subroutine. The same would be true with respect to an output device. That is, the output device (say a printer or cassette tape) would tell the microcomputer, by means of an interrupt request, that it was ready to receive a character or a bit from the accumulator. The microcomputer would respond by departing from the main program to go to a service subroutine which would implement outputting of the character or bit to the I/O. This allows the microcomputer to work at optimum efficiency: the computer would be occupied with its main program at all times until interrupted by the I/O device requesting service in a service subroutine (an example of "increased thru-put").

The request to go to a subroutine for special service necessitates that at the moment the interrupt request is made an instruction of the *type* of a call be "jammed" from the outside (i.e., from the I/O device itself—the interrupt port) into the instruction register of the microprocessor. When the IR receives this call type instruction it treats it as *if* it were just another instruction coming from the next location in memory and executes it, forcing a call to the desired subroutine. Jamming in to the IR can only be accomplished if this call-type instruction has been sitting on the tristate (interrupt) buffer in its hi Z state waiting to flow on to the data bus and in to the IR of the CPU. The need for the tristate is clear: the jam instruction byte must not interfere with the normal flow of fetched instruction bytes occurring on the data bus as the program is executed. When the *interrupt request* is made by the standby device this tristate buffer must, somehow, be made to go to the low impedance state, thus dumping its stored D_7, D_6, ... D_0 call-type instruction on to the data bus for routing to the IR for decoding to effect the call to the subroutine. (The detristating, as in the last two experiments, comes about from software/interfacing control.) In fact, the "jam" instruction that does this is called a "Restart." It is similar to a Call and simply has the IR/ID, and control section tell the PC to effect a restart of the program at the location indicated (i.e., at the subroutine), where servicing of the standby device(s) can proceed.

The exact definition* of the RSTN (Restart) instruction is

$$RSTN = 3N7 \ (N = 0, 1, 2, \ldots, 7)$$

$$M_{SP-1} \leftarrow (PCH), M_{SP-2} \leftarrow (PCL), SP \leftarrow SP-2,$$

$$PC \leftarrow 000,0N0. \ (N = 0, 1, 2, \ldots, 7)$$

Here (PCH) and (PCL) are the hi and lo address of the *next* instruction in the main program at *the time the RSTN=3N7 is jammed on to the data bus to the IR*. They are saved on the stack and will be popped back to the PC at the end of the subroutine (by means of a 311=RET instruction there) so that we can return to that address for continuation of the main program after servicing of the standby devices has been completed. 000,0N0 is the

---

*Intel Corp. "8080 Microcomputer Systems User's Manual," Sept. 1975, pp. 4-12, 2-18.

"anchor" for getting to our subroutine: loading PC and the address bus with 000,0N0 forces the program to divert to KEX, then to the subroutine in RAM (003,0N0). For the MMD-1 N=0 and N=7 are not allowed: 307 jumps to 000,000 in KEX and the first instruction there is a jump to 000,070 which is the start of the KEX program—no subroutine could be written there. Likewise jumping directly to 000,070 (3N7 with N=7) would not permit writing a subroutine. 317 up to 367 are allowed RSTN instructions with the MMD-1, for a study of KEX (Appendix C) shows that at 000,0N0 (N=1, 2, . . . , 6) there are jump instructions $\begin{pmatrix} 303 \\ 0N0 \\ 003 \end{pmatrix}$ which take us from 000,0N0 to *003,0N0* and into RAM where subroutines can be written. Thus 003,0N0 (N=1, 2, . . . , 6) can be used by *Restarts* (RSTN=3N7) and *vectored interrupts* for subroutine writing to service the requesting device. Since a Call is a 3-byte instruction and a RSTN is one byte, the hardware required to jam in a RST N instruction is of necessity simpler than that needed to jam in 3 bytes, as the interfacing in the experiment shown below will indicate.

In order that an interrupt request be accepted and an RST N instruction jammed in to the IR of the microprocessor, it is necessary to first enable the interrupt flag INTE in the CPU (output pin 16 of the 8080). This is accomplished by loading the instruction 373=EI ("Enable the Interrupt Flag") into the *main* program. This *sets* the INTE flag (flip flop) following execution of the next instruction in the program. An Interrupt request, if made, will now be acknowledged and the 3N7 instruction can be jammed in to the IR for immediate execution (i.e., go to 000,0N0 → 003, 0N0). Once acknowledged, the EI flag is then disabled. Thus, *one and only one request for service can be made*, unless 373 *again* appears somewhere in the program. Hence to allow for future interrupt requests after the first one has been serviced it is essential that EI=373 be programmed into the *end* of the *subroutine* thereby re-setting INTE=1 again after the first interrupt request has been made and honored. If some part has been entered in which it is essential that an interrupt request should not be honored, but 373 has *already* been loaded into the main program, then 363=DI ("Disable the Interrupt Flag") must be programmed in for *that* part of the program or subroutine, followed by 373 at the *end* of that subroutine.

On the SK-10 bus socket of the MMD-1 there are three important quantities that are available to us which are vital in all jamming interrupt experiments and applications. They are INTE ("Interrupt Enable Flag"—also pin 16 of the 8080—a control output), INT ("Interrupt Request"—also pin 14 of the 8080—a control input), and $\overline{IACK}$* (Intel's "$\overline{INTA}$" ("Interrupt Acknowledge"—derived from the output of a Nand Gate whose inputs are *DBIN** ("Data Bus Input"—pin 17 of the 8080—a control input) and *INTA*** (Status bit** Do acknowledging an interrupt request—INTA is 1 when INT= ⊓ request is made). For realization** of $\overline{IACK}$ (or $\overline{INTA}$), see Fig. 11, Chap. 2 or Fig. 69, Chap. 5. The timing among these quantities is shown in Fig. 57 and is based on Fig. 58 reproduced from the Intel 8080 Microcomputer Systems User's Manual, Sept. 1975, p. 2-11. Included with Fig. 58 is a discussion of interrupt sequences, courtesy Intel Corp.

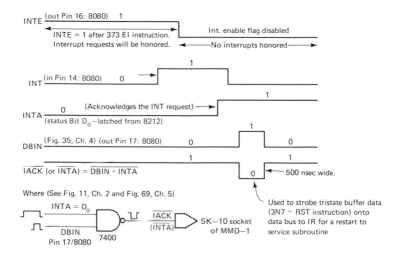

Figure 57. Timing among INTE, INT, INTA, DBIN, $\overline{IACK}$, ($\overline{INTA}$), and construction of $\overline{IACK}$ ($\overline{INTA}$). (See section 5-2(g).) $\overline{IACK}$ is used to de-tristate the interrupt port holding the RST N instruction.

  When INT= ⊓ (request made) the microprocessor recognizes it (if INTE=1) at the end of the current instruction it is executing. $\overline{IACK}$ ⊔ ($\overline{INTA}$) is formed and is used to de-tristate the 8095 buf-

---

*See section 5-2(g), Chap. 5 and Fig. 35, Chap. 4.
**More on status bits and how they are latched in Experiment 5-2(l) and section 5-2(G); for generation of $\overline{IACK}$ and other control signals see also section 5-2(G). See also Intel Manual, Sept. 1975, pp. 2-6, 3-4, and 3-5.

INTERRUPT SEQUENCES

The 8080 has the built-in capacity to handle external interrupt requests. A peripheral device can initiate an interrupt simply by driving the processor's interrupt (INT) line high.

The interrupt (INT) input is asynchronous, and a request may therefore originate at any time during any instruction cycle. Internal logic re-clocks the external request, so that a proper correspondence with the driving clock is established. As Figure 2-8 shows, an interrupt request (INT) arriving during the time that the interrupt enable line (INTE) is high, acts in coincidence with the ϕ_2 clock to set the internal interrupt latch. This event takes place during the last state of the instruction cycle in which the request occurs, thus ensuring that any instruction in progress is completed before the interrupt can be processed.

The INTERRUPT machine cycle which follows the arrival of an enabled interrupt request resembles an ordinary FETCH machine cycle in most respects. The M₁ status bit is transmitted as usual during the SYNC interval. It is accompanied, however, by an INTA status bit (D₀) which acknowledges the external request. The contents of the program counter are latched onto the CPU's address lines during T₁, but the counter itself is not incremented during the INTERRUPT machine cycle, as it otherwise would be.

In this way, the pre-interrupt status of the program counter is preserved, so that data in the counter may be restored by the interrupted program after the interrupt request has been processed.

The interrupt cycle is otherwise indistinguishable from an ordinary FETCH machine cycle. The processor itself takes no further special action. It is the responsibility of the peripheral logic to see that an eight-bit interrupt instruction is "jammed" onto the processor's data bus during state T₃. In a typical system, this means that the data-in bus from memory must be temporarily disconnected from the processor's main data bus, so that the interrupting device can command the main bus without interference.

The 8080's instruction set provides a special one-byte call which facilitates the processing of interrupts (the ordinary program Call takes three bytes). This is the RESTART instruction (RST). A variable three-bit field embedded in the eight-bit field of the RST enables the interrupting device to direct a Call to one of eight fixed memory locations. The decimal addresses of these dedicated locations are: 0, 8, 16, 24, 32, 40, 48, and 56. Any of these addresses may be used to store the first instruction(s) of a routine designed to service the requirements of an interrupting device. Since the (RST) is a call, completion of the instruction also stores the old program counter contents on the STACK.

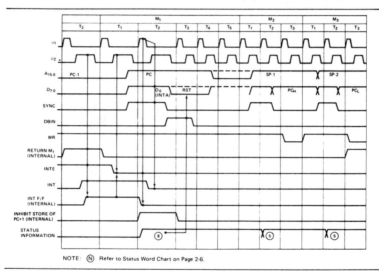

Figure 58. Interrupt timing and discussion of interrupt sequences. (Courtesy Intel Corp.)

fers which have been holding the 3N7 jam instruction in the hi Z state. $\overline{\text{IACK}}$ strobes the 8095's pin DIS₂ thereby sending the byte 3N7 on to the data bus and into the IR causing the program to jump to 000,0N0 (KEX) and then to the subroutine 003,0N0 in RAM. The quantities depicted and explained above are vital in the programming and interfacing in the following experiment.

The following experiment will illustrate the above discussion and should involve just about everything: an Interrupt Enable, an Interrupt Request, $\overline{IACK}$, a jam instruction into the IR (RSTN), tristating, inputting and outputting data to and from the micro-processor, $\overline{In}$ and $\overline{Out}$ pulses, and device selecting. In short, total interfacing.

Experiment 5-2(i)   Jamming and Interrupt Requesting. Inter-rupting a Main Program to Service Two Standby Devices (in this case, inputting their status or data to the microcomputer)— Elements of Data Acquisition, Read-out and Storage. Avoidance of Multiple Interrupts.

a)   The Program

000	$\left(\begin{array}{c} 076 \end{array} \right.$	MVI, A
001	$\left. \begin{array}{c} 111 \end{array} \right)$	
002	$\left(\begin{array}{c} 323 \end{array} \right.$	
003	$\left. \begin{array}{c} 001 \end{array} \right)$	111 to Port 1
004	373	EI
005	$\left(\begin{array}{c} 303 \end{array} \right.$	*Main program* (simulated by a wait loop).
006	$\left(\begin{array}{c} 005 \end{array} \right)$	A wait loop. Stays here until INT request ⊓ is made by standby devices. RST 327 is then jammed in to IR
007	$\left. \begin{array}{c} 003 \end{array} \right)$	taking main program to subroutine at 003,020.

Service Subroutine:

020	$\left(\begin{array}{c} 333 \end{array} \right.$	Generate $\overline{IN}$ and device code 003: input (D′) from de-
021	$\left. \begin{array}{c} 003 \end{array} \right)$	vice 003 to A
022	$\left(\begin{array}{c} 323 \end{array} \right.$	
023	$\left. \begin{array}{c} 001 \end{array} \right)$	(D′) → Port 1
024	$\left(\begin{array}{c} 041 \end{array} \right.$	
025	$\left(\begin{array}{c} 200 \end{array} \right)$	LXI H, L
026	$\left. \begin{array}{c} 003 \end{array} \right)$	
027	167	Mov $\overset{\frown}{M,A}$
030	043	INX H, L
031	$\left(\begin{array}{c} 333 \end{array} \right.$	Generate $\overline{IN}$ and device code 004: input (D) from de-
032	$\left. \begin{array}{c} 004 \end{array} \right)$	vice 004 to A
033	$\left(\begin{array}{c} 323 \end{array} \right.$	
034	$\left. \begin{array}{c} 002 \end{array} \right)$	(D) → Port 2
035	167	Mov $\overset{\frown}{M,A}$
036	373	EI to prepare for future interrupts
037	311	Ret to wait loop where program was interrupted by RST 2

Device 003 will be an 8095 tristate buffer holding data D' (D'C'B'A') from 4 switches and device 004 will be another 8095 tristate buffer holding data D (DCBA) from 4 other switches. Device code pulses ⎍ applied to their pin 1 (DIS$_1$) with $\overline{\text{In}}$ applied to their pin 15 (DIS$_2$) will get them off their hi Z and send this data into the accumulator via data bus, then to ports 1 and 2, respectively, and also into memory locations 200L and 201L, respectively. This will all occur only if we can get to subroutine at 020L where the service described above is performed. What gets us to 003H, 020L will be an interrupt request (INT=⎍) made to the 8080 (pin 14) which will generate (see Figs. 11 and 57) $\overline{\text{IACK}}$ = ⎍ to strobe the RST2=327 instruction waiting on a pair of 8095's into the IR. The IR/ID control then loads the PC with 000,020 and that, together with KEX takes us to 003,020.

b) The circuitry.   Remember (see Ref. 12).

Pin 1	Pin 15		
Dis$_1$	Dis$_2$	In$_i$	Out$_i$
0	0	0	0
0	0	1	1
0	1	X	HZ
1	0	X	HZ
1	1	X	HZ

8095

b-1)   The Interfacing for the JAM Interrupt (RST2=327):

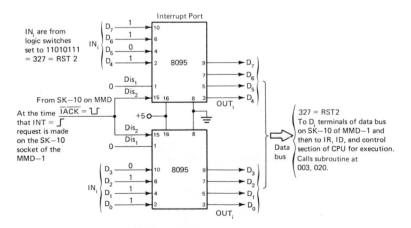

Figure 59. Interfacing for an RST 2 interrupt: Expt. 5-2(i). See relevant 8095 truth table above.

b-2) *The Interfacing to Input the Data from the Two Input Devices After the RST2 is Jammed in*

Tristating and device selecting are now essential. The interfacing below in conjunction with the program in the subroutine will do the job. Again we employ absolute device selecting by means of the device codes 003 and 004 available near the 7442 on the face of the MMD-1 together with $\overline{IN}$ available from the SK-10 bus socket and the employment of the internal NOR gate in the 8095 (Fig. 55).

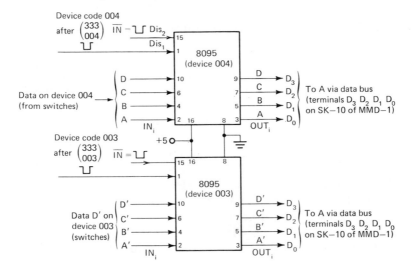

Figure 60. Interfacing for data inputting—Expt. 5-2(i). $\sqcup = \overline{IN}$ occurs after $\begin{pmatrix} 333 \\ 003 \end{pmatrix}$ and $\begin{pmatrix} 333 \\ 004 \end{pmatrix}$. Device selects 003 and 004 are generated just after NOR gate within the 8095 (see Fig. 55). Device codes 003, 004 are from pins 4, 5 of 7442 decoder.

The sequence of events is the following: an INT= $\sqcap$ request (with INTE=1) causes $\overline{IACK}= \sqcup$ to bring the 8095's off their hi Z tristate and jams the 327 instruction into the IR-ID, control section of the CPU via the data bus. This forces the program to go to 000, 020, and then to 003, 020. At that point $\begin{pmatrix} 333 \\ 003 \end{pmatrix}$ causes $\overline{IN}= \sqcup$ to be applied to the 8095 which, together with the device *code* 003= $\sqcup$ from the MMD-1's 7442, produces the device *select* pulse 003= $\sqcup$ after the internal 8095 NOR gate bringing it off tristate, allowing its data $D'C'B'A'$ to be sent to the accumulator via the data bus and from there on to port 1 and into memory location 003,200. After that $\left(\dfrac{333}{004}\right)$ does the same thing to device 004 (the other 8095) containing the data DCBA, thereby inputting DCBA into the accumulator then to port 2, and finally to memory location 003,201. Take

$$D'C'B'A' = 0110 = \text{data on device 3}$$

$$D\,C\,B\,A\ = 0011 = \text{data on device 4}$$

Run the program at full speed with no interrupt request made. Observe $(111)_8$ at port 1. Then observe some "garbage" in memory locations 200 and 201. This confirms that we were in the wait loop and never did get to the subroutine. Rerun and make an interrupt request by setting INT= ⊓ on the SK-10 bus socket. Observe ports 1 and 2. The LSN (nibble) should change to 0110 at port 1 (device 3 data) and be 0011 at port 2 (device 4 data). Reset and examine the data in memory locations 200 and 201. They too should contain 0110 and 0011 as LSN's, respectively. If you observe these results, then your software and interfacing were interacting properly when (and after) the interrupt request was made. Try other combinations of DCBA on device 4 and $D'C'B'A'$ on device 3. Examine ports 1 and 2 and memory locations 200 and 201 in every case.

It is *most* instructive to single step this experiment. Do so first with no interrupt request made. The single stepping should reveal how we are caught up in the wait loop at 005, 006, 007. Then make an interrupt request, INT= ⊓ , and note how single stepping immediately reveals the pushing of (PC) = 003H,005L on to the stack at 377L and 376L, respectively, the restarting of the program at 000,020, then the jump to 003,020, then on through the subroutine, and from there back to the wait loop at 005 *after* 005L,003H are popped from the stack at 376 and 377 back to the PC. It is also instructive to make another interrupt request and single step again. Observe that we again go to the service subroutine after this second request is made. Why? Now change the instruction at 036L from 373 to 000 (NOP). Run the program, single step it, make an interrupt request and note that you again go through the service subroutine and back to wait loop. Make still another interrupt request. What does single stepping now reveal? Did you get to the service subroutine this time? Why?

In this experiment almost every basic facet of interfacing the microcomputer to an I/O is encountered and the intimate interaction with the controlling program demonstrated: interrupts, interrupt enables, device select generation, $\overline{\text{IACK}}$ pulse generation, tristating a jam (RSTN) instruction onto the data bus, inputting/outputting to and from the microcomputer via tristate buffers (8095's) and latches (7475's) at the ports, and the need for software instructions such as "Out" (323), "In" (333), RST (3N7), RET (311), EI (373), and so on to interact with the I/O.

P.S.: A Note on the Need for Debouncing:

The application of the INT = $\sqcap$ request to the 8080 INT terminal on the SK-10 socket carries with it the danger that the switch, or whatever, asking for an interrupt might not be debounced so that INT=$\sqcap\sqcap\sqcap$due to several contact bounces. This would cause multiple jamming interrupts during the program-run causing the subroutine service to be called many times. Now in our particular experiment [5-2(i)] this poses no problems because (see program) this would simply input repeatedly the *same* data hanging on devices 3 and 4 (the 8095's) and then output that same data to ports 1 and 2 and to memory locations 200 and 201. Hence, no change in results would occur due to these multiple interrupts. Programs of the type of *this* experiment cause no problems in this regard. Still they are undesirable in general because they take time away from the main program. Where multiple interrupts cannot *in any way* be tolerated is the case where the service subroutine has in it an instruction of the type, say, 0D4 (increment a register) or an INX H, L instruction with no further resetting of H, L to their prior state (as was the case in this experiment to 003, 200), and *also ends with a 373 (EI) for future interrupts*. A multiple interrupt in such a case would surely produce final results not at all compatible with the *single* interrupt request that had to be made at the time the I/O requested servicing—in this case registers or memory locations would increment many times with one interrupt request. A single data acquisition point might then "plaster" all of memory with the same byte. Part of the answer to this problem is to make sure the mechanism requesting the interrupt is 'debounced." One way of accomplishing this is with NAND gates as follows:*

---

*See also Ref. 24, p. 212; Ref. 20, p. 11-6, 7, 8; and Ref. 25, p. 133.

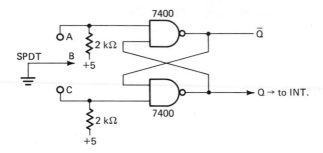

Figure 61. A circuit for SPDT debouncing.

Starting with the switch at A, Q will be 0 (verify it). When the switch is released to position B, Q stays at 0. (Verify it.) When the switch hits C, Q goes to 1 and *stays* at 1 no matter how many bounces off C the switch makes provided it does not hit A again. (Verify it.) Thus Q = ⌐ , debounced, for a valid interrupt request, while C=⎍⎍⎍ (bouncing). Debouncing of the Interrupt Request is advisable in all cases.

There is, however, another aspect to the problem. If the Interrupt Request Pulse width⎍⎍, *even though debounced*, is greater than the time length of the subroutine (*which ends with a 373 EI before returning to the main program*), then as soon as we return from the subroutine after the interrupt request was honored, *INTA will still be 1* and another interrupt request will be made, so the program again jumps to the subroutine. This is so because (Figs. 57 and 58) INTA= ⌐ due to INT=1, and, therefore, $\overline{\text{IACK}}$ = ⎍ will again be generated since INTE = 1 due to 373 at the end of the subroutine. This will repeat as long as INT=1 and INTE was enabled.

To demonstrate this, it is most instructive to modify the experiment:* Change the program listed in part (a) so that LXI H,L is put somewhere in the main program *before* the wait loop. *Be sure it does not now appear in the subroutine.* Leave 043=INX after the first 167 instruction in the subroutine *and add another 043 after the second 167 instruction before EI=373.* We now have a program for *data logging;* i.e., *every time data changes on devices 003 and on 004 and an interrupt request is made these data will be stored in successively higher locations in memory, and, of course, be successively output at ports 1 and 2.* Try the experiment as follows. Make INT= ⏜long by simply connecting INT on the SK-10

---

*Suggested by Tom Tommet, Chemistry Dept., Princeton University.

socket to ground and then to +5 V for the interrupt, and *leaving it there*. The data will appear, momentarily, at ports 1 and 2 and then disappear. Something went wrong. Reset the MMD-1 and examine locations 200, 201, 202, 203, . . . *all the way up* and on to 000, 001, . . . 007. You will find they are occupied, alternately, by the data on input devices 003 and 004, so much so that the program itself (including the most important 373) got wiped out by the successive INX and Mov M̂,A instructions which were implemented many, many times because of the multiple interrupts produced by the long INT= ⌐̄ . Thus, interrupt requests are made as long as INT=1 and INTE=1 is reset by the 373 instruction. A means must be found to make INT short, say of the width of $\overline{IACK}$ (500 ns) to produce a single interrupt.

The practical solution is to use the 8212 Input-Output IC (see Fig. 66). The 8212 is essentially a latch as well as tristate buffer with an added feature that will shortly emerge. Try the modified experiment again with the 8212 wired up for tristating as shown in Fig. 62.

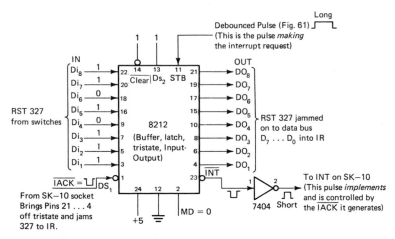

Figure 62. Using the 8212 chip to input a RSTN instruction and prevent multiple interrupts. See text below for relevant 8212 truth tables. The 8212 is here used as a tristate interrupt port holding RSTN. See also Fig. 66.

The 8212 here serves as the tristate buffer holding the jam interrupt 327 at pins 22, . . . 3. Upon an interrupt request at STB, $\overline{IACK}$= ⊔ at DS_1 (pin 1) will de-tristate it and allow 327 to flow on the data bus to the IR of the CPU. The debounced pulse making the interrupt request at STB (pin 11) is presumed to be long (but doesn't have to be). DS_2 at pin 13 and $\overline{clear}$ at pin 14 are both kept high. With these conditions a study of the $\overline{INT}$-producing logic inside the 8212 (see Fig. 66) will show that $\overline{INT}$= ⌐L at pin 23 will be produced when STB= ⌐⌐, from the interrupt requesting switch, is applied to the clock of the D flip flop (the Service Request FF) (up to this moment $\overline{IACK}$=1 at DS_1). This $\overline{INT}$ signal is inverted by the 7404 in Fig. 62 and this is the INT = ⌐⌐ pulse that implements the request inside the 8080 chip (pin 14) via the SK-10 socket (see Figs. 57 and 58). This immediately generates $\overline{IACK}$ (or $\overline{INTA}$) ⌐⌐ (Fig. 57) which is fed back from the SK-10 socket (see Fig. 11, Chap. 2) to DS_1 of the 8212 for detristating. Study of the $\overline{INT}$ circuit of the 8212 (Fig. 66) now shows that when $\overline{IACK}$=DS_1 goes from 1 to 0 and back to 1 (with STB providing *no more* ↑ clocks to the service flip flop) $\overline{INT}$ *goes back to 1*. Thus $\overline{INT}$= ⌐⌐, with a pulse width somewhat larger than $\overline{IACK}$= ⌐⌐ which is controlling it through DS_1. Hence, the long requesting pulse at STB ⌐⌐ has been shortened to an INT pulse ⌐⌐ for the 8080 (after the 7404) of the order of $\overline{IACK}$'s width (500 nsec), and this produces *single interrupts* (Fig. 57). The key, of course, was the leading edge triggering of STB= ⌐⌐ which causes a transition of Q at the D (service) flip flop of the 8212 from 1 to 0 (Fig. 66) and then the appearance of $\overline{IACK}$= ⌐⌐, which immediately causes the Preset on that flip flop to go to 0 making its Q output go back to 1. Multiple interrupts are thus prevented.

It is highly instructive to do the modified data logging experiment suggested, first with 8095's using IACK on their pins 15 with a long ⌐⌐ interrupt request, and then with the 8212 as the tristate buffer, connected as in Fig. 62, with the same long interrupt request, this time applied to pin 11 (STB) of the 8212 and with $\overline{IACK}$= ⌐⌐ fed back to pin 1 (DS_1) from the SK-10 socket. The convenience and advantage of the 8212 will be seen clearly: as you change the data at will or input devices 003 and 004, with the previously suggested modified program being executed, you will see that memory locations 200, 201; 202, 203; 204, 205; etc. have logged the changing input data correctly and in sequence as successive interrupt requests are made, *once* after each data change. Multiple interrupts have been prevented.

Note: the relevant truth tables for the 8212 for the conditions of this experiment follow ($\overline{clear}$=1.)

$\overline{DS_1} \cdot DS_2$	DS_1	DS_2	MD	STB	Out
1	0	1	0	1	$D_0 = D_i$
0	1	1	0	X	hi Z

and

DS_1 Pin 1 $\overline{IACK}$	DS_2	MD	STB	$\overline{INT}$
1	1	0	0	1
1	1	0	↑	0
0	1	0	↑	0
1	1	0	↑	1

Verify these entries by examining the 8212 chip logic in Fig. 66 and again by making *static tests* on the 8212 as suggested by the inputs and outputs presented in the above truth tables. Use a pulser and/or switches and a probe and follow the pin drawings in Fig. 62 or 66.

    In the last table the listing is presented in the order in which the events occur when a request ⌐ is made at STB. ↑ signifies no further *leading edge* pulses.

    As a simple alternative to the 8212 you can use a 7474 flip flop with the 8095's. Thus:*

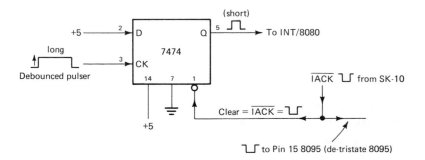

*Courtesy Tom Tommet, Princeton University.

As soon as $\overline{\text{IACK}}$ is generated Q is cleared making INT short, thereby allowing one data input only. This is essentially the method employed with the 8212 service request flip flop (Fig. 66). $\overline{\text{IACK}}$ also serves to detristate the RST from the 8095 on to the data bus to the IR. The 8212 service FF works with "Preset" on the 7474 instead of "Clear" as it generates $\overline{\text{INT}}$ (Pin 23) instead of INT.

Experiment 5-2(j)   Interrupting a Main Routine to Allow the Microcomputer to Output Data (or Status) to Two Standby Devices

This is basically the same experiment as the last one, only now an interrupt is made to jam an RSTN instruction into the IR which will *output* the microcomputer's data to two standby devices (LED's or numeric displays at ports 4 and 5).

a) **Program**

000	373	EI
001	303	
002	001	Wait loop till RST2=327
003	003	jam is made. (Simulates main program.)

Service Subroutine

020	076	Service for device 004
021	111	
022	323	See 111 at device 004
023	004	
024	076	Service for device 005
025	222	
026	323	See 222 at device 005
027	005	
030	373	EI
031	311	Ret to wait loop

b-1) *Interfacing the jam interrupt RST=327*

Exactly the same as in the previous experiment (Fig. 59).

b-2) Interfacing the microcomputer to output devices 004,005

Interfacing is exactly the same as the circuit in Experiment 5-2(e). (Fig. 50.)

Results: Run at full speed. When the interrupt is made you should immediately see 111 appear at display 004 and 222 at display 005. Single step, first with the program as is, then with the interrupt request made. Convince yourself that you get to 020 after (PC)=003,001 is pushed on the stack at 377, 376 and after we get to 000,020, then to 003,020. Make another request. Do you get to 020 again? Replace instruction 373 at 030 by NOP=000. Run, single step, interrupt. Continue to single step. Do you get to the subroutine and back to wait? Interrupt again. Do you get to the subroutine? Why?

5-2(F) Data Acquisition

Experiment 5-2(k) An Experiment on Data Logging.
(Acquisition-Storage-Read-out)

The purpose of this experiment is to demonstrate some of the principles of data acquisition, storage, and read-out. The situation could apply, for example, to changing data being input to, and stored in, a microcomputer from a measurement system, an instrument or test set-up, or from a data transmission system; or to a changing inventory or power demand/usage situation, or generally to the problem of acquisition and storage of changing information and/or data of any sort. For the purposes of this experiment the input device is taken to be a single 8095 tristate buffer containing changing data input to it from a set of 4 switches (the data byte is thus of the form $1111D_3D_2D_1D_0$—the one's are floating). The switches simulate the feeding in of data from transducers in a real system. In every case, read-out and/or storage for future retrieval is essential and provision should be made for their implementation. Interfacing into and out of the microcomputer, as well as the programming, are of paramount importance.

In this experiment we shall be concerned with the acquisition of data bytes, each simulated by 4 switches $D_3 D_2 D_1 D_0$ ($D_7 D_6 D_5 D_4$ will remain high, for simplicity), which are to be displayed one after the other on a single 7-segment display (HP5082-7740) in decimal form (4 switches$\equiv$DCBA $\rightarrow$ $D_3 D_2 D_1 D_0$ $\rightarrow$ BCD number); they are also to be stored in successive memory locations. We employ a time delay routine and it is within one time delay interval that the input data byte is changed. We can accommodate any rate of data change by merely changing the timing byte in the time delay routine to match it. More on this later. In Experiment 5-2(i) data logging was initiated by the requesting device when it jammed an interrupt request. Here we sample the input device at times of *our* choosing.

We first present the program, then analyze it as it pertains to the formulation and solution of the problem, and then show the interfacing required to implement and solve the problem. Variations of this program are possible to accommodate the acquisition and storage of a larger number of data bytes as well as faster or slower rates of acquisition of the data; i.e., synchronizing of the time delay interval to the rate at which data is changing. You can address yourself to these questions after this experiment is performed. Note that *a "nesting" of subroutines is employed* in which the main program calls a subroutine at 100 (part of the time delay structure), which in turn calls another subroutine at 150 (the rest of the time delay structure). This saves memory space and programming steps, especially since the read-out also uses the same "sub-subroutine" at 150.

The Program

	000	⎛ 041 ⎞	LXI H/L
	001	⎜ 200 ⎟	H,L points to memory address
	002	⎝ 003 ⎠	
	003	⎛ 016 ⎞	MVI C
	004	⎝ 005 ⎠ =	number of data bytes = C to be acquired
	005	⎛ 315 ⎞	
	006	⎜ 100 ⎟	Call $\rightarrow$ T.D.
	007	⎝ 003 ⎠	
† Acquisition	010	⎛ 333 ⎞	Generates $\overline{\text{IN}}$ and the device code 006 for the 8095. Inputs data from 006 to A after device select 006 is formed (see Fig. 55 and Fig. 63a).
	011	⎝ 006 ⎠	

$\leftarrow$ Ret

Storage[†]:

012	167	Mov M͡,A
013	⎛ 323 ⎞	
014	⎝ 001 ⎠	(A) → Port 1
015	043	INX H,L
016	015	DCR C
017	⎛ 312 ⎞	
020	⎜ 040 ⎟	JZ (to "Read-out")
021	⎝ 003 ⎠	
022	⎛ 303 ⎞	
023	⎜ 005 ⎟	JMP
024	⎝ 003 ⎠	for next data.

Read-out (Go to 040)

Time Delay (see Experiment 3-2(d) and Table 3-1) during which port 2 is on (377) for 2 seconds and then off for 5 seconds. Data is input during the 5 seconds off-period.

100	365	Push PSW

Port 2 on 2 seconds

101	⎛ 076 ⎞	
102	⎝ 377 ⎠	
103	⎛ 323 ⎞	
104	⎝ 002 ⎠	
105	⎛ 006	
106	B_2=024 ⎠	Port 2 on 2 seconds
107	⎛ 315 ⎞	
110	⎜ 150 ⎟	CALL →
111	⎝ 003 ⎠	

Port 2 off 5 seconds

112	⎛ 076 ⎞	
113	⎝ 000 ⎠	← RET

[†]To debug the acquisition and storage part of the program and interfacing: Place 166 at 040 and examine ⟨M⟩ at 200, 201, 202, 203, and 204. Results should correspond to the five data bytes input from switches (Fig. 63a).

114	$\left.\begin{array}{c}323\\002\end{array}\right)$	
115		
116	$\left(\begin{array}{c}006\\B_2'=062\end{array}\right)$ Port 2 off 5 seconds	
117		
120	$\left(\begin{array}{c}315\\150\\003\end{array}\right)$ CALL $\rightarrow$	
121		
122		
123	361	Pop PSW ← RET
124	311	Ret
150	$\left(\begin{array}{c}021\\046\\015\end{array}\right)$ LXI D/E	
151		
152		
153	033	
154	172	Mov $\widehat{A,D}$
155	263	ORA,E
156	$\left(\begin{array}{c}302\\153\\003\end{array}\right)$	
157		
160		
161	005	DCR B
162	$\left(\begin{array}{c}302\\150\\003\end{array}\right)$	
163		
164		
165	311	Ret

Read-out:[††]

Read-out:[††]

040	$\left(\begin{array}{c}041\\200\\003\end{array}\right)$	LXI H/L
041		H,L Points to memory location
042		
043	$\left(\begin{array}{c}016\\005\end{array}\right)=$	MVI C
044		number of data points = C to be read out
045	176	Mov $\widehat{A,M}$

[††]To test Read-out: Load 200–204 with specific data. Run program from 040 to 066 and observe the 7-segment display. Note the instructions 062–065. 377 causes the 7448 to *blank* the display (see 7448 truth table, Fig. 64).

046   $\begin{pmatrix} 323 \\ 003 \end{pmatrix}$ out (A) to 7475 latch and display
047   Generates $\overline{\text{out}}$ pulse to device select the latch

050   $\begin{pmatrix} 006 \\ 017 \end{pmatrix} =$ B$_2''$ for *1.5 second T.D.*
051

052
053   $\begin{pmatrix} 315 \\ 150 \\ 003 \end{pmatrix}$ Call T.D. at 150 →
054

055   043   INX H,L ← Ret
056   015   DCR C

057
060   $\begin{pmatrix} 302 \\ 045 \\ 003 \end{pmatrix}$ JNZ
061

062   $\begin{pmatrix} 076 \\ 377 \end{pmatrix}$ MVI A
063   blank   Byte placed in A

064   $\begin{pmatrix} 323 \\ 003 \end{pmatrix}$ (A) → latch and display. *Display   blanks.*
065   (See Fig. 64.)

066   166   Halt (or a JMP back to 040 for continuous read-out of the data; or JMP to 000 to prepare for new data).

The required interfacing is presented in two parts: a) the circuitry needed for the acquisition and storage of the data, b) the circuitry for the read-out of the data.

a) *Interfacing for Acquisition and Storage of Data*

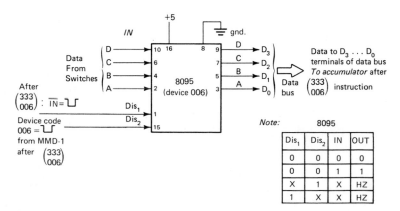

Figure 63(a). Acquisition and storage of data (Expt. 5-2R). Device selected generated after NOR gate within 8095 (see Fig. 55).

b)   Read-Out of the Acquired-stored Data

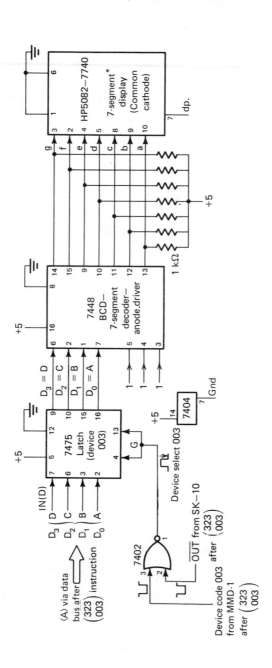

Figure 63(b). Read-out—Expt. 5-2(k).* Note—You can also insert the E & L LR-4 7-segment display with 7447 decoder on board (see Ch. 4 and Fig. 40) in place of the 7448/HP 5082-7440 shown above. In that case simply wire pins 9, 10, 15, 16 of the 7475 to DCBA of the LR-4 display.

For the 7475 $Q = D$ when $G = 1$, and $Q = Q_0$ when $G = 0$ (i.e., latch for $G = \Lambda$). Device selecting is necessary here to avoid outputting data during the acquisition and storage part of the program where $\overline{\text{out}}$ are generated by the $\left(\dfrac{323}{001}\right)$ instruction at 013 and (A) appears on the data bus; also to avoid data appearing on the display during programming or resetting when $\overline{\text{out}}$ and $\overline{\text{in}}$ are generated. Details on the 5082-7740 can be found in Appendix A; the 7448 BCD to 7-segment decoder-anode driver truth table is given below in Fig. 64 (Refs. 10 and 12):

D	C	B	A	a	b	c	d	e	f	g	Display
0	0	0	0	1	1	1	1	1	1	0	0
0	0	0	1	0	1	1	0	0	0	0	1
0	0	1	0	1	1	0	1	1	0	1	2
0	0	1	1	1	1	1	1	0	0	1	3
0	1	0	0	0	1	1	0	0	1	1	4
0	1	0	1	1	0	1	1	0	1	1	5
0	1	1	0	0	0	1	1	1	1	1	6
0	1	1	1	1	1	1	0	0	0	0	7
1	0	0	1	1	1	1	0	0	1	1	9
1	1	1	1	0	0	0	0	0	0	0	Blank

Input → ← Output →

→ Useful to clear

* - 1010 thru 1110 give "strange" symbols which do not concern us here.

Figure 64. BCD to 7 segment decoder/driver truth table (7447 or 7448).

Procedure

1) Load the program

2) Run at full speed

3) Note the first off interval of the LED's at port 2 just after they are all lit (377). Set the switches DCBA=*0000*= $D_3 D_2 D_1 D_0$ during this off interval (0000 appears at port 1)

4) Watch for the next off interval at port 2 and set DCBA= $D_3 D_2 D_1 D_0 = 0001$ during this interval. (0001 appears at port 1)

5) During next off interval (the third one) set DCBA= $D_3 D_2 D_1 D_0 = 0011$ and observe 0011 at port 1.

6) During next off interval (the fourth one) set DCBA= $D_3 D_2 D_1 D_0 = 0111$ and observe 0111 at port 1.

7) During the fifth and last off interval set DCBA=$D_3 D_2 D_1 D_0 = 0110$ and observe 0110 at port 1.

The program now jumps to read-out after the acquisition of the 5 data bytes. The 7-segment display should read in turn:

DCBA = $D_3 D_2 D_1 D_0$ = 0000 (dec. 0), then 0001 (dec. 1), then 0011 (dec. 3), then 0111 (dec. 7), and finally 0110 (dec. 6), in that order: *0, 1, 3, 7, 6.*

Reset, and examine memory locations 200, 201, 202, 203, 204. They should show 11110000, 11110001, 11110011, 11110111, 11110110. (The four 1's at $D_7 \ldots D_4$ are floating for input device 006).

Repeat the experiment with data input in the following order:

$$DCBA=D_3 D_2 D_1 D_0 = 0001 \rightarrow 1$$
$$= 1001 \rightarrow 9$$
$$= 1000 \rightarrow 8$$
$$= 0000 \rightarrow 0$$
$$= 0100 \rightarrow 4$$

The read-out should now be 1, 9, 8, 0, 4, in that order. Again, reset, and examine memory locations 200, 201, 202, 203, 204 and see 11110001, 11111001, 11111000, 11110000, and 11110100.

Do not take DCBA > 1001. The 7448 decoder truth table gives "weird" symbols for DCBA=1010 up to 1110 (not shown in the truth table on preceding page).

The number of data bytes acquired and read out can be increased or decreased simply by changing the byte C at 004 and correspondingly at 044 in the program. Likewise the time available for capturing each byte of data can be varied by changing B_2' at 117 in the time delay ("port 2 off") program. In this way we can accommodate a faster or slower data sampling rate.

It is suggested that, if you have an HP multi-digit display available (HP 5082-7402/3/4/5 or 5082-7412/3/4/5, see Appendix A), you work out a read-out program starting at 040 which will display several acquired data bytes *all at once* rather than one after the other. In this case no call for a time delay is needed at location 052. The interfacing for readout will now be a bit more complicated. The 7475 and 7448 are still necessary but device select pulses will be needed for *each* of the cathodes of the multi-digit display. Since the MMD-1 has a total of 5 device codes available

(003 to 007) and two are being used for selecting the 8095 input device (006) and the 7475 output device (003), you will not have enough device selects left if the display contains more than 3 digits. In this case you will have to resort to wiring up the 74154 Hexa decoder to provide the necessary device selects. This should present no difficulty. See Appendix A for details on the 5082-7400 3, 4, or 5 digit displays for pin connections to the 7448.

5-2(G)   Status Bits* and Control Signals.

Implicit in the proper working of a microcomputer (the writing in and execution of a program and the implementation of an I/O interfacing set-up) is the existence or generation of certain *control signals* at the precise time during a machine cycle which will allow *that* machine cycle to be carried out and eventually lead to the successful execution of a full instruction comprising one or more machine cycles (sections 2-2 and 4-1). Thus, for example, during execution of a CALL in a program run five machine cycles must be executed and they require 1) a $\overline{\text{MEMR}}$ ⊐ signal to allow reading from memory to *fetch* the instruction (315) there for IR/ID identification, 2) another $\overline{\text{MEMR}}$ signal to allow *reading* from memory of the second byte B_2 (subroutine low address) stored there, 3) ditto with respect to B_3 (subroutine high address), 4) a $\overline{\text{MEMW}}$ ⊐ signal to allow *writing* into the stack the high part of the *return address* $(PCH)_r$ for saving until the RET instruction at the end of the subroutine returns $(PCH)_r$ to the PC, and 5) ditto with respect to $(PCL)_r$ and the stack.

In an input instruction a $\overline{\text{MEMR}}$ ⊐ signal would have to be generated to fetch 333 from memory for subsequent decoding in the ID; another $\overline{\text{MEMR}}$ would be needed to read the device number B_2 stored in memory; and an $\overline{\text{I/O R}}$ $(\overline{\text{IN}})$ ⊐ signal will be needed to form a *detristating device select* to allow the I/O to send its information into the CPU. A similar analysis holds for the output instruction 323 except that an $\overline{\text{I/O W}}$ $(\overline{\text{OUT}})$ signal will be needed to form a device select to allow the I/O to *latch* the output data going to I/O from CPU via the data bus. In an instruction like Mov M, r the fetch of the operation code from memory to the IR and ID requires a $\overline{\text{MEMR}}$ signal to enable reading from memory, while its *execution* requires a $\overline{\text{MEMW}}$ signal to allow the contents of register r to be written into memory via the data bus.

---

*Not to be confused with PSW (Process Status Word) which consists of ⟨A⟩ and ⟨Flags⟩— see Chap. 3, section 3-6(B).

Finally, an interrupt request needs an $\overline{\text{IACK}}$ ($\overline{\text{INTA}}$) signal ⊔ to allow reading (detristating) into the IR (via data bus) the RST N instruction hanging on the interrupt port (a tristate buffer), and also two $\overline{\text{MEMW}}$ signals to write the return address $(\text{PCH})_r$ and $(\text{PCL})_r$ one after the other into two stack locations in memory (so as to know where in the main program to return at the end of the service subroutine initiated by the RST N instruction). Note that in an interrupt the flow of RST N into the IR is a *fetch*, albeit from an I/Θ (the interrupt port) and not from memory (we assume the INTE flag is enabled).

In all of the above you can surely see that one or more of the signals $\overline{\text{MEMR}}$, $\overline{\text{MEMW}}$, $\overline{\text{I/OR}}$, $\overline{\text{I/OW}}$, or $\overline{\text{IACK}}$ must be generated at precise times for each and every machine cycle of a program if the microprocessor is to successfully control reading from and writing into memory or I/O's or read from interrupt ports. *These signals must be interfaced with the memory and I/O's (see Fig. 11 and all the experiments in this chapter)* to effect the pertinent read/write enables on memories or I/O's.

In what follows you are urged to review carefully the material on machine cycles in sections 2-2 and 4-1 and the experiments in section 4-2. See also pp. 2-16 thru 2-19, Intel 8080 Manual, Sept. 1975 (and App. I and J here).

How are these signals generated as they are needed? To make possible their synthesis the microprocessor generates *"Status Bits"* $D_7 \ldots D_0$ during the beginning (T_1) of *every* machine cycle and outputs them on to the data bus just during $T_1 - T_2$. These bits tell completely the requirements of the machine cycle and the activity that *will* take place on the address and data bus or in memory and I/O during that machine cycle *to come*. Different status bits will be generated at the beginning of the next machine cycle. They will be characteristic of *its* activities on the data and address busses. As we shall see, these status bits must be latched and then used with certain other signals ("control signals") output at certain times by the microprocessor (DBIN, SYNC, $\overline{\text{WR}}$—see below) in order to synthesize the control signals $\overline{\text{MEMW}}$, $\overline{\text{MEMR}}$, $\overline{\text{I/O R}}$, $\overline{\text{I/O W}}$, and $\overline{\text{IACK}}$ ($\overline{\text{INTA}}$). Before discussing how the status bits are latched and the control signals synthesized we first define the 8 status bits and describe what they indicate and then discuss how they are generated (really no big mystery).

The eight status bits are:

INTA (D_0) = 1 when interrupt request is made at pin 14, 8080.
RST N will flow on data bus to IR. Zero otherwise (see Figs. 57, 58).

$\overline{\text{WO}}$ (D$_1$)   (Write output) = 0 when current machine cycle will write into memory or I/O; 1 otherwise (read memory or I/O).

Stack (D$_2$) = 1 to indicate data will flow between CPU and Stack (Push or Pop). 0 otherwise.

HLTA (D$_3$) = 1 to indicate a Halt instruction will be executed, 0 otherwise.

Out (D$_4$) = 1 to indicate *address bus* has an *output device number* on it and that the data bus will contain the outgoing data *to the I/O* when $\overline{\text{WR}}$ (see below) = 0; 0 otherwise.

M$_1$ (D$_5$) = 1 *only* during the *fetch* of the *first* byte (the OP code) of an instruction; 0 otherwise.

INP (D$_6$) = 1 to indicate *address bus* has the *input device number* on it and that input data will be on the data bus when DBIN (see below) = 1; 0 otherwise.

MEMR (D$_7$) = 1 when data bus will have data coming in *from memory*. 0 otherwise.

A word on Sync, $\overline{\text{WR}}$, and DBIN. They are "control signals" somewhat similar to status bits generated by the 8080 at certain times (see Figs. 35, 68 and some timing diagrams, Chap. 2, Intel 8080 User's Manual, Sept. 1975):

Sync: = $\sqcap$ at the *beginning* of *each* machine cycle (T$_1$ – T$_2$). Pin 19–8080.

$\overline{\text{WR}}$:   = $\sqcup$ whenever there is stable data on the data bus going *to* memory or an I/O (T$_3$). It is 1 otherwise. Pin 18–8080.

DBIN: = $\sqcap$ whenever data is on the data bus coming *from* memory or an I/O to the CPU (T$_3$). 0 otherwise. Pin 17–8080.

If we were the microprocessor designer and had to sit down to ensure that the CPU will indeed put out the proper status bits characteristic of a particular machine cycle belonging to an instruction, how would we go about it? We would first make a table of status bits belonging to each machine cycle for a given instruc-

tion and then repeat that for every single instruction in the in-
struction set. Let us take $\begin{pmatrix} 315 \\ B_2 \\ B_3 \end{pmatrix}$ = CALL as an example. The *first*
thing the CPU must do is *fetch* the OP code stored in memory, in
this case 315, and decode it via the IR/ID. We, and the CPU, *now*
know that a call is in progress. *We* know that a byte B_2 and then a
byte B_3 will be successively *read* from memory. We *also* know that
$\langle PCH \rangle_{ret}$ and $(PCL)_{ret}$ will be successively *written* into successive
stack locations (SP–1, SP–2) for saving in memory. These facts
would allow us to make up a table of status bits vs. machine cycle
as shown in Table 5-1 below (we have included the case of an
input instruction $\begin{pmatrix} 333 \\ B_2 \end{pmatrix}$ in which there are two reads from memory, the first being a fetch, followed by a read (input) from an
I/O).

	M_1	M_2	M_3	M_4	M_5	M_1	M_2	M_3
Status Bits	*315 fetch for IR/ID*	*Read B_2*	*Read B_3*	*Stack Write SP–1*	*Stack Write SP–2*	*333 fetch for IR/ID*	*Read B_2*	*Read I/O*
INTA, D_0	0	0	0	0	0	0	0	0
$\overline{WO}$, D_1	1	1	1	0	0	1	1	1
Stack, D_2	0	0	0	1	1	0	0	0
HLTA, D_3	0	0	0	0	0	0	0	0
Out, D_4	0	0	0	0	0	0	0	0
M_1, D_5	1	0	0	0	0	1	0	0
INP, D_6	0	0	0	0	0	0	0	1
MEMR, D_7	1	1	1	0	0	1	1	0

Table 5-1: Status Bit Chart for the 315 and 333 instructions. M_i are
machine cycles for the given instruction. The fetch of the
OP. code during M_1 is the key to telling us the nature of the
machine cycles to follow.

Our next step would be to incorporate *all* such tables for *all* the instructions as "look-up" tables in a vast microprogram stored in a control memory (ROM) in the CPU. The status bits would be stored for M_1, then for M_2 (if any), and so on up to the last machine cycle for *each* instruction with M_1, M_2, . . . being given successive addresses in the microprogram. All instructions have exactly the same status bits for M_1 (see Table 5-1: i.e., a *fetch* of an *Op. Code byte* from *memory*) with the exception of the interrupt. (In the case of the interrupt there are 3 machine cycles, with M_1 a *fetch from the I/O interrupt port* holding the RSTN = 3N7 instruction and M_2, M_3 two write cycles into the Stack in memory to save the return address $(PCH)_r$ and $(PCL)_r$. The fetch involves 3N7 going from I/O interrupt port via data bus to the IR in the CPU. INP = 0 because the interrupt port has no device number on the address bus during its execution. Hence the status bits *for M_1* will be D_0 = 1 (INTA), $\overline{WO}$ = 1, Stack = 0, HLTA = 0, Out = 0, M_1 = 1 (fetch), INP = 0, MEMR = 0). Coming back to program execution and the appearance of status bits on the data bus at the beginning of each machine cycle, this no longer poses a mystery. As the program is being executed the first byte (e.g., OP. Code 315) would be decoded by the IR/ID so that *one* of the decoder's outputs q_i (i = 1, . . . 256) would go low. A search and compare routine in the microprogram would establish which of the q_i went low and on the basis of its finding would take us to *that* instruction's (here the CALL's) look-up tables for the status bits associated with its various machine cycles which we have *previously* written in to the control memory on the basis of tables like 5-1. The control and *timing* section of the CPU would then direct the spilling out of the status bits from the look-up tables on to the data bus at the beginning (T_1) of each of the 5 machine cycles. Thus it is only a question for the CPU to establish the OP. Code (first byte of the instruction) by means of the IR/ID and then consult the look-up tables for that OP. Code which have been programmed into the control memory in order to find the status bits belonging to each M_i of that instruction, and then dump them on to the data bus for successive M_i. All this, of course, has been done for us already.

We reproduce below material (courtesy Intel Corp.) which may further elucidate this subject (see also Fig. 65). (See Intel 8080 User's Manual, Sept. 1975, pp. 2-6 and 5-9.) Note particularly the status word chart and the timing diagram relationships

Instructions for the 8080 require from one to five machine cycles for complete execution. The 8080 sends out 8 bit of status information on the data bus at the beginning of each machine cycle (during SYNC time). The following table defines the status information.

STATUS INFORMATION DEFINITION

Symbols	Data Bus Bit	Definition
INTA*	D_0	Acknowledge signal for INTERRUPT request. Signal should be used to gate a restart instruction onto the data bus when DBIN is active.
$\overline{WO}$	D_1	Indicates that the operation in the current machine cycle will be a WRITE memory or OUTPUT function ($\overline{WO}$ = 0). Otherwise, a READ memory or INPUT operation will be executed.
STACK	D_2	Indicates that the address bus holds the pushdown stack address from the Stack Pointer.
HLTA	D_3	Acknowledge signal for HALT instruction.
OUT	D_4	Indicates that the address bus contains the address of an output device and the data bus will contain the output data when $\overline{WR}$ is active.
M_1	D_5	Provides a signal to indicate that the CPU is in the fetch cycle for the first byte of an instruction.
INP*	D_6	Indicates that the address bus contains the address of an input device and the input data should be placed on the data bus when DBIN is active.
MEMR*	D_7	Designates that the data bus will be used for memory read data.

*These three status bits can be used to control the flow of data onto the 8080 data bus.

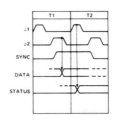

STATUS WORD CHART

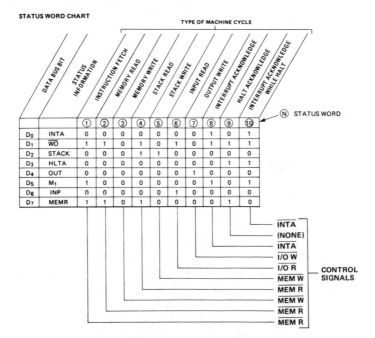

Data Bus Bit	Status Information	① Instruction Fetch	② Memory Read	③ Memory Write	④ Stack Read	⑤ Stack Write	⑥ Input Read	⑦ Output Write	⑧ Interrupt Acknowledge	⑨ Halt Acknowledge	⑩ Interrupt Acknowledge While Halt
D_0	INTA	0	0	0	0	0	0	0	1	0	1
D_1	$\overline{WO}$	1	1	0	1	0	1	0	1	1	1
D_2	STACK	0	0	0	1	1	0	0	0	0	0
D_3	HLTA	0	0	0	0	0	0	0	0	1	1
D_4	OUT	0	0	0	0	0	0	1	0	0	0
D_5	M_1	1	0	0	0	0	0	0	1	0	1
D_6	INP	0	0	0	0	0	1	0	0	0	0
D_7	MEMR	1	1	0	1	0	0	0	0	1	0

CONTROL SIGNALS:

Cycle	Control Signal
①	MEM R
②	MEM R
③	MEM W
④	MEM R
⑤	MEM W
⑥	I/O R
⑦	I/O W
⑧	INTA
⑨	(NONE)
⑩	INTA

among ϕ_1, ϕ_2, Sync, status data, and status latching ("data" represents the onset of status bits on to the bus at T_1 and "status" represents *latching* the status bits when Sync $\cdot$ ϕ_1 = $\sqcap$ *at the time the status bits are stable on the data bus just after* T_1).

A good exercise for you would be to draw up status bit tables like 5-1 for instructions such as XTHL, Mov A, M, SHLD, etc.

The next question is how we latch the status bits (this is necessary to synthesize the control signals $\overline{\text{MEMR}}$, etc. as we shall soon see). The reproduced material above indicates that the bits should be latched when Sync $\cdot$ ϕ_1 = $\sqcap$ to ensure status bit stability on the data bus. The 8224 clock generator and driver for the 8080 (see Fig. 67) generates a *TTL* signed $\overline{\text{STSTB}}$ (status strobe) which is precisely $\overline{\text{Sync} \cdot \phi_1}$ = $\sqcup$ (it does so by bringing sync = from pin 19 of the 8080 and gating it with an internal timing signal Q_{1A}). If we use $\overline{\text{STSTB}}$ as input to DS_1 (pin 1) of the 8212 with DI input pins 3, 5, . . . 22 tied to D_0, D_1, . . . D_7 on the data bus and keep DS_2 (pin 13) = MD (pin 2) = 1 with STB (pin 11) = X, as shown in Fig. 65 below, then D_0 pins 4, 6, . . . 21 of the 8212 will output the latched status bits INTA, $\overline{\text{WO}}$, . . . MEMR precisely at the beginning of each machine cycle when they are available and stable. Notice the 8212 truth table in Fig. 65 (both its latch and tristate properties). With the truth table as shown and the pin connections as indicated, $\overline{\text{STSTB}}$ = $\sqcup$ will latch D_0 . . . D_7 from the data bus just after T_1. See also Fig. 66 for the logic details of the 8212 and Fig. 68 for 8080 pin connections used in the generation of control signals taken up shortly.

Figure 65 is important and will be used in Experiment 5-2(l) that follows.

Now that we have the latched status bits, how do we generate the desired control signals from them? The diagrams below and the discussion following them will indicate how this is done (see also Fig. 11, Chap. 2, and Fig. 69 reproduced from Fig. 3-5, Intel 8080 Manual, Sept. 1975, p. 3-4). In the diagrams DBIN and $\overline{\text{WR}}$ are available at pins 17 and 18 of the 8080 (Fig. 68). Their significance and meaning were discussed earlier in this section. The status bits needed are D_4, D_6, D_0, and D_7 (latched—Fig. 65).

Thus, for example, to generate $\overline{\text{I/O W}}$ $\overline{\text{(OUT)}}$ we Nand D_4 with WR, for when $\begin{pmatrix} 323 \\ B_2 \end{pmatrix}$ has to be executed, D_4 = Out = 1 (indicating B_2 is on the address bus) and $\overline{\text{WR}}$ = $\sqcup$ (indicating data will be on the data bus to be written out). When *both* occur we want $\overline{\text{I/O W}}$ to be generated and the Nanding does just that. Likewise with respect to $\overline{\text{I/O R}}$, except that here DBIN is employed to indi-

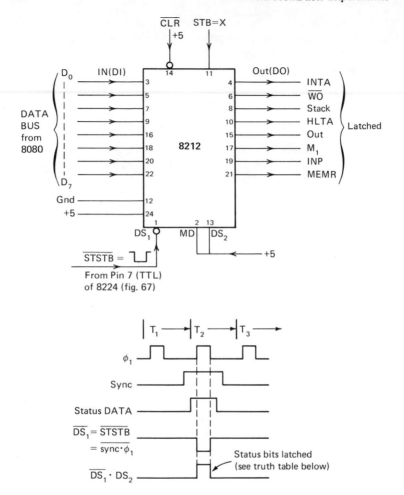

Figure 65. Latching of status bits with the 8212. Relevant timing diagrams and truth table. You can apply pins 4-21 to LED's and observe them as they change while single stepping the machine cycle.

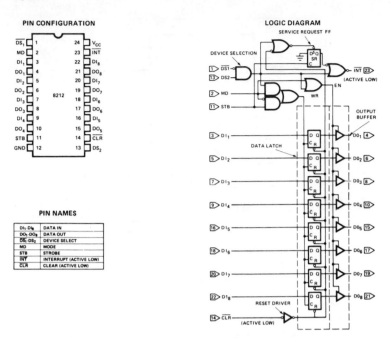

Figure 66. The 8212 buffer, latch, tristate I/O port. (Courtesy Intel Corp.).

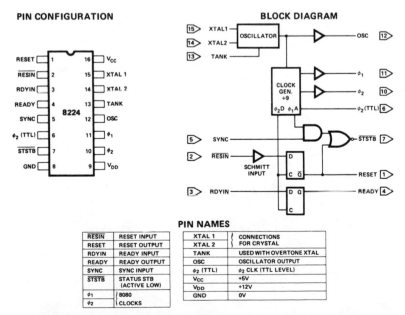

Figure 67. The 8224 clock/generator driver for the 8080 (Courtesy Intel Corp.).

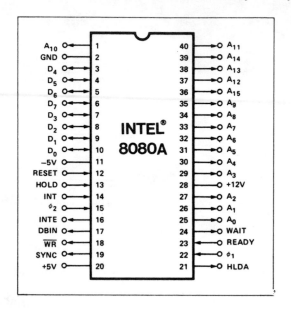

Figure 68. Pin configuration of 8080 showing power, control, clock, data bus, and address bus pins. (Courtesy Intel Corp.).

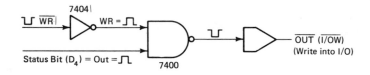

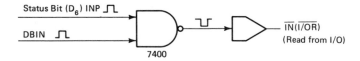

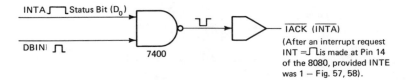

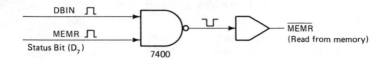

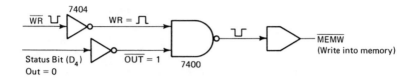

cate data will be coming in from *an I/O* to the CPU after $\left(\dfrac{333}{B_2}\right)$ is executed. To generate $\overline{\text{MEMR}}$ is similar to generating $\overline{\text{I/O R}}$ except one uses $D_7 = \text{MEMR}$ which indicates the machine cycle will be reading from *memory* (stack read or fetch or memory read). In generating $\overline{\text{MEMW}}$ *we use* $D_4 = Out$ with WR because in a *memory* write operation Out $= 0$ (it is 1 only when data is on the data bus going out to an *I/O* with an *I/O* address on the address bus) so that after inverting Out and Nanding with $\overline{\text{WR}}$ (= ⊔ because we are writing out) we indeed produce $\overline{\text{MEMW}}$ = ⊔ as desired. In the case of $\overline{\text{INTA}}$ ($\overline{\text{IACK}}$) the existence of RSTN = 3N7 on an interrupt port means DBIN will go ⊓ when an interrupt request (INT = ⊓) is made at pin 14 of 8080 (provided INTE = 1). This is certainly so since RSTN's data (3N7) will be going into the IR from the interrupt port via the data bus. In that case Nanding of DBIN and INTA (D_0)—which goes ⊓ to acknowledge the interrupt request— will generate $\overline{\text{IACK}}$ ($\overline{\text{INTA}}$) = ⊔ which is then the very signal used to detristate the interrupt port to send in 3N7 to the IR.

Now that we have these control signals what do we do with them? Remember they are generated to comply with the nature of the machine cycle just fetched and to help execute that machine cycle. The machine cycle(s) for any instruction will want to do one of several things: read from memory (stack read, memory read, or fetch); write into memory (stack write or memory write); write into or read from an I/O; interrupt (fetch from interrupt port and write into stack). These cover the essential tasks confronting the microcomputer during programming/bootstrapping, program execution, peripheral interfacing, and interrupting (service subroutine requests). To promote the execution of these tasks we simply connect $\overline{\text{MEMR}}$ from the control bus to chip selects or chip enables on ROMs and RAMs (with proper address decoding to distinguish between various memory blocks) and tie $\overline{\text{MEMW}}$ to R/W inputs of RAMs (see Fig. 11). Then any machine cycle that needs to read from or write into specific memory will be serviced by the above control (read/write) signals which enable the desired memory to be written into or read from. Likewise $\overline{\text{I/O W}}$ ($\overline{\text{OUT}}$) and $\overline{\text{I/O R}}$ ($\overline{\text{IN}}$) signals are used to generate device selects (Figs. 46, 51, 52) after input/output (333, 323) instructions. They will allow the output device to latch outgoing data from the data bus or de-tristate an input device in order to have it send its data into the CPU. Figure 11 gives examples with respect to three output ports (000, 001, 002) and one input port (000—the keyboard) of the MMD-1. $\overline{\text{I/O W}}$ and $\overline{\text{I/O R}}$, and device selects derived from them, have been used throughout the experiments in this chapter. Finally $\overline{\text{IACK}}$ is needed to detristate interrupt ports when an interrupt request is made in order to send RSTN = 3N7 in to the IR for subroutine service. We have used that, too, in the experiments.

Note that in lieu of using the 8212 as a status latch and then doing your own Nanding to derive the control signals, you can use an 8224, 8080, 8228 system (see Appendix A on the 8228 and p. 5-12, Intel Manual). The 8228 is a system controller and bus driver which has its own status latch and Nand gating array built in to latch the status bits and generate the control signals exactly in the fashion described above. It, too, gets driven by $\overline{\text{STSTB}}$ from the 8224.

A good summary of the material in section 5-2(G) is obtained by studying Fig. 69 below (Fig. 3-5 p. 3-4 Intel 8080 Manual, Sept. 1975).

Experiment 5-2(I)   An Experiment on Status Bits and Their Significance

In this experiment we wish to write a simple program containing a variety of instructions that differ sufficiently from each other, latch the status bits (Fig. 65) from the data bus using the 8212 chip and observe them on 8 LED's as they change from instruction to instruction as we single step our way through the program. An understanding of the results should go a long way in revealing the meaning and significance of the 8 status bits MEMR (D_7), INP (D_6), M_1 (D_5) Out (D_4), HLTA (D_3), Stack (D_2), $\overline{\text{Wo}}$ (D_1), and INTA (D_0) and their relation to data or

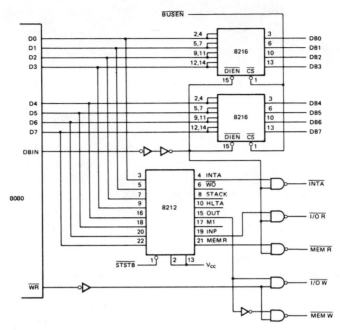

Figure 69. Latching of status bits and synthesis of control bus using the 8212. (8216 serves as bi-directional data bus buffer to drive I/O's and memories.) Courtesy Intel Corp.

address byte flow from CPU to and from memory and/or I/O instruction. It is suggested that each of these status bits, as observed on the LED's, be entered in the table shown and each one then plotted as a function of each step, with each step identified by address and data bus monitor readings plotted on the horizontal axis. It is also instructive to record with a fast probe the Sync pulses (pin 19 of the 8080) as they vary with the single stepping of the program as well as the DBIN and $\overline{\text{WR}}$ pulses (pins 17, 18 of the 8080).

The program is simple:

000	⎛ 076 ⎞	
001	⎝ 222 ⎠	
002	373	EI
003	⎛ 333 ⎞	Input to A from non existent device 006,
004	⎝ 006 ⎠	hence 377 goes to A (floating)
005	337	RST 3

$$\begin{matrix} 006 \\ 007 \\ 010 \end{matrix} \left(\begin{matrix} 303 \\ 000 \\ 003 \end{matrix}\right)$$

030   311   RET

The interfacing is shown in Fig. 65. Exhibit the status bits on 8 LED's—this monitors the "control bus." Load the program, run it, then single step it keeping INT on SK-10 equal to 0 (no interrupt request made). Then single step again, this time making an interrupt request* (INT=⎍). Shown in Table 5-2 are the single step address/data bus readings without an interrupt being made. Fill in the table with 1's or 0's for MEMR . . . INTA status bits, as well as $\overline{WR}$, Sync, and DBIN. Then redo this table all over making an interrupt request anywhere you like in the middle of the program. In each case plot MEMR, . . . , INTA vs. each step—a step being identified by address monitor and data monitor readings during the single step. Pay special attention to INTA. Study and interpret the results carefully in the light of the various status bit definitions and the "status word chart" included earlier in this section. This study should reveal a lot of the mysteries and subtleties of status bits and their relation to address and data flow during the machine cycles peculiar to a given instruction.

Read the footnote* carefully. Think of other experimental programs (employ the 5 machine cycle instruction $\left(\begin{matrix} 315 \\ B_2 \\ B_3 \end{matrix}\right)$ = Call) and make up similar tables and re-interpret the status bits. You can appreciate why single stepping is so important in this experiment. Compare your results with the status bits to be expected for each type of machine cycle (see status word chart earlier in this section).

---

*Note that after an interrupt request is made (INT=1), the EI flag (INTE) goes 1→0, and after the next instruction is executed all memory and I/O devices (except the interrupt port) are tristated off the address and data busses. The next instruction from memory *cannot* be fetched. Instead an RSTN=3N7 is to be jammed in. Here we are not enabling a *jam* RSTN instruction (via $\overline{IACK}$) *since we have not provided an 8212 or 8095 interrupt port to hold 3N7*. But the data bus, being high (377) after INTE goes 1→0, *simulates* a 377 jam Instruction into the IR. Hence the program goes to 000, 070 which is *precisely the start of the KEX Program* (061 instruction). Hence further single stepping after INT=1 is made will take us thru KEX—verify this. Note the Extra Bytes on the single step monitors after an interrupt request is made *just before* going into KEX. The data byte 377 should appear (data bus hi) as well as the "Push PC" bytes on to the stack at 377, 376.

	Single Step		D_7	D_6	D_5	D_4	D_3	D_2	D_1	D_0	SYNC Pin 19 8080	DBIN Pin 17 8080	$\overline{WR}$ Pin 18 8080
Hi	Add Bus	Data Bus	MEMR	INP	MI	OUT	HLTA	STACK	$\overline{WO}$	INTA			
003	000	076											
	001	222											
	002	373											
	003	333											
	004	006											
	006	377											
	005	337											
	377	003											
003	376	006											
000	030	303											
000	031	030											
000	032	003											
003	030	311											
	376	006											
	377	003											
	006	303											
	007	000											
	010	003											
	000	076											

Table 5-2. To be filled in relative to Expt. 5-2(I) on status bits. Note address and data bus monitor readings above are for INT = 0. Every entry under address and data bus headings represents another and distinct machine cycle.

5-3 Miscellaneous Experiments

Experiment 5-3(a) Function or Tone Generator (D to A Conversion)*

In this experiment we illustrate the principles of periodic function or tone generation using look-up tables in memory simulating the functions. The period is limited, of course, by the number of clock cycles per instruction and the frequency of the

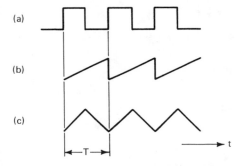

*The author acknowledges the cooperation of Carmine Capone, E. E. senior at Pratt Institute.

processor (2Mhz for 8080, but reduced to 750 khz—1.33 μsec—in the MMD-1). We consider square wave (or pulses), sawtooth, and triangular functions as examples.

We shall simulate these functions with 33 values of t in one period (32 intervals) in which the maximum voltage in cases (a) and (b) will correspond to digital bytes 377 and in case (c) to digital byte 200, while minimum voltage (0) corresponds, of course, to 000. Thus

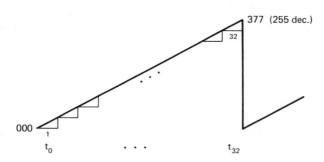

Clearly 32 intervals requires increments of 8_{10} or $(010)_8$ in the above sawtooth to go from 000 to 377. The schematic follows:

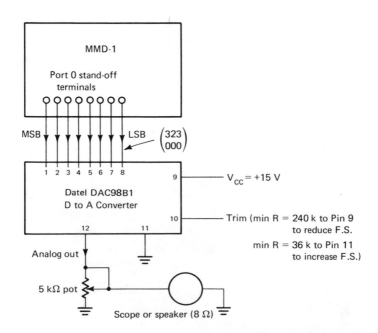

The program follows:

000	041		(X=1: Sawtooth table location	
001	X00	LXI H,L	X=2: Triangle table location	
002	003		X=3: Square wave table location)	
003	006	32 intervals		
004	040			
005	176	Mov A,M	⑦ clocks	
006	043	INX H,L	⑤ clocks	
007	323	⟨A⟩ → Port 0 (Latch for DAC Input)	⑩ clocks	
010	000			
011	005	DCR B	⑤ clocks	
012	312	JZ (Repeat for new cycle)	⑩ clocks	
013	000			
014	003			
015	303	JMP (cycle not complete)	⑩ clocks	
016	005			
017	003			

one interval → indicated for addresses 005–017

time to acquire and display
one point = 47 clocks

From the Intel 8080 Manual Sept. 1975 pp. 4-15 we find the clock cycles per instruction as indicated above. Thus 47 clocks at 1.33 μsec per clock (for the MMD-1) and 32 intervals to complete one period gives a period $T = 47 \times 1.33 \times 10^{-6} \times 32$ or $T \sim 2$ msec ($f \sim 500$ hz). Fewer intervals will yield a larger frequency but give a poorer approximation to the function. The look-up tables follow:

t	← Sawtooth → address	f(t)	← Triangular → address	f(t)	← Pulse or Square Wave → address	f(t)*
0	100	000	200	000	300	377
1	101	010	201	010	301	377
2	102	020	202	020	302	377
3	103	030	203	030	303	377
4	104	040	204	040	304	377
5	105	050	205	050	305	377

*Table shown is for square wave.

t	← Sawtooth →		← Triangular →		← Pulse or Square Wave →	
	address	f(t)	address	f(t)	address	f(t)*
6	106	060	206	060	306	377
7	107	070	207	070	307	377
8	110	100	210	100	310	377
9	111	110	211	110	311	377
10	112	120	212	120	312	377
11	113	130	213	130	313	377
12	114	140	214	140	314	377
13	115	150	215	150	315	377
14	116	160	216	160	316	377
15	117	170	217	170	317	377
16	120	200	220	200	320	000
17	121	210	221	170	321	000
18	122	220	222	160	322	000
19	123	230	223	150	323	000
20	124	240	224	140	324	000
21	125	250	225	130	325	000
22	126	260	226	120	326	000
23	127	270	227	110	327	000
24	130	300	230	100	330	000
25	131	310	231	070	331	000
26	132	320	232	060	332	000
27	133	330	233	050	333	000
28	134	340	234	040	334	000
29	135	350	235	030	335	000
30	136	360	236	020	336	000
31	137	370	237	010	337	000
32	140	377	240	000	340	000

*Table shown is for square wave.

Observe the waveforms on the scope and the corresponding tone generations. Note the measured period agrees with the 2 msec calculated above. Note the tone timbre in each case.

It is suggested that you program for a) a sin wave generator, b) variable duty cycle pulse generator, c) exponential "sawtooth", etc. You can include a loop

$$\begin{pmatrix} 016 \\ C \end{pmatrix} \quad \text{MVI, C}$$

$$015 \quad \text{DCR C}$$

$$\begin{pmatrix} 302 \\ B_2 \\ 003 \end{pmatrix} \quad \text{JNZ back to DCR C}$$

between 010 and 011 in the program to provide for a longer period. C would then control the frequency or period. Consult function tables for sin, exponentials, etc. in the handbooks. You will be surprised at the quality of the wave forms produced.

Experiment 5-3(b)   A Software Simulation of a UART

The purpose of a UART (see Refs. 6, 9, 28, 36) is to convert parallel bits in the μp accumulator to serial bits for transmission to a TTY or cassette type of peripheral; and, vice-versa, to convert serial bits representing data or characters coming from the peripheral into parallel bits to be received by the μp. The AY5-1013 is one such chip that accomplishes these functions.

The same function can be accomplished under software control using the μp and a latch (here port 0 on the MMD-1). We illustrate with a program* for parallel to serial conversion and leave it to you to try to implement a serial to parallel counterpart.

$$\begin{array}{ll} 000 & \begin{pmatrix} 076 \\ 252 \end{pmatrix} & \text{MVI, A} \\ 001 & & \text{Byte to be converted to serial } (D_7 \ldots D_0) \\ 002 & \begin{pmatrix} 323 \\ 001 \end{pmatrix} & \text{Parallel bits exhibited at port 1} \\ 003 & & \end{array}$$

---

*Interchange the instructions at 002, 003 with those at 004, 005, then change byte 006 to 004 at address 022 in the program, run and observe ports 1 and 0. This should vividly demonstrate the register shifting and serial exiting going on inside a UART. The chip has been replaced by software.

004	$\binom{046}{010}$	MVI, H
005		no. bits in one byte
006	117	Mov C͡, A
007	$\binom{346}{001}$	ANI, B$_2$
010		Mask on—all but lowest bit in Accum.
011	$\binom{323}{000}$	Di → lowest stand-off terminal
012		on port 0 (i = 0, 1, 2, . . 7)
013	$\binom{315}{}$	
014	$\binom{100}{}$	Call Time Delay (1 sec).
015	$\binom{003}{}$	
016	171	Mov A͡, C
017	017	RRC
020	045	DCR H
021	$\binom{302}{}$	
022	$\binom{006}{}$	JNZ
023	$\binom{003}{}$	
024	166	Halt (or Jump back to 000).

Time Delay (1 sec)

100	365	Push PSW
101	$\binom{006}{144}$	MVI, B
102		Time Byte
103	$\binom{021}{}$	
104	$\binom{046}{}$	LXI D, E
105	$\binom{001}{}$	Time bytes
106	033	DCX D, E
107	172	Mov A͡, D
110	263	ORA, E
111	$\binom{302}{}$	
112	$\binom{106}{}$	JNZ
113	$\binom{003}{}$	
114	005	DCR B
115	$\binom{302}{}$	
116	$\binom{103}{}$	JNZ
117	$\binom{003}{}$	
120	361	Pop PSW
121	311	Ret

Experiment 5-3(c)   Input Select Control of a Demultiplexer

The 8095 tri-state buffer is used here, together with two switches S_1 and S_0 to control the appearance of a byte at either port 0, 1, or 2 on the MMD-1. The interfacing is simple and follows:

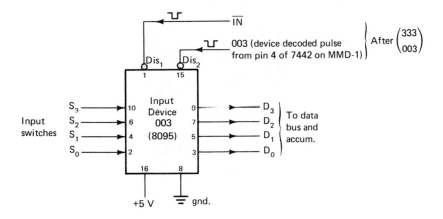

In this experiment switches S_3 and S_2 are kept high (they are needed for experiment 5-3(d)). The program follows:

000	$\left(\begin{matrix} 076 \\ 000 \end{matrix} \right)$	
001		
002	$\left(\begin{matrix} 323 \\ 000 \end{matrix} \right)$	
003		
004	$\left(\begin{matrix} 323 \\ 001 \end{matrix} \right)$	clear ports
005		
006	$\left(\begin{matrix} 323 \\ 002 \end{matrix} \right)$	
007		
010	$\left(\begin{matrix} 333 \\ 003 \end{matrix} \right)$	111111 S_1 S_0 → Acc.
011		
012	$\left(\begin{matrix} 346 \\ 003 \end{matrix} \right)$	Leaves 000000 S_1 S_0 in Acc.
013		

014 $\begin{pmatrix} 062 \\ 022 \\ 003 \end{pmatrix}$ STA in 003, 022.
015
016

017 $\begin{pmatrix} 076 \\ 377 \end{pmatrix}$
020

021 $\begin{pmatrix} 323 \\ X \end{pmatrix}$ 377 → Port X.
022

023 $\begin{pmatrix} 303 \\ 000 \\ 003 \end{pmatrix}$ JMP.
024
025

As you vary switches S_1 and S_0 you should find the following results.

S_1	S_0	*377 appears at Port*
0	0	0
0	1	1
1	0	2
1	1	000 at all ports

Experiment 5-3(d)   Input Control of a Process Rate

Here the process rate may be just about anything: a pulse generator repetition frequency, a tone frequency, on/off times of a motor, etc., etc. We shall illustrate with pulse generator rep. rates. The control is brought about by means of switches $S_3 \ S_2 \ S_1 \ S_0$ *while the program is running.* As in the previous experiment the STA instruction is crucial. The interfacing is identical with that shown in the previous experiment.

000 $\begin{pmatrix} 333 \\ 003 \end{pmatrix}$ 1111 $S_3 \ S_2 \ S_1 \ S_0$ → Accum.
001

002 $\begin{pmatrix} 346 \\ 017 \end{pmatrix}$ 0000 $S_3 \ S_2 \ S_1 \ S_0$ in Acc.
003

004 $\begin{pmatrix} 062 \\ 105 \\ 003 \end{pmatrix}$ Sends 0000 $S_3 \ S_2 \ S_1 \ S_0$
005   to $M_{003, 105}$ as T. D. byte
006

007	⎛076⎞	
010	⎝377⎠	377 → Port 0 (Pulse Gen.)
011	⎛323⎞	
012	⎝000⎠	

013	⎛315⎞	
014	⎜100⎟	Call T. D.
015	⎝003⎠	

016	⎛076⎞	
017	⎝000⎠	000 → Port 0
020	⎛323⎞	
021	⎝000⎠	

022	⎛315⎞	
023	⎜100⎟	Call T. D.
024	⎝003⎠	

025	⎛303⎞	
026	⎜000⎟	JMP
027	⎝003⎠	

Time Delay

100	365	Push PSW
101	⎛006⎞	MVI, B
102	⎝024⎠	= B (T. D. byte)
103	⎛021⎞	LXID, E
104	⎜046⎟	= E (T. D. byte)
105	⎝ X ⎠	= D (T. D. byte)
106	033	DCX D, E
107	172	Mov A, D
110	263	OR A, E
111	⎛302⎞	
112	⎜106⎟	JNZ
113	⎝003⎠	
114	005	DCRB
115	⎛302⎞	
116	⎜103⎟	JNZ
117	⎝003⎠	
120	361	Pop PSW
121	311	

With S_3 S_2 S_1 S_0 = 0000, D = 000 (.03 sec. periods); 0001 gives
D = 001 (.2 sec); 1101 gives D = 015 ($\sim$ 2 sec); etc. Vary the
switch settings and note the control over the pulse generator fre-
quencies.

Appendix A

Some Important IC's and Displays and Their Pin Configurations

Reproductions of IC 7400 series pin drawings are courtesy Texas Instruments Incorporated (The TTL Data Book For Design Engineers, 1976, 2nd Edition); those of the 8093, 8094, 8095 and 8097 IC's are courtesy National Semiconductor Corp. (TTL Data Book, Feb. 1976); those of the other 8000 series chips are courtesy Intel Corp. (8080 Microcomputer Systems User's Manual Sept. 1975); and those of the numeric displays are courtesy Hewlett Packard Corporation (Optoelectronics Designer's Catalog 1976 and 1977).

The author wishes to thank the above sources for their kind cooperation.

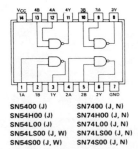

SN5400 (J)   SN7400 (J, N)
SN54H00 (J)   SN74H00 (J, N)
SN54L00 (J)   SN74L00 (J, N)
SN54LS00 (J, W)   SN74LS00 (J, N)
SN54S00 (J, W)   SN74S00 (J, N)

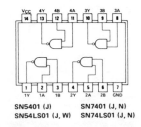

SN5401 (J)   SN7401 (J, N)
SN54LS01 (J, W)   SN74LS01 (J, N)

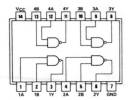

SN54H01 (J)   SN74H01 (J, N)

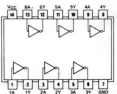

SN5405 (J)   SN7405 (J, N)
SN54H05 (J)   SN74H05 (J, N)
SN54LS05 (J, W)   SN74LS05 (J, N)
SN54S05 (J, W)   SN74S05 (J, N)

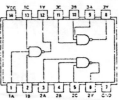

SN5410 (J)   SN7410 (J, N)
SN54H10 (J)   SN74H10 (J, N)
SN54L10 (J)   SN74L10 (J, N)
SN54LS10 (J, W)   SN74LS10 (J, N)
SN54S10 (J, W)   SN74S10 (J, N)

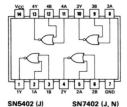

SN5402 (J)   SN7402 (J, N)
SN54L02 (J)   SN74L02 (J, N)
SN54LS02 (J, W)   SN74LS02 (J, N)
SN54S02 (J, W)   SN74S02 (J, N)

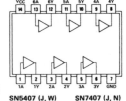

SN5407 (J, W)   SN7407 (J, N)

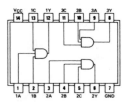

SN54H11 (J)   SN74H11 (J, N)
SN54LS11 (J, W)   SN74LS11 (J, N)
SN54S11 (J, W)   SN74S11 (J, N)

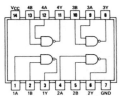

SN5403 (J)   SN7403 (J, N)
SN54L03 (J)   SN74L03 (J, N)
SN54LS03 (J, W)   SN74LS03 (J, N)
SN54S03 (J, W)   SN74S03 (J, N)

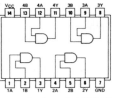

SN5408 (J, W)   SN7408 (J, N)
SN54LS08 (J, W)   SN74LS08 (J, N)
SN54S08 (J, W)   SN74S08 (J, N)

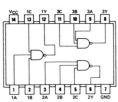

SN5412 (J, W)   SN7412 (J, N)
SN54LS12 (J, W)   SN74LS12 (J, N)

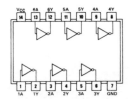

SN5404 (J)   SN7404 (J, N)
SN54H04 (J)   SN74H04 (J, N)
SN54L04 (J)   SN74L04 (J, N)
SN54LS04 (J, W)   SN74LS04 (J, N)
SN54S04 (J, W)   SN74S04 (J, N)

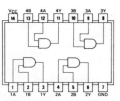

SN5409 (J, W)   SN7409 (J, N)
SN54LS09 (J, W)   SN74LS09 (J, N)
SN54S09 (J, W)   SN74S09 (J, N)

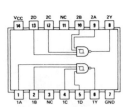

SN5413 (J, W)   SN7413 (J, N)
SN54LS13 (J, W)   SN74LS13 (J, N)

NC—No internal connection

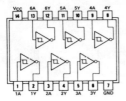

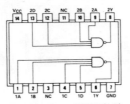

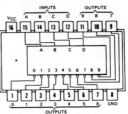

SN5414 (J, W)   SN7414 (J, N)
SN54LS14 (J, W)   SN74LS14 (J, N)

SN5422 (J, W)   SN7422 (J, N)
SN54H22 (J)   SN74H22 (J, N)
SN54LS22 (J, W)   SN74LS22 (J, N)
SN54S22 (J, W)   SN74S22 (J, N)

SN5442A (J, W)   SN7442A (J, N)
SN54L42 (J)   SN74L42 (J, N)
SN54LS42 (J, W)   SN74LS42 (J, N)
SN5443A (J, W)   SN7443A (J, N)
SN54L43 (J)   SN74L43 (J, N)
SN5444A (J, W)   SN7444A (J, N)
SN54L44 (J)   SN74L44 (J, N)

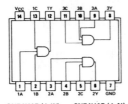

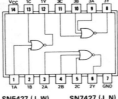

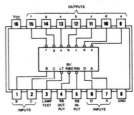

SN54H15 (J, W)   SN74H15 (J, N)
SN54LS15 (J, W)   SN74LS15 (J, N)
SN54S15 (J, W)   SN74S15 (J, N)

SN5427 (J, W)   SN7427 (J, N)
SN54LS27 (J, W)   SN74LS27 (J, N)

SN5446A (J, W)   SN7446A (J, N)
SN54L46 (J)   SN74L46 (J, N)
SN5447A (J, W)   SN7447A (J, N)
SN54L47 (J)   SN74L47 (J, N)
SN54LS47 (J, W)   SN74LS47 (J, N)

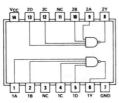

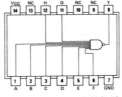

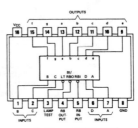

SN5420 (J)   SN7420 (J, N)
SN54H20 (J)   SN74H20 (J, N)
SN54L20 (J)   SN74L20 (J, N)
SN54LS20 (J, W)   SN74LS20 (J, N)
SN54S20 (J, W)   SN74S20 (J, N)

SN5430 (J)   SN7430 (J, N)
SN54H30 (J)   SN74H30 (J, N)
SN54L30 (J)   SN74L30 (J, N)
SN54LS30 (J, W)   SN74LS30 (J, N)
SN54S30 (J, W)   SN74S30 (J, N)

SN5448 (J, W)   SN7448 (J, N)
SN54LS48 (J, W)   SN74LS48 (J, N)

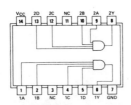

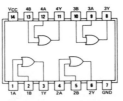

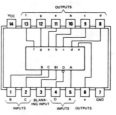

SN54H21 (J)   SN74H21 (J, N)
SN54LS21 (J, W)   SN74LS21 (J, N)

SN5432 (J, W)   SN7432 (J, N)
SN54LS32 (J, W)   SN74LS32 (J, N)
SN54S32 (J, W)   SN74S32 (J, N)

SN5449 (W)
SN54LS49 (J, W)   SN74LS49 (J, N)

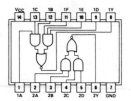

SN54L51 (J)　　SN74L51 (J, N)
SN54LS51 (J, W)　SN74LS51 (J, N)

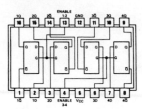

SN5475 (J, W)　　SN7475 (J, N)
SN54L75 (J)　　SN74L75 (J, N)
SN54LS75 (J, W)　SN74LS75 (J, N)

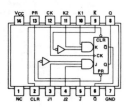

SN5470 (J)　SN7470 (J, N)

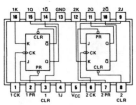

SN5476 (J, W)　　SN7476 (J, N)
SN54H76 (J, W)　SN74H76 (J, N)
SN54LS76 (J, W)　SN74LS76 (J, N)

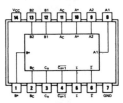

SN5480(J)　SN7480(J,N)

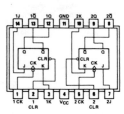

SN5473 (J, W)　　SN7473 (J, N)
SN54H73 (J, W)　SN74H73 (J, N)
SN54L73 (J, T)　SN74L73 (J, N)
SN54LS73 (J, W)　SN74LS73 (J, N)

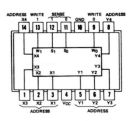

SN5481A (J, W)　SN7481A (J, N)

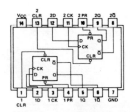

SN5474 (J)　　　SN7474 (J, N)
SN54H74 (J)　　SN74H74 (J, N)
SN54L74 (J)　　SN74L74 (J, N)
SN54LS74A (J, W)　SN74LS74A (J, N)
SN54S74 (J, W)　SN74S74 (J, N)

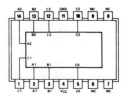

SN5482 (J, W)　SN7482 (J, N)

NC—No internal connection

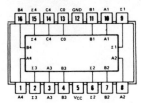

SN5483A (J, W)   SN74 83A (J, N)
SN54LS83A (J, W)   SN74LS83A (J, N)

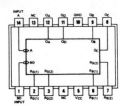

SN5490A (J, W)   SN7490A (J, N)
SN54L90 (J, T)   SN74L90 (J, N)
SN54LS90 (J, W)   SN74LS90 (J, N)
NC — No internal connection

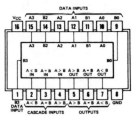

SN5484A (J, W)   SN7484A (J, N)

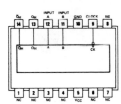

SN5491A (J)   SN7491A (J, N)
SN54L91 (J)   SN74L91 (J, N)
SN54LS91 (J)   SN74LS91 (J, N)

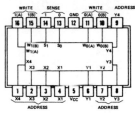

SN5485 (J, W)   SN7485 (J, N)
SN54LS85 (J, W)   SN74LS85 (J, N)
SN54S85 (J, W)   SN74S85 (J, N)

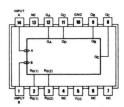

SN5493A (J, W)   SN7493A (J, N)
SN54LS93 (J, W)   SN74LS93 (J, N)

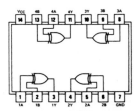

SN54L86 (J)   SN74L86 (J, N)

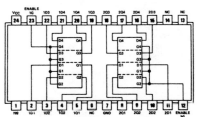

SN54100 (J, W)   SN74100 (J, N)
NC — No internal connection

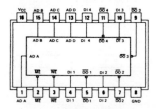

SN7489 (J, N)

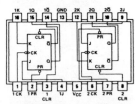

SN54H106 (J, W)   SN74H106 (J, N)

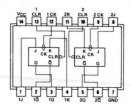

SN54107 (J)   SN74107 (J, N)
SN54LS107 (J)   SN74LS107 (J, N)

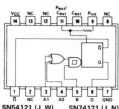

SN54121 (J, W)   SN74121 (J, N)
SN54L121 (J, T)   SN74L121 (J, N)

'121 . . . R_{int} = 2 kΩ NOM
'L121 . . . R_{int} = 4 kΩ NOM

NC—No internal connection

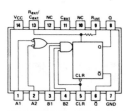

SN54122 (J, W)   SN74122 (J, N)
SN54L122 (J, T)   SN74L122 (J, N)
SN54LS122 (J, W)   SN74LS122 (J, N)

'122 . . . R_{int} = 10 kΩ NOM
'L122 . . . R_{int} = 20 kΩ NOM
'LS122 . . . R_{int} = 10 kΩ NOM

NC—No internal connection

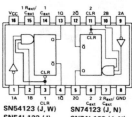

SN54123 (J, W)   SN74123 (J, N)
SN54L123 (J)   SN74L123 (J, N)
SN54LS123 (J, W)   SN74LS123 (J, N)

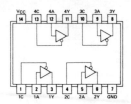

SN54125 (J, W)   SN74125 (J, N)
SN54LS125 (J, W)   SN74LS125 (J, N)

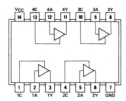

SN54126 (J, W)   SN74126 (J, N)
SN54LS126 (J, W)   SN74LS126 (J, N)

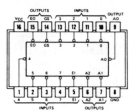

SN54148 (J, W)   SN74148 (J, N)
SN54LS148 (J, W)   SN74LS148 (J, N)

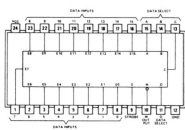

SN54150 (J, W)   SN74150 J, N)

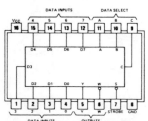

SN54151A (J, W)   SN74151A (J, N)
SN54LS151 (J, W)   SN74LS151 (J, N)
SN54S151 (J, W)   SN74S151 (J, N)

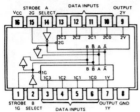

SN54153 (J, W)   SN74153 (J, N)
SN54L153 (J)   SN74L153 (J, N)
SN54LS153 (J, W) SN74LS153 (J, N)
SN54S153 (J, W)   SN74S153 (J, N)

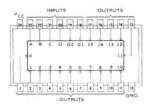

SN54154 (J, W)   SN74154 (J, N)
SN54L154 (J)   SN74L154 (J, N)

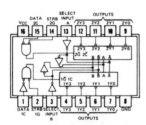

SN54155 (J, W)   SN74155 (J, N)
SN54LS155 (J, W) SN74LS155 (J, N)
SN54156 (J, W)   SN74156 (J, N)
SN54LS156 (J, W) SN74LS156 (J, N)

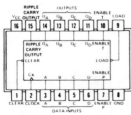

SN54160 (J, W)   SN74160 (J, N)
SN54LS160A (J, W)   SN74LS160A (J, N)
SN54161 (J, W)   SN74161 (J, N)
SN54LS161A (J, W)   SN74LS161A (J, N)
SN54162 (J, W)   SN74162 (J, N)
SN54LS162A (J, W)   SN74LS162A (J, N)
SN54S162 (J, W)   SN74S162 (J, N)
SN54163 (J, W)   SN74163 (J, N)
SN54LS163A (J, W)   SN74LS163A (J, N)
SN54S163 (J, W)   SN74S163 (J, N)

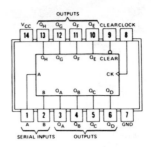

SN54164 (J, W)   SN74164 (J, N)
SN54L164 (J, T)   SN74L164 (J, N)
SN54LS164 (J, W) SN74LS164 (J, N)

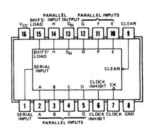

SN54165 (J, W)   SN74165 (J, N)
SN54LS165 (J, W) SN74LS165 (J, N)

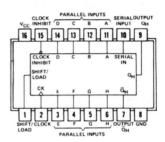

SN54166 (J, W)   SN74166 (J, N)
SN54LS166 (J, W) SN74LS166 (J, N)

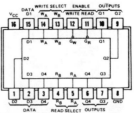

SN54170 (J, W)   SN74170 (J, W)
SN54LS170 (J, W) SN74LS170 (J, N)

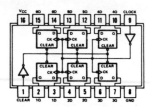

SN54174 (J, W)   **SN74174 (J, N)**
SN54LS174 (J, W)   **SN74LS174 (J, N)**
SN54S174 (J, W)   **SN74S174 (J, N)**

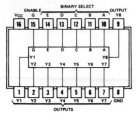

SN54184 (J, W)   **SN74184 (J, N)**
SN54185A (J, W)   **SN74185A (J, N)**

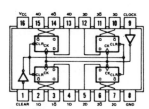

SN54175 (J, W)   **SN74175 (J, N)**
SN54LS175 (J, W)   **SN74LS175 (J, N)**
SN54S175 (J, W)   **SN74S175 (J, N)**

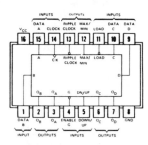

SN54190 (J, W)   **SN74190 (J, N)**
SN54LS190 (J, W)   **SN74LS190 (J, N)**
SN54191 (J, W)   **SN74191 (J, N)**
SN54LS191 (J, W)   **SN74LS191 (J, N)**

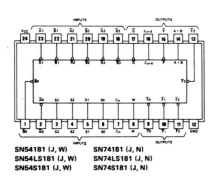

SN54181 (J, W)   **SN74181 (J, N)**
SN54LS181 (J, W)   **SN74LS181 (J, N)**
SN54S181 (J, W)   **SN74S181 (J, N)**

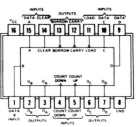

SN54192 (J, W)   **SN74192 (J, N)**
SN54L192 (J)   **SN74192 (J, N)**
SN54LS192 (J, W)   **SN74LS192 (J, N)**
SN54193 (J, W)   **SN74193 (J, N)**
SN54L193 (J)   **SN74L193 (J, N)**
SN54LS193 (J, W)   **SN74LS193 (J, N)**

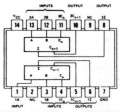

SN54LS183 (J, W)   **SN74LS183 (J, N)**
SN54H183 (J, W)   **SN74H183 (J, N)**

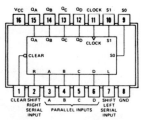

SN54194 (J, W)   **SN74194 (J, N)**
SN54LS194A (J, W)   **SN74LS194A (J, N)**
SN54S194 (J, W)   **SN74S194 (J, N)**

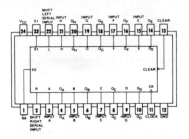

SN54198 (J, W)   SN74198 (J, N)

DM70/DM8093,94

TRI-STATE Quad Buffers

General Description

The DM7093/DM8093 and DM7094/DM8094 are quad two-input buffers which accept normal TTL or DTL input levels; and have outputs which provide either normal low-impedance TTL characteristics, or a high-impedance third logic state. One of the two inputs to each buffer is used as a control line to gate the output into the high-impedance state. The other input simply passes the non-inverted data through the buffer. The DM7093/DM8093 provides the high-impedance state when a high logic level is applied to the control input, the DM7094/DM8094 when a low logic level is applied to the control input. The low output impedance of these devices provides good capacitive-drive capability and rapid transition from the low to the high logic levels, thus assuring both speed and waveform

integrity. It is possible to connect as many as 128 devices to a common bus line, and still have adequate drive capability.

Features

- Pin equivalent to DM54125/74125 (7093/8093) and DM54126/74126 (7094/8094)
- Up to 128 devices can be connected to a common bus line
- High capacitive-drive capability
- Independent control of each buffer
- Typical propagation delay – 12 ns

Connection Diagrams

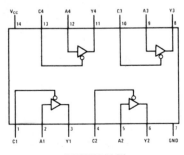

7093/8093(J), (N), (W)

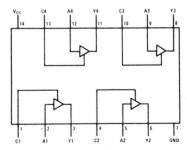

7094/8094(J), (N), (W)

Truth Tables

DM7093/DM8093

DATA	CONTROL	OUTPUT
H	L	H
L	L	L
X	H	Hi-Z

DM7094/DM8094

DATA	CONTROL	OUTPUT
H	H	H
L	H	L
X	L	Hi-Z

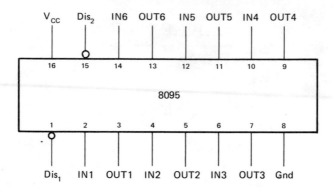

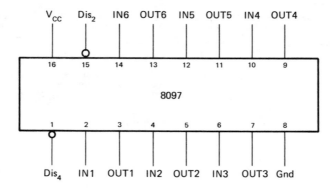

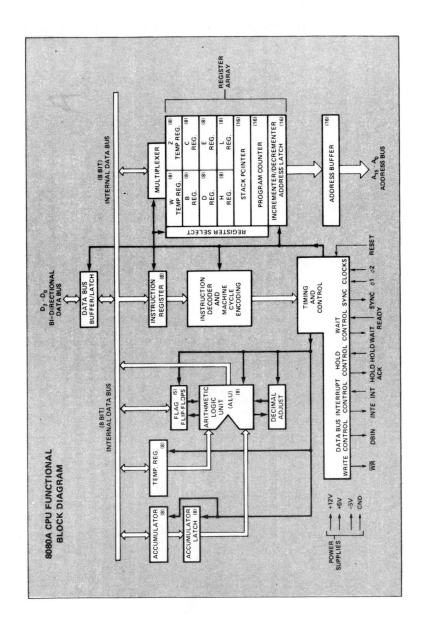

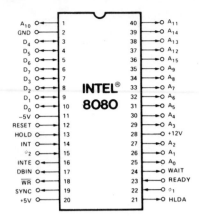

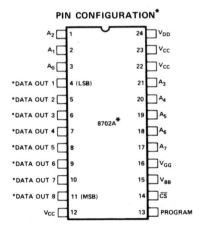

PIN CONFIGURATION*

BLOCK DIAGRAM

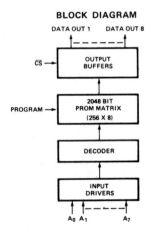

*THIS PIN IS THE DATA INPUT LEAD DURING PROGRAMMING.

PIN NAMES

A_0-A_7	ADDRESS INPUTS
$\overline{CS}$	CHIP SELECT INPUT
DO_1- DO_2	DATA OUTPUTS

*The 8702A is a 256×8 Erasable and Electrically Reprogrammable ROM. It is similar in most respects to the Intel 1702 UV Erasable PROM (see Intel Catalog)

PIN CONFIGURATION*

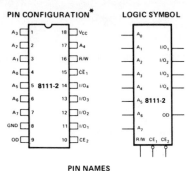

LOGIC SYMBOL

(8111-2)

BLOCK DIAGRAM

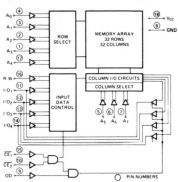

PIN NAMES

A_0-A_7	ADDRESS INPUTS
OD	OUTPUT DISABLE
R/W	READ/WRITE INPUT
$\overline{CE}_1$	CHIP ENABLE 1
$\overline{CE}_2$	CHIP ENABLE 2
I/O_1- I/O_4	DATA INPUT/OUTPUT

PIN CONFIGURATION**

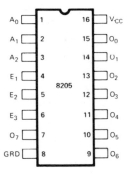

LOGIC SYMBOL

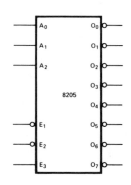

(8205)

PIN NAMES

A_0- A_2	ADDRESS INPUTS
$\overline{E}_1$- $\overline{E}_3$	ENABLE INPUTS
$\overline{O}_0$- $\overline{O}_7$	DECODED OUTPUTS

ADDRESS			ENABLE			OUTPUTS							
A_0	A_1	A_2	E_1	E_2	E_3	0	1	2	3	4	5	6	7
L	L	L	L	L	H	L	H	H	H	H	H	H	H
H	L	L	L	L	H	H	L	H	H	H	H	H	H
L	H	L	L	L	H	H	H	L	H	H	H	H	H
H	H	L	L	L	H	H	H	H	L	H	H	H	H
L	L	H	L	L	H	H	H	H	H	L	H	H	H
H	L	H	L	L	H	H	H	H	H	H	L	H	H
L	H	H	L	L	H	H	H	H	H	H	H	L	H
H	H	H	L	L	H	H	H	H	H	H	H	H	L
X	X	X	L	L	L	H	H	H	H	H	H	H	H
X	X	X	H	L	L	H	H	H	H	H	H	H	H
X	X	X	L	H	L	H	H	H	H	H	H	H	H
X	X	X	H	H	L	H	H	H	H	H	H	H	H
X	X	X	H	L	H	H	H	H	H	H	H	H	H
X	X	X	L	H	H	H	H	H	H	H	H	H	H
X	X	X	H	H	H	H	H	H	H	H	H	H	H

*256×4 Static MOS RAM.

**3×8 Decoder.

int_el®   Schottky Bipolar **8216/8226**

4 BIT PARALLEL BIDIRECTIONAL BUS DRIVER

- Data Bus Buffer Driver for 8080 CPU
- Low Input Load Current — .25 mA Maximum
- High Output Drive Capability for Driving System Data Bus

- 3.65V Output High Voltage for Direct Interface to 8080 CPU
- Three State Outputs
- Reduces System Package Count

The 8216/8226 is a 4-bit bi-directional bus driver/receiver.

All inputs are low power TTL compatible. For driving MOS, the DO outputs provide a high 3.65V V_{OH}, and for high capacitance terminated bus structures, the DB outputs provide a high 50mA I_{OL} capability.

A non-inverting (8216) and an inverting (8226) are available to meet a wide variety of applications for buffering in microcomputer systems.

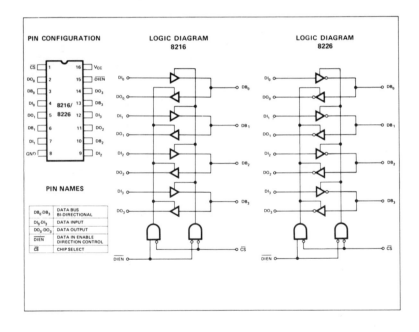

Schottky Bipolar **8224**

CLOCK GENERATOR AND DRIVER
FOR 8080A CPU

- **Single Chip Clock Generator/Driver for 8080A CPU**
- **Power-Up Reset for CPU**
- **Ready Synchronizing Flip-Flop**
- **Advanced Status Strobe**
- **Oscillator Output for External System Timing**
- **Crystal Controlled for Stable System Operation**
- **Reduces System Package Count**

The 8224 is a single chip clock generator/driver for the 8080A CPU. It is controlled by a crystal, selected by the designer, to meet a variety of system speed requirements.

Also included are circuits to provide power-up reset, advance status strobe and synchronization of ready.

The 8224 provides the designer with a significant reduction of packages used to generate clocks and timing for 8080A.

PIN CONFIGURATION

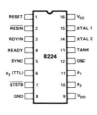

BLOCK DIAGRAM

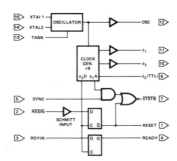

PIN NAMES

RESIN	RESET INPUT	XTAL 1	CONNECTIONS
RESET	RESET OUTPUT	XTAL 2	FOR CRYSTAL
RDYIN	READY INPUT	TANK	USED WITH OVERTONE XTAL
READY	READY OUTPUT	OSC	OSCILLATOR OUTPUT
SYNC	SYNC INPUT	ϕ_2 (TTL)	ϕ_2 CLK (TTL LEVEL)
STSTB	STATUS STB (ACTIVE LOW)	V_{CC}	+5V
		V_{DD}	+12V
ϕ_1	8080	GND	0V
ϕ_2	CLOCKS		

Schottky Bipolar 8212[*]

EIGHT-BIT INPUT/OUTPUT PORT

- **Fully Parallel 8-Bit Data Register and Buffer**
- **Service Request Flip-Flop for Interrupt Generation**
- **Low Input Load Current — .25 mA Max.**
- **Three State Outputs**
- **Outputs Sink 15 mA**

- **3.65V Output High Voltage for Direct Interface to 8080 CPU or 8008 CPU**
- **Asynchronous Register Clear**
- **Replaces Buffers, Latches and Multiplexers in Microcomputer Systems**
- **Reduces System Package Count**

The 8212 input/output port consists of an 8-bit latch with 3-state output buffers along with control and device selection logic. Also included is a service request flip-flop for the generation and control of interrupts to the microprocessor.

The device is multimode in nature. It can be used to implement latches, gated buffers or multiplexers. Thus, all of the principal peripheral and input/output functions of a microcomputer system can be implemented with this device.

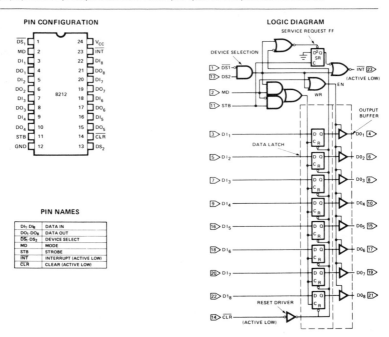

PIN NAMES

$DI_1 \cdot DI_8$	DATA IN
$DO_1 \cdot DO_8$	DATA OUT
$\overline{DS}_1 \cdot DS_2$	DEVICE SELECT
MD	MODE
STB	STROBE
$\overline{INT}$	INTERRUPT (ACTIVE LOW)
$\overline{CLR}$	CLEAR (ACTIVE LOW)

*See also Figs. 62, 65, 69, Chap. 5.

Schottky Bipolar **8228**

SYSTEM CONTROLLER AND BUS DRIVER FOR 8080A CPU

- **Single Chip System Control for MCS-80 Systems**
- **Built-in Bi-Directional Bus Driver for Data Bus Isolation**
- **Allows the use of Multiple Byte Instructions (e.g. CALL) for Interrupt Acknowledge**

- **User Selected Single Level Interrupt Vector (RST 7)**
- **28 Pin Dual In-Line Package**
- **Reduces System Package Count**

The 8228 is a single chip system controller and bus driver for MCS-80. It generates all signals required to directly interface MCS-80 family RAM, ROM, and I/O components.

A bi-directional bus driver is included to provide high system TTL fan-out. It also provides isolation of the 8080 data bus from memory and I/O. This allows for the optimization of control signals, enabling the systems deisgner to use slower memory and I/O. The isolation of the bus driver also provides for enhanced system noise immunity.

A user selected single level interrupt vector (RST 7) is provided to simplify real time, interrupt driven, small system requirements. The 8228 also generates the correct control signals to allow the use of multiple byte instructions (e.g., CALL) in response to an INTERRUPT ACKNOWLEDGE by the 8080A. This feature permits large, interrupt driven systems to have an unlimited number of interrupt levels.

The 8228 is designed to support a wide variety of system bus structures and also reduce system package count for cost effective, reliable, design of the MCS-80 systems.

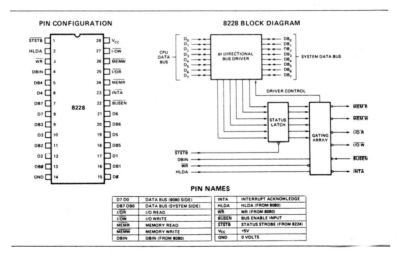

PIN CONFIGURATION

8228 BLOCK DIAGRAM

PIN NAMES

D7-D0	DATA BUS (8080 SIDE)	INTA	INTERRUPT ACKNOWLEDGE
DB7-DB0	DATA BUS (SYSTEM SIDE)	HLDA	HLDA (FROM 8080)
I/OR	I/O READ	WR	WR (FROM 8080)
I/OW	I/O WRITE	BUSEN	BUS ENABLE INPUT
MEMR	MEMORY READ	STSTB	STATUS STROBE (FROM 8224)
MEMW	MEMORY WRITE	Vcc	+5V
DBIN	DBIN (FROM 8080)	GND	0 VOLTS

SCHOTTKY BIPOLAR 8228

FUNCTIONAL DESCRIPTION

General

The 8228 is a single chip System Controller and Data Bus driver for the 8080 Microcomputer System. It generates all control signals required to directly interface MCS-80™ family RAM, ROM, and I/O components.

Schottky Bipolar technology is used to maintain low delay times and provide high output drive capability to support small to medium systems.

Bi-Directional Bus Driver

An eight bit, bi-directional bus driver is provided to buffer the 8080 data bus from Memory and I/O devices. The 8080A data bus has an input requirement of 3.3 volts (min) and can drive (sink) a maximum current of 1.9mA. The 8228 data bus driver assures that these input requirements will be not only met but exceeded for enhanced noise immunity. Also, on the system side of the driver adequate drive current is available (10mA Typ.) so that a large number of Memory and I/O devices can be directly connected to the bus.

The Bi-Directional Bus Driver is controlled by signals from the Gating Array so that proper bus flow is maintained and its outputs can be forced into their high impedance state (3-state) for DMA activities.

Status Latch

At the beginning of each machine cycle the 8080 CPU issues "status" information on its data bus that indicates the type of activity that will occur during the cycle. The 8228 stores this information in the Status Latch when the $\overline{STSTB}$ input goes "low". The output of the Status Latch is connected to the Gating Array and is part of the Control Signal generation.

Gating Array

The Gating Array generates control signals ($\overline{MEM\ R}$, $\overline{MEM\ W}$, $\overline{I/O\ R}$, $\overline{I/O\ W}$ and $\overline{INTA}$) by gating the outputs of the Status Latch with signals from the 8080 CPU (DBIN, $\overline{WR}$, and HLDA).

The "read" control signals ($\overline{MEM\ R}$, $\overline{I/O\ R}$ and $\overline{INTA}$) are derived from the logical combination of the appropriate Status Bit (or bits) and the DBIN input from the 8080 CPU.

The "write" control signals ($\overline{MEM\ W}$, $\overline{I/O\ W}$) are derived from the logical combination of the appropriate Status Bit (or bits) and the $\overline{WR}$ input from the 8080 CPU.

All Control Signals are "active low" and directly interface to MCS-80 family RAM, ROM and I/O components.

The $\overline{INTA}$ control signal is normally used to gate the "interrupt instruction port" onto the bus. It also provides a special feature in the 8228. If only one basic vector is needed in the interrupt structure, such as in small systems, the 8228 can automatically insert a RST 7 instruction onto the bus at the proper time. To use this option, simply connect the $\overline{INTA}$ output of the 8228 (pin 23) to the +12 volt supply through a series resistor (1K ohms). The voltage is sensed internally by the 8228 and logic is "set-up" so that when the DBIN input is active a RST 7 instruction is gated on to the bus when an interrupt is acknowledged. This feature provides a single interrupt vector with no additional components, such as an interrupt instruction port.

When using CALL as an Interrupt instruction the 8228 will generate an $\overline{INTA}$ pulse for each of the three bytes.

The $\overline{BUSEN}$ (Bus Enable) input to the Gating Array is an asynchronous input that forces the data bus output buffers and control signal buffers into their high-impedance state if it is a "one". If $\overline{BUSEN}$ is a "zero" normal operation of the data buffer and control signals take place.

8228 BLOCK DIAGRAM

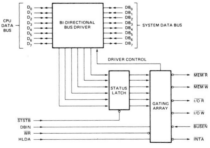

SCHOTTKY BIPOLAR 8228

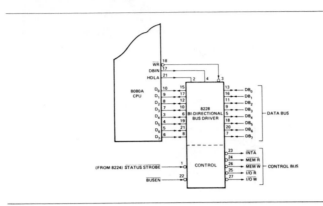

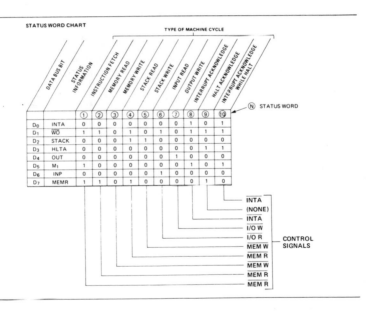

SCHOTTKY BIPOLAR 8228

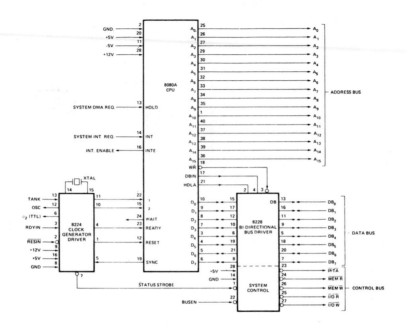

8080A CPU Standard Interface

NUMERIC and	5082-7300
HEXADECIMAL	5082-7302
INDICATORS	5082-7304
	5082-7340

TECHNICAL DATA   APRIL 1977

Features

- **NUMERIC 5082-7300/-7302**
  0-9, Test State, Minus
  Sign, Blank States
  Decimal Point
  7300 Right Hand D.P.
  7302 Left Hand D.P.
- **HEXADECIMAL 5082-7340**
  0-9, A-F, Base 16
  Operation
  Blanking Control,
  Conserves Power
  No Decimal Point
- **DTL/TTL COMPATIBLE**
- **INCLUDES DECODER/DRIVER WITH 5 BIT MEMORY**
  8421 Positive Logic Input
- **4 x 7 DOT MATRIX ARRAY**
  Shaped Character, Excellent Readibility
- **STANDARD .600 INCH x .400 INCH DUAL-IN-LINE PACKAGE INCLUDING CONTRAST FILTER**
- **CATEGORIZED FOR LUMINOUS INTENSITY**
  Assures Uniformity of Light Output from
  Unit to Unit within a Single Category

Description

The HP 5082-7300 series solid state numeric and hexadecimal indicators with on-board decoder/driver and memory provide a reliable, low-cost method for displaying digital information.

The 5082-7300 numeric indicator decodes positive 8421 BCD logic inputs into characters 0-9, a "–" sign, a test pattern, and four blanks in the invalid BCD states. The unit employs a right-hand decimal point. Typical applications include point-of-sale terminals, instrumentation, and computer systems.

The 5082-7302 is the same as the 5082-7300, except that the decimal point is located on the left-hand side of the digit.

The 5082-7340 hexadecimal indicator decodes positive 8421 logic inputs into 16 states, 0-9 and A-F. In place of the decimal point an input is provided for blanking the display (all LED's off), without losing the contents of the memory. Applications include terminals and computer systems using the base-16 character set.

The 5082-7304 is a (± 1.) overrange character, including decimal point, used in instrumentation applications.

Package Dimensions

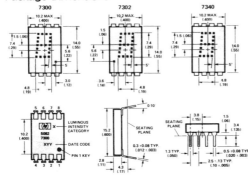

PIN	FUNCTION	
	5082-7300 and 7302 Numeric	**5082-7340 Hexadecimal**
1	Input 2	Input 2
2	Input 4	Input 4
3	Input 8	Input 8
4	Decimal point	Blanking control
5	Latch enable	Latch enable
6	Ground	Ground
7	V_{cc}	V_{cc}
8	Input 1	Input 1

NOTES:
1. Dimensions in millimetres and (inches).
2. Unless otherwise specified, the tolerance on all dimensions is ±.38mm (±.015").
3. Digit center line is ±.25mm (±.01") from package center line.

TRUTH TABLE					
BCD DATA [1]				5082-7300/7302	5082-7340
X_8	X_4	X_2	X_1		
L	L	L	L	0	0
L	L	L	H	1	1
L	L	H	L	2	2
L	L	H	H	3	3
L	H	L	L	4	4
L	H	L	H	5	5
L	H	H	L	6	6
L	H	H	H	7	7
H	L	L	L	8	8
H	L	L	H	9	9
H	L	H	L	A	A
H	L	H	H	(BLANK)	B
H	H	L	L	(BLANK)	C
H	H	L	H	----	D
H	H	H	L	(BLANK)	E
H	H	H	H	(BLANK)	F
DECIMAL PT. [2]			ON	$V_{DP} = L$	
			OFF	$V_{DP} = H$	
ENABLE [1]			LOAD DATA	$V_E = L$	
			LATCH DATA	$V_E = H$	
BLANKING [3]			DISPLAY-ON	$V_B = L$	
			DISPLAY-OFF	$V_B = H$	

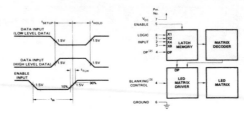

Figure 1. Timing Diagram of 5082-7300 Series Logic.

Figure 2. Block Diagram of 5082-7300 Series Logic.

Notes:
1. H = Logic High; L = Logic Low. With the enable input at logic high changes in BCD input logic levels have no effect upon display memory or displayed character.
2. The decimal point input, DP, pertains only to the 5082-7300 and 5082-7302 displays.
3. The blanking control input, B, pertains only to the 5082-7340 hexadecimal display. Blanking input has no effect upon display memory.

HEWLETT **hp** PACKARD

COMPONENTS

0.3 INCH RED SEVEN SEGMENT DISPLAY

5082-7730 SERIES
5082-7740

TECHNICAL DATA APRIL 1977

Features

* **5082-7730**
  Common Anode
  Left Hand D.P.
* **5082-7731**
  Common Anode
  Right Hand D.P.
* **5082-7736**
  Polarity and Overflow Indicator
  Universal Pinout
  Right Hand D.P.
* **5082-7740**
  Common Cathode
  Right Hand D.P.
* **EXCELLENT CHARACTER APPEARANCE**
  Continuous Uniform Segments
  Wide Viewing Angle
  High Contrast
* **IC COMPATIBLE**
  1.6V dc per Segment
* **STANDARD 0.3" DIP LEAD CONFIGURATION**
  PC Board or Standard Socket Mountable
* **CATEGORIZED FOR LUMINOUS INTENSITY**
  Assures Uniformity of Light Output from
  Unit to Unit withing a Single Category

Description

The HP 5082-7730/7740 series devices are common anode LED displays. The series includes a left hand and a right hand decimal point numeric display as well as a polarity and overflow indicator. The large 7.62 mm (0.3 in.) high character size generates a bright, continuously uniform seven segment display. Designed for viewing distances of up to 3 meters (9.9 feet), these single digit displays provide a high contrast ratio and a wide viewing angle.

The 5082-7730 series devices utilize a standard 7.62 mm (0.3 in.) dual-in-line package configuration that permits mounting on PC boards or in standard IC sockets. Requiring a low forward voltage, these displays are inherently IC compatible, allowing for easy integration into electronic instrumentation, point of sale terminals, TVs, radios, and digital clocks.

Devices

Part No. 5082-	Description	Package Drawing
7730	Common Anode Left Hand Decimal	A
7731	Common Anode Right Hand Decimal	B
7736	Universal Overflow ±1 Right Hand Decimal	C
7740	Common Cathode Right Hand Decimal	D

Note: Universal pinout brings the anode and cathode of each segment's LED out to separate pins. See internal diagram C.

Package Dimensions

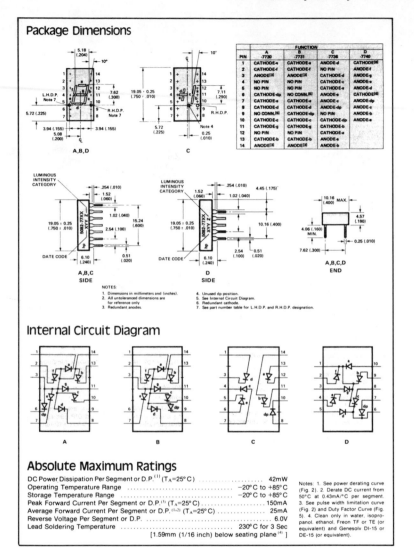

	FUNCTION			
PIN	**A** -7730	**B** -7731	**C** -7736	**D** -7740
1	CATHODE-c	CATHODE-a	ANODE-d	CATHODE[5]
2	CATHODE-f	CATHODE-f	NO PIN	ANODE-f
3	ANODE[3]	ANODE[3]	CATHODE-d	ANODE-g
4	NO PIN	NO PIN	CATHODE-c	ANODE-a
5	NO PIN	NO PIN	CATHODE-e	ANODE-d
6	CATHODE-dp	NO CONN.[6]	ANODE-c	CATHODE[5]
7	CATHODE-e	CATHODE-e	ANODE-e	ANODE-dp
8	CATHODE-d	CATHODE-d	ANODE-dp	ANODE-c
9	NO CONN.[6]	CATHODE-dp	ANODE-b	ANODE-b
10	CATHODE-c	CATHODE-c	CATHODE-dp	ANODE-e
11	CATHODE-g	CATHODE-g	CATHODE-b	
12	NO PIN	NO PIN	CATHODE-a	
13	CATHODE-b	CATHODE-b	ANODE-a	
14	ANODE[3]	ANODE[3]	ANODE-b	

A,B,D

C

LUMINOUS INTENSITY CATEGORY

A,B,C SIDE

LUMINOUS INTENSITY CATEGORY

D SIDE

A,B,C,D END

NOTES:
1. Dimensions in millimeters and (inches).
2. All untoleranced dimensions are for reference only
3. Redundant anodes.
4. Unused dp position.
5. See Internal Circuit Diagram.
6. Redundant cathode.
7. See part number table for L.H.D.P. and R.H.D.P. designation.

Internal Circuit Diagram

A

B

C

D

Absolute Maximum Ratings

DC Power Dissipation Per Segment or D.P.[1] (T_A=25°C) 42mW
Operating Temperature Range .... −20°C to +85°C
Storage Temperature Range .... −20°C to +85°C
Peak Forward Current Per Segment or D.P.[3] (T_A=25°C) 150mA
Average Forward Current Per Segment or D.P.[1,2] (T_A=25°C) 25mA
Reverse Voltage Per Segment or D.P. 6.0V
Lead Soldering Temperature .... 230°C for 3 Sec
[1.59mm (1/16 inch) below seating plane[4]]

Notes: 1. See power derating curve (Fig. 2). 2. Derate DC current from 50°C at 0.43mA/°C per segment. 3. See pulse width limitation curve (Fig. 2) and Duty Factor Curve (Fig. 5). 4. Clean only in water, isopropanol. ethanol. Freon TF or TE (or equivalent) and Genesolv DI-15 or DE-15 (or equivalent).

SOLID STATE NUMERIC INDICATOR (7 Segment Monolithic)	5082-7400 SERIES

HEWLETT **hp** PACKARD
COMPONENTS

TECHNICAL DATA APRIL 1976

Features

- **ULTRA LOW POWER**
  Excellent Readability at Only 500 μA
  Average per Segment
- **CONSTRUCTED FOR STROBED OPERATION**
  Minimizes Lead Connections
- **STANDARD DIP PACKAGE**
  End Stackable
  Integral Red Contrast Filter
  Rugged Construction
- **CATEGORIZED FOR LUMINOUS INTENSITY**
  Assures Uniformity of Light Output from
  Unit to Unit within a Single Category
- **IC COMPATIBLE**

Description

The HP 5082-7400 series are 2.79mm (.11''), seven segment GaAsP numeric indicators packaged in 3, 4, and 5 digit end-stackable clusters. An integral magnification technique increases the luminous intensity, thereby making ultra-low power consumption possible. Options include either the standard lower right hand decimal point or a centered decimal point for increased legibility in multi-cluster applications.

Applications include hand-held calculators, portable instruments, digital thermometers, or any other product requiring low power, low cost, minimum space, and long lifetime indicators.

Device Selection Guide

Digits per Cluster	Configuration			Part Number	
	Device			Center Decimal Point	Right Decimal Point
3 (right)				5082-7402	5082-7412
3 (left)				5082-7403	5082-7413
4				5082-7404	5082-7414
5				5082-7405	5082-7415

Package Description

NOTES: 1. Dimensions in millimeters and (inches).
2. Tolerances on all dimensions are ±0.038mm (±.015 in.) unless otherwise noted.

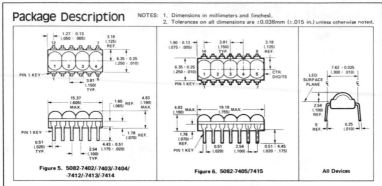

Figure 5. 5082-7402/-7403/-7404/
-7412/-7413/-7414

Figure 6. 5082-7405/7415

All Devices

Magnified Character Font Description

DEVICES
5082-7402
5082-7403
5082-7404
5082-7405

Figure 7. Center Decimal Point Configuration.

DEVICES
5082-7412
5082-7413
5082-7414
5082-7415

Figure 8. Right Decimal Point Configuration

Device Pin Description

PIN NO.	5082-7402/7412 FUNCTION	5082-7403/7413 FUNCTION	5082-7404/7414 FUNCTION	5082-7405/7415 FUNCTION
1	N/C	CATHODE 1	CATHODE 1	CATHODE 1
2	ANODE e	ANODE e	ANODE e	ANODE e
3	ANODE c	ANODE c	ANODE c	ANODE c
4	CATHODE 3	CATHODE 3	CATHODE 3	CATHODE 3
5	ANODE dp	ANODE dp	ANODE dp	ANODE dp
6	CATHODE 4	N/C	CATHODE 4	ANODE d
7	ANODE g	ANODE g	ANODE g	CATHODE 5
8	ANODE d	ANODE d	ANODE d	ANODE g
9	ANODE f	ANODE f	ANODE f	CATHODE 4
10	CATHODE 2	CATHODE 2	CATHODE 2	ANODE f
11	ANODE b	ANODE b	ANODE b	(See Note 1)
12	ANODE a	ANODE a	ANODE a	ANODE b
13	–	–	–	CATHODE 2
14	–	–	–	ANODE a

Note 1. Leave Pin 11 unconnected.

Electrical

Character encoding can be performed by commercially available BCD-7 segment decoder/driver circuits. Through the use of a strobing technique, only one decoder/driver is required for each display. In addition, the number of interconnection lines between the display and the drive circuitry is minimized to 8 + N, where N is the number of characters in the display.

Each of the segments on the display is "addressable" on two sets of lines — the "character enable" lines and the "segment enable" lines. Displays are wired so that all of the cathodes of all segments comprising one character are wired together to a single character enable line. Similarly, the anodes of each of like segments (e.g., all of the decimal points, all of the center line anodes, etc.) are wired to a single line. Therefore, a single digit in the cluster can be illuminated by connecting the appropriate character enable line, with the appropriate segment enable lines for the character being displayed. When each character in the display is illuminated in sequence, at a minimum of 100 times a second, flicker free characters are formed.

The decimal point in the 7412, 7413, 7414, and 7415 displays is located at the lower right of the digit for conventional driving schemes.

The 7402, 7403, 7404 and 7405 displays contain a centrally located decimal point which is activated in place of a digit. In long registers, this technique of setting off the decimal point significantly improves the display's readability. With respect to timing, the decimal point is treated as a separate character with its own unique time frame.

A detailed discussion of display circuits and drive techniques appears in Application Note 937.

Mechanical

The 5082-7400 series package is a standard 12 or 14 Pin DIP consisting of a plastic encapsulated lead frame with integral molded lenses. It is designed for plugging into DIP sockets or soldering into PC boards. The lead frame construction allows use of standard DIP insertion tools and techniques. Alignment problems are simplified due to the clustering of digits in a single package. The shoulders of the lead frame pins are intentionally raised above the bottom of the package to allow tilt mounting of up to 20° from the PC board.

To improve display contrast, the plastic incorporates a red dye that absorbs strongly at all visible wavelengths except the 655 nm emitted by the LED. In addition, the lead frames are selectively darkened to reduce reflectance. An additional filter, such as Plexiglass 2423, Panelgraphic 60 or 63, and Homalite 100-1600, will further lower the ambient reflectance and improve display contrast.

The devices can be soldered for up to 5 seconds at a maximum solder temperature of 230°C(1/16" below the seating plane). The plastic encapsulant used in these displays may be damaged by some solvents commonly used for flux removal. It is recommended that only Freon TE, Freon TE-35, Freon TF, Isopropanol, or soap and water be used for cleaning operations.

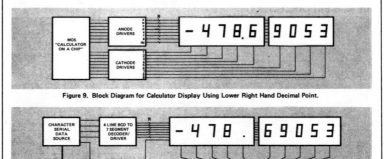

Figure 9. Block Diagram for Calculator Display Using Lower Right Hand Decimal Point.

Figure 10. Block Diagram for Display Using Center Decimal Point.

Appendix B

Intel 8080 Instruction List[†]

The list that follows is the complete set of 8080 Instructions from 000 to 377, showing octal and hexadecimal code, with Intel Mnemonic and a brief description of the instruction. Note that (r) ≡ "contents of register r" where

r = A, B, C, D, E, H, or L (A=accumulator).

(SP) or (PC) ≡ "contents of stack pointer" (16 bits) or "contents of program counter" (16 bits).

(r, p) = "Contents of register pair r, p"; i.e., B,C; D,E; H,L.

M* always will mean the memory location whose address is (H), (L) = the contents of the H,L registers.

Thus (M*) = "contents of memory location whose address is (H), (L)."

But M, without *, is a location whose address is determined by the contents of a pair of bytes or of a register pair other than (H),

---

[†] Based on "Intel 8080 Microcomputer Systems User's Manual", Sept. 1975, Chapter 4: "Instruction Set". The full implications in the use of any given instruction can only be understood by studying its *complete* description in the Intel Manual. Note also that the 8085 and 8080 instruction sets are identical except for the addition of RIM and SIM instructions with the 8085 (see Appendix F). For further instruction details see Appendices I and J.

(L), and will be specified. We also use $(M)_{(SP)}$ referring to "the contents of memory location whose address is $(SP)=\langle SPh\rangle, \langle SPl\rangle$". Note also that in a 3-byte instruction $\{-, B_2, B_3\} B_2$ is placed in the *low* register and B_3 in the *high* register of the pair; or, B_2 represents the *low* part of an address and B_3 the *high* part of an address. Thus, "LXI D,$B_2 B_3$" means place B_2 in register E and B_3 in register D even though *we describe* it as "Load reg. pr. D,E with bytes B_2, B_3." Likewise, "Call $B_2 B_3$" means "call subroutine at address B_3 Hi, B_2 Lo," and "STA, $B_2 B_3$" means "store (A) into M whose address is B_3 Hi, B_2 Lo". Be careful about this with 3-byte instructions. They are brought to your attention by + after their descriptions. Note also that results of arithmetic and logical operations are stored in the accumulator while in "compare" instructions (a subtraction) the accumulator *remains unchanged*. We will not repeat this in the descriptions that follow.

OCTAL	*HEX*	*MENOMIC*	*DESCRIPTION*
000	00	NOP	No operation
001	01	LXI B, $B_2 B_3$	Load reg. pr. B,C with bytes B_2,B_3 +
002	02	STAX B	Store (A) into M whose address is (B), (C)
003	03	INX B	Increment (reg. pr. B,C) by 1
004	04	INR B	Increment (B) by 1
005	05	DCR B	Decrement (B) by 1
006	06	MVI B, B_2	Move B_2 into reg. B
007	07	RLC	Rotate (A) one bit to left
010	08	–	No instruction
011	09	DAD B	Add (B,C) to (H,L); store in H,L
012	0A	LDAX B	Load A with (M) whose address is (B), (C)
013	0B	DCX B	Decrement (reg. pr. B,C) by 1
014	0C	INR C	Increment (C) by 1
015	0D	DCR C	Decrement (C) by 1
016	0E	MVI C, B_2	Move B_2 into reg. C
017	0F	RRC	Rotate (A) one bit to right
020	10	–	No instruction
021	11	LXI D, $B_2 B_3$	Load reg. pr. D,E with bytes B_2,B_3 +
022	12	STAX D	Store (A) into M whose address is (D), (E)
023	13	INX D	Increment (reg. pr. D,E) by 1

OCTAL	HEX	MNEMONIC	DESCRIPTION
024	14	INR D	Increment (D) by 1
025	15	DCR D	Decrement (D) by 1
026	16	MVI D, B_2	Move B_2 into reg. D
027	17	RAL	Rotate (A) one bit left thru carry
030	18	–	No instruction
031	19	DAD D	Add (D,E) to (H,L); store in H,L
032	1A	LDAX D	Load A with (M) whose address is (D), (E)
033	1B	DCX D	Decrement (reg. pr. D,E) by 1
034	1C	INR E	Increment (E) by 1
035	1D	DCR E	Decrement (E) by 1
036	1E	MVI E, B_2	Move B_2 into reg. E
037	1F	RAR	Rotate (A) one bit to right thru carry
040	20	–	No instruction
041	21	LXI H, $B_2 B_3$	Load reg. pr. H,L with bytes B_2,B_3 +
042	22	SHLD, $B_2 B_3$	Store (L) into M, (H) into M+1; M's address is B_3, B_2 +
043	23	INX H	Increment (reg. pr. H,L) by 1
044	24	INR H	Increment (H) by 1
045	25	DCR H	Decrement (H) by 1
046	26	MVI H, B_2	Move B_2 into reg. H
047	27	DAA	Decimal adjust (A) to BCD
050	28	–	No instruction
051	29	DAD H	Add (H,L) to (H,L); store in H,L
052	2A	LHLD, $B_2 B_3$	(M) → L, (M+1) → H where M's address is B_3, B_2 +
053	2B	DCX H	Decrement (reg. pr. H,L) by 1
054	2C	INR L	Increment (L) by 1
055	2D	DCR L	Decrement (L) by 1
056	2E	MVI L, B_2	Move B_2 into reg. L
057	2F	CM A	Complement (A) $(0 \to 1, 1 \to 0)$
060	30	–	No instruction
061	31	LXI SP, $B_2 B_3$	Load SP with B_2, B_3 +
062	32	STA, $B_2 B_3$	Store (A) into M whose address is B_3, B_2 +
063	33	INX SP	Increment (SP) by 1
064	34	INR M	Increment (M*) by 1
065	35	DCR M	Decrement (M*) by 1
066	36	MVI M, B_2	Move B_2 into M*

OCTAL	HEX	MNEMONIC	DESCRIPTION
067	37	STC	Set carry flag to 1
070	38	–	No instruction
071	39	DAD SP	Add (SP) to (H,L); store in H,L
072	3A	LDA, B_2B_3	Load A with (M) whose address is B_3, B_2 +
073	3B	DCX SP	Decrement (SP) by 1
074	3C	INR A	Increment (A) by 1
075	3D	DCR A	Decrement (A) by 1
076	3E	MVI A, B_2	Move B_2 into reg. A
077	3F	CMC	Complement the carry flag
100	40	Mov B,B	Move (B) to reg. B
101	41	Mov B,C	Move (C) to reg. B
102	42	Mov B,D	Move (D) to reg. B
103	43	Mov B,E	Move (E) to reg. B
104	44	Mov B,H	Move (H) to reg. B
105	45	Mov B,L	Move (L) to reg. B
106	46	Mov B,M	Move (M*) to reg. B
107	47	Mov B,A	Move (A) to reg. B
110	48	Mov C,B	Move (B) to reg. C
111	49	Mov C,C	Move (C) to reg. C
112	4A	Mov C,D	Move (D) to reg. C
113	4B	Mov C,E	Move (E) to reg. C
114	4C	Mov C,H	Move (H) to reg. C
115	4D	Mov C,L	Move (L) to reg. C
116	4E	Mov C,M	Move (M*) to reg. C
117	4F	Mov C,A	Move (A) to reg. C
120	50	Mov D,B	Move (B) to reg. D
121	51	Mov D,C	Move (C) to reg. D
122	52	Mov D,D	Move (D) to reg. D
123	53	Mov D,E	Move (E) to reg. D
124	54	Mov D,H	Move (H) to reg. D
125	55	Mov D,L	Move (L) to reg. D
126	56	Mov D,M	Move (M*) to reg. D
127	57	Mov D,A	Move (A) to reg. D
130	58	Mov E,B	Move (B) to reg. E
131	59	Mov E,C	Move (C) to reg. E
132	5A	Mov E,D	Move (D) to reg. E
133	5B	Mov E,E	Move (E) to reg. E

OCTAL	HEX	MNEMONIC	DESCRIPTION
134	5C	Mov E,H	Move (H) to reg. E
135	5D	Mov E,L	Move (L) to reg. E
136	5E	Mov E,M	Move (M*) to reg. E
137	5F	Mov E,A	Move (A) to reg. E
140	60	Mov H,B	Move (B) to reg. H
141	61	Mov H,C	Move (C) to reg. H
142	62	Mov H,D	Move (D) to reg. H
143	63	Mov H,E	Move (E) to reg. H
144	64	Mov H,H	Move (H) to reg. H
145	65	Mov H,L	Move (L) to reg. H
146	66	Mov H,M	Move (M*) to reg. H
147	67	Mov H,A	Move (A) to reg. H
150	68	Mov L,B	Move (B) to reg. L
151	69	Mov L,C	Move (C) to reg. L
152	6A	Mov L,D	Move (D) to reg. L
153	6B	Mov L,E	Move (E) to reg. L
154	6C	Mov L,H	Move (H) to reg. L
155	6D	Mov L,L	Move (L) to reg. L
156	6E	Mov L,M	Move (M*) to reg. L
157	6F	Mov L,A	Move (A) to reg. L
160	70	Mov M,B	Move (B) to M*
161	71	Mov M,C	Move (C) to M*
162	72	Mov M,D	Move (D) to M*
163	73	Mov M,E	Move (E) to M*
164	74	Mov M,H	Move (H) to M*
165	75	Mov M,L	Move (L) to M*
166	76	HLT	Halt
167	77	Mov M,A	Move (A) to M*
170	78	Mov A,B	Move (B) to A
171	79	Mov A,C	Move (C) to A
172	7A	Mov A,D	Move (D) to A
173	7B	Mov A,E	Move (E) to A
174	7C	Mov A,H	Move (H) to A
175	7D	Mov A,L	Move (L) to A
176	7E	Mov A,M	Move (M*) to A
177	7F	Mov A,A	Move (A) to A
200	80	Add B	Add (B) to (A)
201	81	Add C	Add (C) to (A)

OCTAL	HEX	MNEMONIC	DESCRIPTION
202	82	Add D	Add (D) to (A)
203	83	Add E	Add (E) to (A)
204	84	Add H	Add (H) to (A)
205	85	Add L	Add (L) to (A)
206	86	Add M	Add (M*) to (A)
207	87	Add A	Add (A) to (A)
210	88	ADC B	Add carry and (B) to (A)
211	89	ADC C	Add carry and (C) to (A)
212	8A	ADC D	Add carry and (D) to (A)
213	8B	ADC E	Add carry and (E) to (A)
214	8C	ADC H	Add carry and (H) to (A)
215	8D	ADC L	Add carry and (L) to (A)
216	8E	ADC M	Add carry and (M*) to (A)
217	8F	ADC A	Add carry and (A) to (A)
220	90	Sub B	Subtract (B) from (A)
221	91	Sub C	Subtract (C) from (A)
222	92	Sub D	Subtract (D) from (A)
223	93	Sub E	Subtract (E) from (A)
224	94	Sub H	Subtract (H) from (A)
225	95	Sub L	Subtract (L) from (A)
226	96	Sub M	Subtract (M*) from (A)
227	97	Sub A	Subtract (A) from (A) i.e., clear A
230	98	SBB B	Subtract carry and (B) from (A)
231	99	SBB C	Subtract carry and (C) from (A)
232	9A	SBB D	Subtract carry and (D) from (A)
233	9B	SBB E	Subtract carry and (E) from (A)
234	9C	SBB H	Subtract carry and (H) from (A)
235	9D	SBB L	Subtract carry and (L) from (A)
236	9E	SBB M	Subtract carry and (M*) from (A)
237	9F	SBB A	Subtract carry and (A) from (A)
240	A0	ANA B	AND (B) with (A) bit by bit
241	A1	ANA C	AND (C) with (A) bit by bit
242	A2	ANA D	AND (D) with (A) bit by bit
243	A3	ANA E	AND (E) with (A) bit by bit
244	A4	ANA H	AND (H) with (A) bit by bit
245	A5	ANA L	AND (L) with (A) bit by bit
246	A6	ANA M	AND (M*) with (A) bit by bit
247	A7	ANA A	AND (A) with (A) bit by bit

OCTAL	HEX	MNEMONIC	DESCRIPTION
250	A8	XRA B	Exclusive-OR (B) with (A) bit by bit
251	A9	XRA C	Exclusive-OR (C) with (A) bit by bit
252	AA	XRA D	Exclusive-OR (D) with (A) bit by bit
253	AB	XRA E	Exclusive-OR (E) with (A) bit by bit
254	AC	XRA H	Exclusive-OR (H) with (A) bit by bit
255	AD	XRA L	Exclusive-OR (L) with (A) bit by bit
256	AE	XRA M	Exclusive-OR (M*) with (A) bit by bit
257	AF	XRA A	Exclusive-OR (A) with (A) bit by bit
260	B0	ORA B	OR (B) with (A) bit by bit
261	B1	ORA C	OR (C) with (A) bit by bit
262	B2	ORA D	OR (D) with (A) bit by bit
263	B3	ORA E	OR (E) with (A) bit by bit
264	B4	ORA H	OR (H) with (A) bit by bit
265	B5	ORA L	OR (L) with (A) bit by bit
266	B6	ORA M	OR (M*) with (A) bit by bit
267	B7	ORA A	OR (A) with (A) bit by bit
270	B8	CMP B	Compare (B) with (A): $(A) - (B)$
271	B9	CMP C	Compare (C) with (A): $(A) - (C)$
272	BA	CMP D	Compare (D) with (A): $(A) - (D)$
273	BB	CMP E	Compare (E) with (A): $(A) - (E)$
274	BC	CMP H	Compare (H) with (A): $(A) - (H)$
275	BD	CMP L	Compare (L) with (A): $(A) - (L)$
276	BE	CMP M	Compare (M) with (A): $(A) - (M^*)$
277	BF	CMP A	Compare (A) with (A): $(A) - (A)$
300	C0	RNZ	Return from subroutine if not zero
301	C1	POP B	$(M)_{(SP)} \to$ reg. C; $(M)_{(SP+1)} \to$ reg. B
302	C2	JNZ B_2B_3	Jump to address B_3, B_2^+ if not zero
303	C3	JMP B_2B_3	Jump to address B_3, B_2+
304	C4	CNZ B_2B_3	Call subroutine at B_3, B_2+ if not zero
305	C5	Push B	$(B) \to M_{(SP-1)}$; $(C) \to M_{(SP-2)}$
306	C6	ADI B_2	Add B_2 to (A)
307	C7	RST 0	Call subroutine at 000,000 (octal)
310	C8	RZ	Return from subroutine if zero
311	C9	RET	Return from subroutine
312	CA	JZ B_2B_3	Jump to address B_3, B_2+ if zero
313	CB	—	No instruction
314	CC	CZ B_2B_3	Call subroutine at B_3, B_2+ if zero

OCTAL	HEX	MNEMONIC	DESCRIPTION
315	CD	Call B_2B_3	Call subroutine at B_3, B_2+
316	CE	ACI B_2	Add B_2 and carry to (A)
317	CF	RST 1	Call subroutine at 000, 010 (octal)
320	D0	RNC	Return from subroutine if no carry
321	D1	POP D	$(M)_{(SP)} \to$ reg. E; $(M)_{(SP+1)} \to$ reg. D
322	D2	JNC B_2B_3	Jump to address B_3B_2+ if no carry
323	D3	Out B_2	Output (A) to device number B_2
324	D4	CNC B_2B_3	Call subroutine at B_3, B_2+ if no carry
325	D5	Push D	$(D) \to M_{(SP-1)}$; $(E) \to M_{(SP-2)}$
326	D6	SUI B_2	Subtract B_2 from (A)
327	D7	RST 2	Call subroutine at 000, 020 (octal)
330	D8	RC	Return from subroutine if carry
331	D9	—	No instruction
332	DA	JC B_2B_3	Jump to address B_3, B_2+ if carry
333	DB	IN B_2	Input data from device number B_2 to A
334	DC	CC B_2B_3	Call subroutine at B_3, B_2+ if carry
335	DD	—	No instruction
336	DE	SBI B_2	Subtract B_2 and carry from (A)
337	DF	RST 3	Call subroutine at 000, 030 (octal)
340	E0	RPO	Return from subroutine if parity is odd
341	E1	POP H	$(M)_{(SP)} \to$ reg. L; $(M)_{(SP+1)} \to$ reg. H
342	E2	JPO B_2B_3	Jump to address B_3, B_2+ if parity is odd
343	E3	XTHL	$(L) \leftrightarrow (M)_{(SP)}$; $(H) \leftrightarrow (M)_{(SP+1)}$, i.e., exchange
344	E4	CPO B_2B_3	Call subroutine at B_3, B_2+ if parity is odd
345	E5	Push H	$(H) \to M_{(SP-1)}$; $(L) \to M_{(SP-2)}$
346	E6	ANI B_2	AND B_2 with (A), bit by bit
347	E7	RST 4	Call subroutine at 000, 040 (octal)
350	E8	RPE	Return from subroutine if parity is even
351	E9	PCHL	$(H) \to PCH$, $(L) \to PCL$, i.e., jump to address (H), (L)
352	EA	JPE B_2B_3	Jump to address B_3, B_2+ if parity is even

OCTAL	HEX	MNEMONIC	DESCRIPTION
353	EB	XCHG	Exchange H,L with D,E: $(H) \leftrightarrow (D)$, $(L) \leftrightarrow (E)$
354	EC	CPE $B_2 B_3$	Call subroutine at B_3, B_2+ if parity is even
355	ED	–	No instruction
356	EE	XRI B_2	Exclusive-OR B_2 with (A), bit by bit
357	EF	RST 5	Call subroutine at 000, 050 (octal)
360	F0	RP	Return from subroutine if positive $(D_7 = 0)$
361	F1	POP PSW	$(M)_{(SP)} \rightarrow$ flag flip flops; $(M)_{(SP+1)} \rightarrow$ reg. A
362	F2	JP $B_2 B_3$	Jump to address B_3, B_2 + if positive $(D_7 = 0)$
363	F3	DI	Disable Interrupts
364	F4	CP $B_2 B_3$	Call subroutine at B_3, B_2 + if positive $(D_7 = 0)$
365	F5	Push PSW	$(A) \rightarrow M_{(SP-1)}$; (flag word) $\rightarrow M_{(SP-2)}$
366	F6	ORI B_2	OR B_2 with (A), bit by bit
367	F7	RST 6	Call subroutine at 000, 060 (octal)
370	F8	RM	Return from subroutine if minus $(D_7 = 1)$
371	F9	SPHL	$(H),(L) \rightarrow$ stack pointer register
372	FA	JM $B_2 B_3$	Jump to address B_3, B_2 + if minus $(D_7 = 1)$
373	FB	EI	Enable Interrupts
374	FC	CM $B_2 B_3$	Call subroutine at B_3, B_2 + if minus $(D_7 = 1)$
375	FD	–	No instruction
376	FE	CPI B_2	Compare B_2 with (A), i.e., $(A) - B_2$
377	FF	RST 7	Call subroutine at 000, 070 (octal)

Appendix C

KEX Prom Bootstrap Program for MMD-1

The KEX program listed below is reprinted courtesy Radio-Electronics May, June, July 1976 © Gernsback Publications, Inc, 1976. Their permission is gratefully acknowledged. (Note: The explanation of the instruction at 000, 115 should read: "Jump if key was ⩾ 010").

KEX PROGRAM LISTING (OCTAL)

```
ADDRESS      DATA
HI  LOW      B7...B0

                         *000 000
000 000      303         JMP
000 001      070         START
000 002      000         0


                         / JUMP UP 10 R/W MEMORY TO BE USED BY
                         / RESTARTS & VECTORED INTERRUPTS

                         *000 010
000 010      303         JMP
000 011      010         010
000 012      003         003
                         *000 020
000 020      303         JMP
000 021      020         020
000 022      003         003
                         *000 030
000 030      303         JMP
000 031      030         030
000 032      003         003
                         *000 040
000 040      303         JMP
000 041      040         040
000 042      003         003
                         *000 050
000 050      303         JMP
000 051      050         050
000 052      003         003
                         *000 060
000 060      303         JMP
000 061      060         060
000 062      003         003


                         / BEGINNING OF MAIN PROGRAM

                         *000 070
000 070      061  START,  LXISP   /SET STACK POINTER TO TOP OF R/W MEM.
000 071      000          000
000 072      004          004
000 073      041          LXIH    /INITIAL VALUE OF H & L
000 074      000          000
000 075      003          003
000 076      116  POINTA, MOVCM   /LOAD MEM DATA INTO TEMP DATA BUFFER
000 077      174          MOVAH   /OUTPUT HI TO LED'S
000 100      323          OUT
000 101      001          001
000 102      175          MOVAL   /OUTPUT LOW TO LED'S
```

KEX PROGRAM LISTING (CONTINUED)

ADDRESS HI LOW	DATA $B_7...B_0$		
000 103	323		OUT
000 104	000		000
000 105	171	POINTB,	MOVAC	/ OUTPUT TEMP. DATA BUFFER DATA TO LED'S
000 106	323		OUT
000 107	002		002
000 110	315	POINTC,	CALL	/ WAIT & INPUT NEXT KEY CLOSURE
000 111	315		KBRD
000 112	000		0
000 113	376		CPI
000 114	010		010
000 115	322		JNC	/ JUMP IF KEY WAS < 010
000 116	134		POINTD	/ (0-7 , OCTAL DIGIT)
000 117	000		0
000 120	107		MOVBA	/ SAVE KEY CODE
000 121	171		MOVAC	/ GET OLD VALUE
000 122	027		RAL	/ ROTATE 3 TIMES
000 123	027		RAL
000 124	027		RAL
000 125	346		ANI	/ MAK OUT LEAST SIG. OCTAL DIGIT
000 126	370		370
000 127	260		ORAB	/ OR IN NEW OCTAL DIGIT
000 130	117		MOVCA	/ PUT NEW DATA BACK INTO BUFFER
000 131	303		JMP
000 132	105		POINTB
000 133	000		0
000 134	376	POINTD,	CPI
000 135	011		011	/ "L" KEY
000 136	302		JNZ	/ JUMP IF NOT AN "L"
000 137	145		POINTE
000 140	000		0
000 141	151		MOVLC	/ PUT BUFFER DATA IN L
000 142	303		JMP
000 143	076		POINTA
000 144	000		0
000 145	376	POINTE,	CPI
000 146	010		010	/ "H" KEY
000 147	302		JNZ	/ JUMP IF NOT AN "H"
000 150	156		POINTF
000 151	000		0
000 152	141		MOVHC	/ PUT BUFFER DATA IN H
000 153	303		JMP
000 154	076		POINTA
000 155	000		0
000 156	376	POINTF,	CPI
000 157	013		013	/ "S" KEY
000 160	302		JNZ	/ JUMP IF NOT "S"
000 161	170		POINTG
000 162	000		0
000 163	161		MOVMC	/ PUT TEMP. DATA INTO MEMORY
000 164	043		INXH	/ INCERMENT H & L
000 165	303		JMP
000 166	076		POINTA
000 167	000		0
000 170	376	POINTG,	CPI

KEX PROGRAM LISTING (CONTINUED)

```
ADDRESS      DATA
HI   LOW     B7...B0

000 171      012            012     / "G" KEY
000 172      302            JNZ     / JUMP IF NOT "G"
000 173      110            POINTC
000 174      000            0
000 175      351            PCHL    / GO EXECUTE PGM POINTED TO BY H & L


                          / THIS 10 MSEC DELAY DISTURBS NO REGISTERS OR FLAG

                           *000 277
000 277      365  TIMEOUT, PUSHPSW / SAVE REGISTERS
000 300      325            PUSHD
000 301      021            LXID    / LOAD D & E WITH VALUE TO BE DECREMENTED
000 302      046            046
000 303      001            001
000 304      033   MORE,    DCXD    / JUMP IN THIS LOOP UNTIL
000 305      172            MOVAD   /    D & E ARE BOTH ZERO
000 306      263            ORAE
000 307      302            JNZ
000 310      304            MORE
000 311      000            0
000 312      321            POPD
000 313      361            POPPSW  / RESTORE REGISTERS
000 314      311            RET


                          / THE KBRD ROUTINE DEBOUNCES KEY CLOSURES
                          /     AND TRANSLATES KEY CODES

                          / FLAGS AND REG A ARE CHANGED
                          / A0-A3= CODE  ; A4-A7= 0000

000 315      333   KBRD,    IN      / INPUT FROM KEYBOARD ENCODERS
000 316      000            000
000 317      267            ORAA    / SET FLAGS
000 320      372            JM      / JUMP BACK IF LAST KEY NOT RELEASED
000 321      315            KBRD
000 322      000            0
000 323      315            CALL    / WAIT 10 MSEC
000 324      277            TIMOUT
000 325      000            0
000 326      333  FLAGCK,   IN
000 327      000            000
000 330      267            ORAA
000 331      362            JP      / JUMP BACK TO WAIT FOR A NEW
000 332      326            FLAGCK  /    KEY TO BE PRESSED
000 333      000            0
000 334      315            CALL    / WAIT 10 MSEC FOR BOUNCING
000 335      277            TIMOUT
000 336      000            0
000 337      333            IN
000 340      000            000
000 341      267            ORAA
000 342      362            JP      / JUMP BACK IF NEW KEY NOT STILL
```

KEX PROGRAM LISTING (CONTINUED)

ADDRESS HI	LOW	DATA $B_7...B_0$		
000	343	326	FLAGCK	/ PRESSED (FALSE ALARM)
000	344	000	0	
000	345	346	ANI	/ MASK OUT ALL BUT KEY CODE
D00	346	017	017	
000	347	345	PUSHH	/ SAVE H&L
000	350	046	MVIH	/ ZERO H REG
000	351	000	000	
000	352	306	ADI	/ADD THE ADDRESS OF THE BEGINNING OF
000	353	360	360	/ THE TABLE TO THE KEY CODE
000	354	157	MOVLA	/
000	355	176	MOVAM	/ FETCH NEW VALUE FROM TABLE
000	356	341	POPH	/ RESTORE H & L
000	357	311	RET	

```
                               / THIS TRANSLATION TABLE CONVERTS THE CODE
                               / GENERATED BY KEY CLOSURES TO THE CODE
                               / USED BY THE MAIN KEX PROGRAM
```

ADDRESS HI	LOW	DATA		
000	360	000	TABLE,	000
000	361	001		001
000	362	002		002
000	363	003		003
000	364	004		004
000	365	005		005
000	366	006		006
000	367	007		007
000	370	013		013 / S
000	371	000		000 / THIS CODE CAN'T BE GENERATED
000	372	017		017 / C
000	373	012		012 / G
000	374	010		010 / H
000	375	011		011 / L
000	376	015		015 / A
000	377	016		016 / B

Appendix D

Some Vendors

The following list of vendors is not intended to be complete. It represents a brief cross-section of some sources of the various components needed in a microprocessor-microcomputer laboratory, particularly for interfacing work as illustrated in the experiments in Chapter 5 of this book.

1. James Electronics - 1021 Howard Ave., San Carlos, California (94070). (415) 592-8092. (IC's, LED's, breadboards, switches, wire, handbooks, probes, power supplies, etc.)

2. Poly Paks - P. O. Box 942, S. Lynnfield, Mass.

3. Solid State Systems, Inc. - P. O. Box 773, Columbia, Mo. 65201.

4. John Meshna Jr. - 19 Allerton St., Lynn, Mass. 01904.

5. Intel Corp. - 3065 Bowers Ave., Santa Clara, California 95051 (408) 987-8080 (and local distributors and representatives).

6. E and L Instruments Inc. - 61 First St., Derby, Conn. 06418 (203) 735-8774 (Microcomputer and digital trainers and kits, IC's, breadboards, the "Bugbooks®," Digital "Outboards®," probes).

7. Hamilton Avnet, Schweber Electronics, Cramer Electronics, Harvey Radio (consult local directory).

8. Samtec - 2652 Charlestown Rd., N. Albany, Indiana 47150 (cable plugs, etc.), (812) 944-6733.

9. Storm Products - 112 S. Glasgow Ave., Inglewood, California 90301 (stripped wire—all gauges and lengths).

10. General Instruments - 600 West John St., Hicksville, N. Y. 11802 - (516) 733-3107. (Game chips, character generators, UARTS, etc.)

11. Hewlett Packard: Palo Alto, California (Displays, probes, pulsers, mini and microcomputers, etc.).

12. National Semiconductor, Signetics, Motorola, Texas Instruments, Fairchild Camera, Mostek, Zilog, Mos Technology, etc.

13. *For Handbooks*: (see also references in Appendix E, i.e., 10, 11, 12, 13, 14, 15, 16, 21, 23).

   a) Texas Instruments, P. O. Box 5012, Dallas, Texas 75222.

   b) Signetics, 811 E. Arques Ave., Sunnyvale, Calif. 94086.

   c) National Semiconductor, 2900 Semiconductor Dr., Santa Clara, Calif. 95051.

   d) Intel Corp., 3065 Bowers Ave., Santa Clara, Calif. 95051.

   e) Motorola Semiconductor Products, Phoenix, Arizona 85036 (Box 20924).

14. Jim-Pak, White Plains, N. Y. 10601.

15. Advanced Computer Products, Inc., Santa Ana, Calif. 92705.

16. Semiconductor Concepts, Hauppage, N. Y.

17. Computer Mart, 118 Madison Ave., New York, N. Y.

18. Computer Warehouse, Boston, Mass.

19. Hoboken Computer Works, Hoboken, N. J.

20. Mini Micro Mart, Syracuse, N. Y.

21. OK Machine Tool (Wire Wrap), 3455 Conner St., Bronx, N. Y. 10475.

22. Computer Emporium, 487 Broadway, New York, N. Y. 10013.

23. Polymorphic Systems, Goleta, Calif. 93017.

24. Digital Group, Denver, Col. 80206

25. Datel Systems, Inc. (A to D, D to A), Canton, Mass. 02021.

Appendix E

References

1. Hilburn and Julich. Microcomputers/Microprocessors: Hardware, Software, and Applications. Prentice Hall 1976.

2. R. Kline. Digital Computer Design. Prentice Hall 1977.

3. J. O'Malley, Introduction to the Digital Computer. Holt, Rinehart, Winston 1972.

4. T. C. Bartee. Digital Computer Fundamentals (4th Ed.). McGraw Hill 1977.

5. B. Soucek. Microprocessors and Microcomputers. J. Wiley & Sons Inc. 1976.

6. J. Peatman. Microcomputer Based Design. McGraw Hill 1977.

7. B. Ward. Microprocessor-Microprogramming Handbook. Tab Books 1975.

8. Caxton Foster. Computer Architecture. Van Nostrand Reinhold Co. 1970.

9. D. Lancaster. TV Typewriter Cookbook. Sams Publics. 1976.

10. Texas Instruments. TTL Data Book for Design Engineers, 2nd ed., 1976.

11. Signetics Corp. Integrated Circuits: Digital, Linear, and MOS Handbook.

12. National Semiconductor Corp. Digital Integrated Circuits Handbook, Jan. 1974 and TTL Data Book, Feb. 1976.

13. Intel Corp. 8080 Microcomputer Systems User's Manual. Sept. 1975; Jan. 1975. MCS 85 User's Manual, June 1977.

14. Blukis and Baker. Practical Digital Electronics. Hewlett Packard Co. 1974.

15. Microdata Corp. Microprogramming Handbook, 1971. Santa Ana, California.

16. D. Lancaster. TTL Cookbook. Sams Publics. 1974.

17. Rony and Larsen. Bugbooks I and II (Logic and Memory Experiments Using TTL Integrated Circuits). E & L Instruments Inc., 1974.

18. Rony and Larsen. Bugbook IIA (Using the UART). E & L Instruments Inc., 1975.

19. Rony, Larsen and Titus. Bugbook III (Microcomputer Interfacing-the Mark 80, an 8080 system). E & L Instruments Inc., 1975.

20. Rony, Larsen and Titus. Bugbooks V and VI. (Introductory Experiments in Digital Electronics, 8080 A Microcomputer Programming, and 8080 A Microcomputer Interfacing). E & L Instruments, Inc., 1977.

21. National Semiconductor Corp. "Memory Data Book", Jan. 1976.

22. Luecke, Mize, and Carr. Semiconductor Memory Design and Applications. McGraw Hill, 1973.

23. J. Lenk. Handbook of Logic Circuits. Reston Publishing Co. 1972.

24. J. Dempsey. Basic Digital Electronics with MSI Applications. Addison Wesley 1977.

25. Altman and Scrupski (Editors). Applying Microprocessors. -Electronics Book Series, McGraw Hill 1976.

26. Periodicals: Interface Age, Byte, Computer Design, Electronics, Personal Computing, Etc.

27. Electronics, July 21, 1977, p. 95-102 (McGraw Hill).

28. Morris Mano. Computer System Architecture. Prentice Hall 1976.

29. Microprocessors: Fundamentals and Applications. Edited by Wen C. Lin. IEEE Press 1977.

30. Fortune Magazine, Nov. 1975, p. 134. "Here Comes The Second Computer Revolution"—G. Bylinsky.

31. Chirlian. Analysis and Design of Digital Circuits and Computer Systems. Matrix Publishers 1976.

32. Miller and Irwin. Digital Electronics for Beginners. dilithium Press, 1978.

33. H. Katzan, Jr. Microprogramming Primer, McGraw Hill 1977.

34. H. Katzan, Jr. Information Technology: The Human Use of Computers. Petrocelli Books N. Y., 1974.

35. Scientific American—"Microelectronics," W.H. Freeman and Co. San Francisco, Sept. 1977.

36. Rodnay Zaks "Microprocessors, from Chips to Systems"; "Microprocessor Interfacing Techniques". Sybex, 1977.

37. Adam Osborne Assoc. Inc.—various books on microprocessors.

38. J. Peatman—The Design of Digital Systems. McGraw-Hill—1972.

Appendix F

The Intel 8085 Microprocessor and Its Relation to the 8080

(See also Appendix H.)

We are including here reproductions from Intel's MCS-85 User's Manual (June 1977, Fig. 2-4 p. 2-3, Fig. 1 p. 3-2, and p. 3-26) and MCS 85 Handbook (June 1977, pp. 1-9, p. 11) giving the essential features of the 8085 Microprocessor and how they relate to the 8080. The 8085 integrates some important functions that are external to the 8080: clock generator, system controller, priority interrupts, and serial I/O ports arc internal to the 8085 CPU. In addition, accessing memory does not require wait states and the speed is higher (3 Mhz). A multiplex data bus also distinguishes the 8085 from the 8080: the address bus contains the 8 high address bits only and the data bus contains the 8 low address bits followed by the 8 bits of data. Aside from two added instructions (RIM and SIM), described below, the 8085 is fully compatible, software-wise, with the 8080—every 8080 program will work equally well with the 8085. Other aspects of the 8085 vs. 8080 will become apparent in the reproduced material. All experiments in this book can be done with the 8085 as far as the programs presented are concerned; the interfacing will be different because of the multiplexed nature of the data/address bus and because of the integration of many auxiliary 8080 functions into the 8085 microprocessor (*see Appendix H*). These matters will be gone into further in another book to appear on 8080/8085 *Applications* experiments.

It is also recommended that the reader consult the article by D. W. Sohn and A. Volk in Electronics, May 12, 1977: "Third-Generation Microcomputer Set Packs It All Into 3 Chips."

The following material is reproduced courtesy Intel Corp. For more details and information on the 8085 consult Intel MCS 85 User's Manual June 1977.

INTRODUCTION TO MCS-85™

EVOLUTION

In December 1971, Intel introduced the first general purpose, 8-bit microprocessor, the 8008. It was implemented in P-channel MOS technology and was packaged in a single 18 pin, dual in-line package (DIP). The 8008 used standard semiconductor ROM and RAM and, for the most part, TTL components for I/O and general interface. It immediately found applications in byte-oriented end products such as terminals and computer peripherals where its instruction execution (20 micro-seconds), general purpose organization and instruction set matched the requirements of these products. Recognizing that hardware was but a small part in the overall system picture, Intel developed both hardware and software tools for the design engineer so that the transition from prototype to production would be as simple and fast as possible. The commitment of providing a total systems approach with the 8008 microcomputer system was actually the basis for the sophisticated, comprehensive development tools that Intel has available today.

THE 8080A MICROPROCESSOR

With the advent of high-production N-channel RAM memories and 40 pin DIP packaging, Intel designed the 8080A microprocessor. It was designed to be software compatible with the 8008 so that the existing users of the 8008 could preserve their investment in software and at the same time provide dramatically increased performance (2 micro-second instruction execution), while reducing the amount of components necessary to implement a system. Additions were made to the basic instruction set to take advantage of this increased performance and large system-type features were included on-chip such as DMA, 16-bit addressing and external stack memory so that the total spectrum of application could be significantly increased. The 8080 was first sampled in December 1973. Since that time it has become the standard of the industry and is accepted as the primary building block for more microcomputer based applications than all other microcomputer systems combined.

A TOTAL SYSTEMS COMMITMENT

The Intel® 8080A Microcomputer System encompasses a total systems commitment to the user to fully support his needs both in developing prototype

systems and reliable, high volume production. From complex MOS/LSI peripheral components to resident high level systems language (PL/M) the Intel® 8080 Microcomputer System provides the most comprehensive, effective solution to today's system problems.

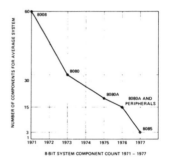

8-BIT SYSTEM COMPONENT COUNT 1971 – 1977

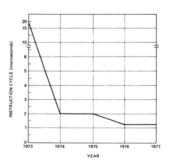

YEAR

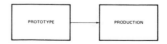

INTRODUCTION TO MCS-85™

THE MCS-85™ MICROCOMPUTER SYSTEM

The basic philosophy behind the MCS-85 microcomputer system is one of logical, evolutionary advance in technology without the waste of discarding existing investments in hardware and sotware. The MCS-85 provides the existing 8080 user with an increase in performance, a decrease in the component count, a single 5 volt operation and still preserves 100% of his existing software investment. For the new microcomputer user, the MCS-85 represents the refinement of the most popular microcomputer in the industry, the Intel 8080, along with a wealth of supporting software, documentation and peripheral components to speed the cycle from prototype to production. The identical development tools that Intel has produced to support the 8080 microcomputer system can be used for the MCS-85, and additional add-on features are available to optimize system development for MCS-85.

This section of the MCS-85 User's Manual will briefly detail the basic differences between the MCS-85 and MCS-80 families. It will illustrate both the hardware and software compatibilities and also reveal some of the engineering trade-offs that were met during the design of MCS-85. More detailed discussion of the MCS-85 bus operation and component specifications are available in Sections: 2,3,4, but the information provided in this section, Section 1, will be extremely helpful in understanding the basic concepts and philosophies behind the MCS-85.

It is important for the reader of the MCS-85 User's Manual to have a solid understanding of the 8080 microcomputer system. Most of the terms and procedures that are used in the MCS-85 User's Manual are based on information in the MCS-80 User's Manual. Please refer to the MCS-80 User's Manual as required.

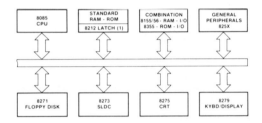

MCS-85™ TOTAL SYSTEM

INTRODUCTION TO MCS-85™

SYSTEM INTEGRATION

The MCS-85 integrates many of the functions that are auxiliary to an 8080A based system. Functions such as: clock generation, system control and interrupt prioritizing are integrated into on-chip features of the **8085** Central Processor. The 8085 is, of course, the central element in the MCS-85 family. It coordinates all bus transfers and operations and executes the instruction set. The 8085 CPU is designed to be the controlling master of a unique, multiplexed bus system. This bus structure will be discussed in detail later in the manual but basically, the information provided on the data bus is time-multiplexed and contains both data and the lower 8 address bits (A7-A0). The address bus contains the remaining 8-bits (A8-A15). The 8085 CPU generates signals that tell peripheral devices what type of information is on the multiplexed bus (Address/Data) and from that point on the operation is almost identical to the MCS-80™ CPU Group. The multiplexed bus structure was chosen because it had no detrimental effect on system performance, allowed complete compatibility to existing peripheral components, provided improved timing margins and access requirements and freed device pins so that more functions could be integrated on the 8085 and other components of the family.

To enhance the system integration of MCS-85, several special components with combined memory and I/O were designed. These new devices have been designed to directly interface to the multiplexed bus of the 8085. It is interesting to note that the pin locations of the 8085 and the special peripheral components were assigned to minimize PC board area and allow for a smooth, efficient layout. The details on the new peripheral components will be discussed later in the manual.

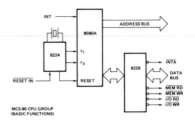

MCS-80™ CPU GROUP (BASIC FUNCTIONS)

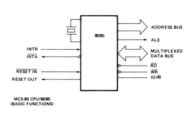

MCS-85™ CPU/8085 (BASIC FUNCTIONS)

MULTIPLEXED BUS TIMING

INTRODUCTION TO MCS-85™

SOFTWARE COMPATIBILITY

As with any computer system the cost of software development far outweighs those of hardware. A microcomputer-based system is traditionally a very cost-sensitive application and the development of software is one of the key areas where success or failure of the cost objectives is vital.

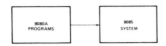

The 8085 CPU is 100% software compatible with the Intel 8080A CPU. The compatibility is at the object or "machine code" level so that existing programs written for 8080A execution will run on the 8085 as is. This becomes even more evident to the user who has mask programmed ROMs and wishes to update his system without the need for new masks.

PROGRAMMER TRAINING

A cost which is often forgotten is that of programmer training. A new, or modified instruction set, would require programmers to relearn another set of mnemomics and greatly effect the productivity during development. The 100% compatibility of the 8085 CPU assures that no re-training effort will be required.

For the new microcomputer user, the software compatibility between the 8085 and 8080A means that all of the software development tools that are available for the 8080A and all software libraries for 8080A will operate with the new design and thus save immeasurable cost in development and debug.

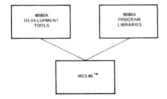

The 8085 CPU does however add two instructions to initialize and maintain hardware features of the 8085. Two of the unused opcodes of the 8080A instruction set were designated for the addition so that 100% compatibility could be maintained.

As mentioned previously, the MCS-85 is designed to be a logical, evolutionary advance that solves problems in the most efficient, cost effective manner available. 100% software compatibility fulfills one of the most important aspects of the overall MCS-85 system philosophy.

HARDWARE COMPATIBILITY

The integration of auxiliary 8080A functions, such as clock generation, system control and interrupt prioritization, dramatically reduces the amount of components necessary for most systems. In addition to integrating some of the MCS-80™ system functions, the MCS-85 operates off a single +5 volt power supply to further simplify hardware development and debug. A close examination of the AC/DC specifications of the MCS-85 systems components shows that each is specified to supply a maximum of 400 micro Amps of source current and a full TTL load of sink current so that a very substantial system can be constructed without the need for extra TTL buffers or drivers. Input and output voltage levels are also specified so that a minimum of 400 microvolts noise margin is provided for reliable, high-performance operation.

PC BOARD CONSIDERATIONS

The 8085 CPU and the 8080A are not pin-compatible due to the reduction in power supplies and the addition of integrated auxiliary features. However the pinouts of the MCS-85 system components were carefully assigned to minimize PC board area and thus yield a smooth, efficient layout. For new designs this incompatibility of pinouts presents no problems and for upgrades of existing designs the reduction of components and board area will far offset the incompatibility.

INTRODUCTION TO MCS-85™

MCS-85™ SPECIAL PERIPHERAL COMPONENTS

The MCS-85 was designed to minimize the amount of components required for most systems. Intel designed several new peripheral components that combine memory, I/O and timer functions to fulfill this requirement. These new peripheral devices directly interface to the multiplexed MCS-85 bus structure and provide new levels in system integration for today's designer.

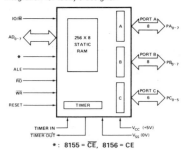

* : 8155 = $\overline{CE}$, 8156 = CE

8155/8156 RAM, I/O and Timer

　256 bytes RAM
　2- 8-bit ports
　1- 6-bit port (programmable)
　1- 14-bit programmable interval timer
　Single +5 volt supply operation
　40 pin DIP plastic or cerdip package

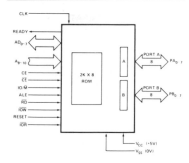

8355 ROM and I/O

　2K bytes ROM
　2- 8-bit ports (direction programmable)
　Single +5 volt supply operation
　40 pin DIP plastic or cerdip package

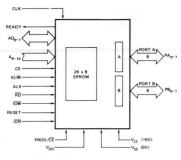

8755 EPROM and I/O

　Socket compatible with 8355
　2K bytes EPROM
　2- 8-bit ports (direction programmable)
　Single +5 volt supply read operation
　U.V. Erasable
　40 pin DIP package

8755/8355

One of the most important advances made with the MCS-85 is the socket-compatibility of the 8355 and 8755 components. This allows the systems designer to develop and debug in erasable PROM and then, when satisfied, switch over to mask-programmed ROM 8355 with no performance degradation or board relayout. It also allows quick prototype production for market impact without going to a "kluge" solution.

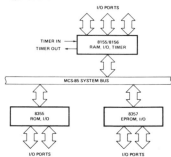

SYSTEM EXPANSION

Each of these peripheral components has features that allow a small to medium system to be constructed without the addition of buffers and decoders to further reduce the component count.

INTRODUCTION TO MCS-85™

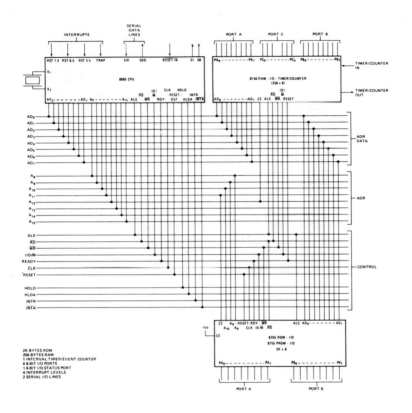

MCS-85™ BASIC SYSTEM

INTRODUCTION TO MCS-85™

INTERFACING TO MCS-80™ PERIPHERAL COMPONENTS

The MCS-80 has a wide range of peripheral components that solve system problems and provide the designer with a great deal of flexibility in his I/O, Interrupt and DMA structures. The MCS-85 is directly compatible with these peripherals, and, with the exception of the 8257 DMA controller, needs no additional circuitry for their interface. The 8257 DMA controller uses an 8212 latch and some gating to support the multiplexed bus of MCS-85.

MULTIPLEX BUS

To understand the exact interface between the MCS-85 and the MCS-80™ peripheral components, recall that the 8080A CPU issues the address of the I/O device on its 16-bit address bus. The I/O address appears on both the upper and lower 8-bits of the address bus. The 8085 CPU utilizes a multiplexed bus structure where the address bus contains only the upper 8-bits of the address. The data bus contains both data and the lower 8-bits of information. Since the read/write control signals are only issued when there is data on the bus and the address bus contains the I/O device address, then all of the MCS-80 peripherals will interface directly with no hardware or software problems. In fact, due to the manner in which the 8085 control signals were implemented, memory-mapped I/O becomes simpler to use than with MCS-80 and combinations of memory-mapped and standard I/O techniques will provide the designer with new flexibilities to maximize system efficiency.

MCS-80™ PERIPHERALS

8251	Programmable Communications Interface
8253	Programmable Interval Timer
8255A	Programmable Peripheral Interface
8257	Programmable DMA Controller
8259	Programmable Interrupt Controller

This compatibility also assures the designer that all new peripheral components from Intel will interface to the MCS-85 bus structure to further expand the application spectrum of MCS-85.

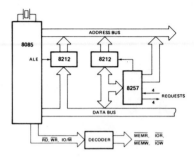

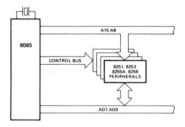

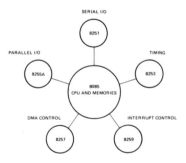

INTRODUCTION TO MCS-85™

INTERFACING TO STANDARD MEMORY

The MCS-85 was designed to support the full range of system configurations from small 3 chip applications to large memory and I/O applications. The 8085 CPU issues advanced timing signals (S0 & S1) so that, in the case of large systems, these signals could be used to simplify bus arbitration logic and dynamic RAM refresh circuitry.

The multiplexed bus structure of the MCS-85 provides direct interface to MCS-80™ peripheral components, but in large, memory intensive systems, standard ROM and RAM memory will be present due to the economies of such devices when used in large quantities per system. In most memory intensive systems I/O requirements do not generally track memory space. Thus standard memory is a more cost effective solution for these applications than the special 8155, 8355 devices.

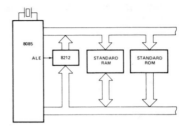

DEMULTIPLEXING THE BUS

In order to interface standard memory components such as Intel® 8102A, 8101A, 8111A, 8316A, 8308, 2104 and 2116 the MCS-85 bus must be "de-multiplexed". This is accomplished by connecting an Intel® 8212 latch to the data bus and strobing the latch with the ALE signal from the 8085 CPU. The ALE signal is issued to indicate that the information on the data bus is actually the lower 8-bits of the address bus, and the 8212 simply latches this information so that a full 16-bit address is now available to interface standard memory components.

USE OF 8212

The additional component may at first seem wasteful but large, memory intensive systems are usually multi-card implementations and require some form of TTL buffering to provide necessary current and voltage levels. Therefore, the additional 8212 will probably be required for the buffering task and the de-multiplexing of the data bus is incidental.

SYSTEM PERFORMANCE

The true benchmark of any microcomputer-based system is the amount of tasks that can be assigned to the software execution and still meet the overall product performance requirements. Speed of CPU instruction execution has been the common approach to system through-put problems but this puts a greater strain on the memory access requirement and bus operation than is usually practical for most applications. A much more desirable method would be to distribute the task-load to peripheral devices and free the systems software to simply initializing and maintaining these devices on a regular basis.

DISTRIBUTED PROCESSING

The concept of distributed task processing is not new to the computer designer, but until recently little if any task distribution was available to the microcomputer user. The MCS-85 is fully supported by Intel's MCS-80™ peripheral components. All are programmable and each can relieve the systems software of many of the bookkeeping I/O and timing tasks common to any system.

INSTRUCTION CYCLE/ACCESS

The basic instruction cycle of the 8085 is 1.3 microseconds. It is the same speed as the 8080A-1 and a closer look at the MCS-85 bus operation shows that the access requirement for this speed is only 450 nanoseconds. The MCS-80™ access requirements for this speed would be under 300 nanoseconds to illustrate the efficiency and improved timing margins of the MCS-85 bus structure.

THROUGHPUT/COST

When a total system through-put analysis is taken, the MCS-85 with its programmable peripheral components will yield the most cost-effective, reliable and producible system available.

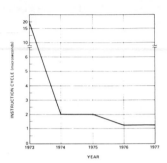

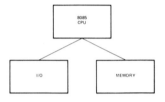

8085
SINGLE CHIP 8-BIT N-CHANNEL MICROPROCESSOR

- Single +5V Power Supply
- 100% Software Compatible with 8080A
- 1.3 μs Instruction Cycle
- On-Chip Clock Generator (with External Crystal or RC Network)
- On-Chip System Controller

- Four Vectored Interrupts (One is non-Maskable)
- Serial In/Serial Out Port
- Decimal, Binary and Double Precision Arithmetic
- Direct Addressing Capability to 64K Bytes of Memory

The Intel® 8085 is a new generation, complete 8 bit parallel central processing unit (CPU). Its instruction set is 100% software compatible with the 8080A microprocessor, and it is designed to improve the present 8080's performance by higher system speed. Its high level of system integration allows a minimum system of three IC's: 8085 (CPU), 8155 (RAM) and 8355/8755 (ROM/PROM).

The 8085 incorporates all of the features that the 8224 (clock generator) and 8228 (system controller) provided for the 8080, thereby offering a high level of system integration.

The 8085 uses a multiplexed Data Bus. The address is split between the 8 bit address bus and the 8 bit data bus. The on-chip address latches of 8155/8355/8755 memory products allows a direct interface with 8085.

8085 CPU FUNCTIONAL BLOCK DIAGRAM

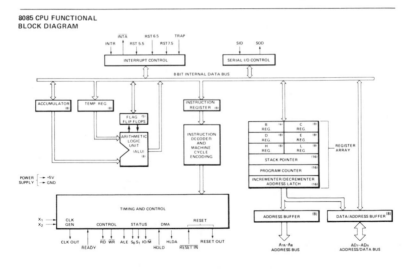

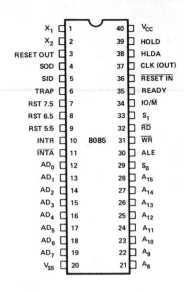

8085 PINOUT DIAGRAM

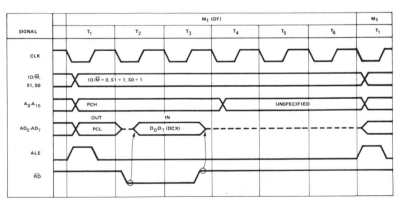

OPCODE FETCH MACHINE CYCLE.

8085

RIM   (Read Interrupt Mask)

After the execution of the RIM instruction, the accumulator is loaded with the restart interrupt masks, any pending interrupts, and the contents of the serial input data line (SID).

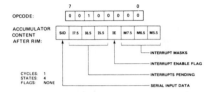

SIM   (Set Interrupt Masks)

During execution of the SIM instruction, the contents of the accumulator will be used in programming the restart interrupt masks. Bits 0–2 will set/reset the mask bit for RST 5.5, 6.5, 7.5 of the interrupt mask register, if bit 3 is 1 ("set"). Bit 3 is a "Mask Set Enable" control.

Setting the mask (i.e. masked bit = 1) disables the corresponding interrupt.

	Set	Reset
RST 5.5 MASK	if bit 0 = 1	if bit 0 = 0
RST 6.5 MASK	bit 1 = 1	bit 1 = 0
RST 7.5 MASK	bit 2 = 1	bit 2 = 0

RST 7.5 (edge trigger enable) internal request flip flop will be reset if bit 4 of the accumulator = 1; regardless of whether RST 7.5 is masked or not.

RESET IN input (pin 36) will set all RST MASKs, and reset/disable all interrupts.

SIM can, also, load the SOD output latch. Accumulator bit 7 is loaded into the SOD latch if bit 6 is set. The latch is unaffected if bit 6 is a zero. RESET IN input sets the SOD latch to zero.

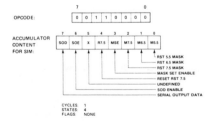

Appendix G

Monitoring of RAM Write/Read or PROM Read vs. Single Stepping

It is convenient to have an octal or hexa monitor of programs as they are being written into memory *or* being read back for inspection. The advantage of octal or hexa monitor displays over binary read-outs is obvious. We can approach the problem two ways (see Chap. 4): Monitor the address and instruction or data bytes as they are being written in or read back, or run the program and then single step it in which case the address and data bus monitors will *read back* address vs. instruction bytes and in addition the "extra bytes" associated with certain instructions. The display connections to the data and address busses and to control signals are different in the two cases. An appreciation of the bootstrap program (in this case KEX—Appendix C) is vital to understanding the difference, particularly as it applies to the first case above. We illustrate the approach for octal displays although the description that follows is easily applied to hexadecimal displays (two for address and two for data). We assume the displays are such (HP 5082-7300 or LR-4 seven segment artboards) that strobe "low" enables (Data Out = Data In) and strobe "high" disables (latches) (Data Out = Q_0, no change as Data In changes).

Address, Instruction Monitoring During Writing or Reading Back

BA, CBA, CBA of the three octal address bus displays must be tied to the stand-off terminals $b_7 \ldots b_0$, respectively, of port 0 on the MMD-1 (see KEX) and the strobes should be kept low (or tied to $\overline{\text{Out}}$) to allow the last address latched to the terminals to be displayed (DC, D, D are grounded). BA, CBA, CBA of the three octal data bus displays must be tied to the data bus D_7 . . . D_0. The strobes should be tied to $\overline{\text{Out}}$ to enable *and then latch*. Study KEX carefully to see why this is so. See also Experiment 4-2(a). Writing a program into RAM will then be displayed as octal address/data as you write in. Likewise reading the program back (Reset and repeatedly press "S" key) will show the complete program address/data bytes on the displays. You can read back the program in any ROM or PROM this way—the KEX program at 000, 000 or the cassette, TTY load/dump PROM, if you have one, at 001, 000 or the Debug Proms at 020, 000 through 023, 377 on the E & L Memory Interface (Extension) Board if you have that. Just strike the starting address (hi, lo) for that memory, "S" your way through, and read the program on the octal displays.

Single Step Read-Out of Address vs. Instruction— The "Extra Bytes".

BA, CBA, CBA of the three octal address displays must be tied to A_7 . . . A_0 of the address bus with strobes kept low. BA, CBA, CBA of the data bus displays are tied to the data bus D_7 . . . D_0 with strobes kept low. "Ready" and "Wait" from the 8224 (RDYIN) and 8080, respectively, are tied to appropriate pins of the 7476 or 7474 flip flop or LR-50 outboard (Fig. 34). The program is run full speed, then single stepped with a pulser. Address and instruction bytes are read back together with any extra bytes. The low on both strobes will allow the *last* address and fetched data (or any other read/write memory or I/O machine cycle data) to show on the displays. State T_3 of a machine cycle is the state during which incoming or outgoing data of any kind is placed on the data bus, and being the last time during the machine cycle that such data appears on the data bus, the lo on the enable will allow the display to capture it. Likewise with respect to the address byte and states T_1 through T_3 (see Fig. 35). See also Experiment 4-2(a).

Appendix H

Conditions Necessary to Perform the Experiments in This Book on Other 8080 Based Microcomputers. Using the 8085 with Standard Memories/Peripherals to do the Experiments

1. Three latched output ports with 8 LED's each are most useful in all the experiments *especially* in demonstrating software control in Chap. 3. (See Fig. 11 for design.)

2. A keyboard/encoder/bootstrap PROM to program 8080 instructions in either octal or hexa. (See Fig. 11, Chap. 2, Section 2-2, and Appendix C for ideas.)

3. Control signals ($\overline{\text{MEMR}}$, $\overline{\text{MEMW}}$, $\overline{\text{I/OW}}$, ($\overline{\text{Out}}$), $\overline{\text{I/OR}}$ ($\overline{\text{IN}}$), and $\overline{\text{INTA}}$ ($\overline{\text{IACK}}$)) are needed. See Section 5-2(G) for their synthesis.

4. Accessability to address and data busses is a must. A terminal board to facilitate this access and the I/O interfacing via IC's is necessary.

5. Device selects must be generated (use either 74154 or 7442 decoders with either $\overline{\text{I/OR}}$ or $\overline{\text{I/OW}}$ ($\overline{\text{IN}}$, $\overline{\text{Out}}$) control signals). See Sections 5-2(C), 5-2(G), Figs. 11, 46, 51, 52, 69, and 70.

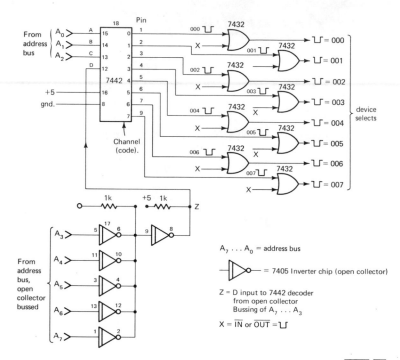

Figure 70. Absolute device selects generated with 7442, 7432, and $\overline{\text{OUT}}/\overline{\text{IN}}$ control signals. (Courtesy E & L Instruments—p. 33 MMD-1 operating Manual.)

6. $\overline{\text{MEMR}}$ and $\overline{\text{MEMW}}$ control signals as well as decoded memory chip selects to enable one memory block at a time. They are used to enable or disable R/W and OD pins on RAMS. $\overline{\text{MEMR}}$ is also used to enable-disable the ROM chip select. (See Fig. 11 for decoding scheme with the 74155 and for proper $\overline{\text{MEMW}}$, $\overline{\text{MEMR}}$ connections.)

7. You will need to access RDYIN at pin 3 of the 8224 and WAIT at pin 24 of the 8080 to implement single stepping with the 7474 or 7476 flip flop. See Fig. 34, Chap. 4. Data and address bus monitors are essential (see Chap. 4).

8. The 8085 microprocessor can be used in these experiments either with its 8085 family of peripherals/memories (8155 or 8156 RAM and 8355 ROM/PROM) or with standard memories/I/O's of the types encountered in these experiments and used in Figs. 11, 12, etc. Naturally, adaptations must be made in interrupt experiments. They are easier with the 8085 as vec-

tored interrupts are built in and $\overline{\text{INTA}}$ is generated for us. You are advised to consult pp. 1-5, 1-6, 1-7, 3-1 through 3-6, and p. 2-20, 2-21 of the Intel MCS-85 User's Manual June 1977, as well as Appendix F of this book. They will give you the necessary information to use the 8085 in an all 8085 system (8155, 56 plus 8355, 8755) or with standard memories/peripherals (8080 types, for example).

To use the 8085 with standard peripherals/memories in these experiments, it is basically a matter of 1) latching A_7 ... A_0 from the AD_7 ... AD_0 multiplexed address/data bus to form the usual 8080 type A_{15} ... A_0 address bus, and 2) generating the 8080 type control signals $\overline{\text{I/OR}}$ ($\overline{\text{IN}}$), $\overline{\text{I/OW}}$ ($\overline{\text{Out}}$), $\overline{\text{MEMR}}$, $\overline{\text{MEMW}}$, ($\overline{\text{INTA}}$ is already available on the 8085). Once the latter are generated, device selects for I/O's can be generated as explained in Chap. 5 and Fig. 70. Item (1) above is accomplished with the 8212. ALE (pin 30) from the 8085 (address latch enable) is applied to DS_2 of the 8212 and will latch the inputs A_7 ... A_0 to the 8212 at the beginning of each machine cycle (see pp. 2-20, 21, MCS 85 Manual June 1977). Item (2) above is accomplished by using a 3×8 decoder (8205, for example) in which $\overline{\text{WR}}$, $\overline{\text{RD}}$, and I/O$\overline{\text{M}}$ from pins 31, 32, and 34 are inputs and the control signals $\overline{\text{I/OW}}$, $\overline{\text{I/OR}}$, $\overline{\text{MEMW}}$, $\overline{\text{MEMR}}$ are generated at the outputs O_6, O_5, O_2, and O_1 of the decoder (see p. 2-20 MCS 85 Manual June 1977).

The next book on Applications Experiments will go further into the use of the 8085 with standard memories/peripherals.

Appendix I

The 8080 Instruction Set Micro-operation 'Legalisms' (Machine Cycle* States)

The following four pages are reproduced courtesy Intel Corp. (8080 Microcomputer Systems User's Manual, pp. 2-16, 17, 18, 19; Sept. 1975). They detail the states and microoperations (data bus flow, address bus flow, register to register, memory to register, register to memory, register to I/O, I/O to register, etc., flow) involved in each of the up to five machine cycles which may be necessary to fetch and execute each 8080 instruction. These pages should be carefully consulted when there is any doubt about what happens during execution of a particular instruction. Together with the *"Description Format"* of every instruction reproduced in Appendix J, they should help considerably in the correct use of 8080 instructions in your program.

*See also Chaps. 1, 2, and 4.

MNEMONIC	OP CODE		M1[1]					M2		
	D7 D6 D5 D4	D3 D2 D1 D0	T1	T2[2]	T3	T4	T5	T1	T2[2]	T3
MOV r1,r2	0 1 D D	D S S S	PC OUT STATUS	PC = PC +1	INST→TMP/IR	(SSS)→TMP	(TMP)→DDD			
MOV r, M	0 1 D D	D 1 1 0	↑	↑	↑	X[3]		HL OUT STATUS[6]	DATA——►DDD	
MOV M, r	0 1 1 1	0 S S S				(SSS)→TMP		HL OUT STATUS[7]	(TMP)——►DATA BUS	
SPHL	1 1 1 1	1 0 0 1				(HL) _____	SP			
MVI r, data	0 0 D D	D 1 1 0				X		PC OUT STATUS[6]	B2 ——►DDDD	
MVI M, data	0 0 1 1	0 1 1 0				X		↑	B2——►TMP	
LXI rp, data	0 0 R P	0 0 0 1				X			PC = PC + 1	B2 ——►r1
LDA addr	0 0 1 1	1 0 1 0				X			PC = PC + 1	B2 ——►Z
STA addr	0 0 1 1	0 0 1 0				X			PC = PC + 1	B2 ——►Z
LHLD addr	0 0 1 0	1 0 1 0				X			PC = PC + 1	B2 ——►Z
SHLD addr	0 0 1 0	0 0 1 0				X		PC OUT STATUS[6]	PC = PC + 1	B2 ——►Z
LDAX rp[4]	0 0 R P	1 0 1 0				X		rp OUT STATUS[6]	DATA——►A	
STAX rp[4]	0 0 R P	0 0 1 0				X		rp OUT STATUS[7]	(A) ——►DATA BUS	
XCHG	1 1 1 0	1 0 1 1				(HL)◄──►(DE)				
ADD r	1 0 0 0	0 S S S				(SSS)→TMP (A)→ACT		[9]	(ACT)+(TMP)→A	
ADD M	1 0 0 0	0 1 1 0				(A)→ACT		HL OUT STATUS[6]	DATA——►TMP	
ADI data	1 1 0 0	0 1 1 0				(A)→ACT		PC OUT STATUS[6]	PC = PC + 1	B2 ——►TMP
ADC r	1 0 0 0	1 S S S				(SSS)→TMP (A)→ACT		[9]	(ACT)+(TMP)+CY→A	
ADC M	1 0 0 0	1 1 1 0				(A)→ACT		HL OUT STATUS[6]	DATA——►TMP	
ACI data	1 1 0 0	1 1 1 0				(A)→ACT		PC OUT STATUS[6]	PC = PC + 1	B2 ——►TMP
SUB r	1 0 0 1	0 S S S				(SSS)→TMP (A)→ACT		[9]	(ACT)-(TMP)→A	
SUB M	1 0 0 1	0 1 1 0				(A)→ACT		HL OUT STATUS[6]	DATA——►TMP	
SUI data	1 1 0 1	0 1 1 0				(A)→ACT		PC OUT STATUS[6]	PC = PC + 1	B2 ——►TMP
SBB r	1 0 0 1	1 S S S				(SSS)→TMP (A)→ACT		[8]	(ACT)-(TMP)-CY→A	
SBB M	1 0 0 1	1 1 1 0				(A)→ACT		HL OUT STATUS[6]	DATA——►TMP	
SBI data	1 1 0 1	1 1 1 0				(A)→ACT		PC OUT STATUS[6]	PC = PC + 1	B2 ——►TMP
INR r	0 0 D D	D 1 0 0				(DDD)→TMP (TMP) + 1→ALU	ALU→DDD			
INR M	0 0 1 1	0 1 0 0				X		HL OUT STATUS[6]	DATA ——►TMP (TMP)+1 ——► ALU	
DCR r	0 0 D D	D 1 0 1				(DDD)→TMP (TMP)+1→ALU	ALU→DDD			
DCR M	0 0 1 1	0 1 0 1				X		HL OUT STATUS[6]	DATA——►TMP (TMP)-1 ——► ALU	
INX rp	0 0 R P	0 0 1 1				(RP) + 1 _____	RP			
DCX rp	0 0 R P	1 0 1 1				(RP) - 1 _____	RP			
DAD rp[8]	0 0 R P	1 0 0 1				X		(rl)→ACT	(L)→TMP, (ACT)+(TMP)→ALU	ALU→L, CY
DAA	0 0 1 0	0 1 1 1				DAA→A, FLAGS[10]				
ANA r	1 0 1 0	0 S S S				(SSS)→TMP (A)→ACT		[9]	(ACT)+(TMP)→A	
ANA M	1 0 1 0	0 1 1 0	PC OUT STATUS	PC = PC + 1	INST→TMP/IR	(A)→ACT		HL OUT STATUS[6]	DATA ——► TMP	

	M3			M4			M5				
T1	T2[2]	T3	T1	T2[2]	T3	T1	T2[2]	T3	T4	T5	
HL OUT STATUS[7]	(TMP) → DATA BUS										
PC OUT STATUS[6]	PC = PC + 1 B3 → rh										
	PC = PC + 1 B3 → W		WZ OUT STATUS[6]	DATA → A							
	PC = PC + 1 B3 → W		WZ OUT STATUS[7]	(A) → DATA BUS							
	PC = PC + 1 B3 → W		WZ OUT STATUS[6]	DATA → L, WZ = WZ + 1		WZ OUT STATUS[6]	DATA → H				
PC OUT STATUS[6]	PC = PC + 1 B3 → W		WZ OUT STATUS[7]	(L) → DATA BUS, WZ = WZ + 1		WZ OUT STATUS[7]	(H) → DATA BUS				
[9]	(ACT)+(TMP)→A										
[9]	(ACT)+(TMP)→A										
[9]	(ACT)+(TMP)+CY→A										
[9]	(ACT)+(TMP)+CY→A										
[9]	(ACT)−(TMP)→A										
[9]	(ACT)−(TMP)→A										
[9]	(ACT)−(TMP)−CY→A										
[9]	(ACT)−(TMP)−CY→A										
HL OUT STATUS[7]	ALU → DATA BUS										
HL OUT STATUS[7]	ALU → DATA BUS										
(rh)→ACT	(H)→TMP (ACT)+(TMP)+CY→ALU	ALU→H, CY									
[9]	(ACT)+(TMP)→A										

MNEMONIC	OP CODE		M1 [1]					M2		
	D7 D6 D5 D4	D3 D2 D1 D0	T1	T2[2]	T3	T4	T5	T1	T2[2]	T3
ANI data	1 1 1 0	0 1 1 0	PC OUT STATUS	PC = PC + 1	INST→TMP/IR	(A)→ACT		PC OUT STATUS[6]	PC = PC + 1	B2→TMP
XRA r	1 0 1 0	1 S S S				(A)→ACT (SSS)→TMP		[9]	(ACT)+(TMP)→A	
XRA M	1 0 1 0	1 1 1 0				(A)→ACT		HL OUT STATUS[6]		DATA→TMP
XRI data	1 1 1 0	1 1 1 0				(A)→ACT		PC OUT STATUS[6]	PC = PC + 1	B2→TMP
ORA r	1 0 1 1	0 S S S				(A)→ACT (SSS)→TMP		[9]	(ACT)+(TMP)→A	
ORA M	1 0 1 1	0 1 1 0				(A)→ACT		HL OUT STATUS[6]		DATA→TMP
ORI data	1 1 1 1	0 1 1 0				(A)→ACT		PC OUT STATUS[6]	PC = PC + 1	B2→TMP
CMP r	1 0 1 1	1 S S S				(A)→ACT (SSS)→TMP		[9]	(ACT)-(TMP), FLAGS	
CMP M	1 0 1 1	1 1 1 0				(A)→ACT		HL OUT STATUS[6]		DATA→TMP
CPI data	1 1 1 1	1 1 1 0				(A)→ACT		PC OUT STATUS[6]	PC = PC + 1	B2→TMP
RLC	0 0 0 0	0 1 1 1				(A)→ALU ROTATE		[9]	ALU→A, CY	
RRC	0 0 0 0	1 1 1 1				(A)→ALU ROTATE		[9]	ALU→A, CY	
RAL	0 0 0 1	0 1 1 1				(A), CY→ALU ROTATE		[9]	ALU→A, CY	
RAR	0 0 0 1	1 1 1 1				(A), CY→ALU ROTATE		[9]	ALU→A, CY	
CMA	0 0 1 0	1 1 1 1				(Ā)→A				
CMC	0 0 1 1	1 1 1 1				C̄Y→CY				
STC	0 0 1 1	0 1 1 1				1→CY				
JMP addr	1 1 0 0	0 0 1 1				X		PC OUT STATUS[6]	PC = PC + 1	B2→Z
J cond addr[17]	1 1 C C	C 0 1 0				JUDGE CONDITION		PC OUT STATUS[6]	PC = PC + 1	B2→Z
CALL addr	1 1 0 0	1 1 0 1				SP = SP - 1		PC OUT STATUS[6]	PC = PC + 1	B2→Z
C cond addr[17]	1 1 C C	C 1 0 0				JUDGE CONDITION IF TRUE, SP = SP - 1		PC OUT STATUS[6]	PC = PC + 1	B2→Z
RET	1 1 0 0	1 0 0 1				X		SP OUT STATUS[15]	SP = SP + 1	DATA→Z
R cond addr[17]	1 1 C C	C 0 0 0			INST→TMP/IR	JUDGE CONDITION[14]		SP OUT STATUS[15]	SP = SP + 1	DATA→Z
RST n	1 1 N N	N 1 1 1			ɸ→W INST→TMP/IR	SP = SP - 1		SP OUT STATUS[16]	SP = SP - 1	(PCH)→DATA BUS
PCHL	1 1 1 0	1 0 0 1			INST→TMP/IR	(HL) ——→ PC				
PUSH rp	1 1 R P	0 1 0 1				SP = SP - 1		SP OUT STATUS[16]	SP = SP - 1	(rh)→DATA BUS
PUSH PSW	1 1 1 1	0 1 0 1				SP = SP - 1		SP OUT STATUS[16]	SP = SP - 1	(A)→DATA BUS
POP rp	1 1 R P	0 0 0 1				X		SP OUT STATUS[15]	SP = SP + 1	DATA→r1
POP PSW	1 1 1 1	0 0 0 1				X		SP OUT STATUS[15]	SP = SP + 1	DATA→FLAGS
XTHL	1 1 1 0	0 0 1 1				X		SP OUT STATUS[15]	SP = SP + 1	DATA→Z
IN port	1 1 0 1	1 0 1 1				X		PC OUT STATUS[6]	PC = PC + 1	B2→Z, W
OUT port	1 1 0 1	0 0 1 1				X		PC OUT STATUS[6]	PC = PC + 1	B2→Z, W
EI	1 1 1 1	1 0 1 1				SET INTE F/F				
DI	1 1 1 1	0 0 1 1				RESET INTE F/F				
HLT	0 1 1 1	0 1 1 0				X		PC OUT STATUS	HALT MODE[20]	
NOP	0 0 0 0	0 0 0 0	PC OUT STATUS	PC = PC + 1	INST→TMP/IR	X				

	M3			M4			M5			
T1	T2[2]	T3	T1	T2[2]	T3	T1	T2[2]	T3	T4	T5
[9]	(ACT)+(TMP)→A									
[9]	(ACT)+(TMP)→A									
[9]	(ACT)+(TMP)→A									
[9]	(ACT)+(TMP)→A									
[9]	(ACT)+(TMP)→A									
[9]	(ACT)−(TMP); FLAGS									
[9]	(ACT)−(TMP); FLAGS									
PC OUT STATUS[6]	PC = PC + 1	B3 →W						WZ OUT STATUS[11]	(WZ) + 1 → PC	
PC OUT STATUS[6]	PC = PC + 1	B3 →W						WZ OUT STATUS[11,12]	(WZ) + 1 → PC	
PC OUT STATUS[6]	PC = PC + 1	B3 →W	SP OUT STATUS[16]	(PCH) SP = SP - 1	→DATA BUS	SP OUT STATUS[16]	(PCL)	→DATA BUS	WZ OUT STATUS[11]	(WZ) + 1 → PC
PC OUT STATUS[6]	PC = PC + 1	B3 →W[13]	SP OUT STATUS[16]	(PCH) SP = SP - 1	→DATA BUS	SP OUT STATUS[16]	(PCL)	→DATA BUS	WZ OUT STATUS[11,12]	(WZ) + 1 → PC
SP OUT STATUS[15]	SP = SP + 1	DATA →W						WZ OUT STATUS[11]	(WZ) + 1 → PC	
SP OUT STATUS[15]	SP = SP + 1	DATA →W						WZ OUT STATUS[11,12]	(WZ) + 1 → PC	
SP OUT STATUS[16]	(TMP = 00NNN000) (PCL)	→Z →DATA BUS						WZ OUT STATUS[11]	(WZ) + 1 → PC	
SP OUT STATUS[16]		(rl) →DATA BUS								
SP OUT STATUS[16]		FLAGS →DATA BUS								
SP OUT STATUS[15]	SP = SP + 1	DATA →rh								
SP OUT STATUS[15]	SP = SP + 1	DATA →A								
SP OUT STATUS[15]		DATA →W	SP OUT STATUS[16]	(H)	→DATA BUS	SP OUT STATUS[16]	(L)	→DATA BUS	(WZ) →HL	
WZ OUT STATUS[18]		DATA →A								
WZ OUT STATUS[18]		(A) →DATA BUS								

Appendix J

Description Format of the 8080 Instruction Set. Clock Cycles

The following pages are reproduced courtesy Intel Corp. (8080 Microcomputer Systems Manual, Sept. 1975, pp. 4-4 through 4-15). Together with Appendix I they should help in the correct use of all 8080 instructions when programming. Note also the last page summarizes the instruction set and gives the number of clock cycles per instruction.

MVI r, data   (Move Immediate)

(r) ←— (byte 2)

The content of byte 2 of the instruction is moved to register r.

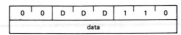

0	0	D	D	D	1	1	0
data							

Cycles: 2
States: 7
Addressing: immediate
Flags: none

Data Transfer Group:

This group of instructions transfers data to and from registers and memory. **Condition flags are not affected** by any instruction in this group.

MOV r1, r2   (Move Register)

(r1) ←— (r2)

The content of register r2 is moved to register r1.

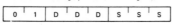

0	1	D	D	D	S	S	S

Cycles: 1
States: 5
Addressing: register
Flags: none

MOV r, M   (Move from memory)

(r) ←— ((H) (L))

The content of the memory location, whose address is in registers H and L, is moved to register r.

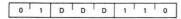

0	1	D	D	D	1	1	0

Cycles: 2
States: 7
Addressing: reg. indirect
Flags: none

MOV M, r   (Move to memory)

((H) (L)) ←— (r)

The content of register r is moved to the memory location whose address is in registers H and L.

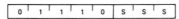

0	1	1	1	0	S	S	S

Cycles: 2
States: 7
Addressing: reg. indirect
Flags: none

MVI M, data   (Move to memory immediate)

((H) (L)) ←— (byte 2)

The content of byte 2 of the instruction is moved to the memory location whose address is in registers H and L.

0	0	1	1	0	1	1	0
data							

Cycles: 3
States: 10
Addressing: immed./reg. indirect
Flags: none

LXI rp, data 16   (Load register pair immediate)

(rh) ←— (byte 3),

(rl) ←— (byte 2)

Byte 3 of the instruction is moved into the high-order register (rh) of the register pair rp. Byte 2 of the instruction is moved into the low-order register (rl) of the register pair rp.

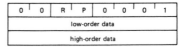

0	0	R	P	0	0	0	1
low-order data							
high-order data							

Cycles: 3
States: 10
Addressing: immediate
Flags: none

LDA addr   (Load Accumulator direct)

(A) ←— ((byte 3)(byte 2))

The content of the memory location, whose address is specified in byte 2 and byte 3 of the instruction, is moved to register A.

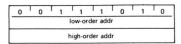

Cycles: 4
States: 13
Addressing: direct
Flags: none

STA addr   (Store Accumulator direct)

((byte 3)(byte 2)) ←— (A)

The content of the accumulator is moved to the memory location whose address is specified in byte 2 and byte 3 of the instruction.

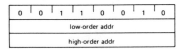

Cycles: 4
States: 13
Addressing: direct
Flags: none

LHLD addr   (Load H and L direct)

(L) ←— ((byte 3)(byte 2))
(H) ←— ((byte 3)(byte 2) + 1)

The content of the memory location, whose address is specified in byte 2 and byte 3 of the instruction, is moved to register L. The content of the memory location at the succeeding address is moved to register H.

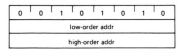

Cycles: 5
States: 16
Addressing: direct
Flags: none

SHLD addr   (Store H and L direct)

((byte 3)(byte 2)) ←— (L)
((byte 3)(byte 2) + 1) ←— (H)

The content of register L is moved to the memory location whose address is specified in byte 2 and byte 3. The content of register H is moved to the succeeding memory location.

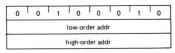

Cycles: 5
States: 16
Addressing: direct
Flags: none

LDAX rp   (Load accumulator indirect)

(A) ←— ((rp))

The content of the memory location, whose address is in the register pair rp, is moved to register A. Note: only register pairs rp=B (registers B and C) or rp=D (registers D and E) may be specified.

Cycles: 2
States: 7
Addressing: reg. indirect
Flags: none

STAX rp   (Store accumulator indirect)

((rp)) ←— (A)

The content of register A is moved to the memory location whose address is in the register pair rp. Note: only register pairs rp=B (registers B and C) or rp=D (registers D and E) may be specified.

Cycles: 2
States: 7
Addressing: reg. indirect
Flags: none

XCHG   (Exchange H and L with D and E)

(H) ←→ (D)
(L) ←→ (E)

The contents of registers H and L are exchanged with the contents of registers D and E.

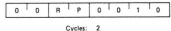

Cycles: 1
States: 4
Addressing: register
Flags: none

Arithmetic Group:

This group of instructions performs arithmetic operations on data in registers and memory.

Unless indicated otherwise, all instructions in this group affect the Zero, Sign, Parity, Carry, and Auxiliary Carry flags according to the standard rules.

All subtraction operations are performed via two's complement arithmetic and set the carry flag to one to indicate a borrow and clear it to indicate no borrow.

ADD r   (Add Register)

(A) ◄── (A) + (r)

The content of register r is added to the content of the accumulator. The result is placed in the accumulator.

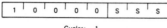

Cycles:	1
States:	4
Addressing:	register
Flags:	Z,S,P,CY,AC

ADD M   (Add memory)

(A) ◄── (A) + ((H) (L))

The content of the memory location whose address is contained in the H and L registers is added to the content of the accumulator. The result is placed in the accumulator.

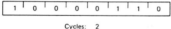

Cycles:	2
States:	7
Addressing:	reg. indirect
Flags:	Z,S,P,CY,AC

ADI data   (Add immediate)

(A) ◄── (A) + (byte 2)

The content of the second byte of the instruction is added to the content of the accumulator. The result is placed in the accumulator.

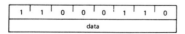

Cycles:	2
States:	7
Addressing:	immediate
Flags:	Z,S,P,CY,AC

ADC r   (Add Register with carry)

(A) ◄── (A) + (r) + (CY)

The content of register r and the content of the carry bit are added to the content of the accumulator. The result is placed in the accumulator.

Cycles:	1
States:	4
Addressing:	register
Flags:	Z,S,P,CY,AC

ADC M   (Add memory with carry)

(A) ◄── (A) + ((H) (L)) + (CY)

The content of the memory location whose address is contained in the H and L registers and the content of the CY flag are added to the accumulator. The result is placed in the accumulator.

Cycles:	2
States:	7
Addressing:	reg. indirect
Flags:	Z,S,P,CY,AC

ACI data   (Add immediate with carry)

(A) ◄── (A) + (byte 2) + (CY)

The content of the second byte of the instruction and the content of the CY flag are added to the contents of the accumulator. The result is placed in the accumulator.

Cycles:	2
States:	7
Addressing:	immediate
Flags:	Z,S,P,CY,AC

SUB r   (Subtract Register)

(A) ◄── (A) − (r)

The content of register r is subtracted from the content of the accumulator. The result is placed in the accumulator.

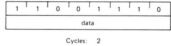

Cycles:	1
States:	4
Addressing:	register
Flags:	Z,S,P,CY,AC

SUB M (Subtract memory)

(A) ← (A) − ((H) (L))

The content of the memory location whose address is contained in the H and L registers is subtracted from the content of the accumulator. The result is placed in the accumulator.

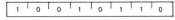

1	0	0	1	0	1	1	0

Cycles: 2
States: 7
Addressing: reg. indirect
Flags: Z,S,P,CY,AC

SUI data (Subtract immediate)

(A) ← (A) − (byte 2)

The content of the second byte of the instruction is subtracted from the content of the accumulator. The result is placed in the accumulator.

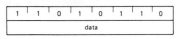

1	1	0	1	0	1	1	0
data

Cycles: 2
States: 7
Addressing: immediate
Flags: Z,S,P,CY,AC

SBB r (Subtract Register with borrow)

(A) ← (A) − (r) − (CY)

The content of register r and the content of the CY flag are both subtracted from the accumulator. The result is placed in the accumulator.

1	0	0	1	1	S	S	S

Cycles: 1
States: 4
Addressing: register
Flags: Z,S,P,CY,AC

SBB M (Subtract memory with borrow)

(A) ← (A) − ((H) (L)) − (CY)

The content of the memory location whose address is contained in the H and L registers and the content of the CY flag are both subtracted from the accumulator. The result is placed in the accumulator.

1	0	0	1	1	1	1	0

Cycles: 2
States: 7
Addressing: reg. indirect
Flags: Z,S,P,CY,AC

SBI data (Subtract immediate with borrow)

(A) ← (A) − (byte 2) − (CY)

The contents of the second byte of the instruction and the contents of the CY flag are both subtracted from the accumulator. The result is placed in the accumulator.

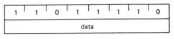

1	1	0	1	1	1	1	0
data

Cycles: 2
States: 7
Addressing: immediate
Flags: Z,S,P,CY,AC

INR r (Increment Register)

(r) ← (r) + 1

The content of register r is incremented by one. Note: All condition flags **except CY** are affected.

0	0	D	D	D	1	0	0

Cycles: 1
States: 5
Addressing: register
Flags: Z,S,P,AC

INR M (Increment memory)

((H) (L)) ← ((H) (L)) + 1

The content of the memory location whose address is contained in the H and L registers is incremented by one. Note: All condition flags **except CY** are affected.

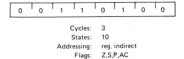

0	0	1	1	0	1	0	0

Cycles: 3
States: 10
Addressing: reg. indirect
Flags: Z,S,P,AC

DCR r (Decrement Register)

(r) ← (r) − 1

The content of register r is decremented by one. Note: All condition flags **except CY** are affected.

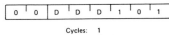

0	0	D	D	D	1	0	1

Cycles: 1
States: 5
Addressing: register
Flags: Z,S,P,AC

DCR M   (Decrement memory)

((H) (L)) ◄— ((H) (L)) − 1

The content of the memory location whose address is contained in the H and L registers is decremented by one. Note: All condition flags **except CY** are affected.

Cycles:	3
States:	10
Addressing:	reg. indirect
Flags:	Z,S,P,AC

INX rp   (Increment register pair)

(rh) (rl) ◄— (rh) (rl) + 1

The content of the register pair rp is incremented by one. Note: **No condition flags are affected.**

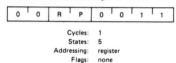

Cycles:	1
States:	5
Addressing:	register
Flags:	none

DCX rp   (Decrement register pair)

(rh) (rl) ◄— (rh) (rl) − 1

The content of the register pair rp is decremented by one. Note: **No condition flags are affected.**

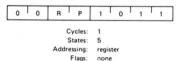

Cycles:	1
States:	5
Addressing:	register
Flags:	none

DAD rp   (Add register pair to H and L)

(H) (L) ◄— (H) (L) + (rh) (rl)

The content of the register pair rp is added to the content of the register pair H and L. The result is placed in the register pair H and L. Note: **Only the CY flag is affected.** It is set if there is a carry out of the double precision add; otherwise it is reset.

Cycles:	3
States:	10
Addressing:	register
Flags:	CY

DAA   (Decimal Adjust Accumulator)

The eight-bit number in the accumulator is adjusted to form two four-bit Binary-Coded-Decimal digits by the following process:

1. If the value of the least significant 4 bits of the accumulator is greater than 9 or if the AC flag is set, 6 is added to the accumulator

2. If the value of the most significant 4 bits of the accumulator is now greater than 9, or if the CY flag is set, 6 is added to the most significant 4 bits of the accumulator.

NOTE: All flags are affected.

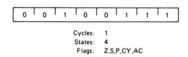

Cycles:	1
States:	4
Flags:	Z,S,P,CY,AC

Logical Group:

This group of instructions performs logical (Boolean) operations on data in registers and memory and on condition flags.

Unless indicated otherwise, all instructions in this group affect the Zero, Sign, Parity, Auxiliary Carry, and Carry flags according to the standard rules.

ANA r   (AND Register)

(A) ◄— (A) ∧ (r)

The content of register r is logically anded with the content of the accumulator. The result is placed in the content of the accumulator. **The CY flag is cleared.**

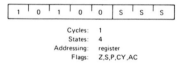

Cycles:	1
States:	4
Addressing:	register
Flags:	Z,S,P,CY,AC

ANA M   (AND memory)

(A) ◄— (A) ∧ ((H) (L))

The contents of the memory location whose address is contained in the H and L registers is logically anded with the content of the accumulator. The result is placed in the accumulator. **The CY flag is cleared.**

Cycles:	2
States:	7
Addressing:	reg. indirect
Flags:	Z,S,P,CY,AC

ANI data   (AND immediate)

(A) ⬅— (A) ∧ (byte 2)

The content of the second byte of the instruction is logically anded with the contents of the accumulator. The result is placed in the accumulator. **The CY and AC flags are cleared.**

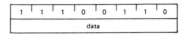

1	1	1	0	0	1	1	0
data

Cycles: 2
States: 7
Addressing: immediate
Flags: Z,S,P,CY,AC

XRA r   (Exclusive OR Register)

(A) ⬅— (A) ∀ (r)

The content of register r is exclusive-or'd with the content of the accumulator. The result is placed in the accumulator. **The CY and AC flags are cleared.**

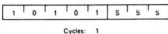

1	0	1	0	1	S	S	S

Cycles: 1
States: 4
Addressing: register
Flags: Z,S,P,CY,AC

XRA M   (Exclusive OR Memory)

(A) ⬅— (A) ∀ ((H) (L))

The content of the memory location whose address is contained in the H and L registers is exclusive-OR'd with the content of the accumulator. The result is placed in the accumulator. **The CY and AC flags are cleared.**

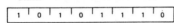

1	0	1	0	1	1	1	0

Cycles: 2
States: 7
Addressing: reg. indirect
Flags: Z,S,P,CY,AC

XRI data   (Exclusive OR immediate)

(A) ⬅— (A) ∀ (byte 2)

The content of the second byte of the instruction is exclusive-OR'd with the content of the accumulator. The result is placed in the accumulator. **The CY and AC flags are cleared.**

1	1	1	0	1	1	1	0
data

Cycles: 2
States: 7
Addressing: immediate
Flags: Z,S,P,CY,AC

ORA r   (OR Register)

(A) ⬅— (A) V (r)

The content of register r is inclusive-OR'd with the content of the accumulator. The result is placed in the accumulator. **The CY and AC flags are cleared.**

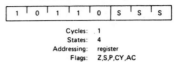

1	0	1	1	0	S	S	S

Cycles: 1
States: 4
Addressing: register
Flags: Z,S,P,CY,AC

ORA M   (OR memory)

(A) ⬅— (A) V ((H) (L))

The content of the memory location whose address is contained in the H and L registers is inclusive-OR'd with the content of the accumulator. The result is placed in the accumulator. **The CY and AC flags are cleared.**

1	0	1	1	0	1	1	0

Cycles: 2
States: 7
Addressing: reg. indirect
Flags: Z,S,P,CY,AC

ORI data   (OR Immediate)

(A) ⬅— (A) V (byte 2)

The content of the second byte of the instruction is inclusive-OR'd with the content of the accumulator. The result is placed in the accumulator. **The CY and AC flags are cleared.**

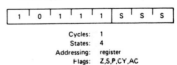

1	1	1	1	0	1	1	0
data

Cycles: 2
States: 7
Addressing: immediate
Flags: Z,S,P,CY,AC

CMP r   (Compare Register)

(A) — (r)

The content of register r is subtracted from the accumulator. The accumulator remains unchanged. The condition flags are set as a result of the subtraction. **The Z flag is set to 1 if (A) = (r). The CY flag is set to 1 if (A) < (r).**

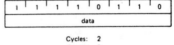

1	0	1	1	1	S	S	S

Cycles: 1
States: 4
Addressing: register
Flags: Z,S,P,CY,AC

CMP M   (Compare memory)

(A) − ((H) (L))

The content of the memory location whose address is contained in the H and L registers is subtracted from the accumulator. The accumulator remains unchanged. The condition flags are set as a result of the subtraction. The Z flag is set to 1 if (A) = ((H) (L)). The CY flag is set to 1 if (A) < ((H) (L)).

Cycles:	2
States:	7
Addressing:	reg. indirect
Flags:	Z,S,P,CY,AC

CPI data   (Compare immediate)

(A) − (byte 2)

The content of the second byte of the instruction is subtracted from the accumulator. The condition flags are set by the result of the subtraction. The Z flag is set to 1 if (A) = (byte 2). The CY flag is set to 1 if (A) < (byte 2).

Cycles:	2
States:	7
Addressing:	immediate
Flags:	Z,S,P,CY,AC

RLC   (Rotate left)

$(A_{n+1}) \leftarrow (A_n)$; $(A_0) \leftarrow (A_7)$

$(CY) \leftarrow (A_7)$

The content of the accumulator is rotated left one position. The low order bit and the CY flag are both set to the value shifted out of the high order bit position. **Only the CY flag is affected.**

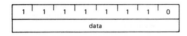

Cycles:	1
States:	4
Flags:	CY

RRC   (Rotate right)

$(A_n) \leftarrow (A_{n-1})$; $(A_7) \leftarrow (A_0)$

$(CY) \leftarrow (A_0)$

The content of the accumulator is rotated right one position. The high order bit and the CY flag are both set to the value shifted out of the low order bit position. **Only the CY flag is affected.**

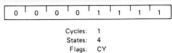

Cycles:	1
States:	4
Flags:	CY

RAL   (Rotate left through carry)

$(A_{n+1}) \leftarrow (A_n)$; $(CY) \leftarrow (A_7)$

$(A_0) \leftarrow (CY)$

The content of the accumulator is rotated left one position through the CY flag. The low order bit is set equal to the CY flag and the CY flag is set to the value shifted out of the high order bit. **Only the CY flag is affected.**

Cycles:	1
States:	4
Flags:	CY

RAR   (Rotate right through carry)

$(A_n) \leftarrow (A_{n+1})$; $(CY) \leftarrow (A_0)$

$(A_7) \leftarrow (CY)$

The content of the accumulator is rotated right one position through the CY flag. The high order bit is set to the CY flag and the CY flag is set to the value shifted out of the low order bit. **Only the CY flag is affected.**

Cycles:	1
States:	4
Flags:	CY

CMA   (Complement accumulator)

$(A) \leftarrow (\overline{A})$

The contents of the accumulator are complemented (zero bits become 1, one bits become 0). **No flags are affected.**

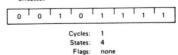

Cycles:	1
States:	4
Flags:	none

CMC (Complement carry)

(CY) ◄— (CY̅)

The CY flag is complemented. **No other flags are affected.**

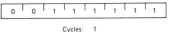

0	0	1	1	1	1	1	1

Cycles: 1
States: 4
Flags: CY

STC (Set carry)

(CY) ◄— 1

The CY flag is set to 1. **No other flags are affected.**

0	0	1	1	0	1	1	1

Cycles: 1
States: 4
Flags: CY

Branch Group:

This group of instructions alter normal sequential program flow.

Condition flags are not affected by any instruction in this group.

The two types of branch instructions are unconditional and conditional. Unconditional transfers simply perform the specified operation on register PC (the program counter). Conditional transfers examine the status of one of the four processor flags to determine if the specified branch is to be executed. The conditions that may be specified are as follows:

CONDITION		CCC
NZ	— not zero (Z = 0)	000
Z	— zero (Z = 1)	001
NC	— no carry (CY = 0)	010
C	— carry (CY = 1)	011
PO	— parity odd (P = 0)	100
PE	— parity even (P = 1)	101
P	— plus (S = 0)	110
M	— minus (S = 1)	111

JMP addr (Jump)

(PC) ◄— (byte 3) (byte 2)

Control is transferred to the instruction whose address is specified in byte 3 and byte 2 of the current instruction.

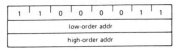

1	1	0	0	0	0	1	1
low-order addr							
high-order addr							

Cycles: 3
States: 10
Addressing: immediate
Flags: none

Jcondition addr (Conditional jump)

If (CCC),

(PC) ◄— (byte 3) (byte 2)

If the specified condition is true, control is transferred to the instruction whose address is specified in byte 3 and byte 2 of the current instruction; otherwise, control continues sequentially.

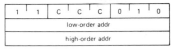

1	1	C	C	C	0	1	0
low-order addr							
high-order addr							

Cycles: 3
States: 10
Addressing: immediate
Flags: none

CALL addr (Call)

((SP) − 1) ◄— (PCH)

((SP) − 2) ◄— (PCL)

(SP) ◄— (SP) − 2

(PC) ◄— (byte 3) (byte 2)

The high-order eight bits of the next instruction address are moved to the memory location whose address is one less than the content of register SP. The low-order eight bits of the next instruction address are moved to the memory location whose address is two less than the content of register SP. The content of register SP is decremented by 2. Control is transferred to the instruction whose address is specified in byte 3 and byte 2 of the current instruction.

1	1	0	0	1	1	0	1
low-order addr							
high-order addr							

Cycles: 5
States: 17
Addressing: immediate/reg. indirect
Flags: none

Ccondition addr   (Condition call)
   If (CCC),
     ((SP) − 1) ◄— (PCH)
     ((SP) − 2) ◄— (PCL)
     (SP) ◄— (SP) − 2
     (PC) ◄— (byte 3) (byte 2)
If the specified condition is true, the actions specified in the CALL instruction (see above) are performed; otherwise, control continues sequentially.

     Cycles: 3/5
     States: 11/17
     Addressing: immediate/reg. indirect
     Flags: none

RET   (Return)
   (PCL) ◄— ((SP));
   (PCH) ◄— ((SP) + 1);
   (SP) ◄— (SP) + 2;
The content of the memory location whose address is specified in register SP is moved to the low-order eight bits of register PC. The content of the memory location whose address is one more than the content of register SP is moved to the high-order eight bits of register PC. The content of register SP is incremented by 2.

     Cycles: 3
     States: 10
     Addressing: reg. indirect
     Flags: none

Rcondition   (Conditional return)
   If (CCC),
     (PCL) ◄— ((SP))
     (PCH) ◄— ((SP) + 1)
     (SP) ◄— (SP) + 2
If the specified condition is true, the actions specified in the RET instruction (see above) are performed; otherwise, control continues sequentially.

     Cycles: 1/3
     States: 5/11
     Addressing: reg. indirect
     Flags: none

RST n   (Restart)
   ((SP) − 1) ◄— (PCH)
   ((SP) − 2) ◄— (PCL)
   (SP) ◄— (SP) − 2
   (PC) ◄— 8 • (NNN)
The high-order eight bits of the next instruction address are moved to the memory location whose address is one less than the content of register SP. The low-order eight bits of the next instruction address are moved to the memory location whose address is two less than the content of register SP. The content of register SP is decremented by two. Control is transferred to the instruction whose address is eight times the content of NNN.

     Cycles: 3
     States: 11
     Addressing: reg. indirect
     Flags: none

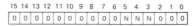

Program Counter After Restart

PCHL   (Jump H and L indirect — move H and L to PC)
   (PCH) ◄— (H)
   (PCL) ◄— (L)
The content of register H is moved to the high-order eight bits of register PC. The content of register L is moved to the low-order eight bits of register PC.

     Cycles: 1
     States: 5
     Addressing: register
     Flags: none

Stack, I/O, and Machine Control Group:

This group of instructions performs I/O, manipulates the Stack, and alters internal control flags.

Unless otherwise specified, **condition flags are not affected by any instructions in this group.**

FLAG WORD

D_7	D_6	D_5	D_4	D_3	D_2	D_1	D_0
S	Z	0	AC	0	P	1	CY

PUSH rp   (Push)

$((SP) - 1) \leftarrow (rh)$
$((SP) - 2) \leftarrow (rl)$
$(SP) \leftarrow (SP) - 2$

The content of the high-order register of register pair rp is moved to the memory location whose address is one less than the content of register SP. The content of the low-order register of register pair rp is moved to the memory location whose address is two less than the content of register SP. The content of register SP is decremented by 2. **Note: Register pair rp = SP may not be specified.**

1	1	R	P	0	1	0	1

Cycles: 3
States: 11
Addressing: reg. indirect
Flags: none

PUSH PSW   (Push processor status word)

$((SP) - 1) \leftarrow (A)$
$((SP) - 2)_0 \leftarrow (CY) , ((SP) - 2)_1 \leftarrow 1$
$((SP) - 2)_2 \leftarrow (P) , ((SP) - 2)_3 \leftarrow 0$
$((SP) - 2)_4 \leftarrow (AC) , ((SP) - 2)_5 \leftarrow 0$
$((SP) - 2)_6 \leftarrow (Z) , ((SP) - 2)_7 \leftarrow (S)$
$(SP) \leftarrow (SP) - 2$

The content of register A is moved to the memory location whose address is one less than register SP. The contents of the condition flags are assembled into a processor status word and the word is moved to the memory location whose address is two less than the content of register SP. The content of register SP is decremented by two.

1	1	1	1	0	1	0	1

Cycles: 3
States: 11
Addressing: reg. indirect
Flags: none

POP rp   (Pop)

$(rl) \leftarrow ((SP))$
$(rh) \leftarrow ((SP) + 1)$
$(SP) \leftarrow (SP) + 2$

The content of the memory location, whose address is specified by the content of register SP, is moved to the low-order register of register pair rp. The content of the memory location, whose address is one more than the content of register SP, is moved to the high-order register of register pair rp. The content of register SP is incremented by 2. **Note: Register pair rp = SP may not be specified.**

1	1	R	P	0	0	0	1

Cycles: 3
States: 10
Addressing: reg. indirect
Flags: none

POP PSW   (Pop processor status word)

$(CY) \leftarrow ((SP))_0$
$(P) \leftarrow ((SP))_2$
$(AC) \leftarrow ((SP))_4$
$(Z) \leftarrow ((SP))_6$
$(S) \leftarrow ((SP))_7$
$(A) \leftarrow ((SP) + 1)$
$(SP) \leftarrow (SP) + 2$

The content of the memory location whose address is specified by the content of register SP is used to restore the condition flags. The content of the memory location whose address is one more than the content of register SP is moved to register A. The content of register SP is incremented by 2.

1	1	1	1	0	0	0	1

Cycles: 3
States: 10
Addressing: reg. indirect
Flags: Z,S,P,CY,AC

XTHL   (Exchange stack top with H and L)

(L) ⟷ ((SP))

(H) ⟷ ((SP) + 1)

The content of the L register is exchanged with the content of the memory location whose address is specified by the content of register SP. The content of the H register is exchanged with the content of the memory location whose address is one more than the content of register SP.

Cycles: 5
States: 18
Addressing: reg. indirect
Flags: none

SPHL   (Move HL to SP)

(SP) ⟵ (H) (L)

The contents of registers H and L (16 bits) are moved to register SP.

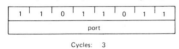

Cycles: 1
States: 5
Addressing: register
Flags: none

IN port   (Input)

(A) ⟵ (data)

The data placed on the eight bit bi-directional data bus by the specified port is moved to register A.

Cycles: 3
States: 10
Addressing: direct
Flags: none

OUT port   (Output)

(data) ⟵ (A)

The content of register A is placed on the eight bit bi-directional data bus for transmission to the specified port.

Cycles: 3
States: 10
Addressing: direct
Flags: none

EI   (Enable interrupts)

The interrupt system is enabled **following the execution of the next instruction.**

Cycles: 1
States: 4
Flags: none

DI   (Disable interrupts)

The interrupt system is disabled **immediately following the execution of the DI instruction.**

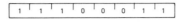

Cycles: 1
States: 4
Flags: none

HLT   (Halt)

The processor is stopped. The registers and flags are unaffected.

Cycles: 1
States: 7
Flags: none

NOP   (No op)

No operation is performed. The registers and flags are unaffected.

Cycles: 1
States: 4
Flags: none

INSTRUCTION SET

Summary of Processor Instructions

Mnemonic	Description	D7	D6	D5	D4	D3	D2	D1	D0	Clock[2] Cycles
MOV r1,r2	Move register to register	0	1	D	D	D	S	S	S	5
MOV M,r	Move register to memory	0	1	1	1	0	S	S	S	7
MOV r,M	Move memory to register	0	1	D	D	D	1	1	0	7
HLT	Halt	0	1	1	1	0	1	1	0	7
MVI r	Move immediate register	0	0	D	D	D	1	1	0	7
MVI M	Move immediate memory	0	0	1	1	0	1	1	0	10
INR r	Increment register	0	0	D	D	D	1	0	0	5
DCR r	Decrement register	0	0	D	D	D	1	0	1	5
INR M	Increment memory	0	0	1	1	0	1	0	0	10
DCR M	Decrement memory	0	0	1	1	0	1	0	1	10
ADD r	Add register to A	1	0	0	0	0	S	S	S	4
ADC r	Add register to A with carry	1	0	0	0	1	S	S	S	4
SUB r	Subtract register from A	1	0	0	1	0	S	S	S	4
SBB r	Subtract register from A with borrow	1	0	0	1	1	S	S	S	4
ANA r	And register with A	1	0	1	0	0	S	S	S	4
XRA r	Exclusive Or register with A	1	0	1	0	1	S	S	S	4
ORA r	Or register with A	1	0	1	1	0	S	S	S	4
CMP r	Compare register with A	1	0	1	1	1	S	S	S	4
ADD M	Add memory to A	1	0	0	0	0	1	1	0	7
ADC M	Add memory to A with carry	1	0	0	0	1	1	1	0	7
SUB M	Subtract memory from A	1	0	0	1	0	1	1	0	7
SBB M	Subtract memory from A with borrow	1	0	0	1	1	1	1	0	7
ANA M	And memory with A	1	0	1	0	0	1	1	0	7
XRA M	Exclusive Or memory with A	1	0	1	0	1	1	1	0	7
ORA M	Or memory with A	1	0	1	1	0	1	1	0	7
CMP M	Compare memory with A	1	0	1	1	1	1	1	0	7
ADI	Add immediate to A	1	1	0	0	0	1	1	0	7
ACI	Add immediate to A with carry	1	1	0	0	1	1	1	0	7
SUI	Subtract immediate from A	1	1	0	1	0	1	1	0	7
SBI	Subtract immediate from A with borrow	1	1	0	1	1	1	1	0	7
ANI	And immediate with A	1	1	1	0	0	1	1	0	7
XRI	Exclusive Or immediate with A	1	1	1	0	1	1	1	0	7
ORI	Or immediate with A	1	1	1	1	0	1	1	0	7
CPI	Compare immediate with A	1	1	1	1	1	1	1	0	7
RLC	Rotate A left	0	0	0	0	0	1	1	1	4
RRC	Rotate A right	0	0	0	0	1	1	1	1	4
RAL	Rotate A left through carry	0	0	0	1	0	1	1	1	4
RAR	Rotate A right through carry	0	0	0	1	1	1	1	1	4
JMP	Jump unconditional	1	1	0	0	0	0	1	1	10
JC	Jump on carry	1	1	0	1	1	0	1	0	10
JNC	Jump on no carry	1	1	0	1	0	0	1	0	10
JZ	Jump on zero	1	1	0	0	1	0	1	0	10
JNZ	Jump on no zero	1	1	0	0	0	0	1	0	10
JP	Jump on positive	1	1	1	1	0	0	1	0	10
JM	Jump on minus	1	1	1	1	1	0	1	0	10
JPE	Jump on parity even	1	1	1	0	1	0	1	0	10
JPO	Jump on parity odd	1	1	1	0	0	0	1	0	10
CALL	Call unconditional	1	1	0	0	1	1	0	1	17
CC	Call on carry	1	1	0	1	1	1	0	0	11/17
CNC	Call on no carry	1	1	0	1	0	1	0	0	11/17
CZ	Call on zero	1	1	0	0	1	1	0	0	11/17
CNZ	Call on no zero	1	1	0	0	0	1	0	0	11/17
CP	Call on positive	1	1	1	1	0	1	0	0	11/17
CM	Call on minus	1	1	1	1	1	1	0	0	11/17
CPE	Call on parity even	1	1	1	0	1	1	0	0	11/17
CPO	Call on parity odd	1	1	1	0	0	1	0	0	11/17
RET	Return	1	1	0	0	1	0	0	1	10
RC	Return on carry	1	1	0	1	1	0	0	0	5/11
RNC	Return on no carry	1	1	0	1	0	0	0	0	5/11

Mnemonic	Description	D7	D6	D5	D4	D3	D2	D1	D0	Clock[2] Cycles
RZ	Return on zero	1	1	0	0	1	0	0	0	5/11
RNZ	Return on no zero	1	1	0	0	0	0	0	0	5/11
RP	Return on positive	1	1	1	1	0	0	0	0	5/11
RM	Return on minus	1	1	1	1	1	0	0	0	5/11
RPE	Return on parity even	1	1	1	0	1	0	0	0	5/11
RPO	Return on parity odd	1	1	1	0	0	0	0	0	5/11
RST	Restart	1	1	A	A	A	1	1	1	11
IN	Input	1	1	0	1	1	0	1	1	10
OUT	Output	1	1	0	1	0	0	1	1	10
LXI B	Load immediate register Pair B & C	0	0	0	0	0	0	0	1	10
LXI D	Load immediate register Pair D & E	0	0	0	1	0	0	0	1	10
LXI H	Load immediate register Pair H & L	0	0	1	0	0	0	0	1	10
LXI SP	Load immediate stack pointer	0	0	1	1	0	0	0	1	10
PUSH B	Push register Pair B & C on stack	1	1	0	0	0	1	0	1	11
PUSH D	Push register Pair D & E on stack	1	1	0	1	0	1	0	1	11
PUSH H	Push register Pair H & L on stack	1	1	1	0	0	1	0	1	11
PUSH PSW	Push A and Flags on stack	1	1	1	1	0	1	0	1	11
POP B	Pop register pair B & C off stack	1	1	0	0	0	0	0	1	10
POP D	Pop register pair D & E off stack	1	1	0	1	0	0	0	1	10
POP H	Pop register pair H & L off stack	1	1	1	0	0	0	0	1	10
POP PSW	Pop A and Flags off stack	1	1	1	1	0	0	0	1	10
STA	Store A direct	0	0	1	1	0	0	1	0	13
LDA	Load A direct	0	0	1	1	1	0	1	0	13
XCHG	Exchange D & E, H & L Registers	1	1	1	0	1	0	1	1	4
XTHL	Exchange top of stack, H & L	1	1	1	0	0	0	1	1	18
SPHL	H & L to stack pointer	1	1	1	1	1	0	0	1	5
PCHL	H & L to program counter	1	1	1	0	1	0	0	1	5
DAD B	Add B & C to H & L	0	0	0	0	1	0	0	1	10
DAD D	Add D & E to H & L	0	0	0	1	1	0	0	1	10
DAD H	Add H & L to H & L	0	0	1	0	1	0	0	1	10
DAD SP	Add stack pointer to H & L	0	0	1	1	1	0	0	1	10
STAX B	Store A indirect	0	0	0	0	0	0	1	0	7
STAX D	Store A indirect	0	0	0	1	0	0	1	0	7
LDAX B	Load A indirect	0	0	0	0	1	0	1	0	7
LDAX D	Load A indirect	0	0	0	1	1	0	1	0	7
INX B	Increment B & C registers	0	0	0	0	0	0	1	1	5
INX D	Increment D & E registers	0	0	0	1	0	0	1	1	5
INX H	Increment H & L registers	0	0	1	0	0	0	1	1	5
INX SP	Increment stack pointer	0	0	1	1	0	0	1	1	5
DCX B	Decrement B & C	0	0	0	0	1	0	1	1	5
DCX D	Decrement D & E	0	0	0	1	1	0	1	1	5
DCX H	Decrement H & L	0	0	1	0	1	0	1	1	5
DCX SP	Decrement stack pointer	0	0	1	1	1	0	1	1	5
CMA	Complement A	0	0	1	0	1	1	1	1	4
STC	Set carry	0	0	1	1	0	1	1	1	4
CMC	Complement carry	0	0	1	1	1	1	1	1	4
DAA	Decimal adjust A	0	0	1	0	0	1	1	1	4
SHLD	Store H & L direct	0	0	1	0	0	0	1	0	16
LHLD	Load H & L direct	0	0	1	0	1	0	1	0	16
EI	Enable Interrupts	1	1	1	1	1	0	1	1	4
DI	Disable interrupt	1	1	1	1	0	0	1	1	4
NOP	No operation	0	0	0	0	0	0	0	0	4

NOTES: 1. DDD or SSS — 000 B — 001 C — 010 D — 011 E — 100 H — 101 L — 110 Memory — 111 A.
2. Two possible cycle times, (5/11) indicate instruction cycles dependent on condition flags.

Appendix K

Examples of Keyboard Control Using the Bootstrap Monitor

Almost every bootstrap monitor will have a "keyboard" subroutine which, if called, will place the key code of a key that is pressed into the accumulator and then return to the main program. This can be a very powerful tool in controlling by means of a keyboard, and helps in simplifying programming and interfacing problems. Experiment 3-13 gave one illustration of the employment of the "KBRD" routine in KEX (see also Appendix C, location 000, 315). Another follows here (see also App. F in the "Applications Experiments" book by Boyet and Katz, for further examples).

Controlled Branching (Demultiplexer)

000	$\left.\begin{array}{l} 315 \\ 315 \\ 000 \end{array}\right\}$	Call "KBRD" in KEX
001		Then press Key 2 or Key 4 (Codes 002 or 004)
002		
003	007	RLC
004	007	RLC
005	007	RLC (leaves 020 or 040 in Acc.)
006	$\left.\begin{array}{l} 062 \\ 012 \\ 003 \end{array}\right\}$	STA
007		
010		
011	$\left.\begin{array}{l} 303 \\ \text{X} \\ 003 \end{array}\right\}$	JMP to 020 or 040
012		
013		

020	$\left(\begin{array}{c} 076 \\ 000 \end{array}\right)$	
021		
022	$\left(\begin{array}{c} 323 \\ 002 \end{array}\right)$	clears Port 2
023		
024	075	DCR A
025	$\left(\begin{array}{c} 323 \\ 001 \end{array}\right)$	377 → Port 1
026		
027	$\left(\begin{array}{c} 303 \\ 000 \\ 003 \end{array}\right)$	JMP
030		
031		

040	$\left(\begin{array}{c} 076 \\ 000 \end{array}\right)$	
041		
042	$\left(\begin{array}{c} 323 \\ 001 \end{array}\right)$	clears Port 1
043		
044	075	
045	$\left(\begin{array}{c} 323 \\ 002 \end{array}\right)$	377 → Port 2
046		
047	$\left(\begin{array}{c} 303 \\ 000 \\ 003 \end{array}\right)$	JMP
050		
051		

Run, press Key 2 or 4 and note how 377 appears either at port 001 or 002, respectively, with the other port cleared.

Devise your own keyboard control experiment to illustrate, for example, a keyboard controlled one-shot multivibrator (controlled pulse width). Other keyboard control experiments will surely come to mind.

Index